ETHICS and PROFESSIONAL ISSUES in COUPLE and FAMILY THERAPY

Ethics and Professional Issues in Couple and Family Therapy, Second Edition, builds upon the strong foundations of the first edition. This new edition addresses the 2015 American Association for Marriage and Family Therapy Code of Ethics as well as other professional organizations' codes of ethics, and includes three new chapters: one on in-home family therapy, a common method of providing therapy to clients, particularly those involved with child protective services; one chapter on Health Insurance Portability and Accountability Act of 1996 (HIPAA) and Health Information Technology for Economic and Clinical Health (HITECH) regulations that practicing therapists need to know; and one chapter on professional issues, in which topics such as advertising, professional identity, supervision, and research ethics are addressed. This book is intended as a training text for students studying to be marriage and family therapists.

Megan J. Murphy, PhD, LMFT, is an associate professor and director of the Marriage and Family Therapy Program at Purdue University Northwest in Hammond, Indiana. She currently serves as a commissioner on the Commission on Accreditation for Marriage and Family Therapy Education and was a coeditor of *Families Across Time: A Life Course Perspective* (Oxford University Press, 2000).

Lorna Hecker, PhD, LMFT, is a professor and director of the Couple and Family Therapy Center at Purdue University Northwest in Hammond, Indiana. She is Certified in Healthcare Privacy and Security expertise in HIPAA and HITECH regulations. She edited the first edition of *Ethics and Professional Issues in Couple and Family Therapy*, and her previous publications include *The Therapist's Notebook: Homework, Handouts, and Activities for Use in Psychotherapy* (Volumes 1, 2, and 3), *The Therapist's Notebook for Children and Adolescents*, and *An Introduction to Marriage and Family Therapy* (Routledge). She also authored the book *HIPAA Demystified: HIPAA Compliance for Mental Health Professionals* (Loger Press).

"The second edition of the Murphy and Hecker book is excellently written with illustrative case vignettes and is even more comprehensive than the original version. The additional chapters about HIPAA and HITECH, home-based therapy, and professional private practice issues make the book a must for all C/MFT training programs and private practitioners."

—**Volker Thomas, PhD, LMFT**, *professor of couple and family therapy, University of Iowa (retired)*

"*Ethics and Professional Issues in Couple and Family Therapy* is full of preventive care and interventions for couple and family therapists in clinical practice. The distinguished editors and contributors provide pages of practical suggestions and recommendations to maintain best practices. The authors took great care to untangle complex ethical, legal, and technical issues, which makes the book an easy, but informative read for experienced clinicians and CFT students. The culturally diverse case examples illustrate how therapists can avoid common pitfalls inherent in clinical practice and the importance of self-care. This book should be a required reading for students in CFT programs!"

—**Stephanie Brooks, PhD, LCSW, LMFT**, *chair, Couple and Family Therapy Department; associate dean, Graduate Health Professions, Drexel University*

"This is an indispensable resource on ethical issues in the practice of couple and family therapy. The second edition includes a comprehensive review of new HIPAA and HITECH regulations, and the latest AAMFT code of ethics. Clear and concrete examples are used to drive home major points. I highly recommend this book to any couple and family therapy student, instructor, or licensed provider."

—**Andrea K. Wittenborn, PhD**, *graduate director, associate professor, Human Development and Family Studies, Michigan State University*

ETHICS and PROFESSIONAL ISSUES in COUPLE and FAMILY THERAPY

Second Edition

Edited by Megan J. Murphy
and Lorna Hecker

NEW YORK AND LONDON

Second edition published 2017
by Routledge
711 Third Avenue, New York, NY 10017

and by Routledge
2 Park Square, Milton Park, Abingdon, Oxon, OX14 4RN

Routledge is an imprint of the Taylor & Francis Group, an informa business

First edition published by Routledge 2009

Library of Congress Cataloging-in-Publication Data
Names: Murphy, Megan J., editor. | Hecker, Lorna L., editor.
Title: Ethics and professional issues in couple and family therapy / edited by
Megan J. Murphy and Lorna Hecker.
Description: Second edition. | New York, NY: Routledge, 2017.
Includes bibliographical references and index.
Identifiers: LCCN 2016019391 | ISBN 9781138645257 (hbk: alk. paper) |
ISBN 9781138645264 (pbk: alk. paper) | ISBN 9781315628240 (ebk)
Subjects: LCSH: Family psychotherapy—Moral and ethical aspects. | Marital
psychotherapy—Moral and ethical aspects. | Family therapists—Professional ethics. |
Marriage counselors—Professional ethics.
Classification: LCC RC488.5 .E87 2017 DDC 616.89/1562—dc23
LC record available at https://lccn.loc.gov/2016019391

ISBN: 978-1-138-64525-7 (hbk)
ISBN: 978-1-138-64526-4 (pbk)
ISBN: 978-1-315-62824-0 (ebk)

Typeset in Minion Pro
by codeMantra

Printed and bound in Great Britain by
TJ International Ltd, Padstow, Cornwall

Contents

Preface

Primum non nocere—First, do no harm.

Hippocrates (c. 460–400 BC)

You likely chose the field of couple and family therapy because of a desire to help people and would likely be aghast at the notion of harming your clients. Yet without proper knowledge, you can make decisions that can indeed cause harm to clients, your own professional practice, the larger professional field, and yourself. The chapters in this book have been chosen to educate you on the most salient topics regarding the intertwining of ethical, legal, clinical, and professional issues faced by couple and family therapists.

This book is a revision on the first edition, edited by Hecker in 2010. This book grapples with contemporary ethical and professional issues, some of which have changed or recently arisen or transformed since that writing. For example, in this edition, linear decision-making is replaced with a relationally focused ethical decision-making process that relies much more on clients' context and the responsibilities therapists have to consider when making ethical decisions with clients. Power and privilege issues have been updated to include a focus on power issues that arise in choice of our theories, the therapeutic relationship, and in clients' relationships with each other. The power of a therapist with regard to maintaining sexual boundaries and how to handle sexual harassment is detailed. The complexity reflected in intersectionality is introduced.

A new standard of care has arisen with privacy protections for our clients' oral, written, or digital private information, with the advent of the Health Insurance Portability and Accountability Act of 1996 (HIPAA) as well as the subsequent Health Information Technology for Economic and Clinical Health (HITECH) Act of 2009. HIPAA audits were mandated by HITECH, and lawsuits are beginning to occur using HIPAA regulations as the standard of care for client privacy protection, whether or not you are a "covered entity" under the regulations. HIPAA security regulations stress the importance of maintaining privacy of digitally stored client data, which can be overlooked by more of us who favor "high touch" over "high tech." Specific information around ethical issues within e-therapy is also discussed, with a framework from which to conceptualize e-therapy clinical and ethical issues presented.

Couple and family therapists' entwinement with the legal system is explored, educating the reader on properly responding to a subpoena, while still focusing on the ever-important duty to warn or protect. Additionally, career opportunities that intersect with the legal system such as the role of a couple and family therapist as mediator and parent coordinator are explored. As we look at CFT involvement with custody issues on children, we also address the increasingly recognized phenomenon of parental alienation from a child.

In our first edition, office policies and procedures were explained; in this book, we also delve into requirements to establish a private practice, including information on opening a business, applying to insurance panels, and necessary documentation.

We recognize that more and more therapists are providing in-home family therapy, which evokes particular attention to ethical principles, including confidentiality, boundaries, and safety. Self-of-the-therapist issues are addressed and include knowing one's own values, implementing a program of self-care, and warning signs for burnout and compassion fatigue. Finally, we have added a chapter on ethics of professionalism—to remind us that we represent our professional fields through our actions and behaviors. We are indeed connected to something larger than ourselves—the field of family therapy.

This is a book for professionals who want to understand the context of complex situations in which couple and family therapists find themselves. It is a book for couple and family therapists who, consistent with their systems training, will grasp multilevel problems, grapple with them, and go through a reasoned analysis to find a solution that best meets the needs of the people involved. As in the 2010 edition of this book, readers are introduced to ethical principles for consideration in ethical deliberation and decision-making. In an ideal world, all therapists would be trained in moral philosophy; that ideal is clearly outside the scope of this book. This book can be used as an introductory graduate text in marriage and family therapy graduate programs, professionals wishing to expand their depth and understanding of the field, or by those refreshing their knowledge of professional issue and ethics for licensing exams.

You will no doubt have quandaries when faced with ethical dilemmas posed in this book. Answers to ethical dilemmas often introduce complexity for which answers to those dilemmas also result in a refrain of "it depends." Many variables contribute to evaluation when making sound ethical decisions. A tolerance of ambiguity is necessary for anyone who truly wishes to struggle with ethical dilemmas. You have to be able to juggle many diverging solutions (and viewpoints) at once before the best action can be chosen. Sometimes the best solution is obvious; other times, there are competing "best" courses of action. Sometimes, all alternatives to an ethical dilemma simply are not satisfying or can even be repugnant. Early foreclosure on decisions to decrease your accompanying anxiety can lead to situations (ethical, clinical, or legal) that are worse than the predicament that was initially raised. Although some ethical/clinical decisions need to be made quickly, there are many situations in which the therapist can decelerate the process to thoroughly scrutinize the situation at hand.

In this book, you will find numerous case scenarios, many based on actual experiences to give the reader a sense of the richness of ethical issues that may present themselves in therapy. In some, the ethical or legal issues at hand may be quite evident, whereas in others it may be subtle and you will need to search for the shades of gray that continuously make ethics a challenging but worthwhile pursuit. All case scenarios have had identifying information of the clients and case-specific information altered to protect the confidentiality of the client.

Unfortunately, in our personal experience, we have encountered therapists who have not followed the "do no harm" dictate and have hurt people when they violate their professional and moral responsibilities. In some circumstances, there has been egregious harm. We have seen others believe that they are without moral fault—this alone is a dangerous stance. The people who believe themselves to be without moral fault put themselves outside the realm of dialogue, and relationships become secondary to their agenda. Dialogue is key to resolving most ethical dilemmas. It our hope that you engage in much dialogue as you traverse this book. It is our quest, then, that therapists be educated about ethics for the very positive goal of helping clients, but at the very least, *Primum non nocere*. This book provides education, insight, and tools to help you adequately prepare for ethical practice as a couple and family therapist.

1

Introduction

Lorna Hecker and Megan J. Murphy

> The Lincoln family attends therapy for concerns about their oldest daughter, Elise, who is 15 years old. Elise has been breaking curfew, and the family fears she is using drugs. Dr. Shindell sees all the family members, parents Kelly and Sam Lincoln, Elise, and her younger sister, Macy, age 12. Family therapy focuses on getting the parents to synchronize their parenting efforts to strengthen the parental hierarchy. As therapy progresses, Dr. Shindell receives a voicemail from Sam's mother, Mrs. Lincoln, stating her concern that Kelly and Sam are unfit parents, and that she and her husband would like to try to gain custody of the girls. The elder Mrs. Lincoln states in the message that Sam has been known to hit Elise out of frustration for her misbehavior.

Ethics is about what actions we should take, which rules govern our conduct, what "right thing" we should do, and what we ought not to do. It is also about how we justify our actions. When making ethical decisions, couple and family therapists need well-founded reasons to support their actions. Our sense of ethics is influenced by scholarship and evidence, and is shaped by our values, worldview, and context (Roberts & Dyer, 2004). Ethics involves cognition *and* affect, and a "moral sensitivity" that includes the recognition that our actions affect the welfare of others (Welfel & Kitchener, 2003). Clients' values and morals also need to be clearly understood so that empowering, collaborative decisions can be made.

When facing situations that may have ethical quandaries, couple and family therapists can make decisions using the following four criteria:

- What are the *ethical* components?
- What are the *clinical* components?
- Are there any potential *legal* issues?
- Are there any *professional* issues to reflect upon?

Ethical components inform how professionals should conduct themselves within the context of the professional relationship and the specific situation. Ethical dilemmas arise most often when the welfare of people may be at stake. For example, when a therapist sees a family and suspects that the parents are abusing their child, an ethical issue is posed because the welfare of the child is at stake, as one can imagine Dr. Shindell, in our case scenario, must be contemplating. However, the ethical dilemma is embedded within the clinical issues at hand and is entangled in legal issues because of reporting statutes.

Clinical components relate to the therapeutic context in which the ethical issue is occurring. Ethical issues typically arise out of the clinical context and can affect the therapist–client relationship. The effect of ethical issues may have a positive or negative valence. For example, a therapist who ethically and legally must report parents to child protective services may severely damage the therapist–client relationship because this violates the confidentiality and trust the parents put in the therapist. Additionally, clients may feel betrayed and angry that the therapist involved authorities in the therapeutic relationship. Steinberg, Levine, and Doueck (1997) found that 27% of people leave therapy when they are reported to child protective services. Conversely, the vast majority of parents may understand that the therapist had a legal obligation to report to child protective services and are interested in bettering their parenting skills so that the abuse never happens again.

There may or may not be legal issues in an ethical situation. In the case of the parents who abuse a child, all 50 states have child abuse reporting statutes, but even though this may be a legal requirement, apparently not all therapists find this ethical or advisable in all situations. Jankowski and Martin (2003) found that, in cases of child maltreatment, family therapists in Illinois made the decision to report child abuse based on their worldview assumptions, ethical principles, prior clinical and life experiences, situational factors including type and severity of abuse, the amount of evidence presented to them, client characteristics such as age and personal history, and interactional factors including willingness on the part of adult clients to comply with therapy. Even though therapists realize they are legally bound to report abuse, the legal requirement may not appear ethical to the therapist. In other cases, it would be unethical to the therapist if they do not report actual, ongoing abuse.

Last, there are professional components to any situation. How the therapists conducts themselves reflect on the profession as a whole. For example, a therapist who is constantly late to sessions, while strictly not generating an ethical issue, is behaving in a way that reflects poorly on the professional and the profession. If, as discussed previously, the therapist does not report abuse and the child continues to be abused or dies, it would be both a tragedy and a poor reflection on couple and family therapists.

Consider the scenario at the beginning of this chapter. Dr. Shindell is faced with potential ethical issues. First, she may not speak to Sam's mother without a written release from her clients. This is an ethical issue, but because confidentiality is statutorily defined, it is also a legal issue. Clinically, Dr. Shindell will need to be cautious about how she handles the issue of the voicemail. She wants to avoid the perception of an alliance or coalition developing with Sam's mother that will derail therapy and erode therapeutic trust. Yet she now holds some information that may be relevant to therapy—either if there is actual abuse, or if this is not true, the sabotage of the parents by Mrs. Lincoln is of import. Legally, in Dr. Shindell's state, she is bound to report suspected child abuse. Professionally, if Dr. Shindell speaks to Sam's mother about Sam, Kelly, and Elise, she will have acted in an unprofessional manner; confidentiality is the foundation on which therapy is built. If the public cannot count on confidentiality being upheld, there is no reason for clients to confide in couple and family therapists. Ultimately, Dr. Shindell cannot "confirm or deny" to Sam's mother that the Lincoln family is a client.

All ethical decisions should be evaluated in these four realms. The process of *ethical decision-making* is much more complex and is discussed by Elisabeth Shaw in Chapter 2, *Ethical Decision-Making from a Relational Perspective*. In her chapter, she describes a more contextual, relationally based way of making ethical decisions, as opposed to the step-by-step models familiar to many therapy professionals. Professional codes of ethics provide some guidance on our basic ethical responsibilities; they provide a floor of protection for clients. Codes give us specific "dos" and "don'ts," but do not aid the couple and family therapist in making ethical decisions when the complexities extend beyond the professional code.

Philosophical Roots to Ethical Decision-Making

Historically, in analyzing ethical decisions, therapists have borrowed from philosophy and use the moral principles of autonomy, nonmaleficence, justice, beneficence (Beauchamp & Childress, 2013), veracity, and fidelity (Nash, 2002; Sidgwick, 1981):

- *Autonomy* refers to respecting individuals and their right to make decisions for themselves with regard to their own health and well-being.

When we ask clients to give informed consent for treatment, we are respecting their autonomy, providing information so that they may make an autonomous decision about their care. Even the labeling of "client" vs. "patient" has shades of the level of autonomy we believe clients should hold.

- *Nonmaleficence* means "above all, do no harm." We educate clients in our informed consent about the risks and benefits of treatment. An assumption of nonmaleficence is that the benefits of treatment outweigh the risks.
- *Justice* means all humans should be treated fairly. When ethical codes dictate that therapists provide services without discrimination (e.g., on the basis of race, age, ethnicity, gender, religion, sexual orientation) the principle of justice is employed.
- *Beneficence* refers to actions intended to do good for others; the value of caring in couple and family therapist is derived from this principle.
- *Veracity* refers to the importance of truth telling. We want to be honest and transparent with our clients. There has long been questioning of the use of paradoxical interventions and emotional manipulation (e.g., strategic family therapy), and whether or not these types of interventions are ethical, because of deceit/lack of transparency (Lakin, 1988).
- *Fidelity* refers to honoring commitments and promoting trust. For example, when therapists promise confidentiality, clients expect that promise to be honored (within legal limits).

Now, let us again consider our case scenario with the Lincoln family. When considering client autonomy, Dr. Shindell may be evaluating how much therapy time to devote to Elise individually to honor her developing autonomy as a teenager. She may also be evaluating the autonomy of Kelly and Sam to seek treatment without the involvement of Sam's mother. Yet, Dr. Shindell does not want to cause harm (nonmaleficence) and must work to keep Elise safe (beneficence) both from abuse and involvement with harmful substances. Likewise, in evaluating the principle of justice, Dr. Shindell may wonder if it is fair to report Kelly and Sam based on the report of a potentially maligned grandparent who may be acting in her own interests, not those of the family. Dr. Shindell wishes to do well by this family, help the parents regain their parental role in relation to their child, and keep her from harm (beneficence). There is also the question of reporting the grandmother's allegation of abuse to the authorities, as is legally required in her state (e.g., reporting of suspected abuse and neglect). Dr. Shindell's first allegiance is to the family and she fears revealing the phone call with Sam's mother may cause harm to her relationship with the Lincoln family; likewise, she may be rightly concerned about the effect on the therapeutic relationship should she report Kelly and Sam to child protection authorities (fidelity). These are but a few examples of ethical components that may go into one ethical decision. Couple and family therapists make daily decisions with ethical ramifications.

Historically, ethical decision-making has been done in a linear fashion with basic steps including defining the problem, fact gathering, weighing the ethical principles mentioned previously, and then making a decision. Yet as Elisabeth Shaw (see Chapter 2) notes, our cognitive, linear decision-making models do not take into account the context of our relationships. One can imagine that culture and specific family rules can vary in what benevolent acts are believed to be. One culture may see the death penalty as a form of justice, whereas another sees it as morally repugnant. Although some ethical decisions may seem easy to discern with little thought (e.g., keep therapy information confidential), others will require an examination of a client's relational context in order to evaluate the "right" thing to do. Our context shapes our ethical thinking. For example, those who ground their ethical beliefs in the notion of a divine being are likely to view the source of their morality as external and objective, whereas those who do not are more likely to view ethics as internal and subjective; in U.S. culture, we can see this difference in the impasse between conservative and liberal ideologies (Goodwin & Darley, 2008). Cultural context and worldviews are inherent in all ethical decisions. In the following chapters, information is presented on ethical decision-making around a variety of issues couple and family therapists confront daily.

Case Examples of Ethical Issues

What follows are examples of ethical issues relevant to chapters in this book.

Most scenarios are variations on actual case events. Names and details have been changed to maintain client confidentiality.

> Martin was a family therapy intern at a university Couple and Family Therapy Center working with a young man, Jared, who was referred for anger management counseling. Jared, initially wary of counseling, revealed that he had been involved in a gang, but had changed his ways and was now a father with a partner and two young children. It was clear he had given up his gang activities, had obtained a job, and stated interest in couple's therapy for him and his partner. Jared exhibited symptoms of posttraumatic stress disorder, having witnessed significant violence during his involvement with gangs. Although outwardly he portrayed bravado, the more he became comfortable with therapy, the more vulnerable he became with his therapist. Jared began to talk about how he had few friends and trusted

> no one. He described a chaotic family of origin whose members attacked each other frequently and only contacted Jared when they needed money. He trusted his partner the most, but he was even wary of her. He said he had made a pact with three gang buddies, and that was the deepest trust he had experienced. He began to discuss to the fact that these three friends of his had a secret that they had agreed to tell no one. It became clear to the therapist, over time, that this event was a criminal act. Jared eventually talked in terms that left no doubt to the therapist the men had murdered a rival gang member.

Sometime later, Martin was subpoenaed to testify in court about Jared's involvement in the murder. Although Jared had thought what he shared was *confidential*, there was an exception to Jared's legal right to *privilege* that was specified in the state statute. Specifically, the state statute read in part:

> Matters communicated to the Couple and Family Therapist in the couple and family therapist's official capacity by a client are privileged information and may not be disclosed by the couple and family therapist to any person, except under the following circumstances: (1) In a criminal proceeding involving a homicide if the disclosure relates directly to the fact or immediate circumstances of the homicide… (adapted from Indiana Code IC 25–23.6–6).

Although this exception had been detailed in the Couple and Family Therapy Center's *informed consent*, Jared had unburdened himself of the information anyway, putting Martin in a very tenuous legal position. The judge ordered Martin to testify as to what Jared had confided to him in the therapy sessions. Martin was forced to comply. Confidentiality and legal privilege will be defined and discussed further in Chapter 3; informed consent to treatment will be detailed in Chapter 12.

> Mrs. Lee attended therapy with her 10-year-old daughter, Rose, stating that she wanted therapy for Rose because of the divorce she had experienced the year prior. Rose seemed to be an outgoing and friendly fourth grader. Mrs. Lee stated she wanted a neutral place for Rose to talk about any concerns she had about the divorce. The family therapist, Dr. Snow, asked for a copy of the most recent custody order, which Mrs. Lee brought to the subsequent session. Dr. Snow ascertained that Mrs. Lee had sole legal custody of Rose. Rose lived with Mrs. Lee and only visited with Mr. Lee on alternate weekends plus one night per week. Dr. Snow saw Mrs. Lee and Rose conjointly for two sessions, and Rose alone for two sessions. Mrs. Lee stated that she had asked Mr. Lee to join therapy, but he had said that he was not interested. Dr. Snow made no attempt to contact Mr. Lee. During the fifth week of treatment, Dr. Snow received an irate phone call from Mr. Lee, who had learned from Rose that she was in therapy. Mr. Lee demanded to know why he was not notified his daughter was in treatment.

Dr. Snow correctly assumed that he only needed Mrs. Lee's legal consent to treat Rose because Mrs. Lee had *sole legal custody* of Rose. However, Mr. and Mrs. Lee shared *joint physical custody* of Rose, indicating involvement in her parenting on a regular basis. Mrs. Lee was deceitful when she said Mr. Lee was not interested in therapy; she had never asked Mr. Lee to join them in therapy. Dr. Snow acted within proper legal guidelines, but he was not clinically sound in his decision to exclude Mr. Lee from treatment. This error could predictably lead to an ethical complaint, a growing concern when dealing with custody issues (Greenberg, Martindale, Gould, & Gould-Saltman, 2004). Chapter 10 will address *Ethics in Therapy with Children in Families.*

A counseling center in Wisconsin was forced to notify 509 of its patients of breach of personal information after a burglary occurred and someone stole a center psychologist's unsecured laptop. The laptop had outpatient mental health records, mental health status examinations, and psychological evaluations. It also included client names, social security numbers, medical histories, diagnoses, and statements of work capacity, as well as personal information of the psychologist himself. In addition to notifying clients of the loss of their personal information, the counseling center was required by federal law to notify the local news media and post information about the breach on the counseling center's website (Shuda, 2015).

Because we live in an increasingly digital era, couple and family therapists now have a responsibility to be diligent about protecting client information held in digital format (Hecker & Murphy, 2015). In the previous scenario, clients not only had their personal counseling information breached, but also additional information that would leave the clients open to identity theft. The Health Insurance Portability and Accountability Act (HIPAA) of 1996 requires covered entities to protect both paper and electronic protected health information. In the event of a breach, the Health Information Technology for Economic and Clinical Health (HITECH) Act of 2009 requires that breaches of more than 500 records be disclosed to the involved clients, news media informed, and a notification be placed on the organization's website. HITECH also set penalties and fines for breaches of privacy. Had the psychologist encrypted his laptop, by regulation it would not have been considered a breach and no action would need to be taken by the counseling center. HIPAA and HITECH regulations are introduced in Chapter 4.

Dr. Stephen was a successful couple and family therapist who treated a young couple that subsequently decided to divorce. He continued to see the young woman, Jill, after the husband dropped out of therapy. During the course of treatment, Dr. Stephen often complimented Jill and told her how no one in her life seemed to

> appreciate how special she was. He said she was really much more intelligent than her husband had given her credit for. Jill was flattered by the compliments, as her emotional life was fairly destitute and she was vulnerable because of her pending divorce. He also sympathized with her feelings regarding her divorce. He seemed like a good friend to Jill, rather than a therapist. He began to sit by her during sessions and hold her hand. Their sessions began to increase in length, and she was often his last client of the day. He eventually began to rub Jill's arms and back, and in future sessions had Jill lie back into his arms so he could hold her and stroke her. He stated he wanted her to be comfortable and in charge. Jill was confused; she did not think this was part of therapy, but she trusted Dr. Stephen. Eventually, Jill dropped out of therapy. Several months later, Jill reentered therapy with a different therapist. Jill suffered depression and anger, she was suicidal at times, and she suffered flashbacks to the situation.

All of the mental health professional codes (e.g., American Association for Marriage and Family Therapy, American Counseling Association, National Association for Social Workers, American Psychological Association) prohibit sexual intimacy with clients. What codes do not state is the long-term damage caused by this type of violation. The damage to Jill was immense. A therapist must always be in charge of the therapeutic boundaries in therapy. A supervisor must always be in charge of the boundaries between the supervisor and the therapist who seeks supervision with them. Professors and clinical supervisors must always be in charge of the boundaries with their students. In Chapter 6, *Power, Privilege, and Ethics*, the responsibility that accompanies the power and privilege held by a therapist is discussed. Likewise in Chapter 7, *Sexuality, Boundaries, and Ethics*, management of therapeutic boundaries around sexuality is explored. The need for the therapist to stay in tune with oneself to avoid disastrous situations such as this one is discussed in Chapter 5, *Self of the Therapist.*

> Jasmine and Dorian attend couple therapy with a couple and family therapist, Joe, citing communication difficulties often emanating from arguments about Jasmine's waitressing at a local bar. Dorian would become jealous when Jasmine's customers would pay "too much" attention to her. Dorian believed Jasmine dressed too suggestively for work. Jasmine disagreed and thought she received better tips if she dressed nicely. Joe soon learned that the discussions became loud and included slapping, pushing, and name-calling, especially when Jasmine had been drinking. Dorian had scratches on his neck and neighbors had called the police on one occasion.

The therapist, Joe, in this scenario is left with the decision of whether to treat Jasmine and Dorian as a couple or individually. The couple is experiencing intimate partner violence (IPV), and in some cases, couples therapy is indicated, and in others, couples therapy could increase risk. Risk and liability for the therapist is also a consideration when treating IPV. In Chapter 8, risk management through adequate assessment of potential IPV is discussed to aid the reader in making treatment decisions to decrease risks to clients (and one's practice).

> Jack brought his 72-year-old father, Robert, to therapy because of his growing concern for his father's depression after the death of the Robert's wife. The therapist, Dr. McDonald, saw Robert for six sessions, who then dropped out of therapy. During those six sessions, he stated to the therapist frequently that he simply wanted to join his wife. Robert did not improve in therapy, and Dr. McDonald made a referral to a psychiatrist for an evaluation for an antidepressant. Dr. McDonald did not attempt to contact the psychiatrist, nor did he inform Jack of his father's suicidality. The Robert took an overdose of sleeping medication prescribed by the psychiatrist and died. His son sued Dr. McDonald for malpractice.

Dr. McDonald did not follow an appropriate *standard of care* when treating Robert. He would have been legally justified to breach confidentiality and tell Jack of his father's suicidality (although he could have simply asked his permission to do this). He also did not contact the other treating party to provide important information regarding the client. It is likely the court will see his care as *malpractice*. In Chapter 8, risk factors and suicide are discussed.

> Amisha, a licensed marriage and family therapist (LMFT), was seeing Harold, who was separated from his wife, Laura. Harold had been despondent about the separation and was hoping the separation was temporary. He wanted to move back in with Laura and their two children. Laura, however, seemed to have other ideas. According to Harold, she taunted him and said that he was "no man" and that she could find a better man than he was, citing his difficulties earning a decent wage and his excessive drinking. Harold began to suspect that Laura had a boyfriend and frequently ranted about it in therapy with Amisha. He said that if he ever caught her with this man, he would kill them both. Amisha asked Harold if he was serious, and he said he was "half-serious." Two weeks later, Harold came to session, and it was clear he had been drinking. He stated that he had caught Laura in bed with a man, someone Laura worked with, and he was going to "settle the score" with Laura and this man. He thanked the therapist for her help and he left the session abruptly before Amisha could intervene.

Amisha is now faced with a dilemma. She has promised Harold confidentiality, but she is fearful for Laura's well-being and that of Laura's paramour. In addition, according to her state statute and code of ethics, she has a *duty to warn* the intended victims. Had Amisha done a violence assessment on Harold? Could she reasonably predict if Harold was likely to be violent? Did she have contact information for Laura? Should she call the police? Should she call Laura? These risk management issues will also be addressed in Chapter 8.

> Leslie, an LMFT, was seeing Chitra and Gopal, a young Indian couple who grew up in the United States and was living with Gopal's parents, who had immigrated to the United States from India. Chitra and Gopal's marriage had been arranged. The couple's biggest stressor was that Chitra did not get along with Gopal's parents and felt that they treated her unfairly. She was expected to do all of the housework and the majority of the cooking. Gopal felt caught in a loyalty conflict between Chitra and his parents. Leslie surmised that the situation seemed like a "pressure cooker," and the couple agreed. Leslie was concerned about the patriarchal and sexist nature of the environment Chitra was living in. She suggested that Chitra move out for a short time to give the family time apart to relieve some of the pressure.

Leslie was letting her Western values guide therapy. She was not respecting the rights of Chitra and Gopal to make decisions for themselves. Chitra would likely have suffered disastrous consequences for the action Leslie was suggesting. These issues are addressed from several viewpoints, with Chapter 5, addressing *Self of the Therapist*; Chapter 6, *Power, Privilege, and Ethics*; and Chapter 9, *Spirituality and Religion*. Within these chapters, therapists' values are explored in order to understand how we affect therapy as well as how therapy affects us.

> Dr. Moonstone has a private practice that is quite successful. He has cleaning help—Ms. Ingrid, who cleans nightly—who he sees every night as he finishes up with evening clients. Over the years, they have become friendly, and he has come to know her family situation. Ms. Ingrid cleans for a living, and her husband works as an auto mechanic. One evening, Ms. Ingrid shared that her teenage daughter, Iris, was getting in trouble at school and has recently been arrested for using marijuana. Ms. Ingrid turned to Dr. Moonstone for help. She begged Dr. Moonstone to see Iris, and Dr. Moonstone, though uncomfortable with the arrangement, agreed to just one session of therapy to assess Iris and then make a referral based on her needs. Ms. Ingrid and her husband, David, attended the assessment session as Dr. Moonstone requested. During the family assessment, Ms. Ingrid, David, and Iris had a major altercation with which Dr. Moonstone had to intervene decisively and firmly to gain order in the therapy room because the fight nearly turned physical. Dr. Moonstone made the referral, but the next time he saw Ms. Ingrid, she refused to speak to him.

Dr. Moonstone learned the hard way not to engage in a *multiple relationship*. Although Ms. Ingrid's request may have seemed harmless, to mix therapy with someone with whom he already had a prior business relationship created an untenable situation. Dr. Moonstone is in the more powerful position; thus, he is in charge of guarding the boundary around engaging in an appropriate relationship. Power, privilege, and multiple relationships will be discussed in more detail in Chapter 6.

> Simone, a licensed marital and family therapist, was working in a state-funded agency. She was working with a married couple, Jerrick and Tameca, who had lost their baby to sudden infant death syndrome. Jerrick and Tameca both came from homes with strong religious traditions and used prayer as a major coping mechanism for managing their loss. Simone was not particularly religious or spiritual but respected and admired the couple's strong faith. On the first anniversary of the loss of their baby, the couple was grieving. When Simone asked the couple what they thought would help them most on that day, they asked if Simone would pray with them.

The difficulty Simone encountered is that Jerrick and Tameca requested spiritual intervention in therapy, however slight it is, and Simone has never explicitly discussed this or her own spiritual values with Jerrick and Tameca. Thus, she is put in what she perceives to be an awkward position. If she declines to pray, she risks alienating her clients. If she prays, she risks sounding insincere or awkward, and going against her personal values. She must also perform therapy within her *scope of practice* in order to be ethical. In Chapter 9, understanding spirituality and religion as a multicultural issue is discussed, as are the ethical issues that surround spiritual or religious interventions with clients.

> Alex has a new client, a 16-year-old young man, Aiden, and his parents. The parents are concerned that Aiden is developing an unhealthy lifestyle and worry about his choice of friends. He does not seem to have a girlfriend, but appears to be "too familiar" with many of his friends. When Alex sees Aiden alone, Aiden relates that he believes himself to be pansexual (a person who is sexually interested in other people regardless of gender). Aiden sees nothing wrong with this, and relates that many of his friends have similar beliefs. Alex is alarmed by this revelation, both because it goes against his own relationship values, but also because he knows that Aiden's parents would be heartbroken to know their son is so "sinful."

Alex's dilemma is not unusual. Many therapists encounter clients with values different than their own. However, sexual values between therapists and clients can differ greatly, and in this case Alex must decide how to treat Aiden and his family, in the midst of several value clashes including his own. Value dilemmas such as this are discussed in Chapter 9.

> Dr. Rodriquez worked in San Antonio, Texas, helping divorced parents. He worked with Bob and Linda, who were court-ordered to see him; the courts had all but given up on intervening with them because of their acrimonious nature and repeated visits to court to fight over the smallest of details concerning their

> children. Dr. Rodriquez helped Bob and Linda come to an agreement about their parenting plan, and he even worked with them to develop a method for exchanging the children's clothing that both agreed upon. He often acted as a coach and referee because Bob and Linda were so acrimonious at times that they could not communicate directly with each other without third-party intervention. When the couple could not communicate without toxicity, he would have them e-mail each other and copy him to decrease the conflict. Dr. Rodriquez worked with them on solving problems relating to the children's homework and issues surrounding holidays. Dr. Rodriquez was assigned by the court and had authority to make decisions for the couple on some issues, excluding custody, which the couple could not agree on.

Dr. Rodriquez lives in Texas where there is legal provision for therapists to become *parent coordinators*. Couple and family therapists are expanding their roles into other arenas where they can be useful to families in need. These roles with families in distress that interact with the legal system are discussed in detail in Chapter 11.

> Karen, a licensed couple and family therapist, saw the Kramer family for 12 sessions. The Kramer parents were concerned about the depression of their 16-year-old son, Darnell. Karen saw the family regularly, and she also saw Darnell separately for part of each session to evaluate him for depression and suicidal ideation. She methodically and consistently evaluated him for the signs and symptoms of depression, and although he initially showed evidence of depression, as family therapy progressed, his symptoms improved. She also taught the parents what to watch for with regard to Darnell's depression and asked them to let her know if his symptoms worsened. The parents agreed Darnell was improving. The family terminated therapy after the twelfth session, considering therapy to be a success. Three weeks later, Darnell killed himself. Some time passed, and Karen was surprised to be served notice that she was being sued for malpractice in the case. It was being alleged that her treatment fell below the acceptable standard of care. Her records were being subpoenaed as well. Unfortunately for Karen, she recorded only that she had family therapy, not that she met privately with Darnell. She never recorded that she individually assessed him for depression and suicide ideation.

Karen is in trouble. She did not properly document her treatment of Darnell. Simpson and Stacy (2004) noted that whether or not malpractice action goes forward could be determined by the quality of documentation. Karen, essentially, had no documentation to speak of; just the family therapy sessions were documented. She also performed no formal suicide assessment because Darnell's depression improved, and she did not see it as necessary, but her justification for not doing this was not documented either. Documentation will be discussed in Chapter 12.

> Robyn has been contacted by Barb, the concerned mother of Jade, a 25-year-old woman who has been struggling to keep a job. Barb suspects Jade may be using drugs. Also in the family is Don, Jade's father, and Jade's other adult siblings—Tim, Seth, and Wendy, ages 33, 30, and 27, respectively. Barb asks Robyn who should attend therapy. Robyn says that she would like all family members to attend therapy. Barb says that she, Don, and Jade will attend the first session but that Tim, Seth, and Wendy probably won't be interested in therapy.

One of the first decisions a therapist needs to make is who is to participate in therapy. Robyn's answer depends on the role of the therapist that she embraces—which can be different depending on whether one takes a traditional or a postmodern approach to therapy. She may insist that all family members attend—consistent with a traditional approach to therapy—and risk losing the family because for various reasons, not all family members will attend. Or Robyn may collaborate with Barb to discuss who is most likely to attend, and who considers the problem to be a problem—more consistent with a postmodern approach. Her initial response to this phone call has ethical implications for the course of treatment, a topic discussed in Chapter 13, *Ethical Issues with Systemic and Social Constructionist Family Therapies.*

> Lawson is an LMFT (licensed marriage and family therapist) in the state of Wisconsin. He decided to augment his practice by offering an e-therapy practice. He established a website, which he was careful to encrypt. Potential clients e-mail directly from the site, and his secretary then sets up a phone therapy session for him with the client. Even though he is relatively new to his e-therapy practice, he had a session with a client in Idaho. During the session, the client reveals that she took an overdose of sleeping pills.

Lawson now has several challenges. Has he received accurate contact information so he can quickly locate the client to send the person emergency care? Has the client given informed consent so they know that what will happen in case of emergency? Could the client have lied about her contact information, leaving Lawson helpless to intervene? If he does intervene, is his license valid across state lines? If he is not practicing what is "usual and customary" therapy practice, does his malpractice insurance cover him? These issues will be discussed in detail in Chapter 14, *Ethical Couple and Family E-Therapy*.

> Nancy worked at an agency that had state contracts to do in-home family therapy. Families were mandated to treatment. After making an appointment over the phone, Nancy pulled up to the home of a family to whom she had been assigned only to find no one was home. She called the family later that day, whereby they apologized and said that they were grocery shopping and missed their bus home.

> Her clients were two young parents, John and Eilene, who had an infant girl. When Nancy was finally able to have her session with the couple, John's mother, Melba, insisted on sitting in on the sessions, often complaining that the couple was not responsible for the baby, did not understand the needs an infant has, and complaining that she was the only one who thought to change the baby's diaper on a regular basis. The therapist was uncomfortable telling Melba that she could not attend a session in her own home, and worried that requiring this would create a problem in her therapeutic alliance with the family.

In Chapter 15, the ethics of conducting therapy in-home is discussed. In-home therapy offers unique challenges with regard to confidentiality, boundaries, and safety, among others. Nancy's situation is not unique as more agencies and state funding sources are seeing the advantages of providing therapy to families in their own homes.

> Dr. Shannon had a couple and family therapy practice, and had appropriate state licensure as an LMFT. When perusing an ad she had placed in an online advertising venue, she noticed that her ad had listed her qualification to be that of a psychologist, not an LMFT. Thinking that the error was negligible, Dr. Shannon ignored it. Some months later, Dr. Shannon had fraud charges brought against her by a local district attorney trying to "clean up the city" and clamp down on deceptive business practices. Dr. Shannon eventually got the charges dropped, but not before her reputation was damaged, had spent thousands of dollars on an attorney, and had suffered many sleepless nights. Further, each time she renews her liability insurance, she must describe the incident in detail as the insurance company requires.

Dr. Shannon, in her nonchalance about her credentials, paid dearly for her mistake in several ways, including her own mental health and well-being. She should have corrected the error to her credentials quickly, and documented her efforts to do so. In Chapter 16, acting and practicing ethically as a couple and family therapist will be discussed.

Summary

On some issues, couple and family therapists have exquisitely clear direction from professional codes of ethics, such as the dictate that therapists should not engage in sexual intimacy with their clients, but others often fall into gray areas that rely instead on therapists making ethical decisions taking into consideration ethical principles and clients' relational contexts. Therapists need to develop an ethical sensitivity to potential ethical issues to decrease their risk in practice and increase their maneuverability in the therapy room. Therapists are responsible for protecting clients and preserving the sanctuary of the therapeutic relationship. Trust is the foundation of any therapeutic relationship and must be carefully guarded for the profession to survive and thrive. Because of their training in systems theory, couple and family therapists are in an excellent position to understand the complexities of ethical situations, which can include ethical, legal, clinical, and professional components. Couple and family therapists consider the many potential courses of action when evaluating ethical decisions; they evaluate the impact of that decision on the individual, the family, and the relationships between family members and the therapist, and the larger systems involved. Ethics in couple and family therapy is not about moralizing; it is about knowing one's self and biases, working to understand the context and worldview of the client, and making collaborative ethical decisions that best benefit clients.

References

Beauchamp, T. L., & Childress, J. F. (2013). *Principles of biomedical ethics* (7th ed.). New York, NY: Oxford University Press.

Goodwin, G. P., & Darley, J. M. (2008). The psychology of meta-ethics: Exploring objectivism. *Cognition, 106*, 1339–1366. doi: 10.1016/j.cognition.2007.06.007.

Greenberg, L. R., Martindale, D. A., Gould, J. W., & Gould-Saltman, D. J. (2004). Ethical issues in child custody and dependency cases: Enduring principles and emerging challenges. *Journal of Child Custody, 1*(1), 7–30. doi: 10.1300/J190v01n01_02.

Hecker, L. L., & Murphy, M. J. (2015). Contemporary and emerging issues in family therapy. *Australian and New Zealand Journal of Family Therapy, 36*(4), 467–479. doi: 10.1002/anzf.1121.

Indiana Code 25-23.6-6. Chapter 6. Social workers, privileged communications. Retrieved from www.in.gov/legislative/ic/code/title25/ar23.6/ch6.html.

Jankowski, P. J., & Martin, M. J. (2003). Reporting cases of child maltreatment: Decision-making processes of family therapists in Illinois. *Contemporary Family Therapy, 25*(3), 311–332. doi: 10.1023/A:1024511405704.

Lakin, M. (1988). *Ethical issues in the psychotherapies*. New York, NY: Oxford University Press.

Nash, R. J. (2002). *"Real world" ethics: Frameworks for educators and human service professionals*. New York, NY: Teachers College Press.

Roberts, L. W., & Dyer, A. R. (2004). *Concise guide to ethics in mental health care.* Washington, DC: American Psychiatric Publishing.

Shuda, N. (2015, Dec. 21). Counseling clinic warns clients of data breach. *USA Today.* Retrieved from http://www.thenorthwestern.com/story/news/2015/12/21/counseling-clinic-warns-clients-data-breach/77693548/.

Sidgwick, H. (1981). *The methods of ethics* (7th ed.). Indianapolis, IN: Hackett Publishing Company.

Simpson, S., & Stacy, M. (2004). Avoiding the malpractice snare: Documenting suicide risk assessment. *Journal of Psychiatric Practice, 10*(3), 1–5.

Steinberg, K. L., Levine, M., & Doueck, H. J. (1997). Effects of legally mandated child-abuse reports on the therapeutic relationship: A survey of psychotherapists. *American Journal of Orthopsychiatry, 67*(1), 112–122.

Welfel, E. R., & Kitchener, K. S. (2003). Introduction to the special section: Ethics education—An agenda for the 1990s. In D. N. Bersoff (Ed.), *Ethical conflicts in psychology* (pp. 135–139). Washington, DC: American Psychiatric Association.

2

Ethical Decision-Making from a Relational Perspective

Elisabeth Shaw

> Peter is a family therapist in a large country town. Although there were quite a few therapists in town with backgrounds in psychology, social work, and counseling, Peter is the only one, to his knowledge, who had undertaken a master's degree in couple and family therapy. Therefore, his practice is quite busy as he is known to primarily provide relationship-focused work.
>
> Sally and Tom consulted Peter about 10 years ago when their 5-year-old son, David, was refusing to go to school. Additionally, David was frequently picking on his 3-year-old sister. Peter provided parenting strategies and also assisted with strengthening the couple bond, which had become frayed with all the anxiety and tension in the house. Sally and Tom left his service saying they were pleased with the work and that much had changed.
>
> A few months later, Sally contacted Peter for assistance with a workplace concern, and he had agreed to see her for a few sessions. Then, Tom contacted him regarding his grief at his mother dying, and Peter saw him for about 10 sessions. Recently, Sally contacted Peter to ask if he would see David, now age 15, who is again refusing to go to school. After all, Peter was so helpful the first time they tackled that issue together.

Couple and family therapists arguably face more ethical issues in practice than individual therapists, given the multiple variables involved in relational clinical work (Shaw, 2015). There are more relationships to manage, not only in the direct therapeutic contract, but also related to the systems of which each participant in therapy is a part: school, work, church, community. Family therapists are more likely to leave the confines of the therapy room and foray into the life of the client than in individual therapy—we (couple and family therapists) might attend school, workplace, or community venues as part of planned intervention. We might move more fluidly between therapist, advocate, and community partner than is encouraged in individual therapeutic practice. Although couple and family therapists observe relational dynamics, an individually oriented therapist may have only the unilateral perspective from one client. Clients can see their family therapist as akin to their family doctor. That is, all members can attend for individual or relationship concerns, and it is with confidence that the family feels the therapist is holding their individual and group needs in mind: "all for one and one for all". In this way, Sally and Tom's use of Peter's family therapy service is not uncommon, especially in smaller communities. Some therapists may have seen multiple generations of one family, or members with different partners across time. This is a pleasure and a privilege for family therapists.

However, these aspects inevitably mean that ethical issues are numerous and more complicated. For example, how does a family therapist manage informed consent with people at different ages and stages and with different contracts across time? How are notes to be taken and filed, given different contracts and participants, at every session? What sort of privacy and confidentiality can be offered? Are there limits to service, or, like the family doctor, are all new requests welcome and provided? Claxton and Lucas (2007) aptly referred to ethical issues as "more like tangled fishing nets ..." (p. 80). So how do we negotiate our way through ethical dilemmas in practice without getting entangled in the nets?

In our training, we come to understand that, as professionals, decisions rest on our shoulders. When challenged, it will be up to couple and family therapists to demonstrate rigor in our ethical decision-making. There are several tools at our disposal: codes of ethics, the law, and ethical decision-making models with which we engage to varying degrees. However, we can also find these limiting. The specifics of our situations do not always seem well-represented in our codes, with our practice dilemmas sitting between clauses rather than a neat fit with any one person or family. The law is a moral floor beneath which we should not sink; however, when our dilemma is not straightforward, but rather ambiguous, the law can feel like it is also an insufficient guide. Ethical decision-making models can be useful, but their linear, procedural, and cognitive approach can seem at odds with a decision that has us wrought with anxiety.

Yet the biggest problem is that these tools are designed to assist us at the practical end of what is often a highly charged, relationally driven, unique situation. We may be caught unprepared and feel confused by the context, timing, or request. Although we are relational therapists, ethical decisions can lead us to stray from our preferred relationships with clients. Due to legal or regulatory requirements, or our own fears of getting into trouble, we can make decisions that are in our own self-interest; procedural rather than contextual, conservative rather than creative, which may inadvertently injure rather than enhance the relational process under way. Increasing emphases on objective assessment and data management to systematise decision-making has also led practitioners to devalue and even fear their intuitive abilities, which are more likely to foster relationships with clients (Munro, 2002). For couple and family therapists, this can mean that we have unintentionally set aside our best skills and our philosophy of practice.

In this chapter, I explore the philosophical and professional traditions that have led us away from a relational approach to a focus on duty-based ethical decision-making as well as the individual forces at work in this process. I describe how working from a relational ethic, an ethic of care, looks in practice. I also argue that, on an individual level, we will always be impeded in our ethical decision-making if we see the ethics as something we *learn* rather than something we *live*.

Individual Frameworks and Their Limitations

As discussed in Chapter 1, there are six moral principles that form the foundation of functioning at the highest professional level: autonomy, nonmaleficence, justice, beneficence (Beauchamp & Childress, 2013), veracity, and fidelity (Nash, 2002; Sidgwick, 1981). To help us understand these principles in practical terms, our training tends to use "quandary ethics" as a primary training technique; quandary ethics refers to training that uses case studies to highlight various ethical dilemmas using and weighing our key professional principles. The educational aim is to expand our knowledge of what might happen while developing some rules of practice for ourselves. The inherent assumption is that basic moral concepts are literal, well-defined, and easily translated into rules for living that can be consistently applied despite a great deal of evidence to the contrary (Shaw & Carroll, 2016). In practice, dilemmas infrequently seem so straightforward, especially in complex work with multiple parties and with culturally diverse populations.

We are encouraged to use ethical decision-making models to work through dilemmas. Such models are linear in nature and rely largely on the therapist's version of events. Following the traditions of Kohlberg (1982), decision-making models tend to follow a fairly standard formula: (1) Identify the issue: is it an ethical dilemma? (2) What are the facts? Who else is involved? (3) Are there relevant rules or legislative requirements? (4) Scope the options and determine the best fit for the circumstances, and (5) Act on your decision.

Although we are always encouraged to seek guidance when making difficult professional decisions, the nature of being a professional inevitably requires us to make autonomous sound decisions, moment to moment. The philosophical traditions underpinning ethics, forged over thousands of years, have fostered the dominant view that ethical decision-making is at its best if it is sanitised of its emotion while eschewing intuitive responses—solely using rationality, objectivity, and logic. Within this frame, ethical decision-making relies heavily on the cognitive, the concrete, and the ability to separate from the demands of others while ignoring contextual factors. Stripped of personal identity, individuals are required to act as "impersonal calculators" in their interactions with the world. Essentially, it is an ethics of strangers—that is, a "set of rules for governing the interactions of people who neither know nor care about one another" (Hinman, 2013, p. 296).

In our case of Sally's call to request that Peter see her son David, Peter could have followed the model presented and decided to see David for therapy because Peter might believe that Sally has the autonomy to make treatment decisions for her son. Or he might think about the principle of beneficence, and believe that he can truly help David, especially because he understands the family history. He may also reason that his professional code of ethics does not prohibit this behavior. Linear decision-making models rely "heavily on the belief that decision-makers are capable of developing a clear, objective view of what is 'right' and 'wrong' in any given situation. Decisions and acts are seen as deliberate, intentional responses over which individuals have complete control" (Painter-Morland, 2006, p. 90).

As I have noted elsewhere (Shaw, 2011), the dominant traditions surrounding psychotherapy have also emphasised the autonomous individual rather than the collective. Without reflection about the potential of couple and family therapists to foster connectedness and community, couple and family therapists, "...some unwittingly, [will] join the ranks of a political ideology that emphasises the rights of the individual over the larger society" (Inger & Inger, 1994, pp. 10–11). As couple and family therapists, we too can pathologise dependency by negatively framing a family's interdependent interests and involvements. Take for example the Western preoccupation with individuation, which can be at odds with cultures that promote the collective. A common clinical example is when parents are in the terrible position of managing a drug-addicted child, they can be accused of "enabling" the child when trying to keep them close and safe.

Larner (2015) has recently argued that couple and family therapists have long been attuned to the importance of ethics in terms of how we are trained to be sensitive to the use of expertise, knowledge, and power in the therapeutic relationship, as well as how we foster empathy, communication, and ethical relating in therapy. However, our theoretical approach does not inoculate us against the forces at work in our practice context. Although we might be wary about replicating dominant cultures and ideologies, particularly those experienced by clients as oppressive or diminishing of their options, we might be equally compelled to engage in those ideologies to ensure our own professional survival or, seemingly paradoxically, to assist the client. In the case of a family seeking assistance after a trauma, for example, there can be pressure to focus on individual rather than relational needs when there are requests for diagnostic assessment and insurance reports. Some therapists might resolve these difficulties with a purist approach, rejecting such referrals or refusing to participate in some aspects of the work. Although therapists are, of course, welcome to choose their practice focus (and indeed deciding not to do work where one cannot be skilled and authentic is in itself an ethical position), opting out as an ideological position may be limiting. Focusing on hard and fast rules that injure clients who are seeking connection runs contrary to a relational decision-making process. Take for example a rigid application of rules in relation to gift giving. A therapist who refuses to accept any and all gifts (no doubt for good ethical reasons) can miss the cultural and relational nuances and meanings associated with the gift, leading to unnecessary distress for clients.

In the case of Peter's decision to work with David at Sally's request, a more procedural, rule-bound approach to decision-making might start with debating the quandary to oneself: What is Sally's request and should I say yes? Does it suit me to say yes? Is it an appropriate request? In a more relational approach, Peter could instead start his analysis with: Who am I to this family? How does the request fit within the context of our relationship? What are the (various) ways I might be able to respond?

Contemporary systemic practitioners and theorists such as Gergen (1999, 2015), Larner (2015), McNamee (2015), and I (2011, 2015) have argued the impossibility of being able to separate individual action from its relational context. Relationship-based ethical approaches argue that the individualistic, rationalistic dominant discourse has left out the moral wisdom of narrative, interpersonal, and community elements. Several philosophical approaches have attempted to redress this, such as virtue ethics, feminist ethics, and situational ethics (e.g., Bergum & Dossetor, 2005;

Fesmire, 2003; Gilligan, 1982; Hinman, 2013). Within the therapy literature, these themes are also explored through relational ethics and social constructionist theory (e.g., Cottone, 2001; McNamee & Gergen, 1999). This literature emphasises that an individual's ethical landscape is inextricably linked to the relationships in which they exist, and that the preservation of connectedness is a crucial component in ethical decision-making (Painter-Morland, 2006). Within this frame, ethical decisions are always interactional, operating within a consensual domain (Cottone, 2001).

Indeed, as Gergen (2015) argues, if as systemic therapists we accept that meaning is created within coordinated actions then the very concepts of "the individual," "individual minds," and "moral thought" are problematic because all are peripheral to relational traditions. Likewise, he argues that moral action is never accomplished alone. Consider for example the meaning of and responses to a relationship infidelity, an ethical issue within the couple relationship (Shaw 2011, 2015). As therapists, we may have judgements about such behaviour as well as theories of change. The transgressor will have a view, as will the person betrayed. Creating understanding around the relational breach, managing the pain and pursuit of recovery, fostering discussion about what it means for connection, means no one person unilaterally determines the work (although at any point any might choose to do so). Even with issues more pointedly ethical/legal, there are good arguments for working them through with clients, rather than away from them, for example when making a notification of child abuse (Mackinnon, 1998).

However, although couple and family therapists value their relationships with clients, and hold at the core of the work relational process, there is something about ethical decision-making that can lead us to retreat into unilateral decision-making, and then deliver our conclusion to clients in a nonrelational fashion. Although Larner (2015) suggests that ethical therapists take care not to use their words like bullets, this is what clients may experience as a result of our individually driven processes.

What Drives Our Responses to Ethical Challenges?

Beyond Logic: Our Emotional, Empathic, and Intuitive Responses

It is tempting to think that therapists are, by their nature, ethical. The assumption that we are kind, caring, and client-focused makes sense on an intuitive level. However, we are human first and therapists second. Our moral identity has been forged from our histories and experiences, and its coherence and robustness will be one of our strongest resources for ethical action (Detert, Trevino, & Sweitzer, 2008; Schlenker, 2008). Moral sensitivity can vary from person to person and situation to situation. Although our philosophical ancestors might have liked us to display rules, duties, and principles that are consistent across all like decisions, in reality, any two situations can look dissimilar as much as they can look similar, depending on the characters and circumstances involved. Our own self-interest plays a part, and we work with clients who are self-interested, but also have an interest in the collective, relational whole. We are also influenced by the speed at which we have to make decisions and whether the particular situation seems to fall into a familiar area of practice or strikes us as requiring a new and different response.

> Peter talks to Sally about her request to see David. Sally says that the school is insisting that David gets help. As parents, they do not believe they have any power to make him go to school; their sense of efficacy is at an all-time low. They are also angry with David and want him to be seen on his own to "sort him out." They say that David is refusing to attend appointments and they ask Peter for some strategies to get him to attend. Sally also says that the school wants a report including a psychosocial assessment of David, detailing any mental health difficulties, a prognosis, and recommendations for getting him back to school.

When Peter was approached by Sally to talk about her work issues, and when Tom called to seek therapy about his grief, Peter had felt quite comfortable to proceed. There were no "red flags" about these requests, as the work was seen to be distinct and focused. Of course, there is always the risk that the initial request masks another, perhaps an unconscious driver for the therapy, or even that in the course of the work, other life events occur 'out of the blue' and come into the sessions. For example, Sally and Tom could have an unexpected downturn in their relationship, and in the process of seeing one of them, relationship concerns are raised. A relationship therapist can never really know how the excluded other feels about the individual work, even after asking. What is in the conscious mind may belie the lived experience of one's partner seeing the previously shared therapist alone. For all these reasons, and others, moving between individual and relational work is generally discouraged (Shaw, 2015) although in smaller communities, it may be a necessity.

> This new request to see David strikes Peter differently, and it just feels "not quite right." While on the phone he understands Sally's assumption that this new request will be fine; indeed, he is tempted to agree with her. However, he finds

himself saying, "I will think about this and ring you back." Peter has realised he is in different territory, which calls for a slower, more deliberate consideration.

Peter's "red flags" relate to the parents sounding disempowered and tempted to hand the problem of David to Peter. Peter knows this could entrench their disempowerment further in the long-term, even if in the short-term they would be grateful. He hears that David is reluctant to attend therapy. Should Peter join with David's parents and his school, who all insist he attend? How much coercion is permissible in therapy?

Peter was also reluctant to engage in the school's request for an assessment, diagnostic formulation, and singular outcome. Not only was that not his preferred way of working, he had not even met with David yet and heard his side of the story. David's reasons for refusing to attend school at 5 years of age may not be the same reasons at 15 years of age. This may call for a different response and, therefore, different outcomes. Yet, Peter is aware that he has the parents' trust and they see him as part of their extended system; this is potentially advantageous in therapy. But will David see the situation the same way or will he see Peter as his parents' advocate, just one more autocratic adult joining the school and parents against him? Or is Peter free to establish a different sort of connection?

There is no definite ethical problem for Peter at this stage, but there are many ethical dimensions to his decisions that, without consideration, could result in ethical breaches. Peter cannot make the decision simplistically on face value alone: can I meet this request or not? The request cannot be divorced from the history of connection with the family, the series of therapies carried out with the family that laid the groundwork for this request, or the small community in which they live. In effect, Peter's decision-making cannot be linear and procedural, nor can it require only rational considerations, even at this early stage. Peter is taking his own disquiet into account, as his subjective emotional response could be wise intuition about what he should do. He is also empathically attuned to Sally, hearing her confidence in him and her desperation to fix David. Her request to work with the family touches on Peter's ego, yet he realises that previous good work does not transfer to every new request. He also thinks about David, who he does not know in his 15-year-old form, and imagines what this might be like for him. He has questions about Tom, and their other daughter. Might she be a resource?

Peter cannot yet determine a reasoned response, but he does have the precursors to it: intuition, empathy, imagination, and relational responsiveness. Our philosophical ancestors would have eschewed them all, believing them to lead us off the rational path into subjective, irrational, ill-considered terrain. However, we not only know that emotional and intuitive responses are key to knowing we are in ethical territory (Haidt, 2013), that morality is as reliant on emotion, intuition, metaphors, and imagination as it is on rules and principles (Gilligan, 1982; Johnson, 1993; Lakoff & Johnson, 1980), but also that the way our brain functions means we make decisions in relation to our emotional reactions (Haidt, 2013; Kahneman, 2011; Lehrer, 2009). In short, when we ignore our emotional response, we cut ourselves off from one of the key building blocks of the reasoned response we need to ultimately form.

Habits of Practice and Responding to New Challenges

> Peter's experience of his professional community is mixed. On the one hand, he lives and works in a close community, and yet on the other, he can feel quite isolated. Although he was invited to join a peer supervision network, he felt this would be problematic, as he worried that most of his clients would probably have some relationship with the other professionals in the group, just by virtue of being in a small community. Overlapping client and professional relationships could occur via the local school or church, for example. However, he also had his own need for a close community connection and for professional support. Should he accept the offer to join the group or not?

In considering his decision, Peter has a number of options. He could think about his own needs for supervision. Moving to justify his desire to join the group, Peter could well say to himself that it is a professional requirement after all, and everyone living in a small town has to have ways of managing the multiple relationships that occur. He could argue that supervision is in his clients' best interests, that some of the interconnections could enhance his work with clients. He could look at the networks of other professionals, such as the doctors and dentists in town, and wonder if couple and family therapists are being excessively cautious to worry about these issues. He might ask others in the peer group how they manage the boundaries, and he may allow himself to be persuaded by their arguments. Peter may believe he has exhausted his options by talking with others about what to do.

However, we could also consider the flaws in this process. Peter has undertaken a very limited analysis of the decision. He has determined what he wanted and then worked out what sort of analysis best serves the outcome he wants. Self-interest is a part of every decision, much as we might be uncomfortable admitting it. Ethical egoism is an underrecognised aspect in ethical decision-making models. Yet, the very obvious fact that we earn our living by assisting clients means that self-interest is part of every decision we make. Acknowledging this helps us to really think about what role it should play in decision-making. Should self-interest run the decision-making process, or play one small part?

If Peter had asked himself the question 'What ought I do?' rather than 'What do I want?' it might have also led to a different process and conclusion. This would require him to see the decision as more ethically layered. His moral radar would need to be activated, which only happens if we have a strong moral identity (Detert et al., 2008; Schlenker, 2008) or if something in the request alerts us to the fact that there could be complications. If Peter views the question as simply "Will this supervision group suit me?" then he might have a fairly quick decision-making process. Do I usually have supervision? Yes. Do I usually try and work with local, like-minded peers? Yes. Then "perfect match." This is an example of what Kahneman (2011) refers to as "fast thinking"—the way in which we are able to make decisions without much conscious thought, as the information fits long-established mental maps of operation. We use fast thinking to make many of our decisions successfully: shall I get up when the alarm goes off today or call in sick; shall I buy a ticket to take the bus today or try and get away with a free trip; will I stop and give money to the three homeless people I see every day on the way to work or not? Without some internalised means of registering and responding, we would barely get our day under way.

However, the problem with quick decisions is that they can move from being efficient and well-tied to our values and principles, to operating on the basis of blunted moral sensitivity or even moral blindness (Palazzo, Krings, & Hoffrage, 2012). If Peter saw the invitation to join the peer group as only related to his needs, such as his requirement to attend supervision, then that would lead to blunted decision-making.

> Peter realised that one of the members of his peer group is married to his child's teacher. Little Paulie, Peter's son, is having a hard time at school, and Peter has had to speak to the teacher a few times about it. Frankly, he has been unimpressed with her response and has been contemplating speaking to the principal. When he realised the personal connection to the peer group, it made him pause about joining.

This information alerts Peter to the issue of multiple relationships, causing him to wonder if he will be able to talk about his work openly. He desperately needs connection with others, and wishes for the emotional release of speaking with others about his own struggles as a father. Yet he wonders if he can feel free to share his own parenting struggles given that he works with clients who struggle as parents. Will his peers think less of him and not refer to him? This activates what Kahneman (2011) refers to as "slow thinking," where Peter has to stop and actively engage in a more considered process of decision-making. It has triggered something on his moral radar and now he has to work harder. As he thinks about his relationship to others in the peer group, it might lead him to think about his clients' relationships within the peer group. In a small community, if he has connections to the group, he can assume that his clients will also have connections to the group. He asked his peers how they manage these boundaries; he and his peers had an open discussion about the challenges of managing boundaries in a small community. Yet Peter, having registered his own personal discomfort, could no longer be satisfied with a procedural response to this difficulty. Drawn by relational responsiveness to stand in the shoes of his clients, he pictured how they might feel if they knew he was in communication about them with the professionals in this group. He thought about what he could do to preserve confidentiality, to achieve transparency regarding conflicts of interest, and so on. However, he realised that the drawbacks in joining the group outweighed the benefits in relation to his work with his clients. Peter resolved to engage a supervisor in a large city nearby and to have individual supervision via Skype (i.e., video transmission). He could find other ways to connect with his peers.

Self-Knowledge

Self-knowledge has been argued to be critical for couple and family therapists, especially with regard to family-of-origin issues, given that our perceptions and reactions are likely to be influenced by our own family-of-origin issues.

> Therapists who are unaware of their own vulnerabilities are likely to misinterpret their clients or steer clients in a direction that will not arouse their own anxieties. Therapists who are aware of their own emotional issues are less likely to get entangled in the problems of their clients (Corey, Corey, & Callanan, 2011, p. 456).

Research tells us that when interpersonal issues arise, or ethical issues appear, emotion runs higher (Hauser, 2006, 2009). However, while ethical awareness or sensitivity is the first step in ethical decision-making and ethical maturity (Carroll & Shaw, 2012, 2013), research on moral decision-making indicates that strong emotion might actually inhibit decision-making, as people can misread or mistrust it (e.g., Betan & Stanton, 1999; Smith, McGuire, Abbott, & Blau, 1991). High levels of negative emotions have also been related to poor ethical decisions (Krishnakumar & Rymph, 2012).

In such circumstances, people tend not to refer to their codes (Congress & McAuliffe, 2006), but instead will turn to a supervisor or senior colleague (Doyle & Miller, 2009). This is all very well after the fact, but so often we are working moment to moment in the therapy interaction. It is self-knowledge and emotional competence that will be crucial in staying calm under fire in addition to reading oneself and the situation well. Yet, emotional competence is one of the least discussed areas in the literature and in professional development forums posttraining (Tamura, 2012). If Peter is struggling with loneliness in this town, or is vulnerable to calls to his ego—"only you can help us Peter!"—then this will influence his decision, and he needs to be alert enough to recognise it.

The therapist's values will also influence any ethical decision; values are both important and inescapable. Many issues elicit personal, familial, and cultural values in relation to marriage, preservation of the family, diverse family forms and ways of living, cultural differences, equity in relationships, child-rearing, affairs, and sexuality; these values influence us consciously and unconsciously (Corey et al., 2011; Knauss & Knauss, 2012). Through our training and professional culture, which emphasises being "nonjudgmental," we learn to not expose our values to colleagues, and in fact they can slip from our own awareness and common discourse, left in the shadows of professional life. We tend to confuse being "nonjudgmental" with having no strong opinions or values of our own, even though this is far from reality. Rather than pretend that therapy is values-neutral or values-free, we need to acknowledge, explore, and engage more fully with our values in the service of more authentic, relational practice (Knauss & Knauss, 2012; Shaw, 2012).

Decision Making From a Relational Perspective

As is hopefully evident by now, ethical dilemmas have both individual components (*What ought I do? Who shall I be?*) as well as relational components (*What is my duty to others? How do I care for the relationship?*). To make effective decisions, we need to move from processes focused solely on rules and protocols, and duty and principles, to ethics of relational fidelity, and ethics of care.

Nearly 30 years ago, as a student on a family therapy team, I recall keeping a book in which I wrote down every single formal intervention we delivered as part of a Milan systemic approach. I thought this would help me with other families I would see; the assumption being that I would see similar families in similar situations, which of course in broad terms is what happened. At the time, I could have argued this would help me help others, that what I lacked in experience could be recovered by the brilliance of the off-the-shelf intervention. Underpinned by a desperate desire to be helpful and make a difference, I could have argued this was relational responsiveness, but that would have been far from the truth, had I really gone on to get that book out and use it (which I am glad to say I did not!).

What we find in ongoing family practice is that the particulars of the situation, their individual circumstances, our history with the family, and our own emotional response will have a much greater impact on our decision-making than we can prepare for or expect. We can use this information to make the very best decisions, and likewise if we lack a strong moral identity, emotional intelligence, and the ability to shape these data into a reasoned response, we can make poor decisions, or fail to deliver our decisions in action (Detert et al., 2008; Krishnakumar & Rymph, 2012; Schlenker, 2008).

Peter was so caught up by the request to see David that he got stuck in a "will I/won't I?" question, which has little information in it to drive a good decision. It is all about him; he has not allowed himself to engage with a full relational response. At this point, Peter may be concerned that exploring the request with Sally is just making the situation more complicated and harder to refuse; Peter may be worried that the family is indeed making a reasonable request, making it harder for Peter to hold his ground. It is curious that these sorts of fears arise in relation to ethical decisions when the task at hand requires fundamental skills of systemic practice: remaining curious, exploring meaning, asking questions from multiple perspectives, and developing imaginative possibilities.

Peter has a 10-year relationship with Sally and Tom and it has largely been successful. He does not want to let them down and he does not want to turn them down. Professional codes of ethics offer statements on the risks of dual relationships, but how does that work for family therapy in which multiple relationships are inherent in the work? What is seen to be "usual" family practice, and when has Peter taken on more responsibilities than he can manage? He has yet to ask himself about the cost to him or the family of turning down the work. Nor has he considered whom he could consult about this. He could consult his new supervisor to help him think it through. He is stuck in "what shall I do?" at the expense of a fuller engagement with the request.

Relational Ethics

"Responsiveness to self and responsiveness to others are essential components of ethics" (Bergum & Dossetor, 2005, p. 78). The suggestion that we can distinguish ourselves, our thoughts, and our actions separately from the clients with whom we work is flawed. Although our decisions must ultimately be defended by reason, our pathway to rational thought is complex and multifaceted. As previously discussed, the work of Haidt (2013), for example, tells us that decision-making in fact operates at a much more emotional and intuitive level.

Further, we cannot make decisions solely from our own perspective. As soon as we have retreated into our own heads and rely on our interpretations alone, we have lost key aspects of the assessment process. We exist and relate in a web of coordinated action—the "to and fro" of the relational dance. Meaning is created from the coordinated actions between people, whether in language or gestures (Gergen, 2015; Larner, 2015). All that we are is conceived in relationship with others and yet, when we make ethical decisions, we are encouraged to step back and separate the elements, separate ourselves from others, and then to decide on behalf of the parties and deliver that decision unilaterally. There are many decisions for which this process may be important and relevant; however, it has limited application. If we accept that everything we are is in relationship, that there is no meaning outside of relational meaning, then we need to accept that moral action is not accomplished alone. Caught in our own worries about the decisions at hand, fueled by good intentions to be responsible, we can forget to include our clients in the decision. Often, sharing our dilemmas with clients will lead to therapeutically useful, practical outcomes. In Peter's case, rather than take on the decision about working with David, Peter could suggest meeting with Sally and Tom, his primary clients, to collaborate in service of David. This might give him more information about the best way forward.

Relational ethics places connectedness at the center of decision-making. Rather than everyone retreating to their respective corners to think, there is an engagement to think together. However, it is important to be clear about what relational ethics is *not.* Relational responsiveness can be confused with doing what the client requests. I have heard this called "client-centered practice." However, in matters of ethics, the therapist should no more be a hostage to the client requests than the client should necessarily comply with the dictates of the therapist. Either position is one involving misuse of power, not relational decision-making.

Relational responsiveness does not necessarily mean that consensus is reached or that everyone walks away equally happy with the decision. Therapists must always be mindful of their ethical and legal obligations and not breach them; clients may want to push for more, even when they know they are asking too much. However, when engaged in conversation involving all aspects of the decision: the request, its meaning to all family members, the non-negotiable, the imaginative possibilities, and the constraints each might be under individually (e.g., Peter's code of ethics, availability) and outside (e.g., the school), new conclusions may be forged in which the longstanding connection is preserved, whether or not the new work is undertaken.

Ethical Maturity as a Lifelong Process

Ethical decision-making requires more from us than reading our professional ethical code, following a procedure, or talking to our supervisor, even though all are helpful and may in many cases be sufficient. We have to be able to identify when the decision at hand has an ethical dimension, how to read the situation, and to have the courage to implement our decisions into action. Research has demonstrated that this is particularly difficult when relational components intrude, and when we feel particularly reactive to the situation (e.g., Smith et al., 1991). As therapists, we can seek out colleagues to "debrief," and then once we have "cooled off" and had a good hearing, we tend to do nothing more. Debriefing becomes the action we take, rather than seeing our decisions through (Shaw & Carroll, 2016). Good decision-making also involves reflecting on our actions and learning from experience. My colleague, Michael Carroll, and I (Carroll & Shaw, 2012, 2013) have conceptualised ethical maturity as follows:

1. *Fostering ethical sensitivity and watchfulness.* Ethical sensitivity, that "gut response" that something is wrong, provides the first alert that there is an ethical issue at stake. Not to be ethically sensitive is to miss the signs of ethical presences and thus, abandon further stages in the ethical decision-making process. The twin anchors of ethical sensitivity are empathy and compassion. Ethical sensitivity is about what we might do, as well as awareness about what we have not done.
2. *Discerning ethical decisions.* Being able to make an ethical decision aligned with our ethical principles and our values.
3. *Implementing ethical decision(s).* Implementing action may demand moral courage and perseverance/resilience to see a difficult task completed; it

may involve withstanding consequences that seem too high on a personal and relational level.

4. *Being able to articulate and justify the decision to stakeholders.* This ethical component is not about justification, defensiveness, or superficial understandings of our actions, but about knowing ourselves in-depth and being able to own up to what is required—always difficult in the area of ethics. However, as professionals, we must be accountable for our actions.
5. *Ethical peace and sustainability.* Achieving closure on the event, even when there were other possible decisions or "better" decisions that could have been made. Living peacefully with the consequences of ethical decision-making is crucial to ongoing well-being.
6. *Learning from what has happened and "testing" the decision through reflection.* Integrating what we have learned into our lives develops our moral character and extends our ethical wisdom and capacity. Part of the process of developing ethical maturity is learning from experience.

Ultimately, these six components result in ethical maturity. The six components come together in a definition or description of ethical maturity, which we define as:

> Having the reflective, rational, emotional, and intuitive capacity to decide if actions are right and wrong, or good and better; having the resilience and courage to implement those decisions; being accountable for ethical decisions made (publicly or privately); and being able to learn from and live with the experience (Carroll & Shaw, 2013, p. 28).

Conclusion

Couple and family therapists face complex ethical issues as a result of managing multiple relationships and working between multiple systems, some of which may appear to be at odds with each other. In contemporary practice, on our side of the therapeutic fence, we also work across paradigms in delivering service, we work in interdisciplinary teams, and we are obliged to meet the terms of a range of stakeholders: the government, health insurers, organisational compliance officers, and regulators. Despite all of these interrelated and intersecting factors and components, when an ethical consideration is present, anxiety and pressure can lead us to restrict our vision of important components of the decision, excluding key people, resources, and information. Effective ethical decision-making requires us to remain calm under fire, to allow ourselves time to make a fully informed decision, and to stay relationally engaged. Despite our training in relationship work, when the stakes are high, the age-old temptation to take flight or flee is strong. This can lead to poor decisions, but also means we have lost the very best of our traditions and ourselves as systemic practitioners.

Ethical maturity is a lifelong journey, not a destination. Knowing that habits of practice and fast thinking can lead to ethical missteps, we need to attend to self-care and to ensure we are well-connected to colleagues that challenge and inspire us, not just validate our perennial positions. We also need to consider our relationship with ourselves. Emotional responsiveness, accountability, empathy, and moral sensitivity are crucial in relational work, and they require space and time to foster and flourish.

References

Beauchamp, T. L., & Childress, J. F. (2013). *Principles of biomedical ethics* (7th ed.). New York, NY: Oxford University Press.

Bergum, V., & Dossetor, J. (2005). *Relational ethics: The full meaning of respect.* Hagerstown, MD: University Publishing Group.

Betan, E. J., & Stanton, A. L. (1999). Fostering ethical willingness: Integrating emotional and contextual awareness with rational analysis. *Professional Psychology: Research and Practice, 30*(3), 295–301. doi: 10.1037/0735-7028.30.3.295.

Carroll, M., & Shaw, E. (2012). *Ethical maturity in the helping professions: Making difficult life and work decisions.* Melbourne, Australia: PsychOz Publication.

Carroll, M., & Shaw, E. (2013). *Ethical maturity in the helping professions: Making difficult life and work decisions.* London, England: Jessica Kingsley Press.

Claxton, G., & Lucas, B. (2007). *The creative thinking plan.* London, England: BBC Books.

Congress, E., & McAuliffe, D. (2006). Social work ethics. Professional codes in Australia and the United States. *International Journal of Social Work, 49,* 151. doi: 10.1177/0020872806061211.

Corey, G., Corey, M. S., & Callanan, P. (2011). *Issues and ethics in the helping professions* (8th ed.). Belmont, CA: Brooks/Cole Cengage.

Cottone, R. R. (2001). A social constructivism model of ethical decision making in counselling. *Journal of Counselling and Development, 79*(1), 39–45. doi: 10.1002/j.1556-6676.2001.tb01941.x.

Detert, J. R., Trevino, L. K., & Sweitzer, V. L. (2008). Moral disengagement in ethical decision making: A study of antecedents and outcomes. *Journal of Applied Psychology, 93*(2), 374–391. doi: 10.1037/0021-9010.93.2.374.

Doyle, O. Z., & Miller, S. E. (2009). Ethical decision-making in social work: Exploring personal and professional values. *Journal of Social Work Values and Ethics, 6*(1), 4–36.

Fesmire, S. (2003). *John Dewey and moral imagination, pragmatism in ethics.* Bloomington, IN: Indiana University Press.

Gergen, K. J. (1999). *Relational being: Beyond self and community.* New York, NY: Oxford University Press.

Gergen, K. J. (2015). Relational ethics in therapeutic practice. *Australian and New Zealand Journal of Family Therapy, 36*(4), 409–418. doi: 10.1002/anzf.1123.

Gilligan, C. (1982). *In a different voice, psychological theory and women's development.* Cambridge, MA: Harvard University Press.

Haidt, J. (2013). *The righteous mind: Why people are divided by politics and religion.* New York, NY: First Vintage Books.

Hauser, M. D. (2006). The liver and the moral organ. *Social Cognitive and Affective Neuroscience Advance Access, 1*(3), 214–220. doi: 10.1093/scan/nsl026.

Hauser, M. D. (2009, Dec. 2). It seems biology (not religion) equals morality. *Edge.* Retrieved from http://edge.org/conversation/it-seems-biology-not-religion-equals-morality.

Hinman, L. (2013). *Ethics: A pluralistic approach to moral theory* (5th ed.). Boston, MA: Wadsworth Cengage.

Inger, I., & Inger, J. (1994). *Creating an ethical position in family therapy.* London, England: Karnac Books.

Johnson, M. (1993). *Moral imagination: Implications of cognitive science for ethics.* Chicago, IL: University of Chicago Press.

Kahneman, D. (2011). *Thinking fast and slow.* London, England: Allen Lane Publications.

Knauss, L. K., & Knauss, J. W. (2012). Ethical issues in multiperson therapy. In S. Knapp (Ed.), *APA handbook of ethics in psychology: Practice, teaching, and research* (Vol. 2, pp. 29–43). Washington, DC: American Psychological Association.

Kohlberg, L. (1982). *The philosophy of moral development.* San Francisco, CA: Harper and Row.

Krishnakumar, S., & Rymph, D. (2012). Uncomfortable ethical decisions: The role of negative emotions and emotional intelligence in ethical decision-making. *Journal of Managerial Issues, 14*(3), 321–344.

Lakoff, G., & Johnson, M. (1980). *Metaphors we live by.* Chicago, IL: The University of Chicago Press.

Larner, G. (2015). Ethical family therapy: Speaking the language of the other. *Australian and New Zealand Journal of Family Therapy, 36*(4), 434–449. doi: 10.1002/anzf.1131.

Lehrer, J. (2009). *How we decide.* New York, NY: Houghton Mifflin Harcourt Publishing Company.

MacKinnon, L. (1998). *Trust and betrayal in the treatment of child abuse.* New York, NY: Guilford Press.

McNamee, S. (2015). Ethics as discursive potential. *Australian and New Zealand Journal of Family Therapy, 36*(4), 419–433. doi: 10.1002/anzf.1125.

McNamee, S., & Gergen, K. J. (Eds.). (1999). *Relational responsibility: Resources for sustainable dialogue.* London, England: Sage Publications.

Munro, E. (2002). Integrating intuition and analysis in child protection. *Social Welfare at Berkeley, 19*(1), 7–9.

Nash, R. J. (2002). *"Real world" ethics: Frameworks for educators and human service professionals.* New York, NY: Teachers College Press.

Painter-Morland, M. (2006). Redefining accountability as relational responsiveness. *Journal of Business Ethics, 66*(1), 89–98. doi: 10.1007/s10551-006-9046-0.

Palazzo, G., Krings, F., & Hoffrage, U. (2012). Ethical blindness. *Journal of Business Ethics, 109,* 323–338. doi: 10.1007/s10551-011-1130-4.

Schlenker, B. (2008). Integrity and character: Implications of principled expedient ethical ideologies. *Journal of Social and Clinical Psychology, 27*(1), 1078–1125. doi: 10.1521/jscp.2008.27.10.1078.

Shaw, E. (2011). Relational ethics and moral imagination in contemporary systemic practice. *Australian & New Zealand Journal of Family Therapy, 32*(1), 1–14. doi: 10.1375/anft.32.1.1.

Shaw, E. (2012). The place for judgement in postmodern clinical practice. *Psychotherapy in Australia, 19*(1), 28–34.

Shaw, E. (2015). Ethical practice in couple and family therapy: Negotiating rocky terrain. *Australian & New Zealand Journal of Family Therapy, 36*(4), 504–517. doi: 10.1002/anzf.1129.

Shaw, E., & Carroll, M. (2016). Towards ethics in counselling psychology. In B. Douglas, R. Woolfe, S. Strawbridge, E. Kasket, & V. Galbraith (Eds.), *Handbook of counselling psychology* (4th ed.). London, England: Sage.

Sidgwick, H. (1981). *The methods of ethics* (7th ed.). Indianapolis, IN: Hackett Publishing Company.

Smith, T. S., McGuire, J. M., Abbott, D. W., & Blau, B. I. (1991). Clinical ethical decision making: An investigation of the rationales used to justify doing less than one believes one should. *Professional Psychology: Research and Practice, 22*(3), 235–239. doi: 10.1037/0735-7028.22.3.235.

Tamura, L. J. (2012). Emotional competence and well-being. In S. J. Knapp (Ed.), *APA handbook of ethics in psychology: Moral foundations and common themes* (Vol. 1, pp. 175–215). Washington, DC: American Psychological Association.

3

Legal Issues in Couple and Family Therapy

Ruth Ogden Halstead and John H. Halstead

Heather and Jared came into therapy after an intense argument in which the police were called. In therapy, they worked on their emotional reactivity to each other. The therapist has concerns about the effects of Heather and Jared's domestic disputes on her three children from a previous relationship. During the course of therapy, Al, the father of Heather's children, learned about the police report and petitioned the court for a protective order against Jared, asking the court to order Jared to stay away from Heather and Al's children. The therapist was subpoenaed to testify at the hearing by Jared, who opposed the protective order. Later, criminal charges were filed against Jared by the prosecutor for domestic violence. The therapist received a subpoena from the prosecutor for the therapy notes.

Ethics and the Law

Ethics and the law differ. Both ethics and the law govern the practice of couple and family therapy.[1] A therapist's ethical and legal obligations overlap to a degree, but not entirely. When ethics prescribes a higher or more restrictive standard than that required by the law, or vice versa, the therapist should abide by the higher or more restrictive standard.

"Ethics" refers to the standards governing the conduct of members of a certain profession (Committee on Professional Practice and Standards, APA, 2003). Written ethical codes frame these standards for each profession. All major mental health professions have professional associations that publish their own ethical codes, such as the American Association for Marriage and Family Therapy (AAMFT), the American Psychological Association (APA), the National Association of Social Workers (NASW), and the American Counseling Association (ACA).

The "law" refers to the body of statutes, regulations, and ordinances that are passed by a legislature or other governmental body, as well as the written opinions of judges interpreting those statutes. In some cases, an ethical obligation gets adopted into state or federal law—for example, the ethical obligation to maintain client confidentiality. Similarly, some states have criminalized sexual contact between a therapist and a client. In cases in which ethical rules have been codified into law, ethical violations may result in criminal penalties, such as fines or even incarceration. An ethical violation may also result in the filing of a civil lawsuit (i.e. malpractice) seeking monetary compensation for a physical, emotional, or financial injury, which resulted from the therapist's ethical breach.

Clients can file an ethical complaint with a therapist's national professional organization, the state licensing board, or state attorney general. Not all complaints result in formal investigations or disciplinary proceedings; this decision rests with the governing agency. Given the nature of couple and family therapy and the frequent intersection with the legal system, it is not uncommon for unfounded allegations to be made against a therapist when a client is unsatisfied or angry. Again, these allegations may or may not lead to an investigation. However, serious consequence can result when there is an actual violation of ethical or legal standards. National professional organizations can revoke the therapist's membership, the state licensing board can revoke or suspend the therapist's license, and/or the state attorney general can institute criminal proceedings against the therapist. Less severe violations may result in lesser consequences such as mandated supervision of their practice, restrictions on the therapist's practice, or a reprimand.

Confidentiality and Privilege

Communications between a therapist and a client are "confidential." When a communication is "confidential," a therapist may not voluntarily disclose that communication to a third person; it is the therapist's ethical duty to keep the information private. The therapist must obtain a signed release of information to be authorized to break clients' right to their confidential information. A general rule is that even when the therapist releases information about a client, the therapist releases the minimum necessary information to satisfy the need for the release, unless the information is for treatment purposes. This general rule applies to the exceptions to confidentiality as well (see "minimum necessary standard" in Chapter 4).

Exceptions to confidentiality occur when there is a duty to report abuse or neglect. When a client is at an immediate risk of suicide, it may trigger our "duty to protect," or when there is a danger the client will harm another person or group of people, it may trigger our "duty to warn." Although professional ethical codes address limits to confidentiality, many states also have laws imposing a legal duty to report under certain circumstances. These exceptions will be discussed in more detail below.

It is important to understand the difference between confidentiality and privilege. "Confidentiality" is an ethical obligation, not a legal one. A "privilege" is a right owned by the client to not have their private information disclosed in court proceedings. Communications that are protected by law are said to be "privileged." The psychotherapist–client privilege was recognized by the U.S. Supreme Court in the 1996 case of *Jaffee v. Redmond*. The psychotherapist–client relationship is now considered to be "privileged" in every state, in the same way that the attorney–client relationship is considered to be privileged, and for many of the same reasons. If a communication is privileged, the therapist generally has the duty to refuse to testify about the communication and the right to refuse to produce documentation of the communication. Indeed, the therapist is *ethically* required to assert the client's privilege. The client, however, may waive their privilege (in writing or in court), and then the therapist may disclose the information.

However, just as there are exceptions to the ethical rule of confidentiality (which are discussed in the following section), there are exceptions to the legal rule of privilege. A therapist may be compelled by law to disclose confidential information under certain circumstances. Some circumstances in which exceptions to privilege might arise include involuntary commitment hearings and guardianship proceedings in which the client's mental competency is at issue, criminal proceedings where the client has claimed insanity as a defense, divorce or custody proceedings, malpractice lawsuits against the therapist, or civil lawsuits where the client has put their psychological condition at issue (Glosoff, Herlihy, Herlihy, & Spence, 1997). Responding to subpoenas and testifying in court hearing and depositions will be discussed in more detail later.

Duty to Report

The duty to report, also called "mandated reporting," refers to a therapist's obligation to report child abuse, elder abuse, or abuse of other dependents to the proper authorities. Therapists are expected to help protect those who cannot protect themselves from abuse or neglect. This is an exception to the ethical obligation to keep communications with clients confidential. Therapists should make this exception explicit in the informed consent at the beginning of treatment.

Most states have legislated the duty to report, in which case the therapist has both a legal and an ethical duty to report abuse or neglect. Some states may require the therapist to report suspected abuse within a certain amount of time, such as 24 or 48 hours. Failure to report may result in criminal culpability and/or civil liability, especially if an injury results from the therapist's inaction. Some states require the report to be made to the police, others to social services, an abuse hotline, or some other entity. Some states require a written report to follow a phone call within a certain time period. The duty to report cannot be delegated to someone else, such as an employer or employee. No one can perform the reporting on the therapist's behalf. Only the therapist themselves can discharge the duty to report. When multiple health care providers develop a suspicion of abuse or neglect, each of them must make their own report (AAMFT, 2007).

Different states apply different standards for reporting; however, some circumstances that may trigger a duty to report in one state may not trigger it in another state. In some states, all that is required is a "mere suspicion of abuse," whereas other states require something more, such as a "reasonable suspicion" or even "probable cause" to believe that abuse or neglect has occurred. These are objective standards, which means a therapist will be judged by what a reasonable therapist would have done under the same or similar circumstances. In the case example here, the therapist might have a duty to report if the therapist felt that the frequency and severity of Jared and Heather's fighting were such that the children were being harmed.

Therapists should review the laws of the state where they practice to determine under what circumstances the duty to report is triggered (AAMFT, 2007). The website for the state professional licensing agency is a good place to find the statutes and regulations that govern a particular profession. Therapists should consult an attorney to determine how the statutes are applied by the courts of their state.

Different states will also have different definitions of "abuse" or "neglect." In some states, slapping and spanking of children may be considered reasonable discipline, so long as it is done with an open hand and leaves no bruising, whereas hitting with a closed fist or hitting with an object, such as a belt, may be considered abuse, even if it leaves no bruises. When a report is made, the state authorities will initiate an investigation to determine whether the claim is "substantiated" or not. If a claim is substantiated, then the state will most likely offer services or potentially suspend rights of the caregivers until the caregivers show the court that they are ready to resume caregiving without exploitation or abuse. The therapist that made the report may or may not be a part of the court-mandated services once a claim has been "substantiated" by the state investigators. The therapist may have to testify and justify their recommendations to the court.

State law typically grants the therapist immunity from criminal prosecution and/or civil liability for breaking confidentiality and reporting abuse or neglect, depending on the circumstances. Some states have also passed laws that protect the therapist from discipline or retaliation by their employer for reporting suspected abuse. Usually, the therapist will only be immune if they have acted in "good faith." This is a subjective standard, which means that the therapist acted with the best interest of their client and with the public in mind (AAMFT, 2007).

Therapists may have concerns about the effect reporting will have on the therapeutic relationship. If the therapist's client is the perpetrator, the therapist may ask the client to make the report to the authorities, with the therapist present for support. This may help preserve the therapeutic relationship while also being beneficial to the client. Having the client report the abuse in the context of therapy may demonstrate to the authorities that the client is taking responsibility for their actions and is already working to change. However, the client should be aware that self-reporting will likely be considered a confession in any criminal proceeding. The therapist should frankly discuss the pros and cons of self-reporting with the client without any coercion, but the therapist should refrain from giving legal advice to clients (Nestor, Steiner, & Stewart, 2010).

Duty to Warn

The duty to warn refers to the obligation of the therapist to protect third parties from physical harm (and sometimes property damage) from the therapist's own clients. Most states have legislated the duty to warn, which means the therapist has a legal, as well as an ethical duty, to warn an intended victim.

Tarasoff v. Regents of the University of California is the seminal case in duty to warn jurisprudence. The *Tarasoff* case involved University of California student, Prosenjit Poddar, who was being seen by a psychologist, Dr. Lawrence Moore, at University of California Berkeley's Cowell Memorial Hospital in 1969. Prosenjit told the therapist that he was going to kill a fellow student, Tatiana Tarasoff, whom he believed had romantically rebuffed him. Prosenjit did not disclose Tatiana's name to Dr. Moore, but he disclosed that he had recently purchased a gun. Dr. Lawrence reported the threat to the campus police, who questioned the client and subsequently released him. Two months later, Prosenjit killed Tatiana. Tatiana's family sued the University of California. The case was initially dismissed, but then appealed, and the case made its way to the California Supreme Court. The court ultimately found the university to be liable, because neither Dr. Moore nor other staff attempted to identify whom the client's girlfriend was, even though the girlfriend was readily identifiable. Although the legal effect of the *Tarasoff* case was limited to California, it fundamentally changed the understanding of the therapeutic relationship nationwide by limiting a client's right to confidentiality. The court ruling established that a therapist has a duty to protect individuals who are not clients when harm has been threatened by a client and that this duty outweighs a therapist's duty to protect the client's confidentiality. The California Supreme Court explained: "The protective privilege ends where the public peril begins" (*Tarasoff v. Regents of the University of California*, 551 P.2d at 347). This was subsequently termed the "duty to warn." The therapist should explain to clients before treatment starts that the therapist has a duty to break confidentiality if they believe the client is a danger to others or to themselves.

The therapist should keep in mind that the duty to warn is only triggered when there is a serious danger of imminent violence. There must be something more than hyperbolic "venting" of anger by the client. The therapist must make every effort to determine whether the client has an actual intent and whether there is a specific victim in mind. The therapist should also assess whether the client has access to firearms or other weapons.

Therapists are not expected to control the behavior of their clients, but rather they are required to act reasonably to protect others. As the *Tarasoff* case illustrated, even if the client does not identify the intended victim by name, the therapist has a duty to attempt to identify the victim through other means. It is not specified exactly when the duty must be satisfied. As *Tarasoff* illustrated, notifying the police may not discharge the therapist's duty to warn, though in some states the duty is satisfied when the therapist contacts the police (Packman, Andalibian, Eudy, Howard, & Bongar, 2009). Therapists may have a duty to warn the potential victim as well. When a duty to warn arises, the therapist must still make every effort to do so in a way that preserves the confidentiality of the client to the extent that is possible while still protecting the intended victim. Whether the therapist warns the police, notifies the victim, and/or takes other action will depend on the specific circumstances of the case. Therapists will be held to an objective "standard of care," which means they will be judged by what a reasonable therapist would have done under the same situation with the same resources (Moffett & Moore, 2011).

Duty to Protect

A related duty is the duty to protect one's own clients from serious self-harm. Therapists must continually assess their clients' risk for suicide, including their level of suicidal ideation and whether they have an actual intent and ability to follow through. When a therapist believes that a client has become a danger to themselves, they have a duty to protect the client by reporting the risk. The therapist may need to report the risk to a family member of the client or to the police, or they may need to hospitalize the client (Woody, 2000).

There are many ways a therapist may be found to be negligent in failing to protect a client from self-harm (Woody, 2000). The therapist should carefully and continually assess clients' risk of self-harm, including the clients' access to lethal means, their social support system, and what treatment they are receiving from other professionals. A client's circumstances may change at any point, so ongoing assessment is necessary to manage the risk.

Once a therapist determines a client's level of risk for self-harm, they should determine the level of treatment appropriate to that level of risk. A high risk would typically signal the need for hospitalization, where there is 24-hour monitoring and lack of access to dangerous instrumentalities. However, even after hospitalization, continued care of the client will likely still be required, including intensive outpatient care, mandatory check-ins with psychiatrists, removal of weapons from the client's home, and the establishment of a schedule of caregivers and family members who will monitor the client.

Therapist should make themselves reasonably available to clients who are at risk for serious self-harm, and should give clients information about where they can go for help if the therapist is unavailable. The termination of the therapeutic relationship carries with it a special risk of the client feeling abandoned by the therapist, and this may put the therapist at even greater risk. When the therapeutic relationship is terminated, therapists should help the client with appropriate referrals and continue to make themselves available to the client until a new therapeutic relationship is established with another professional.

The duty to protect a client from serious self-harm could also extend to clients who are *not* suicidal, but whose actions could potentially be lethal. Nonsuicidal self-injury, such as cutting, and highly risky behaviors, such as adolescent heavy drinking or reckless driving, may trigger the duty to protect. Although clients' intent may not be suicide, their behaviors may still have lethal consequences. The general rule is that, if a client is at risk of becoming a serious harm to themselves, the therapist has an ethical and legal duty to report the risk to protect the client.

Responding to Subpoenas

The receipt of a subpoena is frequently the first interaction a therapist will have with the legal system. A subpoena or summons is an order to appear in court or at a deposition, or an order to produce documents, such as a therapist's notes. Depending on the jurisdiction, subpoenas may be issued by a judge, by the clerk of the court, or even by an attorney in private practice. Subpoenas may be issued by an attorney representing the therapist's client or by an attorney opposing the therapist's client. A subpoena may be issued in a civil proceeding such as a lawsuit or a divorce or custody dispute, in a criminal proceeding, or in an administrative proceeding such as a worker's compensation claim.

Certain subpoenas are only enforceable within a limited geographical area. For example, subpoenas issued in a state court proceeding may only be enforceable in that state. A subpoena may need to be served in a certain manner to be valid, or the subpoena may need to allow a certain amount of time for compliance so that subpoenas that are served the day before a hearing may not be valid. A therapist who has been served with a subpoena should keep in mind, however, that the consequences of failing to respond to an enforceable subpoena are serious. Failure to appear or respond to a subpoena may result in the therapist being held in contempt of court and fined, or in extreme cases, the issuance of a warrant for the therapist's arrest.

To determine whether a subpoena is enforceable, it is best for a therapist to consult an attorney. The clerk of the court may also be able to tell a therapist whether a subpoena is enforceable. When in doubt, it is always best to assume the subpoena is valid. This does not mean, however, that the therapist should automatically comply with everything the subpoena requests. A therapist may appear for a hearing, for example, but refuse to answer questions that require disclosure of confidential information.

Upon receipt of a subpoena, a therapist should immediately contact the client to inform them about the subpoena. A subpoena does not by itself cancel a client's right to confidentiality. This can only be done by a waiver of the psychotherapist–client privilege from the client or by an order from a judge. In cases of couple's or family therapy where there are multiple clients, each of the clients must individually waive the privilege for the waiver to be effective. In the case example here, the therapist should advise Heather that she has received Jared's subpoena. Jared will likely waive the privilege because he was the one issuing the subpoena, but Heather may not want to waive the privilege, in which case the therapist cannot testify about any joint therapy sessions with the couple or any individual sessions with Heather. Therapists should know that, in cases of treatment of minors, waiver by a parent may not be sufficient without waiver by the minor themselves. When in doubt, a therapist should consult with legal counsel. If unable to do so, the therapist should always err on the side of protecting clients' confidential information.

Clients may not want to have their confidential information revealed in court or in a deposition. To the extent that the therapist is able to anticipate what they will be asked when they testify, they should candidly disclose to the client what their anticipated testimony will be, so that the client can make an informed decision whether to waive the privilege. It is also preferable that clients do not hear what the therapist will say for the first time in court or in a deposition. Waiver of the privilege by a client always should be done in writing. Failure to carefully and sensitively handle these issues early on could result in a malpractice claim or ethical complaint against the therapist later.

The client should be advised that the therapist may be ordered by the judge to disclose confidential information even without the client's consent, in which case the therapist will have no choice but to do so. The therapist should discuss with the client the effect this will have on the therapeutic relationship. The therapist may need to process with the client any feelings of betrayal. The therapist should consult with the client's attorney, if represented. The client's attorney will likely also need to know what the therapist will say so as to prepare how to respond. Remember though that the therapist should not talk to any attorney, even the client's attorney, in the absence of a written waiver from the client. Indeed, the therapist should not even confirm the existence of a therapeutic relationship in the absence of a written waiver. The therapist also should keep in mind that the client's attorney does not represent the therapist. Any advice the attorney gives the therapist will be designed to benefit the client, but not necessarily the therapist (Committee on Legal Issues, APA, 2006). In addition, the therapist's conversations with the client's attorney are not privileged, like conversations between the client and their attorney are.

The client may request the court to "quash" (or cancel) a subpoena or issue a "protective order" limiting the scope of the subpoena. Although the therapist has an obligation to protect the client's confidentiality, the right to confidentiality belongs to the client, not the therapist (Committee on Legal Issues, APA, 2006). Consequently, certain actions taken by the client may unintentionally waive that right. Under certain circumstances, a judge may determine that the client has "waived the privilege," or given up the right to confidentiality. A client may have waived the privilege by making certain claims or raising certain defenses, for example, claims for emotional distress in a personal injury lawsuit. The therapist should remember, however, that even if a privilege is waived for the purpose of a particular court proceeding, it is not necessarily waived for all court proceedings. In addition, even if a therapist is compelled to disclose confidential information in a legal proceeding, it is still unethical to disclose that information in other settings.

That the client has not waived confidentiality does not mean the therapist can ignore the subpoena or fail to appear for a deposition or hearing (Committee on Legal Issues, APA, 2006). Nor does it mean that the therapist will not ultimately have to disclose the confidential information. If the therapist is subpoenaed, they should attend the deposition or hearing even if they intend to invoke the psychotherapist–client privilege and refuse to answer questions. In such a case, a therapist should attend the deposition or hearing and, when asked about confidential information, state that they refuse to answer on the basis of the psychotherapist–client privilege. It is advisable that a therapist who intends to assert the psychotherapist–client privilege be represented by their own legal counsel.

However, whether the therapist is ultimately required to disclose confidential information is a determination that neither the therapist nor the lawyers can make; only a judge can make this determination. A judge's order trumps the client's or therapist's claim of privilege. If a privilege is asserted at a hearing, then the judge may order the therapist to answer, in which case the therapist is required to do so. If the privilege is asserted over documents, then the judge may require the therapist to hand over the records for an "*in camera*" (off the record) review, in which the judge will decide whether the records must be disclosed. If a privilege is asserted at a deposition, then the attorneys may pause the deposition to telephone the judge for a ruling or they may "continue" (suspend) the deposition while they petition the court in writing and seek a ruling another day.

A therapist may also request the court to quash a subpoena if compliance would violate confidentiality, or request a protective order limiting the subpoena in some way, for example, if the subpoena is unreasonably broad or if producing the information would be unduly burdensome to the therapist. A therapist may request that treatment records be kept "under seal," meaning they are not made public and only used for a limited purpose in the context of the legal proceeding, or they may request that certain information be "redacted" (blacked out) from the records, such as information regarding sexually transmitted diseases or other information not relevant to the litigation. In the case example here, the therapist may ask the court in the criminal proceeding to quash the subpoena issued by the prosecutor for the therapist's records on the basis that they include Heather's confidential information, as well as Jared's. The court may need to review the records under seal and redact the references to Heather before they are admitted into evidence in the prosecution of the domestic violence charges against Jared.

Therapists have the right to have legal counsel present during testimony, whether it is in court or in a deposition. However, many therapists will not have an attorney present, often because it is not financially cost-effective for them to do so. A therapist's malpractice insurance carrier may provide legal counsel to assist the therapist in responding to the subpoena. If not, a therapist may wish to consult with their governing professional licensing board, agency, or professional association.

A therapist is not required to speak to any attorney. It is preferable that any communication with an attorney be in writing, especially with an attorney who is "adverse" (opposed) to the therapist's client. With the permission of the client, the therapist may contact the attorney who issued the subpoena to discuss what specifically the attorney wants from the therapist. In some cases, the attorney may only want documentation, not testimony. In other cases, the attorney may want *favorable* testimony. After the therapist speaks with the attorney (with the client's written consent), the attorney may determine that therapist's testimony will not be favorable to their case, in which case the therapist may be released from the subpoena. If the therapist has a legitimate scheduling conflict, the attorney may be willing to reschedule a deposition of the therapist. The attorney issuing the subpoena may also be satisfied with a signed and notarized affidavit in lieu of a deposition. The therapist should request written confirmation of any release from a subpoena. A verbal release will not protect the therapist. If the subpoena is from the court or the clerk, the judge will most likely not be able to speak to the therapist "*ex parte*" (outside the presence of the attorneys), and the clerk will likely have little information to offer the therapist. Because hearings and depositions are frequently rescheduled, it is advisable that the therapist contact the person issuing the subpoena the day before the therapist is to appear to confirm the time and place.

On the day of the hearing, when therapists take the witness stand, they should either orally ask their client to waive their privilege or ask the judge if the privilege has been waived. The therapist should take the initiative in this regard and not expect the judge or any of the attorneys to address this issue because their legal duties do not include protecting therapists. If the therapist does not have a written waiver, this should be done "on the record," meaning during the court proceeding or during the deposition while an official recording is being made. This is to protect the therapist from later claims that the therapist breached confidentiality either in an ethical disciplinary proceeding or in a malpractice lawsuit. As stated previously, in the absence of a waiver or a judge's order, the therapist should refuse to disclose any confidential information, even the existence of a therapeutic relationship.

Preparing to Testify

A therapist may be subpoenaed to testify at a hearing in a courtroom or in a deposition. Depositions differ from court hearings in that they usually take place outside the court and outside the presence of a judge. All the parties and their attorneys may be present at the deposition. There will also be a court reporter (stenographer) present to administer oaths to the witnesses and record the testimony, either manually or electronically. Although depositions are somewhat less formal than a court hearing, the testimony given in a deposition is still under oath and may be just as consequential as testimony given in a courtroom. The deposition may be videotaped. In either case, the therapist should dress professionally. The attorneys will be assessing the therapist's appearance and comportment as well as the substance of the testimony. Deposition testimony may be later read to the judge or jury by an attorney, or shown if the deposition was videotaped. Therapists should know that appearing for a deposition does not release them from the obligation to appear in court later if they are subpoenaed again.

It is normal and natural for people, even professionals, to feel anxiety about testifying. If the therapist is to testify in a court hearing, it may be helpful for the therapist to visit the courtroom where the hearing will take place in advance of the hearing. If the therapist is to testify in a deposition, it will likely take place in an office setting, usually an attorney's office or a court reporter's office. Alternatively, a deposition may take place in the therapist's office, if the attorney issuing the subpoena agrees and the space can accommodate all of the attorneys and parties and the court reporter. Holding the deposition in the therapist's office may help the therapist feel more relaxed about and in control of the process.

In some jurisdictions, therapists are legally entitled to reasonable compensation for their time from the party issuing the subpoena. They may be compensated at their regular hourly rate or, in some cases, may charge more for deposition testimony or court appearances. Therapists can set their own fee schedules, but a court may determine that a reasonable fee is lower than the rate the therapist has established. It is customary for professionals to ask for a retainer before any deposition or court appearance. Even if there is no legal requirement that the therapist be compensated, the therapist may still request compensation. If their clients have the funds, attorneys may be willing to pay therapists for their time to maintain goodwill with the therapist. Requesting compensation may also be used by the therapist as a negotiating tool when a therapist wants to be released from a subpoena. If the party issuing the subpoena refuses to compensate the therapist at the requested rate, the therapist still must respond to the subpoena, but may request the court to compel the party issuing the subpoena to pay a reasonable fee. In the case provided previously, the therapist may request compensation from Jared, but may choose not to because Jared is her client, especially if the therapist knows Jared has limited financial resources. Had the therapist been subpoenaed by Al or his attorney, though, then the therapist could have requested compensation from Al and may ask the court to intervene if Al refuses.

Before testifying, therapists should review their notes and familiarize themselves with their client's case history. They may be able to consult their notes in the course of their testimony, but not always. A subpoena which requires a therapist to appear for a hearing or deposition may also require them to bring certain documents, such as treatment or billing records. Therapists should not bring any other documentation to the hearing or deposition that they do not want to disclose to the court or the attorneys, because they may be compelled to produce it.

Testifying in a Hearing or Deposition

Before testifying in court, there may be a "separation of witness" in effect, which means that the therapist and other witnesses will wait outside of the courtroom until it is their turn to testify and will be ordered not to speak to each other. Whether at a hearing or a deposition, the therapist witness will be "sworn in" or administered an oath to tell the truth. After being sworn in, the therapist will be asked questions by an attorney or multiple attorneys, and sometimes by the judge. Regardless of who is asking the questions, the therapist should address responses to the jury, if one is present, or to the judge if there is no jury. The therapist should speak loudly and clearly enough to be heard by the jury, the judge, the attorneys, and the court reporter.

A therapist may be asked only factual questions, such as what a client said or did in session. But unlike "lay" or nonprofessional witnesses, the therapist may also be called upon to testify as to their own opinion, such as a psychological diagnosis, an opinion as to whether someone is a danger to themselves or others, or which parent is most fit to retain custody of a child. Before answering questions that call for the therapist's opinion, the therapist should assess whether the question calls for an opinion, which is beyond the scope of the therapist's practice. For example, unless a therapist has a medical degree, they should decline to offer an opinion as to whether a client needs medication. They can say that they referred the client to their doctor to assess the need for medication.

For opinion testimony to be admissible, the attorney soliciting the opinion will first have to "lay a foundation" showing that the therapist is professionally competent and has the specific knowledge necessary to render an opinion. The judge decides whether a therapist is "competent" to testify. The therapist should keep in mind that legal competence to testify is not the same thing as professional or clinical competence. Therapists should not try to "bolster" their competence by claiming experience or expertise that they do not have.

Generally speaking, when testifying, short answers are the best. This is true for all witnesses, but especially true when the therapist has an interest in limiting the disclosure of confidential information. The therapist witness should answer only the question that is asked and not volunteer information that is not asked for. This is a skill that the therapist may need to practice, by role playing the question and answer process with someone else before the day of the testimony. The therapist will likely not know the attorney's plans for prosecuting or defending their cases, so a therapist's gratuitous attempt to help a client may end up backfiring and damaging their case. The therapist should keep in mind that although it is natural to feel sympathy for the client, the role of the therapist as a witness is not to advocate for the client. That is the job of the client's attorney or the client, if they are unrepresented. The therapist should be forthright and not to try to hide unflattering or embarrassing facts or opinions, if asked. If the answer to a question damages the client's case, therapists should put their trust in the legal process and in the knowledge and skill of their client's attorney to know whether and how best to respond to damaging testimony. Adopting an adversarial or defensive attitude will only diminish the therapist's credibility with the judge or jury.

If necessary, the therapist may take a moment to think before answering a question. Therapists may ask to have questions repeated if necessary and should ask to have any confusing questions clarified before answering. If the attorney asks the same question multiple times, therapists should respond in the same way each time to the best of their ability. Therapists should not attempt to answer or guess if they do not know the answer to a question. "I don't know" and "I don't remember" are the correct answers to questions if the therapist honestly does not know or does not recall, or if the question is outside the scope of the therapist's expertise. Therapist witnesses are not required to limit their answers to "yes" or "no" if a complete and honest answer requires more of a response. Attorneys are not permitted to interrupt witnesses who are still delivering their answer. If the judge later determines that the therapist's answer was "unresponsive," then it may be stricken from the record later.

Sometimes, during the course of the testimony, an attorney will interrupt with an objection. As soon as any attorney declares, "Objection!," the therapist should stop speaking. If it is a court hearing, the judge will listen to the basis for the objection and the response from the opposing counsel before ruling on the objection. If the objection is "sustained," the therapist should not answer the question. If the objection is "overruled," the therapist should answer, but may have the question repeated before answering. If it is a deposition, the therapist may be required to answer after all of the objections are stated for the record. The judge will later rule on the objections after reviewing the transcript and deciding whether the answer is admissible.

Although most attorneys will be professional and courteous to the therapist, they may become verbally aggressive with a therapist witness in an attempt to intimidate or discredit the therapist. The best strategy for responding to aggressive attorneys is to do the opposite. The more insulting an attorney is, the more polite and respectful the therapist should become. This will have dual the advantage of bolstering the judge's or jury's opinion of the therapist and highlighting the disreputable behavior of the attorney. Under no circumstances should therapists lose their temper or stoop to being insulting or sarcastic with an attorney. If at any time during a deposition the therapist needs to take a break, they may do so by advising the attorneys. During a court hearing, the therapist must ask the judge for permission to take a break.

Malpractice

Malpractice refers to a lawsuit brought by a therapist's client or a third party (i.e., someone injured by the therapist's client) claiming that the therapist acted negligently or recklessly (unintentionally), or that they intentionally injured another. Malpractice lawsuits are distinct from ethical complaints, which are made to the therapist's governing professional board or professional organization, although a negative outcome in one forum may result in complaints being made in another forum. For example, a malpractice lawsuit may prompt an inquiry by a therapist's licensing board or vice versa.

Malpractice lawsuits are becoming increasingly common (Jobes & Berman, 1993). Therapists should know that, although ethical conduct and professional compliance reduces the risk of a malpractice lawsuit, there are no guarantees that they will not be sued. Although the therapist may ultimately prevail in a lawsuit, innocence does not protect a therapist from being sued in the first place. Lawsuits carry their own costs, financial and professional, regardless of the outcome.

Therapists should always maintain malpractice insurance (Montgomery, Cupit, & Wimberley, 1999). Therapists should read their entire malpractice policy to ensure that they are compliant with all the terms and not do anything that would void coverage under the policy. Therapists should also keep their malpractice insurance carrier informed of any changes in their practice, such as the hiring of new employees or changes in the nature of the therapist's practice. Failure to notify the insurance company of certain changes may void coverage.

Most policies impose two duties (obligations) on the insurance company in exchange for the payment of the premium by the therapist: a duty to "indemnify" and a duty to defend. The duty to indemnify means the insurance company will pay a judgment against the therapist (up to the policy limit) or a settlement (if agreed to by the insurance company). Every insurance policy has a "policy limit" or maximum amount of money the company will pay to settle a claim. The therapist must pay any judgment above the policy limit. The right to settle within the amount of the policy limit lies within the discretion of the insurance company. So long as it is within the policy limit, the therapist will not have much say, if any, in whether a case is settled, even though a settlement may have an effect on the therapist's professional standing and/or insurance rates. However, if an insurance company refuses to settle within the policy limit, and a judgment results in excess of the policy limit, then the insured therapist may have a claim against their own insurance company for "bad faith," in which case the insurance company may be compelled to pay the full judgment plus additional damages to the insured therapist. Whenever possible, the therapist should insist that any settlement be confidential and this be an explicit term of the written settlement agreement.

The insurance company also has a duty to defend the therapist, which is a benefit of malpractice insurance that some therapists may not be aware of. The duty to defend means that the insurance company will hire and pay for an attorney to defend the therapist against a malpractice claim. The attorney will be chosen by the insurance company. Therapists may hire an attorney of their own choosing, in which case the insurance company may elect to pay that attorney's fees or may choose another attorney to work in concert with the attorney of the therapists' choosing. It is imperative that therapists notify their insurance company *in writing* as soon as they receive notice of a malpractice lawsuit. Failing to do so may void insurance coverage.

To prove malpractice, the client must prove (1) that the therapist's actions fell below the "standard of care," (2) that the client or a third party was injured ("damages"), and (3) that the client's or the third party's damages were "proximately" or directly caused by a "breach," or violation of the standard of care. The standard of care is an objective one, meaning the standard is what a reasonable therapist would have done in the same or similar circumstances. The standard of care is related to, but not necessarily synonymous with, the therapist's ethical obligations. A therapist may have acted ethically, but still committed malpractice. In most cases, other therapists will be called as expert witnesses to offer opinions as to what the standard of care was in a particular instance and whether the therapist breached the standard of care.

Common forms of malpractice include misdiagnosis, practicing outside of one's area of expertise or competence, failure to refer a client to another professional, failure to obtain informed consent, disclosure of confidential information, certain nonsexual physical contact, any sexual contact with a client, failure to prevent a client from harming themselves or another person, abandonment of a client or other forms of negligence, and failure to supervise subordinate therapists, staff, or students

(Stromberg & Dellinger, 1993). Damages arising from malpractice may include emotional or psychological damage or damage to a person's reputation (such as from a breach of confidentiality).

Lawsuits are extremely stressful events. The outcome of a lawsuit, as well as the process itself, can have serious negative consequences for a therapist, both financially and professionally. Lawsuits can stretch over years, or even decades in some cases. They may require the therapist to appear for depositions, hearings, and trial. The mere existence of a malpractice lawsuit, regardless of the outcome, may affect a therapist's reputation, which may result in a loss of income (Kennedy, Vandehey, Norman, & Diekhoff, 2003). It is common for anyone, including therapists, to experience anxiety, depression, anger, and even somatic disorders as a result of the stress of a lawsuit (Woody, 2000). These effects may impact a therapist's personal life and relationships. Therapists should seek their own professional psychological counseling to deal with the stress of litigation.

Risk Management and Defensive Practice

It is essential that therapists obtain the right kinds of insurance in amounts sufficient to protect their business and personal assets. Malpractice insurance or "errors and omissions" insurance is obviously necessary, but if the therapist is operating a business, they should also have a general business liability policy, which will cover them for non-malpractice-related claims, such as when a client slips and falls on the way into the office. If the therapist has employees, additional coverage may be needed to protect against claims of wrongful termination. If the therapist uses a vehicle as part of their job, then they should inform their automobile insurance carrier and obtain an appropriate "rider" or "endorsement." Therapists should also have an umbrella or "excess" personal liability policy that will provide additional protection of their personal assets.

Therapists should incorporate their business, either as a corporation or a limited liability company, if they are in private practice and they employ other people, including other practitioners, but also assistants or anyone who has access to (and may potentially disclose) confidential information. Therapists who partner with other practitioners should form limited liability partnerships because partners may be held liable for each other's actions. Under the legal doctrine of "*respondeat superior*," employers, including therapist employers, are liable for the negligence or other malfeasance of their employees. Employers are generally not liable for the actions of independent contractors, but whether a person is considered an employee or an independent contractor is a thorny legal issue and is not resolved by the person's status in the tax code.

Incorporation helps protect the therapist's personal assets in the event of a lawsuit. Incorporation protects the therapist's assets in the event an employee or a partner is legally culpable, but it does not protect therapists' personal assets if they themselves commit malpractice. Nor does it protect therapists' business assets. Therapist also should be aware that they may still be held personally liable for the negligent hiring of or the failure to supervise their employees.

In addition to being familiar with and complying with the applicable professional ethical codes, other ways of reducing a therapist's exposure to malpractice claims include using written contracts with clients that clearly explain fees, confidentiality, termination of the therapist–client relationship, using written releases before disclosing information, and identifying multiple relationships early. Therapists should keep detailed treatment notes and assign formal diagnoses, as a matter of ethical practice, but also to avoid allegations of improper billing of insurance.

Good defensive practices include consulting with other professionals on difficult clients and referring clients to other professionals when appropriate. Therapists should incorporate suicide assessment into intakes and sessions, contact clients who fail to appear for appointments or terminate therapy suddenly, and always document the reasons for termination of therapy. Because of the risk of vicarious liability, therapists should do background checks on all employees and carefully supervise all employees, both clinical and administrative. Employees should be instructed regularly on issues of confidentiality and maintaining professional boundaries between themselves and clients (Hecker, 2015; Kennedy et al., 2003; Woody, 2000).

Conclusion

There are myriad ways that a therapist's practice can intersect with the legal system, from being drawn into a custody battle to a malpractice action for failure to warn. It is likely that every therapist will, sometime in their career, have to respond to a subpoena for documents or deposition testimony. Understanding the duty of confidentiality and its exceptions will be crucial in these situations. Learning to deal with attorneys and courts is a skill of its own that many therapists will need to learn. The recommendations in this chapter are just a beginning. A review of the laws and rules of every state would take much more space. There is no substitute for the advice of a competent attorney licensed to practice law in the state where the therapist works. But it is our hope that this chapter will help therapists know what questions they need to ask and when they need to seek the professional advice of an attorney.

Note

1 This chapter does not replace the advice of a licensed attorney.

References

American Association for Marriage and Family Therapy (AAMFT). (2007). *Legal guidelines for family therapists*. Washington, DC: Author.

Committee on Legal Issues, American Psychological Association (APA). (2006). Strategies for private practitioners coping with subpoenas or compelled testimony for client records or test data. *Professional Psychology: Research and Practice, 37*(2), 215–222. doi: 10.1037/0735-7028.37.2.215.

Committee on Professional Practice and Standards, American Psychological Association (APA). (2003). Legal issues in the professional practice of psychology. *Professional Psychology: Research and Practice, 34*(6), 595–600. doi: 10.1037/0735-7028.34.6.595.

Glosoff, H. L., Herlihy, S. B., Herlihy, B., & Spence, E. B. (1997). Privileged communication in the psychologist-client relationship. *Professional Psychology: Research and Practice, 28*(6), 573–558. doi: 10.1037/0735-7028.28.6.573.

Hecker, L. L. (2015). Ethical, legal, and professional issues in marriage and family therapy. In J. L. Wetchler & L. L. Hecker (Eds.), *An introduction to marriage and family therapy* (2nd ed., pp. 505–524). New York, NY: Routledge.

Jaffee v. Redmond, 1996 WL 315841 (U.S. June 13, 1996).

Jobes, D. A., & Berman, A. L. (1993). Suicide and malpractice liability: Assessing and revising policies, procedures, and practice in outpatient settings. *Professional Psychology: Research and Practice, 24*(1), 91–99. doi: 10.1037/0735-7028.24.1.91.

Kennedy, P. F., Vandehey, M., Norman, W. B., & Diekhoff, G. M. (2003). Recommendations for risk-management practices. *Professional Psychology: Research and Practice, 34*(3), 309–311. doi: 10.1037/0003-066X.62.9.993.

Moffett, P., & Moore, G. (2011). The standard of care: Legal history and definitions: The bad and good news. *West Journal of Emergency Medicine, 12*(1), 109–112.

Montgomery, L. M., Cupit, B. E., & Wimberley, T. K. (1999). Complaints, malpractice, and risk management: Professional issues and personal experiences. *Professional Psychology: Research and Practice, 30*(4), 402–410. doi: 10.1037/0735-7028.30.4.402.

Nestor, R. A., Steiner, U. T., & Stewart, J. M. (2010). Legal issues. In L. L. Hecker (Ed.), *Ethics and professional issues in couple and family therapy* (pp. 29–49). New York, NY: Routledge.

Packman, W., Andalibian, H., Eudy, K., Howard, B., & Bongar, B. (2009). Legal and ethical risk management with behavioral emergencies. In P. M. Kleespies (Ed.), *Behavioral emergencies: An evidenced-based resource for evaluating and managing risk of suicide, violence, and victimization* (pp. 405–448). Washington, DC: American Psychological Association.

Stromberg, C., & Dellinger, A. (1993). A legal update on malpractice and other professional liability. *The Psychologist's Legal Update, 3*, 3–15.

Tarasoff v. Regents of the University of California 17 Cal. 3d 425 (1976).

Woody, R. H. (2000). Professional ethics, regulatory licensing, and malpractice complaints. In F. W. Kaslaw (Ed.), *Handbook of couple and family forensics: A sourcebook for mental health and legal professionals* (pp. 461–474). New York, NY: Wiley.

4

The Impact of HIPAA and HITECH Regulations on the Couple and Family Therapist

Lorna Hecker, Courtney L. Miner, and Megan J. Murphy

> At a Midwestern mental health clinic, an employee received an e-mail that informed her that her mailbox was flooded, and that her e-mail service would be suspended unless she clicked on the link provided within the e-mail so that they could provide her with more storage space. When the employee clicked on the link, she unknowingly unlocked Cryptolocker malware, which encrypted all of the data housed on the clinic server, including case notes, but also client social security numbers, birthdates, credit card information, and health insurance information. The clinic had no way to decrypt the data, nor did it have backup files. The clinic was contacted by an anonymous source who offered to decrypt the data for $1000. Because the clinic had no way to get access to the information it needed to run its business, it had no option but to pay the ransom. Further, the clinic lacked basic audit controls such as audit logs, access reports, and data usage reports, so it was unable to ascertain if this information was breached or used by the criminals who extorted the clinic.

In Chapter 3, the ethical mandate that client information is kept confidential was introduced; this dictate is also typically codified into state law. However, as more therapists rely on electronic health records (EHRs), and other forms of digital data, electronic storage and transmission of confidential client information brings a changing paradigm of maintaining client confidences, as this scenario illustrates. The clinic in our example potentially exposed its clients to identity theft, as well as medical identity theft. Identity theft includes criminals using social security numbers, and/or bank or credit card numbers for economic gain (U.S. Department of

Justice, 2015). Additionally, loss of the health insurance information makes individuals vulnerable to medical identity theft. Medical identity theft occurs when health insurance information is used criminally to procure medical or mental health services or obtain government benefits. There are several dangers that can occur as a result of medical identity theft; treatment records may now contain health information of someone other than the client, including a false diagnosis, different medications, they may receive bills for someone else's treatment, or insurance benefits may be exhausted (Synovate, 2007).

In addition to identity theft and medical identity theft, there are other concerns when privacy of client treatment information is lost. An organization or practice may suffer loss of clients, loss of customers (those who pay for therapy services), loss of future clients, and loss of staff. The Ponemon Institute (2014) notes that costs for a data breach per record are around $200 *per individual record*. Although there is no legal cause of action written in Health Insurance Portability and Accountability Act (HIPAA) regulations, state attorneys general may sue and other sources of legal woes include state consumer protection laws, as well as torts for breach of privacy. Case law is still in its infancy with regard to HIPAA regulations; more clarity on legal consequences will occur in the coming decade. However, some lawsuits have prevailed in using HIPAA regulations as the appropriate standard of care in handling of client data. For example, in North Carolina psychiatric and other records were improperly accessed and released in regards to a custody case; a lawsuit was filed in which HIPAA was successfully used as establishing the standard of care (*Acosta v. Byrum*, 2006). Likewise, in *Byrne v. Avery Center for Obstetrics and Gynecology* (2014), a successful argument was made with the Connecticut Supreme Court stipulating that HIPAA could be used in establishing standard of care in a breach of contract suit. In this case, the medical center was cited with improper disclosure of records because the center had not followed HIPAA regulations.

Of equal importance for couple and family therapists (CFTs) is that breaches can damage the therapeutic relationship. One survey study cited that 21% of patients said they withhold their or their family's prescription information, mental illness, or substance abuse history from a health care provider due to privacy concerns (Loria, 2015). If clients do not trust their therapist to maintain the privacy and security of their therapy information, therapy suffers and both clients and CFTs lose.

When the federal government encouraged the adoption of electronic health records, it recognized that people would be uneasy about the privacy of their private, protected information being placed online. HIPAA was enacted to help to ensure this privacy and maintain client trust in health care providers. In this chapter, we introduce the federal regulations of HIPAA, and the Health Information Technology for Economic and Clinical Health Act (HITECH Act), highlighting how these regulations affect the practice of CFTs. HIPAA compliance is an ethical issue, a risk management issue, a legal dictate, and a progressing standard of care. Becoming educated on HIPAA and HITECH regulations is mandatory to ethical CFT practice (Health Insurance Portability and Accountability Act, 1996; Health Information Technology for Economic and Clinical Health Act, 2009).

Enactment of HIPAA and HITECH Regulations

In response to the changing landscape, which includes storage, use, and transmission of electronic health information, HIPAA was enacted in 1996 with two purposes: the first was to make health information portable so that individuals can maintain health insurance between jobs, and the second was to ensure that health care plans and providers are held accountable with regard to keeping health information private. U.S. Health and Human Services (HHS) established the regulations, which are administered by the Office of Civil Rights (OCR).

HIPAA provided federal privacy protections for physical and mental health information, which it termed protected health information (PHI). PHI is any health information used to identify a client that relates to physical or mental health, relating to a past, present, or future condition, for both living and deceased individuals (HIPAA, 45 C.F.R. §160.103). HIPAA regulations protect PHI that is written, oral, or electronic (transmitted or maintained) through privacy and security regulations. HIPAA privacy regulations relate to all forms of PHI, but specifically focus on written and oral PHI. The security regulations focus on protection of electronic PHI (ePHI). In 2009 the HITECH Act was passed, which increased patient rights over their PHI, increased restrictions over disclosure of PHI, increased fines and penalties for HIPAA violations, and brought funding for compliance audits.

How Do Therapists Know If They Need To Be HIPAA Compliant?

If a therapist furnishes, bills, or receives payment for health care in the normal course of business, and any transactions are sent in electronic form, the practice is considered a covered entity (CE). Likewise, if an entity or organization creates, receives, maintains, or transmits PHI on behalf of a CE, that entity is considered a business associate (BA) of the CE. Both CEs and BAs are required to comply with HIPAA regulations. CEs include a health care provider (including therapists), a health plan, or a health care clearinghouse, which transmits PHI in electronic form. For therapists, typically HIPAA is triggered when they bill insurance electronically. BAs are entities that create, receive, maintain, or transmit PHI on behalf of a CE. Common BAs for therapists include billing services, claims processors, attorneys, accountants, outside consultants (e.g., supervisors), or accreditation bodies. CEs must obtain satisfactory assurances that their BAs are abiding by HIPAA regulations, which is done by using a BA agreement (BAA), or another type of written contract. BAs who use subcontractors are responsible for obtaining satisfactory assurances from their subcontractors.

Technically, a therapist who does not bill third-party payers but instead takes private pay clients only is likely not a CE. However, HIPAA is quickly becoming a standard of care for how healthcare providers treat PHI (Hecker & Edwards, 2014); therapists will want to understand the regulations and protect their clients' PHI accordingly. Upon a breach of client PHI, it would be difficult to justify why a therapist did not follow HIPAA guidelines for protecting client information. Additionally, state regulations are beginning to evolve to include HIPAA requirements.

Privacy Regulations

Therapists who are CEs must abide by both HIPAA privacy and security regulations; one requirement of the privacy regulations is that each CE must designate a privacy official (BAs are not required to do this) who oversees administration of and compliance with the privacy rules. Because a full analysis of the privacy regulations is well beyond the scope of this chapter, we cover a few of the regulations that are most salient to CFTs. For more information, see Hecker (2016). Next we discuss the uses and disclosures of PHI, the HIPAA definition of psychotherapy notes, the interplay between state and federal regulations with ethical codes, the Notice of Privacy Practices (NPP), authorizations for release of PHI, the minimum necessary standard, and the accounting of disclosures requirement.

Use and Disclosure of PHI

The privacy rule (Health and Human Services, n.d.b) regulates both use and disclosure of PHI. *Use* includes the sharing, application, utilization, examination, or analysis of PHI within a CE or BA. *Disclosure* refers to the release, transfer, provision of, access to, or divulging PHI in any other manner to any outside entity. With the exception of psychotherapy notes, most treatment information may be shared for purposes of treatment, payment, or health care operations (TPO). *Treatment* includes consultation between providers. *Payment* refers to payment or reimbursement (e.g., claim submission, authorizations, payment postings), and *health care operations* include quality assessment, competency assessment, performance evaluations, credentialing audits, and so on. State law may be more prohibitive to sharing PHI. Because a therapist can share for purposes of TPO, when discussing payment information with an insurance company, a release of information from the client is not needed. However, remember if state law is stricter it will preempt this release of information. Though many states do make exceptions that release of PHI can occur for TPO, state statutes must be consulted.

Psychotherapy Notes

In some ways, HIPAA brings additional federal protection to our clients' sensitive treatment data. Psychotherapy notes are given higher level of privacy protections under HIPAA than most other types of PHI. HIPAA also buttresses federal protection of client privilege established in *Jaffee v. Redmond* (1996) (see Chapter 3). However, HIPAA regulations only protect what it defines as *psychotherapy notes*, which are limited in scope. Psychotherapy notes are defined as

> notes recorded (in any medium) by a health care provider who is a mental health professional documenting or analyzing the contents of conversation during a private counseling session or a group, joint, or family counseling session and that are separated from the rest of the individual's medical record (HIPAA, 45 C.F.R. §164.501).

They are to be kept separate from the medical (i.e., case) record, and cannot be used to substantiate billing. Psychotherapy notes specifically:

- Include the practitioner's impression of the patient,
- Include details of the psychotherapy session inappropriate for the medical record,
- Are solely for the use of the practitioner, for example, for planning future sessions,

- Are kept separate to limit access (including in electronic records) to qualify as psychotherapy notes, and
- Are only accessed by the therapist and possibly a supervisor.

If psychotherapy notes are released at the client's written request, they lose their heightened protection once they are released (and, for example, are kept by another treating entity). Testing also does not qualify for heightened protection. If a therapist is part of an integrated health care network and psychotherapy notes are routinely shared with others, they also lose heightened protection. Thus, psychotherapy notes must be maintained and used only by the originator of the notes (i.e., the therapist), with few exceptions. Psychotherapy notes do not need to be shared with clients upon their request, unless state law dictates the disclosure. HIPAA does not require a therapist to keep psychotherapy notes (state law may differ).

General Treatment Information

Although psychotherapy notes are given special protection under HIPAA, most people are surprised at what treatment information is not considered psychotherapy notes, and thus is not afforded special protection under HIPAA. This includes:

- Summary information, such as the current state of the patient,
- Summary of the theme of the psychotherapy session,
- Medications prescribed and side effects,
- Any other information necessary for treatment or payment,
- Treatment plan, symptoms, and progress,
- Diagnoses and prognosis,
- Counseling session start and stop times,
- The modalities and frequencies of treatment furnished,
- Results of clinical tests, and
- Any other information necessary for treatment or payment.

Although this seems like bad news, it generally does not have as much impact for therapists as most states have stricter laws regarding mental health information than what HIPAA does. When state laws are stricter, that is, when state laws give clients more rights or privacy protections, state laws are to be followed (with some regulated exceptions). There are some exceptions when psychotherapy notes may be disclosed without an authorization. They are:

- For one's own training or supervision,
- For defense in legal proceedings brought by the client or client's representative,
- For HHS to investigate or determine the CEs compliance with the regulations,
- To avert a serious and imminent threat to public health or safety (e.g., reporting abuse),
- To a health oversight agency for lawful oversight of the originator of the psychotherapy notes, and
- For the lawful activities of a coroner or medical examiner or as required by law.

If psychotherapy notes are kept in a second location, they are not considered psychotherapy notes and are not afforded a higher level of protection. Clients may not have access to their own psychotherapy notes under HIPAA; if state law allows client access, state law preempts HIPAA.

The Interface of HIPAA, State Law, and Ethical Codes

As noted previously, psychotherapy notes are narrowly defined under HIPAA, although psychotherapy notes are afforded an increased level of confidentiality. However, state mental health laws typically are stricter than HIPAA and often protect much more information than what the government defines under the "psychotherapy notes" provision. Under HIPAA, information not considered psychotherapy notes could be freely shared for purposes of TPO; this is a significant amount of treatment information! Fortunately, state laws are typically more "stringent" with regard to protection of therapy information. A state law is considered more stringent if it either provides more privacy protections for a patient or gives a patient more access to their own PHI. For example, although HIPAA gives a CFT permission to disclose much psychotherapy information without an authorization, if state law does not, state law preempts HIPAA because of its increased protection. Be aware, however, that some state laws *do* give therapists the right to release information for TPO. To further add confusion, CFTs may rely on their ethical codes for more stringent rules with regard to confidentiality, but mental health ethical codes often are written such that client confidences should be maintained except *where mandated or permitted by law*. A good rule to follow is "When in doubt, don't give information out." This is where a CFT may want to consult an attorney to clarify both client confidentiality and privilege rights and limitations. Additionally, with regard to case records, some states include mental health records under medical records statutes, whereas others have separate record requirements. Last, CFTs should be aware of other regulations that may affect or interact with confidentiality requirements. These include the Federal Confidentiality of Alcohol and Drug Abuse Patient Records regulations (HIPAA, 42 C.F.R. Part II), the Family Education Rights and Privacy Act (FERPA), the Gramm-Leach-Bliley Act (which regulates personal financial information), Sarbanes-Oxley (financial reporting), and/or the payment card industry data security standard (credit card security). Medicaid or Medicare rules may also apply. States may also have specific laws with regard to this type of private information.

Notice of Privacy Practices

The NPP is probably the most familiar aspect of HIPAA, because everyone gets a copy of it when they initially visit their physician. The NPP educates clients as to their privacy rights, as well as potential uses and disclosures of their PHI. Many therapists fail to integrate stricter state law into their NPP; therapists should educate clients in their NPP when state law guarantees them more rights. There is nothing in the regulations that precludes this inclusion. Model NPPs are available at the HHS website (www.hhs.gov). Therapists should stay abreast of any changes to NPP requirements. HHS offers both privacy and security listservs so that CEs may stay abreast of regulation changes. NPPs must be prominently posted on an organization's website, as well as in the office(s). CEs are required to give clients an NPP and attempt to obtain their signature acknowledging receipt of the notice. If a client refuses to sign, a therapist may not withhold services as a result of their refusal.

Authorizations

Psychotherapy notes always require client authorization. There are specific elements set forth by the regulations for authorizations. Authorizations must include (1) a specific description of health information to be disclosed; (2) the name of person or organization authorized to release the information; (3) the name of person authorized to receive the information; (4) a description of each purpose of the requested disclosure, an expiration date or event; (5) signature of the patient or legal representative; (6) a statement that the patient has a right to revoke the authorization, in writing; (7) a statement that the patient's treatment or payment could not be conditioned on their permission to release private information; (8) a statement of the potential for redisclosure of the information by the recipient; and (9) the form must be written in plain language. State laws may require additional elements to authorizations or what may also be termed in state statutes as "release of information." A professional's code of ethics may also have additional requirements. HIPAA does not prevent a CFT from establishing a stricter policy on disclosures than is otherwise allowed under the regulations.

Minimum Necessary Information

Disclosures that are not for TPO typically require authorization, with some exceptions (e.g., abuse or duty to warn/protect). When sharing information with another CE or BA, information shared is to be the minimum necessary information to accomplish the intended purpose of the disclosure. PHI is not to be shared unless it is necessary to satisfy a particular purpose or carry out a function. For example, office staff should only have access to enough PHI to perform their duties. Minimum necessary information is not relevant when information is shared for treatment purposes.

Accounting of Disclosures

Clients have the right to ask for an accounting of disclosures (AoD). An AoD is a record of unauthorized disclosures of their PHI covering the prior 6 years to the date of the request. Types of unauthorized disclosures that should go into the AoD include disclosures for: (1) public health purposes; immunizations, infections or communicable disease reporting; (2) vital statistics such as birth or death statistics or teen suicides; (3) poison control; (4) domestic violence, elder abuse, child abuse, abuse of mentally ill or dependent adults; (5) health oversight activities (e.g., Medicare and Medicaid audits, inspections, oversight reviews); (6) judicial or administrative proceedings (court orders, subpoenas, law enforcement purposes, reporting of gunshot wounds); (7) coroners or medical examiners; (8) cadaveric organ, eye, or tissue donation; (9) some Medicare information; (10) human subject research not subject to previous authorizations, or where a waiver of authorization has been obtained through the institutional review board (IRB); (11) research regarding decedents; (12) to the U.S. Food and Drug Administration for purposes related to quality, safety, or effectiveness of a Food and Drug Administration–regulated product or activity or enable product recalls, repairs or replacements, to report adverse events; (13) for worker's compensation; (14) to registries such as cancer, trauma, immunizations; (15) a serious threat to health or safety; (16) to advisory boards; (17) state crime laboratories; (18) misdirected fax or e-mail; (19) release of information based on an invalid authorization; and (20) any other disclosures required or permitted by law.

Disclosures of PHI that are excluded in the AoD include those:

- For TPO purposes,
- Made to the individual or their personal representative,
- Made for directory purposes,
- Made of persons involved in the individual's care,
- For national security or intelligence purposes,
- Made to correctional institutions or law enforcement officials, or
- Made before the date of compliance with the privacy standards (Dougherty, 2001).

Clients may request AoDs only on information for the past 6 years. Software vendors can typically help set up a way for CFTs to compile an AoD. A client may have one disclosure free of charge within a 1-year period.

Security Regulations

HIPAA was in part enacted to protect privacy and security of PHI (HHS, n.d.b, n.d.c). Security of ePHI has become a concern of epic proportions in the health care industry. In the largest breach of PHI (at the time of this publication), the database of Anthem Blue Cross Blue Shield generated a loss of 8.8 to 18.8 million records (Pepitone, 2015a). Premera Blue Cross Blue Shield lost data of up to 11 million customers (Pepitone, 2015b). Although mental health data were likely breached in these incidents, mental health agencies and practices have also been targeted. Comprehensive Psychological Services in South Carolina had PHI of 3,500 patients breached when an unencrypted laptop was stolen, containing both psychological records and custody evaluations (Dissent, 2013). PHI of 500 patients was breached from Arizona Counseling and Treatment Services when an employee had an unencrypted laptop stolen from their home (Davis, 2013). Client concern about the privacy of their treatment data is well-founded; CFTs must educate themselves and be good stewards of data management.

HIPAA security regulations cover ePHI, with three types of safeguards to ePHI: administrative, physical, and technical. Therapists should be aware that there are 54 safeguards and implementation specifications. Some safeguards are "required" and some are considered "addressable." Required safeguards are just that—you must implement the safeguard as directed. Addressable means that the therapist may take into consideration their practice or organization's size, capabilities, and the costs of the security measures. A therapist in private practice for example, would not be required to provide the same security measures as larger companies with more resources (if the measure is cost prohibitive). As with the privacy regulations, the security regulations require that each CE (as well as BAs) must designate a security official. This can be the same person as the privacy official, but need not be.

Administrative Safeguards

Administrative safeguards include administrative actions, policies, and procedures that a CE puts in place to safeguard ePHI. One administrative safeguard standard is security management process with implementation specifications including completing a risk analysis (required), risk management strategies (required), and information system activity review (required), which includes audit logs, access reports, and security incident tracking reports, among others. A sanction policy (required) is needed for workforce that violates the regulations. "Workforce" includes "employees, volunteers, trainees, and other persons whose conduct, in the performance of work for a covered entity, is under the direct control of such entity, whether or not they are paid by the covered entity" (HIPAA, 45 C.F.R. §160.103). Workforce security (required) must be addressed, which includes three addressable specifications: authorization and/or supervision (e.g., determining when a particular user or system has the right to carry out an activity), workforce clearance procedure (e.g., determining access to ePHI by person or role), and termination procedures (e.g., when access ends because of a workforce member quitting or being terminated). An individual or entity must be assigned as the security official (required) who oversees implementation of the security regulations.

The standard "information access management" has three implementation specifications. The first is access authorization (addressable), when a CE or BA defines who has the right to carry out a certain activity, which involves ePHI, such as reading electronic health records of a client. The second is access establishment and modification (addressable), which are policies and procedures that "establish, document, review and modify a user's right to access a workstation, program, or process" (HHS, 2007, p. 13). Third, in the unlikely event an organization is housing a Healthcare Clearinghouse (which processes health care claims), the clearinghouse functions must be separated from the rest of the organization (required).

Security awareness training is an administrative safeguard with four addressable specifications: Workforce must receive security reminders, that is, reminders of the various security safeguards within the organizations policies and procedures. These may take the form of printed or electronic materials, discussions at staff meetings, and bulletin board postings. Retraining should occur whenever environmental or operational changes affect the security of ePHI. For example, retraining should occur if the following changes occur:

- There is new or upgraded software or hardware,
- There is new security technology,
- There are changes to the security rule (HHS, n.d.c)
- There are new or updated policies and procedures, or
- There are environmental or operational changes that affect the security of ePHI.

Measures to protect the entity from malicious software also need to be taken, and third, login monitoring must occur, which signals the user when login attempts are inappropriate and block access after a designated number of access attempts. Last, training must include password management. Password management training includes creating strong passwords, safeguarding passwords, the importance of not sharing passwords, etc. Another administrative safeguard that is required is that the CE/BA must implement policies and procedures to address any security incidents (i.e., HIPAA violations or incidents that lead to, or could have led to a breach of PHI).

The Contingency Plan standard includes plans for data backup (required), disaster recovery (required), emergency mode operations plans (required), and testing and revision procedure (addressable). In our case scenario, had the agency properly backed up client data as required, it would not have been forced to pay "ransom" for retrieval of its data.

Emergency plans need to be in place for instances such as power outages, natural or man-made disaster, or computer system failures.

Last, the standard regarding business associate agreements or other written contracts has one required implementation specification. "Written contracts or another arrangement" must be made between a CE and a BA. CEs are responsible for doing due diligence on their BAs to assure the BA is also complying with HIPAA. A BA contract outlines requirements for the BA to protect PHI and be compliant with the security regulations.

Physical Safeguards

Every CE must put physical safeguards in place to protect ePHI from unauthorized intrusion, as well as natural, human, and environmental hazards. Natural threats include floods, earthquakes, tornadoes, landslides, fires, and so on. Human threats include network and computer-based attacks, hacking, malicious software, and unauthorized access to ePHI (intentional or unintentional). It may also include advertent or inadvertent unauthorized data entry. Environmental threats include issues such as power failures, liquid leakage, pollution, floods, and chemical damage (HHS, n.d.c). Physical safeguards include: contingency operations (addressable), a facility security plan (addressable), access control and validation procedures (addressable), and maintenance records (addressable). Generally these safeguards refer to the physical facilities of an organization, including physical access to the building and operations, and keep ePHI safe from physical hazards and intrusions. Physical safeguards also require policies and procedures for protecting workstations (e.g., computer and surrounding area), and policies around workstation security; both are required standards. Last, device and media controls are also considered physical safeguards. These safeguards include disposal of ePHI (required), media reuse (required), accountability (addressable), and data backup and storage (addressable). All physical safeguards are meant to counteract threats or potential threats to ePHI.

Technical Safeguards

Technical safeguards are policies and procedures put into place to control access to ePHI. The first standard is access control, with specifications that CEs and BAs have the following: unique user identification (required), emergency access procedure (required), automatic logoff (addressable), and encryption and decryption (addressable). All of these procedures confirm that the person or entity trying to access the ePHI is indeed authorized for access to that data. Audit controls are a required standard, which means ePHI controls are needed to monitor ePHI, such as hardware, software, and procedural mechanisms to examine information system activity. Note that if the Midwestern clinic in the initial case scenario had audit controls in place, it could have examined whether or not data had been accessed or altered, which would have given an indication of the level of breach that occurred. The Integrity Standard directs that there be mechanisms to authenticate ePHI (addressable), ensuring both the accuracy of the data and protecting it from improper alteration or destruction. Person or entity authentication is a required standard, requiring policies and procedures be in place to ensure that the person or entity who is accessing ePHI has been confirmed with proof of identity (e.g., password, PIN). Transmission security is a required standard, whereby a CE or BA needs to address integrity controls (addressable) and encryption (addressable). Integrity controls ensure that ePHI has not been modified until end stage disposal, typically addressed by network communication protocols (such as monitoring access methods).

Although encryption of PHI is an addressable standard, it is important to note that if a data device is encrypted, chances of having a breach greatly decrease. That is, when a device is encrypted, such as a desktop, laptop, USB flash drive, and so on, and the device is lost or stolen, the breach falls under the "safe harbor exemption." This means that you are not required to report the loss to HHS or to the client.

Policies and Procedures and Documentation

Policies and procedures on the security standards are required and are accompanied by a documentation requirement. The documentation requirement has three implementation specifications: the first is a time limit (required) for documentation; documentation regarding compliance efforts must be kept for 6 years from the time or origin or revision. Second, policies and procedures documentation must be made available to the workforce (required). Third, policies and procedures updates are required when the regulations change, or there is a material or operational change in an organization.

Security Risk Assessment

A security risk assessment (SRA) is at the nexus of HIPAA compliance. A SRA is a process whereby a CE/BA must evaluate security measures that are currently in place to protect PHI/ePHI. This is an intensive process whereby CEs/BAs must assess vulnerabilities and threats, and prioritize remediation of the threats based on the level of risk (from high to low), and take steps to remediate threats to PHI. The SRA allows CEs/BAs to develop strategies to prevent, correct, and contain security risks. HHS does not expect perfection; they understand some breaches are unavoidable, however, an entity must evidence risk management strategies, decreasing vulnerabilities to a "reasonable and appropriate" level, based on the size of the organization, capabilities, and costs of security measures.

Breach of PHI

Breach is an impermissible acquisition, use, access, and/or disclosure of PHI, and compromises the security of PHI. There are numerous consequences that occur when PHI is breached; first and foremost is the damage that may occur to the therapeutic relationship when personal information is lost or stolen. There are also consequences set by OCR in the forms of fines and penalties. Additionally, for breaches that affect more than 500 individuals, the organizations' name and type of breach is publicized on the HHS website, often termed the "wall of shame." Breaches of less than 500 records get reported to HHS within 60 calendar days of the end of a calendar year in which the breach was discovered. For breaches of more than 500 individuals, HHS must be notified within 60 days of discovery, local media must be notified, and information about the breach must be posted on the organization's website.

The highest amount of breached data occurs through hacking (Redspin, 2015). The most common reason for breach of PHI is theft of unencrypted computing devices such as laptops, tablets, smart phones, or storage devices such as flash drives or CDs (Ponemon Institute, 2014). A few examples of breaches include the following.

Consider the following examples of loss of ePHI, starting with loss of laptops:

> Aspire Indiana, a nonprofit community mental health center based in Noblesville, had a breach of approximately 45,000 patients when several laptops were stolen from its administrative offices (Dissent, 2015).

> Cancer Care Group, P.C., had a laptop bag with an unencrypted laptop and unencrypted backup media with identity and health information of 55,000 patients. HHS fined the company $750,000, and required it to adopt a corrective action plan (HHS, 2013b).
>
> An employee at the Alaska Department of Health and Human Services had a USB drive that may have contained PHI stolen from the employee's vehicle. When OCR investigated, it found that DHHS had not completed a risk analysis or implemented sufficient risk management measures, or completed security training for its workforce members, and not implemented device and media controls, or addressed encryption as required by the security rule. It was fined $1,700,000 (HHS, n.d.a).

Any source of an electronic memory can be a source of breach, depending upon the technology. For example, both copiers and fax machines can have digital memories, upon which PHI will be written with each use. Consider the following breaches:

> Affinity Health Plan, Inc., returned multiple photocopiers to a leasing agent without erasing the data contained on the copier hard drives, breaching records of upwards of 344,579 individuals. They were fined $1,215,780 (HHS, 2013a).

Malware and software glitches can also be source of breach of PHI. For example:

> Anchorage Community Mental Health Services suffered a breach affecting 2,743 individuals due to malware; the company failed to identify basic risks, and failed to update their information technology resources with available patches, and were running outdated, unsupported software. They were fined $150,000 (HHS, 2014).
>
> Milwaukee Froedtert Hospital is alerting patients that up to 43,000 patient files may have been accessed by unauthorized people after an employee's computer was infected with a virus (WISN.com Staff, 2013).

Lack of risk analysis, risk remediation, investigation of a breach, and subsequent follow-up has led to some CEs/BAs being assessed fines by OCR. For example:

> St. Elizabeth's Medical Center (SEMC) was investigated after a workforce member complained that staff was using an Internet-based document sharing application to store documents containing ePHI. SEMC did not report this incident as a breach or take action to address the breach of PHI. Approximately 2 years later, SEMC notified OCR of unsecured PHI on a workforce member's personal laptop and USB containing data on 595 individuals. The settlement with OCR was $218,400 whereby OCR cited disclosure of PHI of at least 1,093 individuals, lack of sufficient securing measures regarding transmission and storage of ePHI,

> and failure to identify and respond to the incident, mitigate harmful effects of the breach, and document the incident and outcome in a timely manner (HHS, 2015).
>
> In Columbia St. Mary's Ozaukee Hospital of Mequon, Wisconsin, a janitor sold patient records to gang members. The janitor was able to use a master key to access boxes of sensitive information that were due to be shredded (Superadmin, 2011).

Fines and Penalties

HIPAA fines range from \$100 to \$50,000 with an annual maximum of \$1.5 million. Penalties can include jail time for more egregious and malicious violations. For example:

> In 2003, Dr. Huping Zhou, a researcher in Los Angeles received notice he was being fired from the UCLA School of Medicine. On the same day, he accessed and read his immediate supervisor's medical records, as well of those of celebrities UCLA had treated—Drew Barrymore, Arnold Schwarzenegger, Tom Hanks, and Leonardo DiCaprio; accessing records 323 times for no legitimate reason. He was sentenced to 4 months in prison, and fined \$2,000 (Dimick, 2010).

Individuals are not allowed to bring suit for violations, but states' attorneys general are able to. However, CFTs may be subject to state breach statutes, accrediting body sanctions, and state consumer protection laws. Additionally, some states have specific laws regarding reporting of loss of social security numbers and other types of private information. Case law is just beginning to be established over security and privacy issues, and lawsuits are beginning to occur for breach of privacy.

Breach Notification

The HITECH Act compels CEs to provide notification to a client if a breach has occurred (Breach Notification for Unsecured Protected Health Information, 2009). Additionally, BAs must notify a CE of a breach. Both must occur within 60 days after the discovery of the incident. If a risk analysis determines a low probability that PHI has been breached, notification need not occur. The risk analysis must examine the nature and extent of the PHI, whether the PHI was acquired or viewed, and to whom it was impermissibly disclosed or accessed. Extremely low-risk breaches do not need to be reported to clients or HHS. Some incidents qualify as exceptions to the definition of breach. One is incidental disclosures (a byproduct of permissible or required disclosures). For example, calling a client's name in the waiting room is not considered a breach. A second is unintentional or inadvertent access or disclose of PHI within a CEs/BAs organization, such as if an internal e-mail is sent to the wrong person and not further disclosed. The third occurs when the information is impermissibly accessed or disclose outside of an organization, but the individual would not be expected to retain the information. For example, if assessment results are handed to the wrong client, but the error is quickly discovered and the document retrieved, it is not considered a breach.

Summary

This chapter is only a summary of HIPAA requirements, giving an overview of the more salient compliance issues of which a CFT needs knowledge of to satisfy the regulations. There are numerous aspects to HIPAA regulations, with privacy and security regulations of most concern to CFTs. Privacy regulations deal with uses and disclosures of PHI, minimum necessary information, the notice of privacy practices, and psychotherapy notes, among others. Security regulations cover administrative, physical and technical safeguards, as well as documentation and organizational requirements. CEs are required to be compliant with the privacy and security regulations, BAs need only be compliant with the security regulations, and any privacy requirements set forth in the business associate agreement.

Each CE and BA must assign a privacy official; CEs and BAs both must assign a security official. The privacy and security officials can be the same person, but this is not required. For CFTs, there is a convergence of numerous requirements with regard to privacy of PHI; therefore, they must be cognizant of state statutes, other federal laws, and our codes of ethics as they converge on the handling of confidentiality of client PHI. Most breaches of PHI must be reported to HHS; larger breaches are publicized through the news and the HHS website. Hacking is responsible for the largest number of breached records, with portable data devices such as laptops or USB flash drives account for the most common type of breach.

HITECH clarified fines and penalties for noncompliance with the regulations and increased client's privacy rights. Breach notification rules outline what needs to occur should client(s) PHI be breached (i.e., impermissibly used or disclosed). Fines and penalties can occur for noncompliance; penalties can include jail time when there is malicious intent (such as for financial gain). Although implementing HIPAA can seem daunting, it is an extension of client confidentiality, helping CFTs to protect clients' right to privacy, but also aiding in maintaining the electronic security of this information as well.

References

Acosta v. Byrum, 180 N.C. App. 562, 638 S.E.2d 246 (North Carolina, 2006).

Breach Notification for Unsecured Protected Health Information, 45 C.F.R. § 164 & §161 (2009). Retrieved from http://www.hhs.gov/ocr/privacy/hipaa/administrative/Breach%20Notification%20Rule/index.html.

Byrne v. Avery Center for Obstetrics and Gynecology, No. 18904, 2014 WL 5507439 (Conn. Nov. 11, 2014).

Davis, H. (2013, April 16). Laptop with patient info stolen from employee's home. *Yuma Sun* Retrieved from http://www.yumasun.com/laptop-with-patients-info-stolen-from-home/article_71ff7535-ff5d-5aa3-afa4-8a2e70f89a2c.html.

Dimick, C. (2010). Californian sentenced to prison for HIPAA violation. *Journal of the American Health Information Management Association*. Retrieved from http://journal.ahima.org/2010/04/29/californian-sentenced-to-prison-for-hipaa-violation/.

Dissent. (2013, December 17). Psychological assessments provider notifies patients after laptop with PHI stolen in office burglary. Retrieved from http://www.phiprivacy.net/psychological-assessments-provider-notifies-patients-after-laptop-with-phi-stolen-in-office-burglary/.

Dissent. (2015, February 9). Aspire Indiana notifies over 45,000 employees and clients after burglars nab office laptops. Retrieved from http://www.databreaches.net/aspire-indiana-notifies-over-45000-employees-and-clients-after-burglars-nab-office-laptops/.

Dougherty, M. (2001). Accounting and tracking disclosures of protected health information. *Journal of AHIMA*, *72*(10), 72E–H.

Health and Human Services. (n.d.a). *Alaska DHSS settles HIPAA security case for $1,700,000*. Retrieved from http://www.hhs.gov/ocr/privacy/hipaa/enforcement/examples/alaska-agreement.html0.

Health and Human Services. (n.d.b). *The privacy rule*. Retrieved from http://www.hhs.gov/ocr/privacy/hipaa/administrative/privacyrule/.

Health and Human Services. (n.d.c). *The security rule*. Retrieved from http://www.hhs.gov/ocr/privacy/hipaa/administrative/securityrule/.

Health and Human Services. (2007). Security standards: Administrative safeguards. *HIPAA Security Series*, 2 *(paper 2)*, 1–29.

Health and Human Services. (2013a). *HHS settles with health plan in photocopier case*. Retrieved from https://wayback.archive-it.org/3926/20150618191048/http://www.hhs.gov/news/press/2013pres/08/20130814a.html.

Health and Human Services. (2013b). *$750,000 HIPAA settlement emphasizes the importance of risk assessment and device and media controls.* Retrieved from http://www.hhs.gov/about/news/2015/09/02/750,000-dollar-hipaa-settlement-emphasizes-the-importance-of-risk-analysis-and-device-and-media-control-policies.html.

Health and Human Services. (2014). *Bulletin: HIPAA settlement underscores the vulnerability of unpatched and unsupported software.* Retrieved from http://www.hhs.gov/ocr/privacy/hipaa/enforcement/examples/acmhs/acmhsbulletin.pdf.

Health and Human Services. (2015). *Bulletin: HIPAA settlement highlights importance of safeguards when using Internet applications.* Retrieved from http://www.hhs.gov/sites/default/files/bulletin.pdf.

Health Information Technology for Economic and Clinical Health Act of 2009. 2009 Public Law, 111–5, 111th Congress. Retrieved from https://www.gpo.gov/fdsys/pkg/PLAW-111publ5/pdf/PLAW-111publ5.pdf.

Health Insurance Portability and Accountability Act of 1996. 1996 Public Law, 104–191, 104th Congress. Retrieved from http://www.hhs.gov/ocr/privacy/hipaa/administrative/statute/hipaastatutepdf.pdf.

Hecker, L. (2016). *HIPAA demystified: HIPAA compliant practice for mental health professionals.* Crown Point, IN: Loger Press.

Hecker, L. L., & Edwards, A. A. (2014). The impact of HIPAA and HITECH: New standards for confidentiality, security, and documentation for marriage and family therapists. *American Journal of Family Therapy, 42*(2), 95–113. doi: 10.1080/01926187.2013.792711.

HIPAA, Public Law 104–191, 42 C.F.R. Part II.

HIPAA, Public Law 104–191, 45 C.F.R. §160.103.

HIPAA, Public Law 104–191, 45 C.F.R. §164.501.

Jaffee v. Redmond, 1996 WL 315841 (U.S. June 13 1996).

Loria, G. (2015). *HIPAA breaches: Minimizing risks and patient fears industry view.* Retrieved from http://www.softwareadvice.com/medical/industryview/hipaa-breaches-report-2015/.

Pepitone, J. (2015a). Anthem hack: Millions of non-Anthem customers could be victims. *NBC News.* Retrieved from http://www.nbcnews.com/tech/security/anthem-hack-millions-non-anthem-customers-could-be-victims-n312051.

Pepitone, J. (2015b). Premera Blue Cross hacked: 11 million customers could be affected. *NBC News.* Retrieved from http://www.nbcnews.com/tech/security/premera-blue-cross-hacked-11-million-customers-affected-n325231.

Ponemon Institute. (2014). *Fourth annual benchmark study on patient privacy and data security.* Retrieved from http://www.ponemon.org/blog/fifth-annual-benchmark-study-on-patient-privacy-and-data-security.

Redspin. (2015). *Breach report 2014: Protected Health Information (PHI).* Retrieved from https://www.redspin.com/resources/whitepapers-datasheets/request-2014-breach-report-protected-health-information-phi-redspin.php.

Superadmin. (2011, December 28). Columbia-St. Mary's Ozaukee Hospital. *Privacy Rights. Clearinghouse.* Retrieved from https://www.privacyrights.org/node/9154.

Synovate. (2007, November). *Federal Trade Commission – 2006 identity theft survey report.* Retrieved from https://www.ftc.gov/reports/federal-trade-commission-2006-identity-theft-survey-report-prepared-commission-synovate.

U.S. Department of Justice. (2015). *Identity theft.* Retrieved from http://www.justice.gov/criminal-fraud/identity-theft/identity-theft-and-identity-fraud.

WISN.com Staff. (2013, February 14). Milwaukee Froedtert hospital warning 43,000 patients their files may have been accessed. *WISN ABC 12 News.* Retrieved from http://www.wisn.com/news/south-east-wisconsin/milwaukee/Froedtert-Hospital-warning-43-000-patients-their-files-may-have-been-accessed/18541500.

5

Self of the Therapist

Being Aware, Prepared, and Ethical

Jared A. Durtschi and Melanie McClellan

> Hillary, a therapist working in private practice, is currently managing many stressors both at home and in her private practice. She is a single mother to her 6-year-old daughter. She is still hurting from the recent loss of her husband in a tragic car accident. Hillary started her private practice a few years ago and is now struggling to figure out how to support her family and keep her private practice up and running. She is finding herself getting behind on paperwork, paying bills, and providing her clients with the quality of care she would prefer. Some of her clients are beginning to recognize that she seems distracted. Before her husband's death, Hillary felt like the pieces of her life were in place, enjoying her family while maintaining a schedule of 20–30 clients a week in her private practice. Now, life has completely changed for Hillary and she is finding herself needing to adjust and accommodate to a different way of living.

Therapists have been described as "wounded healers." This characterization is apropos because while we try to help others heal, we ourselves can be facing serious life challenges, as described in the case scenario. Hillary will likely need to rely on additional self-care and supervision resources to navigate this stressful period of her life so that she can continue providing a high-quality service to her clients. She may need to seek therapy herself, call on family members to help support the care of her daughter, talk to financial advisors regarding the financial stability of her private practice, and adjust her work hours to more effectively complete paperwork and serve clients. She may also need to seek supervision to address and understand how her personal experiences may affect her work with clients. Monitoring signs of compassion fatigue and burnout is prudent—observing how these feelings may be impacting the quality of her clinical work. Hillary can overcome these challenges and provide quality clinical services, but she may need to be deliberate about focusing on issues surrounding the self of the therapist to continue serving clients in an ethical manner. Perhaps most germane to maintaining a high quality of clinical services and ethical behavior is to be vigilantly aware of all the potential self of the therapist issues that may arise that make us susceptible to poor clinical decisions and behaviors.

The self of the therapist is the instrument through which interventions and therapeutic models are provided to clients. Thus, just as a musical instrument must be properly tuned and maintained to successfully provide good music, the self of the therapist must also be carefully tuned and maintained to successfully provide good therapy. When a therapist's self is out of balance or tune, the therapist may not be fully effective, or may even be harmful to clients. An adage attributed to Abraham Lincoln states, "If I had eight hours to chop down a tree, I'd spend six sharpening my axe." Therapists should carefully attend to what can be done to sharpen our clinical tools, including the self of the therapist. The use of self in therapy has the power to dramatically enhance the quality of therapy provided, such as through discussions of process and accessing deeper emotions (Johnson, 2004). Aponte and colleagues (2009) developed the Person of the Therapist Model that focuses on how to use the self of the therapist to enhance clinical intervention. The clinical salience of the self of the therapist is cited in most of the prominent theories in mental health treatment. In fact, some have suggested that one of the most important therapeutic tools available is the therapist's use of self in guiding the process of change (Minuchin, Reiter, & Borda, 2014). Although the self of the therapist can be one of our most valuable clinical tools, problems with the self of the therapist can result in serious ethical violations and harm to clients. We propose that the self of the therapist is a critical ingredient for (1) the process of change and growth in clients and (2) ethical decision-making of the therapist. The purpose of this chapter is to discuss how the self of the therapist can be linked with ethical behavior of the therapist. We start by discussing how self-care is associated with good ethical behavior.

Clinical Opportunities and Challenges

Couple and family therapists (CFTs) believe helping people grow, change, and improve through therapy is noble work that is meaningful for our clients, their partners and children, and many others who are connected with these individuals. Through the process of therapy, clinicians have the chance to be on the front lines witnessing people's symptoms of depression transforming into increased joy, those at risk for suicide finding a reason to keep living, marriages improving to benefit each spouse and the children, trauma survivors finding strength, and in general, helping people transition into their preferred ways of living and being. This process of successful therapy has the potential to change lives, relationships, expected trajectories, and reduce risk for our clients and others in our communities. Many therapists gain a great deal of satisfaction from being a part in this process. However, this professional opportunity to help in such a meaningful way comes with a price. The process of therapy is often slow and uneven. Clients are not always ready to change. Some clients present with a great deal of hostility and threats. Other clients share their trauma that can result in therapists also feeling pain through this process. Despite professional challenges, therapists persevere with the hope of helping, although knowing that this process will frequently stretch us to our limits.

Just like everyone else, therapists experience minor personal stresses, such as a car breaking down or forgetting something important. Therapists also experience more serious personal stressors such as divorce, litigation, and financial hardship. In addition to the everyday life stressors, mental health professionals may have one of the most stressful professions in the world, along with air traffic controllers, police officers, fire fighters, and bomb squad units (Dattillio, 2015). The nature of therapy requires a deep level of emotional investment, and a high level of stress that accompanies working with people with a variety of mental and relational health challenges. Some of the most common stressors cited by mental health practitioners include countertransference, secondary trauma, personal losses, problems with collecting fees, and conflict with coworkers (Bearse, McMinn, Seegobin, & Free, 2013). The experience of professional stress starts in graduate training programs and continues throughout one's clinical career. For example, 73% of psychologist trainees reported clinically significant levels of distress (Stafford-Brown & Pakenham, 2012). In a sample of practicing clinicians, approximately one third had experienced anxiety or depression, whereas more than 40% reported emotional exhaustion in the past year (Mahoney, 1997). Mental health professionals are no strangers to experiencing stress as a byproduct of their clinical work.

Although most careers would presumably be negatively impacted by heightened stress, depression, and anxiety, therapists are especially at risk when experiencing these symptoms because it makes helping other people with similar symptoms more challenging. Unfortunately, despite therapists knowing the negative impact their distress has on the quality of their therapy, and knowing that practicing under undue distress is unethical, a surprising majority of therapists report working with clients while simultaneously recognizing they are too distressed to be effective with their clients (Pope, Tabachnick, & Keith-Spiegel, 1987).

This distress has significant ramifications. In a study of more than 230 occupations, male psychologists were 3.5 times more likely to commit suicide than the general public (Ukens, 1995). Sadly, suicidal ideation has been reported in 29% of mental health professionals, and almost 4% indicated they had made at least one suicide attempt during their professional life (Pope & Tabachnick, 1994). More recent surveys indicate that the percentage of suicide ideation in mental health practitioners is not only stable, but may be rising, as 42% of mental health practitioners reported suicidal ideation or behaviors (Gilroy, Carroll, & Murra, 2002). Ignoring or denying professional work stress is dangerous and unhealthy for the self of the therapist and for clients. Therapists overwhelmed with their own distress, depression, anxiety, or suicide ideation are not in an ethically sound position to provide treatment to others facing similar struggles.

Therapists' continued experience of untreated stressors is expected to have significant impacts on the self of the therapist and on the quality of the therapy provided. Life stressors and professional stressors tend to overwhelm our thinking and emotions, resulting in therapists who may be less focused on their client than usual, and less likely to remember and act upon what they know to be the highest standard of care. In this precarious situation, therapists are at an elevated risk for ethical violations. For example, researchers found that beginning therapists who were experiencing severe personal life stress became more distracted, were less observant, and overall were less effective in their therapy (Bischoff, Barton, Thober, & Hawley, 2002). Therefore, calls have been made for therapists to deal with their personal issues in relation to the therapy that they provide (Aponte et al., 2009).

Compassion Fatigue and Burnout

Compassion fatigue can be defined as a state experienced by therapists characterized by a preoccupation with the suffering of those being helped that may result in a secondary traumatic stress for the therapist (Figley, 2002). On the other hand, burnout is a psychological syndrome in response to chronic stressors on that job that may result from feeling overworked and overstressed (Steel, Macdonald, Schröder, & Mellor-Clark, 2015). Thus, compassion fatigue and burnout may commonly coexist among therapists experiencing a great deal of stress. Compassion fatigue tends to make it more difficult for therapists to experience empathy for a client; this could be the result from a protective wall therapists put up to shield themselves from the pain and suffering of clients. This lack of empathy has serious implications for the therapeutic alliance and the overall quality of therapy services provided. Unfortunately, therapists with compassion fatigue tend to have an emotional reserve that is usually largely depleted, leaving little left to give to the client (Dattillio, 2015).

Several characteristics of the therapist and client create conditions favorable to the development of compassion fatigue. Some clinicians have caseloads that include primarily extreme trauma; for example, some clinicians work exclusively with sexual trauma survivors who have been raped dozens of times through sex trafficking. Carrying a caseload with a high proportion of trauma survivor clients is linked with higher compassion fatigue (Sprang, Clark, & Whitt-Woosley, 2007). Mental health practitioners with a personal history of trauma are more likely to experience compassion fatigue as part of their clinical work (Cunningham, 2003). Some therapists may be drawn to help certain types of clients with a trauma history because of their own personal experiences with trauma. Thankfully, specialized trauma training for therapists can reduce levels of compassion fatigue that may be experienced from hearing similar stories of trauma to their own (Cunningham, 2003). Unique training for trauma-informed therapists has been described in reference to self of the therapist experience (Jordan, 2016). Another factor is isolation. Therapists who work in relative isolation, without regular contact with professional colleagues, or therapists who do not receive supervision may be at elevated risk for developing secondary trauma from clients (Macchi, Johnson, & Durtschi, 2014).

It is important to be aware of the symptoms of compassion fatigue to identify in ourselves so that we know when this process may be affecting us. In a review of the literature on compassion fatigue, it has been noted that symptoms of compassion fatigue include chronic physical and emotional exhaustion, depersonalization, irritability, negative feelings toward work and others, self-contempt, low job satisfaction, headaches, and weight loss (Negash & Sahin, 2011).

The onset of burnout tends to be more gradual and cumulative, whereas compassion fatigue may develop more rapidly, perhaps from exposure to a single traumatic event (Figley, 2002). Excessive exposure to stress and anxiety can leave a therapist feeling fatigued with the therapy process if their stress is not handled well (Azar, 2000). Burnout is typically experienced with a high degree of emotional exhaustion, minimized sense of personal accomplishment from work, and may involve increased apathy and cynicism for clients, the profession, and life in general (Dattillio, 2015). Burnout typically includes three components: emotional exhaustion, cynicism (e.g., an impersonal response to clients), and ineffectiveness (Leiter & Maslach, 2015). In such situations, one can feel an inadequate sense of personal achievement and reduced self-esteem, with a tendency to evaluate oneself negatively with regard to one's work (Leiter & Maslach, 2015). Rosenberg and Pace (2006) reviewed some of the physical and emotional symptoms of burnout in CFT, including chronic fatigue, gastrointestinal problems, insomnia, headaches, hypertension, feelings of hopelessness, futility, boredom, anxiety, and withdrawal. Similarly, Azar (2000) addressed some common indications of burnout, which included: becoming easily angered, frustrated, or irritated; crying often and having difficulty managing feelings; frequently engaging in risky situations; substance abuse; showing extreme rigidity in thinking; displaying signs of depression; spending a great amount of time on tasks, but with decreased amounts of accomplishment; and living to work. The therapist must be sufficiently self-aware to be able to identify these burnout risk factors. Therapists working together in a group practice can help each other as well by being cognizant of these risk factors in their colleagues. These symptoms of burnout may be associated with conditions such as compassion fatigue, secondary traumatic stress and vicarious traumatization through "reexperiencing" clients' trauma and emotional pain that can also have negative effects on therapists' services.

The origins of burnout can be attributed to the characteristics of the client, the practitioner, and the setting. Menniger (1990) surveyed psychotherapists regarding anxiety-provoking therapy situations. He found that client suicide or violence, a difficult client, clients challenging their competence, clients' anger, sexual issues in therapy, litigation, and testifying in court were among the most frequent causes of anxiety for the psychotherapist. Additionally, working with chronically depressed clients and cases of child abuse can be challenging for therapists (Rosenberg & Pace, 2006). Meeting with depressed, hostile, suicidal, borderline, and dependent clients on a regular basis can also have a detrimental impact on the emotional well-being of the therapist. In light of all these stressful work situations the therapist may encounter, it is possible that this level of demand can drain therapists of their emotional resources (Dattillio, 2015).

Burnout can occur in those therapists that have had many years of practice; however, it can also occur in beginning practitioners.

With experienced therapists, burnout can occur when their sense of accomplishment and achievement is no longer adequate (Shapiro, Brown, & Biegel, 2007). Conversely, inexperienced therapists may experience stress and burnout because they are not psychologically prepared for the work (Shapiro et al., 2007). When beginning practitioners encounter unavoidable failures in treating clients or the client's needs exceed the therapist's skills, the beginning practitioner may experience feelings of ineptitude and diminished self-confidence (Lee, Eppler, Kendal, & Latty, 2001). Thus, years of professional experience are positively correlated with a lower risk for compassion fatigue and burnout (Cunningham, 2003). Similarly, therapists with more years of clinical experience are significantly more likely to have a higher quality of professional life (Macchi et al., 2014). Up to 40% of surveyed psychologists met burnout level thresholds, suggesting a substantial number of therapists were overstressed (Fortener, 1999). The more burned out therapists feel, the more likely they may be to provide a diminished quality of therapy, and therefore are more prone to ethical violations.

Therapists Attending Therapy

Despite the fact that therapists are professionals in helping others with their personal and relational problems, therapists are not impervious to experiencing personal and relational problems in their own lives that may require help. If a therapist is feeling burned out or overstressed, one useful resource is for the therapist to attend therapy. Too often, therapists are reticent to get help for themselves, despite knowing how important it is to get help. We speculate that contributing factors to this problem include therapists denying they are as stressed as they actually are, the stigma of seeing a therapist for a personal problem, and having overly full schedules that make it difficult to carve out the time to go to therapy. In a sample of psychologists, 59% admitted that there had been periods of their life when they could have benefited from therapy, but did not seek out therapy services (Bearse et al., 2013). A survey of clinicians found that 95% of those clinicians seeking therapy expressed that their experience was at least somewhat successful, and 99.4% reported they would seek therapy again if necessary (Deacon, Kirkpatrick, Wetchler, & Niedner, 1999). Thus, therapists seeking therapy generally found the process helpful and recommend this to other therapists who may be struggling. More specifically, another study (Linley & Joseph, 2007) surveyed therapists to identify factors related to increased levels of therapist well-being and personal growth. They found that those therapists who received personal therapy experienced more personal growth, increased positive life changes, and less burnout. Also, even seasoned therapists who sought clinical supervision experienced more personal growth in their clinical career. Women reported more personal growth than men, and those therapists who reported a greater number of hours per week spent with clients reported more personal growth. Mental health practitioners receiving their own therapy have been shown to be helpful for reducing burnout, and may even help prevent unethical behaviors from occurring (Grimmer & Tribe, 2001). Therapists receiving their own therapy and supervision were part of what helped therapists who had violated state licensure boards of ethical conduct get back on track (Coy, Lambert, & Miller, 2015). When therapists are under stress, receiving clinical supervision can increase therapist effectiveness (Eastwood & Ecklund, 2008).

Remaining competent to act as a proficient therapist remains the ultimate goal, and receiving therapy should be seen as a key ingredient to maintaining competence in the face of life stresses from work and personal life. Blow and colleagues (2007) note:

> Intense self of the therapist work is required that will bring to awareness the unresolved issues and biases that contribute to a lack of effectiveness with clients, as well as therapist strengths and resources that can help the therapist be more effective (p. 311).

Students in training agree that personal therapy is important (Aponte et al., 2009). Put most bluntly, it is required of therapists to seek professional help in response to their own individual and relational problems that may impinge upon their work. Several mental health professional codes of ethics indicate that a therapist must seek appropriate professional help for personal issues that may affect their clinical work. Therefore, it may be unethical for a therapist with their own mental health issues to continue to provide therapy without receiving treatment to overcome these challenges. In addition, it may also be helpful to consult a professional colleague about personal stressors that may arise.

Self-Care

Self-care can be defined as the deliberate behaviors a therapist engages in to maintain a high functioning self, capable of providing valuable and effective clinical services to clients. Ironically, although mental health professionals are experts on what techniques are helpful in treating challenges with stress, relationships, and mental health in others, many clinicians do not use these principles for themselves. This is unfortunate because caring for oneself helps therapists to prevent ethical violations from occurring, improve clinical outcomes, and enhance personal lives. Self-care is expected to decrease the chances of making an ethical violation through improving our ability to focus on what is best for the client. Recently, a survey of mental health practitioners found that more frequent self-care behaviors was significantly associated with a greater degree of therapists' professional quality of life (Macchi et al., 2014).

However, what types of self-care activities are most helpful? Researchers found that, within a sample of psychologists, the highest rated career-sustaining behaviors included spending time with one's partner and/or family, maintaining a balance between one's personal and professional life, and maintaining a sense of humor (Stevanovic & Ropuert, 2004). Rosenberg and Pace (2006) reviewed many ideas for prevention and treatment of burnout, including engaging in physical exercise, eating a proper diet, taking regular vacations, seeking therapy, setting limits, separating work and private lives, shortening work hours, allowing workday breaks, and improving relations with colleagues and staff members. For a valuable resource on therapist self-care, see Baker (2003).

In addition, we speculate that self-care activities most helpful are activities that aid the therapist to slow down their thinking, focus on the present moment, relax, regain confidence, and gain new clinical skills. Potential helpful types of self-care to achieve these goals may include receiving therapy, seeking out clinical supervision, engaging in mindfulness activities (see Kabat-Zinn, 2005), spending time with family or friends, enjoying a personal hobby or leisure time, getting a massage, attending a clinical training, or reading a clinical article or book. Further, there are some attitudes clinicians have that may minimize our successes and enlarge our failures that hurt our self-care efforts. For example, it seems to be a common belief among clinicians that when a client improves, we attribute that success to the client; however, when a client does not improve, we attribute that to failure to the therapist. This common thought pattern among clinicians could be called the "therapist attribution error." Perhaps a more accurate representation would be to recognize the shared responsibility therapists have in the success of a client, and the client's responsibility in a lack of progress.

We have observed that some therapists report engaging in "self-care" activities that involve binging on watching television (e.g., Netflix), substance use, or sleeping for excessive amounts of time. Of course, certain types of self-care are more useful in achieving the desired end goal than others. In some cases, perhaps the best form of self-care may not be a leisure activity, but rather may involve staying late at the office and completing all the case notes, treatment plans, and billing paperwork before going home, to feel the sweet relief of knowing that it is all done. Despite common stresses of life and work, most often, therapists tend to find their clinical work to be highly fulfilling and growth inspiring, as they share the journey of growth and healing with their clients.

Often, we clinicians may find ourselves feeling somewhat hypocritical when talking with clients about ideas to strengthen their relationships and improve functioning, when we are not engaged in those activities as frequently as we should in our own lives! Self-care involves doing those things we know can help us have a more meaningful life, stronger relationships, and move us toward the people we are trying to become. We suggest using the same theory, research, and clinical techniques to help us care for ourselves that we use to help our clients. For example, we can use the same mindfulness activities for ourselves as we do with our clients to focus our thinking. The concrete goal setting techniques we use with clients can be used on ourselves to help us plan changes we will make. When discussing irrational thoughts with our clients, we can do the same in addressing our own irrational thoughts about ourselves. Dattillio (2015) recommends therapists regularly assessing any changes in our behavior, attitude, thinking, and being aware of changes in us that our friends, family, and colleagues observe in us. Staying vigilantly self-aware of our current functioning can help clinicians know when it might be necessary to engage in more self-care activities.

Therapist and Client Values

In addition to potential ethical concerns that can come from the therapist's life stressors, another potential troublesome area linking self of the therapist with ethics is in the inevitable differences of values and beliefs between the therapist and client. Consider a few examples of potential value differences to be navigated in therapy, such as a religious fundamentalist therapist and a lesbian client (for ideas on handling this, see Paprocki, 2014), a feminist therapist working with a misogynist husband, a therapist who opposes spanking children working with parents who frequently spank, or an overachieving self-driven therapist and a client who struggles finding the energy to get out of bed. The values of therapists and clients strongly influence the course of therapy. Becvar notes "moral values refer to basic beliefs regarding what an individual, group, or society considers good and right; they represent the standards of appropriate behavior" (2001, p. 155). Values are deeply rooted in constituting who we are, what is important to us as individuals, and what directs our course of action throughout life. Values are the standard by which attitudes are formed and decisions are made. Values also color therapists' impressions of what constitutes acceptable behavior for themselves and others; thus, values affect how people behave in most every setting. Everyone has their own unique value system for what they define as important in their lives. These differences in values are evidenced among those who have differing ethnic, religious, racial, sexual, and cultural backgrounds. Even within these differing groups, there is a wide variety of individual diversity in core values. Therapists may find themselves with clients of differing values, and both therapist and client may become cognizant of these inherent value clashes.

To gain integrity as a science, mental health disciplines historically tried to distance themselves from value issues by maintaining that therapeutic neutrality was both possible and optimal. However, a truly "value-free" therapy approach is not possible, and many have critiqued the ideal of purely objective clinical work, as values are always present in the therapeutic process. A fear of imposing values on clients can lead some therapists to sidestep value issues (Tjeltveit, 1986), or feeling unsure of how to address value issues with clients can lead to ignoring values altogether (Fife & Whiting, 2007). Another common way to avoid the influence of values is for therapists to selectively cite research to explain something to their clients that supports the therapist's own personal values (Fife & Whiting, 2007).

Authors have explored and scrutinized how values pervade couple and family therapy (e.g., Fife & Whiting, 2007; Melito, 2003). Becoming more reflective and conscientious about values will help therapists become increasingly effective (Fife & Whiting, 2007). It is clear that values affect therapy, but managing these issues is paramount in protecting against power abuse (Parrott, 1999). In some cases, therapists' values may be more stable than their clients, which may result in clients shifting their values to align with the therapist's values. It has been observed that, during therapy, clients' values tend to converge over time with those of their therapist (Schwehn & Schau, 1990); clients also begin to verbally conceptualize their problems in the same way as their therapist (Davis & Piercy, 2007). These strengthened values of the client may help elicit and maintain positive changes for the client. Conversely, there are serious dangers of the therapist abusing this power by imposing the therapist's values onto their clients, whether intentional or not. Therapists must proceed with great sensitivity in projecting values onto the client. It is tenable that conflicted value systems in therapy between client and therapist can generate emotional reactivity in the therapist, who then refocuses therapy away from the client's presenting problem and towards alleviation of the therapist's own anxiety. Instead, clients could be better served by therapists learning to identify and integrate their personal value system into their professional development (Brosi & Rolling, 2007).

Several theories directly address how to handle value differences. Narrative therapy (Freedman & Combs, 1996), for example, proposes that therapists explore clients' values in a nonjudgmental way, deconstructing where these values come from (e.g., messages from family, the media, and culture), allowing clients to decide what they choose to believe and value and helping them follow their own path. The therapist respects this chosen path, while addressing any potential obstacles of that belief, and helping clients live according to their own values and beliefs. In some cases, this may be challenging for therapists, and supervision can be very instrumental in learning how to handle certain value differences.

Closely related to value differences is helping clients make their own decisions and ensuring that therapists do not make decisions for their clients. Sometimes it may be difficult for therapists who harbor their own strong belief systems to *not* make decisions for clients. For example, if a couple, who is cohabitating, was attending therapy to discuss relationship problems, the therapist cannot encourage the couple to get married or to no longer cohabitate. If a therapist was to direct clients into making life decisions, that therapist would be considered acting in an unethical manner.

Although therapists must not make life decisions for clients, it is expected that therapists will help clients reach an outcome that the client prefers. Sometimes therapists may find it difficult to separate their own values from the clients' values, and this may interfere with the therapeutic process. For example, if a therapist's values are strongly against divorce, and clients want aid in ending their marriage, it would be inappropriate for the therapist to allow their values to be imposed on their clients by pushing them toward saving their marriage. Sometimes value differences may actually halt the progress of therapy. In this case, therapists must seek out supervision or consider whether it is ethical to continue seeing a given client. It is pertinent for the therapist to ensure that the client is benefiting from therapy and the therapist must make every effort to support the client despite any value differences. Therapists must always be cognizant of whether their clients are progressing, and specifically whether value differences between therapists and clients are the reason behind therapy not progressing.

Developing and Maintaining Competence

Another important aspect of the self of the therapist is developing and maintaining therapeutic competence. Therapeutic competence can be defined broadly as therapists' ability to promote positive client change (Shaw & Dobson, 1988). Therapists' competence is critical to providing a beneficial service to clients and is an essential facet of the therapist's ethical responsibility to clients. Therapists must promote beneficence—doing well on the client's behalf. Further, therapists should be vigilant in assuring that they develop strong clinical skills and then maintain therapeutic competence as a professional in providing high-quality service to clients.

The clinician's first step in becoming competent is to obtain the best education and clinical training accessible to them. Through training programs, therapists develop a primary level of expertise with therapeutic theory, clinical skills, the process of change and human development. This training is important for providing the framework from which the therapist will practice. Before graduation and licensure, a therapist will also accumulate many hours of supervision while in the therapeutic training process. Supervision tends to develop and refine therapist's skills and techniques, while also strengthening the therapist's confidence, skill, and experience. Moreover, researchers have identified that more frequent supervision of therapists practicing in the community was associated with a higher degree of therapists' professional quality of life (Macchi et al., 2014).

Supervision is not limited to training programs only, but must be sought in any circumstance throughout one's career in which the therapist may be treating a new population of clients (e.g., Syrian refugees), or using a new clinical approach that the therapist is not yet proficient in (e.g., eye movement desensitization and reprocessing [EMDR]). Put simply, it is unethical to practice outside our scope of training and expertise without additional training and supervision. Therapists' focus must be on doing good for the client, not arrogantly believing we can competently practice a new approach or treat a new clinical population without proper training and supervision.

An important element of therapeutic competence is using evidence-based approaches in clinical work. There is a growing movement toward evidence-based practice in mental health (McCabe, 2006). The core of evidence-based practice is the "systematic preference for those clinical practices for which there has been some documented empirical effectiveness in promoting positive client outcomes" (Hardiman, Theriot, & Hodges, 2005, p. 105). Using clinical methods that have been shown to be effective is a reasonable pursuit for mental health practitioners. Therapy success rates can improve if clinicians focused their interventions on empirically validated treatments rather than on potentially erroneous conceptions of what works. We would all be sorely disappointed if our dentist did not stay abreast of the best way to fill a cavity, and our clients are equally disappointed if therapists do not keep up with new developments in the best ways to help them. Several ways to keep abreast of developments in the field include attending local clinical trainings and conferences, reading articles, and having discussions with colleagues about new ideas.

Cultural competence is an important ingredient closely linked with the self of the therapist. Understanding a client's experience with oppression can help therapists avoid replicating that oppression in the therapy room. Some clinical trainers believe that it is one thing to read or be taught about oppression, but quite another to experience it. Laszloffy and Habekost (2010) suggest several creative ideas for training programs to incorporate as experiential exercises the students do outside of class, and then later discuss with the class. For example, students are asked to apply for welfare, hold hands with someone of the same sex while walking on campus for 15 minutes, attend a community event where they will be a racial minority, attend a church service they do not ascribe to and have a discussion with the ecclesiastical leader, dressing and behaving as someone of the opposite sex for a day, or spending 4 hours in a wheelchair. These type of experiential experiences can serve to help clinicians gain a better sense of the oppression their clients feel, and hopefully develop greater respect and empathy for them. For additional ideas on how to incorporate the use of self in postmodern theories, please see Cheon and Murphy's (2007) article.

Summary

The self of the therapist plays an important role for therapists working in an ethical manner. Ethical violations are more probable when the self of the therapist is out of tune or balance in one way or another. Careful attention to the self of the therapist is expected to not only improve the quality of therapy, but to also facilitate a more ethical clinical practice. Couple and family therapy is a challenging field and clinicians must be prepared to meet these challenges. There are many facets for the person of the therapist to consider throughout their professional career. Specifically, therapists must practice within their specified ethical code, appropriately handle life stress to avoid compassion fatigue, successfully navigate value differences, maintain clients' confidentiality, and develop and maintain strong clinical skills. The person of the therapist is an indispensable component of the outcome of therapy, and as such, must constantly strive to ensure that the therapeutic instrument is finely tuned.

References

Aponte, H., J., Powell, F. D., Brooks, S., Watson, M. F., Litzke, C., Lawless, J., & Johnson, E. (2009). Training the person of the therapist in an academic setting. *Journal of Marital and Family Therapy, 35*(4), 381–394. doi: 10.1111/j.1752-0606.2009.00123.x.

Azar, S. T. (2000). Preventing burnout in professionals and paraprofessionals who work with child abuse and neglect cases: A cognitive behavioral approach to supervision. *JCLP/In Session: Psychotherapy in Practice, 56*(5), 643–663. doi: 10.1002/(SICI)1097-4679(200005)56:5<643::AID-JCLP6>3.0.CO;2-U.

Baker, E. K. (2003). *Caring for ourselves: A therapist's guide to personal and professional well-being.* Washington, DC: American Psychological Association.

Bearse, J. L., McMinn, M. R., Seegobin, W., & Free, K. (2013). Barriers to psychologists seeking mental health care. *Professional Psychology: Research & Practice, 44*(3), 150–157. doi: 10.1037/200311182.

Becvar, D. S. (2001). *Ethics in marriage and family therapy.* Washington, DC: The American Association for Marriage and Family Therapy.

Bischoff, R. J., Barton, M., Thober, J., & Hawley, R. (2002). Events and experiences impacting the development of clinical self-confidence: A study of the first year of client contact. *Journal of Marital and Family Therapy, 28*(3), 371–382. doi: 10.1111/j.1752-0606.2002.tb01193.x.

Blow, A. J., Sprenkle, D. H., & Davis, S. D. (2007). Is who delivers the treatment more important than the treatment itself? The role of the therapist in common factors. *Journal of Marital and Family Therapy, 33*(3), 298–317. doi: 10.1111/j.1752-0606.2007.00029.x.

Brosi, M. W., & Rolling, E. S. (2007). The effect of value conflicts on therapists' work with abusive clients: Implications for the integration of feminist tenets. *Journal of Feminist Family Therapy, 19*(2), 63–89. doi: 10.1300/J086v19n02_03.

Cheon, H., & Murphy, M. J. (2007). The self-of-the-therapist awakened. *Journal of Feminist Family Therapy, 19*(1), 1–16. doi: 10.1300/J086v19n01_01.

Coy, J. S., Lambert, J. E., & Miller, M. M. (2015). Stories of the accused: A phenomenological inquiry of MFTs and accusations of unprofessional conduct. *Journal of Marital and Family Therapy, 42*(1), 139–152. doi: 10.1111/jmft.12109.

Cunningham, M. (2003). Impact of trauma work on social work clinicians: Empirical findings. *Social Work, 48*(4), 451–459. doi: 10.1093/sw/48.4.451.

Dattillio, F. M. (2015). The self-care of psychologists and mental health professionals: A review and practitioner guide. *Australian Psychologist, 50*(6), 393–399. doi: 10.1111/ap.12157.

Davis, S. D., & Piercy, F. P. (2007). What clients of couple therapy model developers and their former students say about change, part 1: Model-dependent common factors across three models. *Journal of Marital and Family Therapy, 33*(3), 318–343. doi: 10.1111/j.1752-0606.2007.00030.x.

Deacon, S., Kirkpatrick, D., Wetchler, J., & Niedner, D. (1999). Marriage and family therapists' problems and utilization of personal therapy. *American Journal of Family Therapy, 27*(1), 73–94. doi: 10.1080/019261899262113.

Eastwood, C. D., & Ecklund, K. (2008). Compassion fatigue risk and self-care practices among residential treatment center childcare workers. *Residential Treatment for Children & Youth, 25*(2), 103–122. doi: 10.1080/08865710802309972.

Fife, S. T., & Whiting, J. B. (2007). Values in family therapy practice and research: An invitation for reflection. *Contemporary Family Therapy, 29*(1), 71–86. doi: 10.1007/s10591-007-9027-1.

Figley, C. R. (2002). Compassion fatigue: Psychotherapists' chronic lack of self-care. *Journal of Clinical Psychology, 58*(11), 1433–1441. doi: 10.1002/5cip.10090.

Fortener, R. G. (1999). *Relationship between work setting, client prognosis, suicide ideation, and burnout in psychologists and counselors.* (Unpublished doctoral dissertation). University of Toledo, Toledo, Ohio.

Freedman, J., & Combs, G. (1996). *Narrative therapy: The social construction of preferred realities*. New York, NY: Norton.

Gilroy, P. J., Carroll, L., & Murra, J. (2002). A preliminary survey of counseling psychologists' personal experience with depression and treatment. *Professional Psychology: Research & Practice, 33*(4), 402–407. doi: 10.1037/0735-7028.33.4.402.

Grimmer, A., & Tribe, R. (2001). Counselling psychologists' perceptions of the impact of mandatory personal therapy on professional development: An exploratory study. *Counselling Psychology Quarterly, 14*(4), 287–301. doi: 10.1080/09515070110101469.

Hardiman, E. R., Theriot, M. T., & Hodges, J. Q. (2005). Evidence based practice in mental health: Important challenges for consumer run programs. *Best Practices in Mental Health, 1*, 105–124.

Johnson, S. M. (2004). *The practice of emotionally focused couple therapy: Creating connection* (2nd ed.). New York, NY: Brunner-Routledge.

Jordan, K. (2016). Training the trauma-informed marriage and family therapist. In K. Jordan (Ed.), *Couple, marriage, and family therapy supervision* (pp. 391–417). New York, NY: Springer.

Kabat-Zinn, J. (2005). *Coming to our senses: Healing ourselves and the world through mindfulness*. New York, NY: Hyperion.

Laszloffy, T., & Habekost, J. (2010). Using experiential tasks to enhance cultural sensitivity among MFT trainees. *Journal of Marital and Family Therapy, 36*(3), 333–346. doi: 10.1111/j.1752-0606.2010.00213.x.

Lee, R. E., Eppler, C., Kendal, N., & Latty, C. (2001). Critical incidents in the professional lives of first year MFT students. *Contemporary Family Therapy, 23*(1), 51–61. doi: 10.1023/A:1007872132292.

Leiter, M. P., & Maslach, C. (2015). Conquering burnout. *Scientific American Mind, 26*(1), 30–35. doi: 10.1038/scientificamericanmind0115-30.

Linley, P. A., & Joseph, S. (2007). Therapy work and therapists' positive and negative well-being. *Journal of Social and Clinical Psychology, 26*(3), 385–403. doi: 10.1521/jscp.2007.26.3.385.

Macchi, C. R., Johnson, M. D., & Durtschi, J. A. (2014). Predictors and processes associated with home-based family therapists' professional quality of life. *Journal of Marital and Family Therapy, 40*(3), 380–390. doi: 10.1111/jmft.12016.

Mahoney, M. (1997). Psychotherapists' personal problems and self-care patterns. *Professional Psychology, Research and Practice, 28*(1), 14–16. doi: 10.1037/0735-7028.28.1.14.

McCabe, O. L. (2006). Evidence based practice in mental health: Accessing, appraising, and adopting research data. *International Journal of Mental Health, 35*(2), 50–69. doi: 10.2753/IMH0020-7411350204.

Melito, R. (2003). Values in the role of the family therapist: Self-determination and justice. *Journal of Marital and Family Therapy, 29*(1), 3–11. doi: 10.1111/j.1752-0606.2003.tb00378.x.

Menniger, W. W. (1990). Anxiety in the psychotherapist. *Bulletin of the Menninger Clinic, 54*(2), 232–247.

Minuchin, S., Reiter, M. D., & Borda, C. (2014). *The craft of family therapy*. New York, NY: Taylor & Francis.

Negash, S., & Sahin, S. (2011). Compassion fatigue in marriage and family therapy: Implications for therapists and clients. *Journal of Marital and Family Therapy, 37*(1), 1–13. doi: 10.1111/j.1752-0606.2009.00147.x.

Paprocki, C. M. (2014). When personal and professional values conflict: Trainee perspectives on tensions between religious beliefs and affirming treatment of LGBT clients. *Ethics and Behavior, 24*(4), 279–292. doi: 10.1080/10508422.2013.860029.

Parrott, C. (1999). Towards an integration of science, art and morality: The role of values in psychology. *Counseling Psychology Quarterly, 12*(1), 5–20. doi: 10.1080/09515079908254074.

Pope, K. S., & Tabachnick, B. G. (1994). Therapists as patients: A national survey of psychologists' experience, problems and beliefs. *Professional Psychology: Research & Practice, 25*(3), 247–258. doi: 10.1037/0735-7028.25.3.247.

Pope, K. S., Tabachnick, B. G., & Keith-Spiegel, P. (1987). Ethics of practice: The beliefs and behaviors of psychologists as therapists. *American Psychologist, 42*(5), 993–1006. doi: 10.1037/0003-066X.42.11.993.

Rosenberg, T., & Pace, M. (2006). Burnout among mental health professionals: Special considerations for the marriage and family therapist. *Journal of Marital and Family Therapy, 32*(1), 87–99. doi: 10.1111/j.1752-0606.2006.tb01590.x.

Schwehn, J., & Schau, C. G. (1990). Psychotherapy as a process of value stabilization. *Counseling and Values, 35*(1), 24–30. doi: 10.1002/j.2161-007X.1990.tb00355.x.

Shapiro, S. L., Brown, K. W., & Biegel, G. M. (2007). Teaching self-care to caregivers: Effects of mindfulness-based stress reduction on the mental health of therapists in training. *Training and Education in Professional Psychology, 1*(2), 105–115. doi: 10.1037/1931-3918.1.2.105.

Shaw, B. F., & Dobson, K. S. (1988). Competency judgments in the training and evaluations of psychotherapists. *Journal of Consulting and Clinical Psychology, 56*(5), 666–672. doi: 10.1037/0022-006X.56.5.666.

Sprang, G., Clark, J. J., & Whitt-Woosley, A. (2007). Compassion fatigue, compassion satisfaction, and burnout: Factors impacting a professional's quality of life. *Journal of Loss and Trauma, 12*(3), 259–280. doi: 10.1080/15325020701238093.

Stafford-Brown, J., & Pakenham, K. I. (2012). The effectiveness of an ACT informed intervention for managing stress and improvising therapist qualities in clinical psychology trainees. *Journal of Clinical Psychology, 68*(6), 592–613. doi: 10.1002/jclp.21844.

Steel, C., Macdonald, J., Schröder, T., & Mellor-Clark, J. (2015). Exhausted but not cynical: Burnout in therapists working within Improving Access to Psychological Therapy Services. *Journal of Mental Health, 24*(1), 33–37. doi: 10.3109/09638237.2014.971145.

Stevanovic, P., & Ropuert, P. A. (2004). Career-sustaining behaviors, satisfactions, and stresses of professional psychologists. *Psychotherapy: Theory, Research, Practice, Training, 41*(3), 301–309. doi: 10.1037/0033-3204.41.3.301.

Tjeltveit, A. C. (1986). The ethics of value conversion in psychotherapy: Appropriate and inappropriate therapist influence on client values. *Clinical Psychology Review, 6*(6), 515–537. doi: 10.1016/0272-7358(86)90035-8.

Ukens, C. (1995). The tragic truth. *Drug Topics, 139,* 66–74.

6

Power, Privilege, and Ethics in Couple and Family Therapy

Megan J. Murphy and Lorna Hecker

Sam is a newly licensed therapist and is working with a couple, Chris and Jessie. The couple has been referred to Sam by the Department of Human Services (DHS) for abuse and neglect of their 4-year-old child, Kendall, who has been removed from the home. Chris and Jessie assert that they never abused their child and that they love Kendall very much, although they admit that Jessie can get quite angry at times, to the point of throwing things. The incident that prompted a call to DHS was that Kendall fell out of a second-story window of their home and suffered severe injuries. Other DHS allegations made upon investigation are that the home was unkempt and that there was not adequate nutritional food in the home for Kendall. Jessie stays at home to care for Kendall while Chris works outside the home.

Introduction

Power, privilege, and ethics permeate all therapeutic encounters. Each of these constructs is complex and multifaceted, which can make it difficult to know how to address and integrate into therapy sessions. Further, because of the overlap in the constructs themselves, it can be hard to recognize and distinguish in the therapeutic process. For these reasons, in this chapter, we first define power, briefly discuss the integration of power in family therapy theories, and then discuss power in the therapeutic relationship as it relates to ethical principles. Next, we explore the definition of privilege, tying privilege to identity and intersectionality. Then, we briefly explore some implications of identity as related to gender, race, class, sexual orientation, and ability. Finally, we return to the idea of intersectionality for some ways that it may impact the scenario described above.

Power

Power is a multidimensional construct that has been defined in many different ways by theorists and researchers over the past several decades (e.g., Cromwell & Olson, 1975; Foucault, 1977; French & Raven, 1959; Hare-Mustin, 1991; Knudson-Martin, 2009). Power exists in relationship between at least two people, as it suggests difference between two (or more) people in some way. Some postmodern definitions of power include the ability to create and make meaning that is differentially held by certain groups of people (Foucault, 1977). Modernist definitions of power include the ability to impose one's will (Blau, 1964), ability to reward another for their behavior (French & Raven, 1959), ability to make decisions (Cromwell & Olson, 1975), and so on. Therapists have power in relation to clients with their ability to provide a diagnosis (or not), the ability to guide the therapeutic conversation in a certain direction (or not), the ability to decide how therapy will unfold, and their role as the expert, among others. Clients hold power as well; for example, they can decide whether or not to follow advice or directives given by the therapist, they may decide to drop out of therapy (even if court mandated), they can write online reviews of therapy, not pay their bill, come late to sessions, or even take legal action against the therapist. Likewise, a child who refuses to leave the car to come into the office for a therapy session or has a tantrum in session holds power. Thus, power is a multidimensional concept; it can be related to a person's characteristics (e.g., gender, race/ethnicity), but can shift with context and relationships. There is a noticeable power shift when therapy that was office-bound becomes in-home therapy; the clients gain some power because they are in charge of their home context, but the therapist can also be seen as gaining power in that they now hold more realistic information about the client's home life. As can be seen, power has many definitions; it certainly impacts participants in the therapeutic process.

Power in Couple and Family Therapy Theories

The concept of power is not ubiquitous throughout couple and family therapy (CFT) theories. One could argue that structural family therapy was the first to consider power (Minuchin, Montalvo, Guerney, Rosman, & Schumer, 1967), at least in terms of reinforcing boundaries and supporting hierarchy between generations. Minuchin and colleagues (1967) believed that power in the family should rest with the parents, and that dysfunction occurs when children hold an inappropriate amount of power in relation to their parents. Structural interventions were developed to enhance the appropriate power structure in the family, but did not consider power as an organizing principle within the parental subsystem (Walsh & Scheinkman, 1989). Strategic family therapists also viewed hierarchy as important in families; again, dysfunction is seen when there is an imbalance in the parent–child hierarchy (Haley, 1976).

In terms of therapy, feminist therapists were the first to apply the idea of power to gender in relationships (Hare-Mustin, 1978). Feminist therapists advocate for CFT theories to be viewed through a feminist lens, which would add an analysis of power to traditional theories. Feminist family therapy also stands on its own as a viable approach to infusing an understanding of power dynamics into clinical work; several current researchers and therapists incorporate power into their approaches. For example, Knudson-Martin and Mahoney's book titled *Couples, Gender, and Power* (2009) provides a research-based model for addressing gendered power in couples' relationships. Similarly, Haddock, Zimmerman, and MacPhee (2000) have developed a gender equity guide that clinicians and supervisors can use to ensure that they are adding a feminist lens to their clinical work. In addition, narrative therapists consider societal power and power in terms of meaning making in their therapeutic approaches. White and Epston (1990), for example, discuss how we, as therapists, can "consider the broader sociopolitical context of the person's experience" (p. 18); they argue that dominant discourses shape the possibilities that clients see for themselves.

Feminist therapists would say that it is highly problematic to fail to consider power dynamics when seeing clients (Kaschak, 1990). Therapists who do not consider or address power issues are taking a stand to uphold the status quo. Given the research establishing links between power imbalances, such as the demand-withdraw pattern, and negative relational outcomes, including a higher risk of divorce (Gottman, Coan, Carrere, & Swanson, 1998) and domestic violence (Berns, Jacobson, & Gottman, 1999), feminists see an ethical mandate for therapists to address power differentials, both within intimate and family relationships, as well as the connection between relationships, families, and larger society.

Power in the Therapeutic Relationship

Because power occurs in relationships, power dynamics are found throughout the therapeutic realm. Most apparent is the relationship between therapist and client. If nothing else, therapists have more power than clients by virtue of their role as a therapist; the role of therapist, at a minimum, includes the fact that the therapist is educated about relationships and may have a license to practice therapy. The therapist gets paid; money is valued by our culture, and is indicative of a one-way relationship on some level. Therapists have the ability to define reality—in this case, mental health. Many clients attend therapy seeking answers to their problems, and presumably therapists can provide those answers, perhaps in the form of a diagnosis. Diagnosing can affect a client's life—sometimes for the better, if such a diagnosis brings relief to the mystery surrounding symptoms and relationship dynamics. Alternatively, a diagnosis can bring shame in being labelled with a mental disorder, or hassle for clients if their jobs are dependent on them being free from a diagnosable mental illness. For example, a pilot who is diagnosed with a mental illness may not be able to fly should the employer learn of the issues (the pilot asking their spouse to take on the diagnosis for insurance purposes also has some interesting power implications!). The potential impact therapists can have on clients' lives is tremendous. Therapists can intervene with a suicidal client and save a life, a therapist can provide much-needed support to clients going through the depths of a depression, or a probation client may return to therapy if the therapist deems them noncompliant with therapy. Therapists can decide whether or not to include children in therapy, but in one early study (as noted in Chapter 10) children were allowed only 3.5% of the spoken words (Cederborg, 1997)! Clearly, therapists' power, by virtue of their role, can be seen as helpful or harmful. There is tremendous responsibility that goes along with the power in the role of the therapist.

Boundaries, Conflict of Interest, Exploitation

One could argue that professional codes of ethics are really about appropriate management of power afforded to therapists via their professional role. Some of the specific provisions in the codes appeared because of misuse of power. For example, the mandate not to have sex with clients came from abuse of the power in which therapists violated a client's world of intimacy, safety, trust, and physical being. Similar scenarios include supervisors having sexual intimacy with supervisees when a training relationship has been established. We may strongly agree as a field that sexual intimacy with clients and students is never acceptable because in these cases the client or student is both in a vulnerable, one-down power position. Part of the responsibility of the therapist is to protect the best interests of the client, regardless of the therapist's sexual desires. Therapists are responsible for setting the limits and boundaries on their relationships, especially when those relationships can benefit the therapist, to the detriment of the client, student, or supervisee, who may not feel as if they can say "no" to a request by the therapist.

Multiple Relationships

First, therapists must be mindful of multiple relationships and the impact this may have on the therapeutic relationship, as well as client outcomes. Couple and family therapists are trained to think systemically about impacts of actions on others in multiple ways; most clients are not likely to think in this manner so part of a therapist's role is to foresee potential negative implications of therapist (and client) actions. One common example is when clients want to be friends with the therapist after therapy has ended. Different professions' codes of ethics may or may not address friendship after termination as a possibility, but it is the therapist's responsibility, via their role and expertise on relationships, to foresee how a friendship may impact the (former) client. As much as a friendship may be desired by both parties, the therapist knows that it is not advisable to form a friendship after therapy ends, for that friendship effectively terminates any future therapeutic relationship that the (former) client may desire. Even if the therapist and client were to discuss this as a possibility, and the client dismisses a future therapeutic relationship as a possibility, the therapist is then in a position to decide if they want to exert their power in deciding not to develop a friendship with the client. This may be a unilateral decision, yet may also be in the client's best interest, even if the client does not agree at the time. Context can also affect navigating this dynamic, as those living in small rural areas will inevitably encounter clients in the community.

Client Autonomy in Decision-making

Clients have the right to decide what is best for them, and to make decisions for themselves, ideally with the therapist's support in evaluating the pros and cons of their decisions. Some codes of ethics explicitly articulate that therapists make it clear that clients are responsible for making major life decisions, such as whether to marry or divorce. Therapist cannot overestimate the power they have in telling clients, for example, that they should divorce (or stay together). The therapist's expertise inherent in that role sets the stage for clients making decisions based on therapists' recommendations. Even an exploration of divorce at the therapist's suggestion, as in "Have you considered divorce as a possible solution?" may be interpreted by the client as suggesting divorce. Therapists can listen carefully to clients' understandings of what is said in session, and make corrections if it is apparent that the client misunderstood the therapist's words.

Therapeutic Relationship Benefits Clients

The various mental health codes of ethics have some language asserting that therapists continue therapeutic relationships only as long as the client is benefitting from the relationship. On the surface, this seems to make sense, yet it can be difficult to ascertain when therapy is no longer benefitting clients. Clients may initially make great progress; yet, if they do not, therapists can continue to work with clients trying different approaches, techniques, and interventions with the hope that clients will change or improve. A common situation is one in which a client comes in to therapy to "vent"; the client may experience relief from this venting, and the therapist can continue to collect fees from clients, leading to a mutually beneficial arrangement. However, "venting" may be difficult to justify clinically; the therapist is the one responsible for assessing the progress of therapy and determining whether therapy should continue. Might it be a therapeutic issue instead that the client has no one else to confide in? Considering the larger picture of therapeutic progress is an ethical use of power by the therapist.

Conflict of Interest and Exploitation

Using relational ethics as a guide (Shaw, 2011), therapists can be mindful of what may benefit them in relation to clients, and take steps to prevent even the "misperception" of actions that benefit the therapist to the detriment of the client, such as conflicts of interest or exploitation of clients and others. Conflicts of interest can be particularly difficult for the couple and family therapist to realize, as there may be a benefit for clients in addition to a benefit for the therapist. For example, let's imagine a therapist hears that a client's car has broken down, and further, the therapist knows that the client's car has had repeated mechanical problems. The therapist subsequently refers the client to the auto-repair shop, which is owned by the therapist's spouse. The intention here by the therapist may be noble and may indeed help the client get their car fixed; however the therapist stands to benefit financially, albeit indirectly, from the client's business at the auto shop. Furthermore, if the car is not repaired to the client's satisfaction, or if the client feels as if they were overcharged, then this could have a negative effect on the therapeutic relationship.

Supervision Boundaries

In terms of supervision, supervisors can keep in mind their influence over supervisees; indeed, the relationship between supervisor and supervisee could possibly be at higher risk for blurred boundaries than is the case for therapist–client relationships. Supervisees may be on more friendly terms with their supervisors; it is not uncommon for supervisors and supervisees to attend the same professional events, professional get-togethers, or go for lunch together. Depending on the supervisor's theoretical orientation, the supervisor may know some personal information about the supervisee that is helpful in furthering the supervisee's clinical skills, yet the boundary between supervision and therapy may blur, to the point where it is uncomfortable for the supervisee. Ultimately, the supervisor is responsible for evaluating the supervisee's clinical work so the supervisor is challenged to be sure that they can be as objective as possible in their evaluations, above and beyond the personal relationships that can occur between supervisor and supervisee.

Authorship

One other area in which the therapist's role may impact students is regarding authorship. Therapists in academia are frequently under pressure to publish, as publication is tied to salary increases, tenure, and/or promotion. This situation can set up a scenario of a conflict of interest, or exploiting a student so that a faculty member either accepts authorship credit when it may not be warranted, or places one's name in authorship order that is not reflective of the faculty member's work on the project. Faculty may exploit students' naiveté about how authorship order is determined, or they may count on a students' unwillingness to challenge authority. Any of these possibilities is an abuse of power of the role of faculty.

Power Between Clients

When working with two or more clients, therapists need to be aware of power differences between clients. Therapists can be mindful of power that exists between partners or spouses, between siblings, between a child and a parent, etc. Power differentials between clients can occur on many levels including income; decision-making around finances, household chores, parenting, and spending time with family and friends. A more direct indicator of power differences between clients is how they handle conflict, including yelling, withdrawing, hitting, threatening, and using other indicators of violence. Unfortunately, despite the high incidence of abuse in intimate relationships, many therapists still do not conduct a routine assessment of violence when working with couples (Schacht, Dimidjian, George, & Berns, 2009). Given the high possibility of violence, it is easy to see that therapists have an ethical responsibility to consider power in relationships, assess for power use in relationships (including domestic violence), as well as to intervene regarding power issues.

Privilege

Privilege can be defined as a set of invisible benefits experienced by members of dominant social groups; privilege is created through and supported by larger systems which benefit members of one group to the detriment of members of other groups (McIntosh, 2008). Certain dominant groups can be said to inherit privilege; privilege is not something that persons actively pursues. Indeed, part of having privilege is having to work very hard to see the privilege that one has. Privilege is built on unseen structural advantages; therefore, it does not feel any "different" to be privileged than not to be privileged. The other side of privilege—oppression—involves members of non-privileged "out" groups experiencing roadblocks or barriers that are supported by larger systems. When a person experiences oppression, they *feel* it because by being silenced, degraded, or limited in opportunity. As a result, it is *much easier* to identify oppressive experiences versus privileges held. Therapists—who have power by virtue of their role as therapists—have an ethical responsibility to examine the privilege that they have in relation to their identity, which occurs in addition to the power that comes with the therapist role.

Peggy McIntosh (2008) has been extremely influential in developing the concept of privilege, particularly White privilege. In her seminal work, she provided a list of benefits she receives on a daily basis because of White privilege—benefits that she is unaware of unless she stops to think about them—based on the color of her skin. An example of White privilege is not having to think that my race, as a White person, has anything to do with me being stopped by the police. Since then, other lists of privileges have been developed, for example, in relation to gender, with men receiving benefits in relation to women. Male privilege is manifested in many ways, including being paid more for the same job, being interrupted less frequently, and being taken more seriously than women. One danger in separating out these parts of our identity is that it can set up a competition of sorts—questions can be raised such as: who is most oppressed, White women or Black men? Given the complexity of privilege and oppression experienced by any one individual, the concept of intersectionality can be a helpful way of understanding parts of identity for both the client and the therapist that impact the therapeutic relationship (Case, Iuzzini, & Hopkins, 2012).

Identity and Intersectionality

Intersectionality refers to "privileged and oppressed social identities that interact simultaneously within each individual" (Wise & Case, 2013, p. 23). One way of understanding identity as it relates to privilege is to examine one's own social location in a number of categories: race, gender, employment, class, sexual orientation, religion, ability, appearance, etc. (Totsuka, 2014). Privilege is associated with the dominant aspects of each of these categories: White, male, employed, middle/upper class, heterosexual, Christian, able-bodied, attractive, etc. When examining ourselves, we are likely to experience a combination of privileged and non-privileged identities. Moreover, our experience of these identities is likely to be brought to the foreground in certain day-to-day interactions whereas some fade to the background. This is particularly relevant for therapists as they develop relationships with clients. Each relationship (and set of relationships) is unique. Each relationship brings forward parts of the therapist's identity that interacts with the client's identity in unique ways. It is an ethical imperative that therapists understand the interplay of identities that play out *in addition to* the power therapists have by virtue of their role. If we were to consider the complexity of intersectionality and various other ways therapists have power, we can see how traditional ethical decision-making models fall short because they cannot account for all of the relational possibilities we may encounter based on power and privilege.

Microaggressions are those seemingly small transgressions that occur in day-to-day interaction that are demeaning and insulting and are directed toward members of marginalized groups; these have been shown to have a deleterious effect on the therapeutic relationship (Constantine, 2007). As can be imagined, therapists' microaggressions can have negative effects on clients and on the therapeutic relationship; they indicate to clients that therapists are not culturally attuned to them as people. Originally, the term was used to refer to mini aggressions made by White people toward people of color, particularly African Americans. Over time, the definition of the term has expanded to include insults and derogatory comments toward any member of an oppressed group. In terms of ethics, therapists need to be vigilant about avoiding microaggressions in all aspects of life, but particularly when providing therapy.

As has been discussed, power is present in all relationships. Furthermore, we carry privilege with us in relationships, although how this privilege plays out can be different depending on the relationship. When a therapist is working with clients, they can assume that the client has had their own experiences of privilege and oppression that they bring to the therapeutic relationship. The picture gets further complicated when there is more than one client in the room—that is, when therapists are working with couples and families. Not only can we assume that power is present in all relationships, but we can assume that power dynamics are impacting clients' presenting problems (Parker, 2009). As mentioned in Chapter 13, from a social constructionist perspective, therapists need to consider the larger sociocultural context in which clients (and the therapist, as well as the treatment system) are embedded. Below, we describe some examples in which ethical issues arise when considering gender, class, race, sexual orientation, and ability.

Gender

Feminist therapists consider gender to be an organizing principle in understanding client concerns (Dickerson, 2013). Several theorists suggest that power be considered a central concept in addressing couple concerns (Esmiol, Knudson-Martin, & Delgado, 2012). Therapists, however, may be reluctant to address gendered power in relationships because of a concern of imposing values on clients. However, therapists guide clients in a direction no matter which intervention they are using; for some reason, power disparities associated with gender seems to be a topic that makes some therapists uncomfortable (Parker, 2009). If therapists do not address gender dynamics because of their own discomfort with the topic, then power dynamics in relationships will remain unexamined, thereby upholding the status quo.

Incidentally, it is often assumed that only men hold patriarchal views about women and relationships; however, research suggests otherwise. In a study of interruptions of men and women clients, therapists (of either gender) were found to interrupt women clients three times more than men clients (Werner-Wilson, Price, Zimmerman, & Murphy, 1997). Indeed, gender impacts the process of therapy, the conceptualization of therapy, and the outcome of therapy. Ethically, therapists do not have the option of ignoring gender; gender is so embedded within cultures across the world that it can be difficult to see and talk about. Therapists, by virtue of their role, have the ability to decide the direction of therapy—they can decide to be collaborative or not; they can decide to explore certain topics to the exclusion of other topics. They can interrupt women clients more frequently than men clients. It is incumbent upon the therapist to attend to gender issues in therapy.

Class

There have been calls for therapists to address class issues in therapy (Kim & Cardemil, 2012; Liu, 2011). Class, or socioeconomic status, is a complex issue that again shifts depending on context. Our values can be greatly impacted by class, although class can be one of the most difficult characteristics to identify in self and others. Socioeconomic class can be associated with a combination of the following: income, education, job classification, access to wealth and resources, and upward mobility. One common value related to class that emerges in therapy is education. For example, many parents bring minor children to therapy out of a concern for truancy or poor grades, and the fear this creates in terms of prospects for the child's future, including college. Therapists may be likely to value education, since earning a master's degree is a requirement of licensure. Therapists who question or do not support parents' concerns about a child's truancy may have difficulty explaining this position to the parents or colleagues. Valuing education is very much a middle-class or upper-class value, a value that is not embraced by all. Similarly, there may be concern for safety of children when parents do not provide fresh fruits and vegetables to children. Again, access to fresh fruits and vegetables is a middle-class value, not to mention the reality that many lower-class families do not have access to nor can afford to provide fresh fruits and vegetables to their children. Therapists and protective services workers who adhere to this expectation are practicing from a middle-class value system.

Race

At the writing of this chapter, racial tensions in the United States are running high. Therapists bring their experiences of race to the table when working with clients; therapists need to be aware of clients' possible experiences with race, which may be different from their own experiences. Even if therapist and client are of the same race, there may be other issues related to race or ethnicity that may be at play, and may subtly impact the therapist–client relationship.

Non-White therapists may have experiences of being oppressed because of their racial/ethnic group. When working with majority clients, therapists of color may need to take extra steps to demonstrate the validity of the therapist role. Moreover, majority White clients may have assumptions or beliefs about their therapists that may impact the therapeutic relationship. Therapists in this situation may face ethical dilemmas in, for example, responding to a client's racial comments directed to the therapist. The therapist must quickly decide how to handle such comments, including how this impacts the therapeutic relationship.

Because White therapists have privilege, they must work to be aware of their privilege and the impact this has in the therapeutic relationship. Therapists have an ethical responsibility to educate themselves about their clients' racial history, while holding this knowledge tentatively, as this knowledge may or may not apply to individual clients. Katz and Hoyt (2014) found that automatic or implicit bias against Blacks had a negative impact on the therapeutic bond, as reported by therapists. Even if race is not directly or indirectly related to the presenting problem, clients of color may have questions about the White therapist's ability to understand their lives and culture. That is, clients may fear that their therapist will be racist (Awosan, Sandberg, & Hall, 2011). Racial questions may subtly impact the therapeutic relationship.

Minority therapists working with minority clients must also be aware of their own privileged positions. Factors such as skin color, immigration history, and class may impact the therapeutic relationship. Experiences of oppression between oppressed racial groups may be similar in some ways, yet also significantly differ so as to create misunderstandings. Yet, there is also the possibility that having some understanding of culture and similar oppressive experiences is helpful to clients.

Majority therapists working with majority clients may also face ethical dilemmas in responding to client comments. There can be an assumption—by both the therapist and the client—that because there is a shared dominant racial background, both will share sociopolitical views. Assumptions that all White people share the same belief glosses over other differences, such as ethnic background, class, gender, etc.

Sexual Orientation

Sexual orientation can be a divisive topic for therapists. According to a recent study by McGeorge, Carlson, and Toomey (2015), 20% of a sample of American Association for Marriage and Family Therapy (AAMFT) members thought that conversion therapy was ethical, despite research and ethical codes to the contrary. Here, assuming therapists are heterosexual, power and privilege combine to affect a negative impact on clients seeking conversion therapy. Therapists have an ethical responsibility to share research with clients, as well as to follow ethical codes to not harm clients—even if a client requests conversion therapy. Aside from conversion therapy, therapists can keep up-to-date on how to provide lesbian, gay, bisexual, and transgender (LGBT)-affirmative therapy; one crucial step is acknowledging heterosexual privilege (McGeorge & Carlson, 2011). Even with legalization of gay marriage at the federal level in the United States, members of the LGBT community will undoubtedly still face discrimination that impacts their lives and relationships.

Religion

Although the number of people identifying with a particular religion is declining, a vast majority of people (therapists and clients included) identify with a religion. Much has been written about how therapists tend not to bring up or address religion with clients. Yet, it still behooves therapists to acknowledge their own religious identity, and to grapple with the privilege tied to that identity if it is Christian. Although there are sometimes stark differences in beliefs depending on denomination, identifying as Christian in United States culture is still privileged. Therapists who are Christian can unwittingly bring beliefs and expectations around their identity into the therapy room, even if religion is not being directly addressed. Clients who are non-Christian, who identify as Wiccan, Jewish, Muslim, Buddhist, or atheist may have to justify their beliefs or traditions if they are different from the therapist's beliefs. Values such as the sanctity of marriage, when life begins, and what happens after death are commonly tied to religious beliefs. Even if therapists do not currently identify as religious, beliefs tied to religion are often embedded in understandings of what is healthy for individuals and relationships.

Ability

Ability refers to a number of areas, including physical ability, mental ability, mobility, ability to read, etc. To navigate the world with full abilities is to not have to worry about how to navigate steps into the therapist's building, whether there will be available materials printed large enough to read and/or available in Braille, or whether corridors are wide enough for a wheelchair to easily pass through, etc. Therapists are privileged when it comes to ability if they do not have to think about any of these things (and much more) on a daily basis, yet they must be prepared to work with clients impacted by difficulty with abilities. As well, this is part of being culturally competent, to be able to work with clients who are impacted by ability status, either as part of a presenting problem or not.

A Return to Intersectionality

It is difficult to capture the complexity of intersectionality within the boundaries of this chapter. The risk in discussing each identity characteristic independently is that the intersections with other characteristics are overlooked. It may be helpful to return to the scenario at the beginning of the chapter to explore further some intersectionality possibilities as it relates to power and privilege.

Suppose that Sam, the therapist in the case scenario, is a White, female, upper-class, heterosexual therapist. Chris is White, male, heterosexual, and lower class and Jessie is Latina, female, bisexual, and lower class. What issues of power and privilege may be at play? Sam has power by virtue of the therapist role; it could be said that by working within the DHS system, she has more power because this couple is mandated to attend therapy. Sam's report to the court about Chris and Jessie's progress in therapy may be very influential in deciding when and if Kendall is returned to the home. Therefore, Sam's understanding of the presenting problem, along with her understanding of Chris and Jessie and the dynamics of their relationship becomes critical. How might privilege play a role between Sam and her clients? Sam is White, as is Chris; although they are both privileged by their race, Jessie is Latina, and her experiences as a Latina depends on many factors, including the geographical area they are located in, her or her family's immigration experience, her family's knowledge and understand of her bisexuality, and her role as mother to Kendall. The decision for Jessie to stay home to care for Kendall could be influenced by job opportunities, affordability of child care, religious beliefs, etc. Chris may have privilege in being male in not understanding how the house could be such a mess when Jessie has been home all day. Further, Sam is upper class, which is a privileged position that may make it difficult for her to understand her clients' lives; she may be likely to connect the events that led up to Kendall's removal from the home exclusively to personal decisions as opposed to considering larger sociopolitical factors that shape her clients' lives—in this case, power and privilege may have life-changing impacts on families, including the decision to remove a child from a home. These are only some possibilities for therapists to consider regarding their own identities, as well as their clients' identities as related to power and privilege—which of course are related to the concerns that brings them into therapy.

What Can Therapists Do?

It is clear by now that therapists have an ethical responsibility to address power and privilege in therapy. What are next steps in addressing these issues? We suggest that embracing a new view of ethics, taking action, and continually learning are steps therapists can take in ensuring that power and privilege are integrated throughout the therapeutic endeavor.

Ethics of Care and Relational Ethics

Given that there are power dynamics at play in all relationships, and given that there are multiple levels of interconnections—between individuals, couples, families, and the larger socio-cultural-political landscape, the question is: where do we go from here? One possibility can be found in the ethics of care. According to Held (2006), ethics of care involves:

- The compelling moral salience of attending to and meeting the needs of particular others for whom we take responsibility,
- The valuing of emotion in understanding and deciding what actions to take, and
- Respecting the claims of particular others with whom we share actual relationships (pp. 10–11).

This view suggests that instead of valuing objectivity, independence, and autonomy, we consider ourselves as being in relationship, valuing emotions, and considering the perspective of those for whom we are responsible. Not to deny and move away from the power inherent in therapeutic relationships, this approach calls for embracing relationships in a way that demonstrates for understanding of and respect for the perspective of the other.

An ethics of care perspective values emotions, and in particular, values *empathy* as a way of connecting ourselves with others (Slote, 2007). If we have more empathy with those who we know rather than those we do not know, then there is a responsibility to learn more about those we do not know; this becomes particularly important for therapists who are working with clients who are, in some significant way, different from themselves.

Embracing an ethics of care perspective can be tremendously helpful in fostering empathy and responsibility, particularly in relationships in which we care for others, as with the therapeutic relationship. One shortcoming of an ethics of care approach is that it fails to integrate a consideration of power within the caring relationship. A relational ethics perspective is one possibility that could be incredibly helpful in navigating the complex dynamics in therapeutic relationships, as context, power, relationships, and dialogue are considered central. Indeed, relational ethics involves a way of *being* that allows for complexity in relationships, while also considering the larger community in which we are all embedded. A relational ethics perspective (Bergum & Dossetor, 2005) suggests that we:

- Take responsibility for the way our communications shape others' understandings,
- Build relationships based on curiosity, openness, respect, and an understanding of the meaning making process,
- Participate in meaning making in ways that allow for creating inclusive positions,
- Understand how our positioning contributes to the creation of social reality, and
- Transparently share our positions of power and their impact on moral decisions that are made, ideally collaboratively.

Taking Action

Therapists can actively address issues of power and privilege in the therapy room. Therapists have this responsibility because of their role as therapist and the associated power that goes along with it (Awosan et al., 2011). Not only must therapists introduce power and privilege as topics in session, they must actively intervene in social processes (Knudson-Martin et al., 2015). Therapists may need extensive training to be able to discuss these topics, as they are sensitive, and may be seen as irrelevant by clients. It can be difficult to know how to intervene. Keeling and Piercy (2007) explored therapists' attention to gender and culture in clinical scenarios. Participants reported seeking balance in addressing these issues; their decisions to raise these topics depended on ethical factors such as client safety, clients being perceived as judgmental, and clients' mental states. Regardless, some assert that therapists have an ethical imperative to address power and culture in therapy (Esmiol et al., 2012). Having a transparent conversation about privileged and oppressed identities can be one way for therapists to incorporate discussions of power into their therapeutic work (Hernandez & McDowell, 2010).

At a minimum, therapists need to be culturally attuned in order to work ethically with clients (Brown & Pomerantz, 2011). It can be argued that to ignore clients' culture is to practice unethically. Cultural competence can be a component of overall clinical effectiveness (Imel et al., 2011). One proposed solution is to match clients on certain characteristics, such as race or gender. Although there are conflicting results on this issue, a recent study found no overall support for matching therapists and clients on gender and race (Johnson & Caldwell, 2011).

Continually Learn

There will never be a time when therapists are finished with their quest to be culturally competent. This stance indicates that therapists must continually and actively be learning about power, privilege, and culture. Stepping outside one's comfort zone on a regular basis is a way to challenge oneself. This may be entering an unfamiliar setting to learn about customs and mores of another culture; engaging in conversation about controversial topics with persons different from oneself—with a goal of understanding the other rather than reifying one's own position; taking a class to learn about recent research as related to power dynamics; consulting with colleagues about ethical dilemmas faced around power and privilege; and reading professional literature. Not only must the therapist learn about others, the therapist must challenge self to acknowledge one's privilege and examine one's own participation in maintaining oppression (Hernandez-Wolfe & McDowell, 2012). Issues of power and privilege are too important in our and our clients' lives to think that we are immune to the larger social context in which we are embedded.

Conclusion

We have argued that therapists have an ethical mandate to attend to power and privilege in their clinical work. Given the complexity of these topics, there are numerous ways that power can play in the therapeutic realm. Self-awareness of one's own identities related to privilege and oppression is important, as is directly addressing these issues in therapy. Relational ethics offers an ongoing perspective and way of being that challenges therapists to reflect on the influence they have in relation to others—both inside and outside the therapy room.

References

Awosan, C. I., Sandberg, J. G., & Hall, C. A. (2011). Understanding the experience of black clients in marriage and family therapy. *Journal of Marital and Family Therapy, 37*(2), 153–168. doi: 10.1111/j.1752-0606.2009.00166.x.

Bergum, V., & Dossetor, J. (2005). *Relational ethics: The full meaning of respect.* Hagerstown, MD: University Publishing Group.

Berns, S. B., Jacobson, N. S., & Gottman, J. M. (1999). Demand-withdraw interaction in couples with a violent husband. *Journal of Consulting and Clinical Psychology, 67*(5), 666–674. doi: 10.1037/0022-006X.67.5.666.

Blau, P. M. (1964). *Exchange and power in social life.* New York, NY: Wiley.

Brown, D. L., & Pomerantz, A. M. (2011). Multicultural incompetence and other unethical behaviors: Perceptions of therapist practices. *Ethics & Behavior, 21*(6), 498–508. doi: 10.1080/10508422.2011.622182.

Case, K. A., Iuzzini, J., & Hopkins, M. (2012). Systems of privilege: Intersection, awareness, and applications. *Journal of Social Issues, 68*(1), 1–10. doi: 10.11 11/j.1540-4560.2011.01732.x.

Cederborg, A. D. (1997). Young children's participation in family therapy talk. *American Journal of Family Therapy, 25*(1), 28–38. doi: 10.1080/01926189 708251052.

Constantine, M. G. (2007). Racial microaggressions against African American clients in cross-racial counseling relationships. *Journal of Counseling Psychology, 54*(1), 1–16. doi: 10.1037/0022-0167.54.1.1.

Cromwell, R. E., & Olson, D. H. (1975). Multidisciplinary perspectives of power. In R. E. Cromwell & D. H. Olson (Eds.), *Power in families* (pp. 15–37). New York, NY: Sage.

Dickerson, V. (2013). Patriarchy, power, and privilege: A narrative/poststructural view of work with couples. *Family Process, 52*(1), 102–114. doi: 10.1111/ famp.12018.

Esmiol, E. E., Knudson-Martin, C., & Delgado, S. (2012). Developing a contextual consciousness: Learning to address gender, societal power, and culture in a clinical practice. *Journal of Marital and Family Therapy, 38*(4), 573–588. doi: 10.1111/j.1752-0606.2011.00232.x.

Foucault, M. (1977). *Power/knowledge: Selected interviews and other writings: 1972–1977.* New York, NY: Pantheon.

French, J. P., Jr., & Raven, B. (1959). The bases of social power. In D. Cartwright (Ed.), *Studies in social power* (pp. 150–167). Ann Arbor, MI: The University of Michigan.

Gottman, J. M., Coan, J., Carrere, S., & Swanson, C. (1998). Predicting marital happiness and stability from newlywed interactions. *Journal of Marriage and Family, 60*(1), 5–22. doi: 10.2307/353438.

Haddock, S. A., Zimmerman, T. S., & MacPhee, D. (2000). The power equity guide: Attending to gender in family therapy. *Journal of Marital and Family Therapy, 26*(2), 153–170. doi: 10.1111/j.1752-0606.2000.tb00286.x.

Haley, J. (1976). *Problem-solving therapy.* San Francisco, CA: Jossey-Bass.

Hare-Mustin, R. T. (1978). A feminist approach to family therapy. *Family Process, 17*(2), 181–194. doi: 10.1111/j.1545-5300.1978.00181.x.

Hare-Mustin, R. T. (1991). Sex, lies, and headaches: The problem is power. In T. J. Goodrich (Ed.), *Women and power: Perspectives for family therapy* (pp. 63–85). New York, NY: Norton.

Held, V. (2006). *The ethics of care: Personal, political, and global.* New York, NY: Oxford University Press.

Hernandez, P., & McDowell, T. (2010). Intersectionality, power, and relational safety in context: Key concepts in clinical supervision. *Training and Education in Professional Psychology, 4*(1), 29–35. doi: 10.1037/a0017064.

Hernandez-Wolfe, P., & McDowell, T. (2012). Speaking of privilege: Family therapy educators' journeys toward awareness and compassionate action. *Family Process, 51*(2), 163–178. doi: 10.1111/j.1545-5300.2012.01394.x.

Imel, Z., Baldwin, S., Atkins, D. C., Owen, J., Baardseth, T., & Wampold, B. E. (2011). Racial/ethnic disparities in therapist effectiveness: A conceptualization and initial study of cultural competence. *Journal of Counseling Psychology, 58*(3), 290–298. doi: 10.1037/a0023284.

Johnson, L. A., & Caldwell, B. E. (2011). Race, gender, and therapist confidence: Effects on satisfaction with the therapeutic relationship in MFT. *The American Journal of Family Therapy, 39*(4), 307–324. doi: 10.1080/01926187.2010.532012.

Kaschak, E. (1990). How to be a failure as a family therapist: A feminist perspective. In H. Lerman & N. Porter (Eds.), *Feminist ethics in psychotherapy* (pp. 70–81). New York, NY: Springer.

Katz, A. D., & Hoyt, W. T. (2014). The influence of multicultural counseling competence and anti-black prejudice on therapists' outcome expectancies. *Journal of Counseling Psychology, 61*(2), 299–305. doi: 10.1037/a0036134.

Keeling, M. H., & Piercy, F. P. (2007). A careful balance: Multinational perspectives on culture, gender, and power in marriage and family therapy practice. *Journal of Marital and Family Therapy, 33*(4), 443–463. doi: 10.1111/j.1752-0606.2007.00044.x.

Kim, S., & Cardemil, E. (2012). Effective psychotherapy with low-income clients: The importance of attending to social class. *Journal of Contemporary Psychotherapy, 42*(1), 27–35. doi: 10.1007/s10879-011-9194-0.

Knudson-Martin, C. (2009). Addressing gendered power: A guide for clinical practice. In C. Knudson-Martin & A. R. Mahoney (Eds.), *Couples, gender, and power: Creating change in intimate relationships* (pp. 317–336). New York, NY: Springer.

Knudson-Martin, C., Huenergardt, D., Lafontant, K., Bishop, L., Schaepper, J., & Wells, M. (2015). Competencies for addressing gender and power in couple therapy: A socio emotional approach. *Journal of Marital and Family Therapy, 41*(2), 205–220. doi: 10.1111/jmft.12068.

Knudson-Martin, C., & Mahoney, A. R. (2009). *Couples, gender, and power: Creating change in intimate relationships.* New York, NY: Springer.

Liu, W. M. (2011). *Social class and classism in the helping professions: Research, theory, and practice.* Thousand Oaks, CA: Sage.

McGeorge, C., & Carlson, T. S. (2011). Deconstructing heterosexism: Becoming an LGB affirmative heterosexual couple and family therapist. *Journal of Marital and Family Therapy, 37*(1), 14–26. doi: 10.1111/j.1752-0606.2009.00149.x.

McGeorge, C. R., Carlson, T. S., & Toomey, R. B. (2015). An exploration of family therapists' beliefs about the ethics of conversion therapy: The influence of negative beliefs and clinical competence with lesbian, gay, and bisexual clients. *Journal of Marital and Family Therapy, 41*(1), 42–56. doi: 10.1111/jmft.12040.

McIntosh, P. (2008). White privilege and male privilege: A personal account of coming to see correspondences through work in women's studies. In M. McGoldrick & K. V. Hardy (Eds.), *Re-visioning family therapy: Race, culture, and gender in clinical practice* (2nd ed., pp. 238–260). New York, NY: Guilford.

Minuchin, S., Montalvo, B., Guerney, B. G., Jr., Rosman, B. L., & Schumer, F. (1967). *Families of the slums: An exploration of their structure and treatment.* New York, NY: Basic Books.

Parker, L. (2009). Disrupting power and privilege in couples therapy. *Clinical Social Work Journal, 37*(3), 248–255. doi: 10.1007/s10615-009-0211-7.

Schacht, R. L., Dimidjian, S., George, W. H., & Berns, S. B. (2009). Domestic violence assessment procedures among couple therapists. *Journal of Marital and Family Therapy, 35*(1), 47–59. doi: 10.1111/j.1752-0606.2008.00095.x.

Shaw, E. (2011). Relational ethics and moral imagination in contemporary systemic practice. *Australian and New Zealand Journal of Family Therapy, 32*(1), 1–14. doi: 10.1375/anft.32.1.1.

Slote, M. (2007). *The ethics of care and empathy.* New York, NY: Routledge.

Totsuka, Y. (2014). 'Which aspects of social GGRRAAACCEEESSS grab you most?' The social GGRRAAACCEEESSS exercise for a supervision group to promote therapists' self-reflexivity. *Journal of Family Therapy, 36*(Suppl. 1), 86–106. doi: 10.1111/1467-6427.12026.

Walsh, F., & Scheinkman, M. (1989). (Fe)male: The hidden gender dimension in models of family therapy. In M. McGoldrick, C. M. Anderson, & F. Walsh (Eds.), *Women in families: A framework for family therapy* (pp. 16–41). New York, NY: Norton.

Werner-Wilson, R. J., Price, S. J., Zimmerman, T. S., & Murphy, M. J. (1997). Client gender as a process variable in marriage and family therapy: Are women clients interrupted more than men clients? *Journal of Family Psychology, 11*(3), 373–377. doi: 10.1037/0893-3200.11.3.373.

White, M., & Epston, D. (1990). *Narrative means to therapeutic ends.* New York, NY: Norton.

Wise, T., & Case, K. A. (2013). Pedagogy for the privileged: Addressing inequality and injustice without shame or blame. In K. A. Case (Ed.), *Deconstructing privilege: Teaching and learning as allies in the classroom* (pp. 17–33). New York, NY: Routledge.

7

Sexuality, Boundaries, and Ethics

Teresa L. Young and René A. Jones

> Iris is a couple and family therapist who is seeing a 30-year-old client named Samuel. The first time she saw Samuel, Iris instantly noticed that he was an extremely handsome man, to whom she instantly found herself attracted. Iris tried to ignore her feelings and proceeded as usual. Weeks passed and Iris could not shake her feelings of attraction. When talking to Samuel, she felt shy and nervous and worried that he could sense her attraction to him. Every time she laughed at something funny Samuel said, she stopped herself so as to not let him catch on that she was having feelings that crossed a therapeutic boundary. As therapy continued, it became so problematic that Iris felt she had to avert Samuel's eye contact so that she did not have to acknowledge her growing feelings of sexual attraction. Iris was overwhelmed with questions. Should she be transparent about her feelings and have a conversation with Samuel? Should she refer Samuel to another therapist, or would the referral do more harm than good?

This scenario is not an uncommon experience for many therapists and demonstrates that sexual ethics in psychotherapy is much more complex than the mandate, "Don't have sex with your clients." Couple and family therapists are likely to face a broad range of sexual ethical dilemmas that comes with the territory of the intimate nature of their work. The need for a wider lens regarding sexual ethics is highlighted by findings that a majority of therapists have experienced feelings of sexual attraction toward clients, but never engaged in sexual relations with clients (Blonna, 2014; Nickell, Hecker, Ray, & Bercik, 1995). This chapter addresses the wider lens of sexual ethics by exploring sexual attraction to clients, sexual harassment, sexual intimacy with current and former clients, discussing sex and sexuality in therapy, and warning signs for couple and family therapists.

Sexual Attraction to Clients

It is well-documented that sexual intimacy between therapist and client is both unethical and potentially harmful (Bates & Brodsky, 1989; Edelwich & Brodsky, 1991; Garrett, 2010; Kim & Rutherford, 2015; Pope, 1988; Rutter, 1989). There is some evidence from previous decades that the number of therapists violating this code has decreased from 9.4% for males and 2.5% for females (Pope, Keith-Spiegel, & Tabachnick, 1986) to 3.6% for males and .05% for females (Pope, Sonne, & Holroyd, 1993). Because there have been no recent data, it is unknown if this trend has continued. Sexual misconduct is the most common allegation in malpractice suits (Eddington & Shuman, 2004) and is the most frequently filed ethical complaint (Pope et al., 1986). Despite the reality that violations happen, many therapists believe that sexual intimacy is something that they will not even remotely consider, which inadvertently can be a red flag that this issue is underexplored and therefore, more of a risk to therapy (Barnett, 2013; Keith-Spiegel, 2014).

Ethical Considerations

Sexual intimacy often begins with attraction, as shown in the scenario with Iris. Iris is not alone in her experience (and her confusion) regarding the ethical dilemma of sexual attraction to clients. In a study of 189 clinical members of the American Association for Marriage and Family Therapy (AAMFT), Nickell et al. (1995) found that a majority of family therapists reported experiencing feelings of attraction to clients. In fact, 100% of male respondents and 73% of female respondents indicated rare to occasional feelings of sexual attraction (Nickell et al., 1995). The researchers also found that 62% of male and 36% of female therapists reported engaging in sexual fantasy about clients within the past 2 years. Additionally, 28% of respondents believed that feeling sexual attraction is "definitely unethical" or "ethical under rare circumstances" (Nickell et al., 1995, p. 323). Many therapists avoid addressing sexual attraction and miss the opportunity to consider important clinical issues (Blonna, 2014). Many experience shame, guilt, and anxiety as a result of the attraction (Ladany, Klinger, & Kulp, 2011). These findings were similar across the field of psychotherapy (Pope, Sonne, & Greene, 2006; Pope, Tabachnick, & Keith-Spiegel, 1987).

Because many believe feelings of sexual attraction to be unethical, it is no wonder that Iris feels ill prepared to manage the situation, let alone divulge her feelings to a colleague or supervisor. As Harris (1998) explained, thoughts such as, "this shouldn't be happening," "I could never tell anyone about this," or "my supervisor will think I wanted it to happen" are typical for therapists in this uncomfortable position (p. 7). In a study of 575 psychotherapists, Pope et al. (1986) reported that half the respondents reported no training regarding sexual attraction to clients. Consequently, to the degree that sexual attraction is considered countertransference, it is particularly regrettable when training systems fail to promote the acknowledgment and examination of this phenomenon (Pope et al., 1986).

Feelings of sexual attraction are common in the therapeutic setting because the therapeutic process by its nature creates intimacy (Strean, 1993). The therapist and client meet alone, sit close to one another, and often meet frequently and regularly, during which time the client often shares intimate details. Clients may share hopes, memories, disappointments, and fears while the therapist carefully listens and empathizes (Edelwich & Brodsky, 1991). These are the stories and feelings that one typically only shares with close intimates, if with anyone else at all. It follows, then, that there is a fine line between the intimate nature of the joining process described previously and sexual attraction (Harris, 1998).

Harris (1998) believes that the greatest problem regarding sexual attraction in therapy is that few acknowledge the potential for sexual feelings to develop during the process of "good" therapy. Not many would argue against the notion that "good" therapy involves joining, and yet joining is part of the process that leads to the intimate nature of therapy that may be confused with feelings of sexual attraction, as described previously. Thus, therapists are left with the ultimate conundrum—the very intimate environment for which they strive is the same environment that may lead them to cross the fine line that is the ethical boundary of sexual attraction toward clients.

So what is a professional like Iris to do? One must first accept that as sexual human beings, therapists are not exempt from experiencing feelings of sexual attraction—even if the attraction is toward a client (Keith-Spiegel, 2014; Strean, 1993). In fact, experiencing sexual attraction to a client is not itself unethical, nor is having a sexual fantasy. It is making the *choice* to act on the attraction or fantasy or to deny the attraction or fantasy to a point at which it impedes therapy that is unethical. Additional advice includes the following.

Acknowledge Your Feelings and Be Self-aware

Thus, in the case of the clinical vignette, Iris must first recognize that her sexual attraction to Samuel does not make her a "bad" or "unethical" therapist; it makes her human (Harris, 1998). It may be helpful for her to consider that if she were to have met Samuel in another context, she would have likely experienced a similar sexual response. Barnett (2013) adds that when therapists know their personal needs and vulnerabilities, they are more aware and more likely to address these challenges in a healthy way. Many therapists minimize or avoid addressing their attraction (Keith-Spiegel, 2014), thus possibly missing the opportunity to consider important clinical issues, which may lead to acting on the attraction. In addition, this avoidance may create a discomfort or anxiety for the therapist that the client may perceive, thus creating confusion or discomfort for the client, which may hinder the therapy (Barnett, 2013).

Know Your Values

Everyone has sexual values. The values may come from a religious or spiritual background, and include edicts such as "no sex before marriage," "sex must be consensual," or "sexual attraction is normal, even if to clients." For therapists to practice in alignment with their values, the values and beliefs need to be known. Couple and family therapists can reflect on how sexual thoughts, emotions, and actions either support or oppose the therapist's values and beliefs (Blonna, 2014).

Do Not Give Your Problems to the Client

The general professional consensus is that it is inappropriate to tell clients of sexual attraction because this can run the risk of harming clients (Fisher, 2004). Edelwich and Brodsky (1991) discussed how some therapists object to this sentiment, arguing that withholding such information leads them to act unnaturally with clients. This may explain the Nickell et al. (1995) finding that 10% of males and 4% of females discussed sexual attraction issues with clients. Edelwich and Brodsky (1991) maintained that it is the therapist's job to act responsibly. In their view, acting responsibly means refraining from discussing sexual attraction issues with clients. Therapists must actively exhibit appropriateness with the client in their overt behaviors while seeking help elsewhere to deal with feelings that may be unintentionally communicated in session. Fisher (2004) also noted there is the potential danger that revealing sexual attraction may put the therapist at increased risk for engaging in activities in therapy that could be defined as sexual harassment, especially for male therapists.

Thus, in the clinical vignette, Iris should not "give" her problem to Samuel by confiding in him about her sexual attraction. To do so would be to burden Samuel with the pressure to respond to a situation that he did not ask for when entering the therapeutic relationship. It may also jeopardize

Samuel's trust in a professional's capability to maintain appropriate boundaries. If Iris feels that she cannot control her behavior that "gives away" her attraction to Samuel, it is her ethical responsibility to follow the next guideline.

Confide in Your Supervisor, Peers, and Professional Consultant, and Use Personal Therapy

Harris (1998) asserted, "When we don't discuss attraction we implicitly underscore, and maybe even reinforce, the idea that experiencing sexual feelings in therapy is unethical" (p. 7). Discussing feelings of sexual attraction with a supervisor or colleague, although initially daunting, often has the effect of normalizing the situation (Harris, 1998) and reconciling the feelings (Pope et al., 2006). Upon speaking with a supervisor or colleague, Iris will likely notice that she is not as nervous about Samuel "catching on" to her attraction, as her feelings are already "out on the table" with someone else. This should calm her worries and refocus her energies on the therapeutic process. Keep in mind that it is common to experience feelings of guilt, anxiety, and confusion related to feelings of sexual attraction to clients (Nickell et al., 1995). Personal therapy can also be used simultaneously as self-care and part of risk management (Fisher, 2004).

Do Not "Refer Out"

Should the client suffer on account of the clinician's problem? Edelwich and Brodsky (1991) discussed how referring a client because of feelings of sexual attraction may lead to the consequences of "discontinuity of care, including uncertainty, loss of time, and possible feelings of rejection," and thus they recommend that a therapist not refer a client (p. 136). Only under the rare circumstances when supervisory or peer support is not sufficient in achieving satisfactory results should the clinician refer. They caution, however, that the therapist must be extremely careful not to imply rejection or abandonment and should allot time to discuss what the referral means to the client. Therapists must take complete blame and explain that they are unable to meet the needs of the client. If therapists chose not to address their attractions and begin acting on their attraction, they will then engage in one form of sexual harassment.

Sexual Harassment

According to Brandenburg (1997), perhaps one of the most challenging aspects of sexual harassment is creating a uniform definition. However, in almost all definitions, *unwanted sexual attention* is a consistent element. The attention can appear on a continuum from name calling to jokes, to physical touch, sexual assault, and rape. The theories regarding sexual harassment describe it as a way to obtain sex and/or to abuse or to increase power (Stringer, Remick, Salisbury, & Ginorio, 1990). Thus, sexual harassment is a boundary violation that can occur from therapist to client and vice versa (Plaut, 2008).

Creating a safe environment for therapy is consistently about creating and maintaining healthy boundaries—this is the therapist's responsibility (Plaut, 2008). To maintain boundaries, Plaut (2008) recommends that therapists be aware of their values and reactions to clients. If the therapist begins to feel uncomfortable about a client's sexual statements or actions, it is material for supervision or professional consultation. As illustrated in the following scenarios, the therapist often can use a client's inappropriate boundaries therapeutically, assisting the client with establishing healthy boundaries both within and outside of therapy.

It is also important to note that the therapist may create a sexually harassing environment, and some clients may not be able to verbalize that the therapist's comments or actions are harassing. Therefore, it is important to pay attention to the client's values and body language (Plaut, 2008); for example, therapists can notice how people respond to jokes, touch, or attire of the therapist. Risk for sexual harassment is high because there is a clear power differential, leaving the client with the inability to freely consent.

Responding to Clients' Sexual Advances

> Anton is a mental health counselor who specializes in working with victims of sexual abuse. He is currently seeing a client named Grace who has a long history of sexual abuse both by family members and intimate partners. Anton noticed early on that Grace tended to dress provocatively. She also exhibited body language that made Anton uncomfortable, such as stroking her leg suggestively when she talked. Sometimes Anton wondered if he was reading too far into Grace's behavior. Other times, however, he felt fairly confident that Grace was coming on to him. She often made suggestive comments and told jokes that were sexual in nature. Anton did not know how to react to these comments or these jokes. He worried that he might revictimize Grace by talking with her about his perceptions that she was making covert sexual advances. At the same time, the sexualized interactions with Grace were jeopardizing the therapeutic relationship. Anton felt paralyzed.

Although the spotlight in research, literature, and media coverage tends to shine on the unethical sexual advances of therapists toward clients, one must also acknowledge that the reverse scenario exists—clients do at times covertly or overtly make sexual advances toward their therapists. Thus, it is imperative that therapists gain awareness as to how to ethically respond to such situations.

To be clear, no matter what a client says or does in terms of sexual advances, the burden to act ethically *always* falls on the professional (sans violence or assault by a client to a therapist). In other words, should sexual relations or sexual mistreatment of a client ensue in a scenario that involves a client's sexual advances, the professional must take responsibility and accountability for their actions. Accordingly, the professional needs to ethically respond to sexual advances in a manner that does not place blame or burden on the client. Furthermore, statements made to describe ways in which clients may attempt to make sexual advances should not be misconstrued as "victim blaming." *Nothing a client says or does justifies a professional's decision to cross a sexual boundary.*

Clients' sexual advances may fall along a continuum that includes extremely obvious, overt advances to more covert, subtle actions that a therapist may or may not perceive as sexual advances. Overt advances may include a client verbally stating that they would like to date, kiss, or sleep with the therapist, or a client making physical advances such as sitting on the therapist's lap or attempting to kiss the therapist. Covert advances may include a client's incessant interest in the therapist's personal life, frequent contacts in the form of phone calls and office visits, flattery in the form of compliments, and body language and physical cues that may include sitting in revealing postures, touching one's body, and wearing provocative clothing. Regardless of where sexual harassment by clients falls on the continuum, the guidelines below will help therapists facing these situations.

Set Limits While Giving the Client a Safe Space For Self-expression

"Clients who act seductively are testing limits" (Edelwich & Brodsky, 1991, p. 128) and therefore need the therapist to create a clear boundary. This allows the client to explore concerns within the safety of the boundary. Clearly delineating appropriate boundaries may look differently depending on the situation. In Anton's position, setting a boundary may involve having a discussion about the limitations of his role as a therapist (e.g., demonstrating with tact that he will not cross a physical boundary with Grace or any other client). Leaving a safe space for self-expression may involve choosing not to comment on Grace's provocative clothing or behavior of stroking her leg. Setting the boundary by discussing Anton's personal ethical limitations is more appropriate than setting a limit by asking Grace to change her behavior for two reasons: (1) it demonstrates to the client that therapists will take it upon themselves to maintain safe boundaries and that the burden to create the safe space is not on the client; and (2) it also lessens the chance that the client will feel embarrassed or personally attacked. Furthermore, once a client understands that the environment is safe (in that the therapist will not respond to advances with sexual exploitation), the client's covert seductive behaviors and limit testing are likely to decrease.

Do Not Be Rejecting

It is not unusual to feel bothered or even disgusted by the overt sexual advances of a client. It may even feel like sexual harassment. However, therapists must proceed with caution when reacting to such behavior. Edelwich and Brodsky (1991) warned, "[a] cold, rejecting manner on the part of the clinician may communicate to the client that his or her sexuality is not acceptable, rather than that it is simply being directed at the wrong person" (p. 130). Edelwich and Brodsky (1991) proposed the following statement: "I appreciate your interest in me—it's flattering, but if you have found our conversations helpful to you, I think I can continue to be helpful by staying away from any other role" (p. 130). The authors also suggest simply stating, "That's not what therapy is" (p. 130); note that the response is neither rejecting nor attacking.

Express Nonsexual Caring

Edelwich and Brodsky (1991) advised "it is a mistake to react to the sexual overture [of a client] by withdrawing from the nurturing role," as the client who acts out sexually is often seeking nurturance (p. 130). By setting a boundary and defining one's role as a nonsexual caregiver, the therapist is communicating to the client that acting out sexually to attain warmth and caring is not necessary (Edelwich & Brodsky, 1991). This may be particularly important for a client who has a history of sexual abuse, like Grace in the case scenario. Thus, Anton need not worry that by having a conversation regarding the limits of his role as a therapist that he is somehow revictimizing Grace. Quite the contrary is true—actively setting such a boundary and continuing to care for Grace in a therapeutic, nonsexual manner is the appropriate, ethical manner in which to proceed.

Do Not Be Drawn into Answering Personal Questions or Giving the Client Other "Double Messages"

Therapists are at risk of sending a "double message" to a client when turning down a sexual advance if they act as though they are setting the limit based on an external rule. In other words, by stating, "I cannot have a sexual relationship with you because it is against the rules," the therapist may inadvertently communicate, "if it weren't for the rule, I would engage in sexual relations with you." Passing off the responsibility to an external "obstacle" may be a tempting option, but it defeats the purpose of delineating a clear, ethical boundary. Edelwich and Brodsky (1991) advised that the therapist should "speak from having internalized [the] tradition, rather than appear to be chafing against an external restraint" (p. 131). Therapists must also be careful when answering personal questions because doing so can be like "quicksand" in that clients take the therapist's gesture as a sign that they can probe more and more (Edelwich & Brodsky, 1991). Thus, it is often necessary to be clear that therapeutic conversations are most helpful if they stay focused on the client and their life and concerns.

Confront the Issue Straightforwardly

It may be unnerving to confront the issue of a client's sexual advances straightforwardly, especially in a situation in which the advances are covert. However, it is ethically appropriate to confront the perceived behavior as soon as it becomes a problem. In Edelwich and Brodsky (1991) assert that "one can have a conversation with one's client without pejorative labeling, without imputation of motive, but simply as a perception of [one's] own that [one] is willing to have corrected" (p. 133). Consider the following statement:

> I may be wrong, but I've noticed something in our interactions together that I want to address. Sometimes it feels like you consider our relationship to be more than professional, and I want to assure you that that is a line that I will not cross with you or any other client, because I respect our therapeutic relationship too much.

Do Not "Refer Out"

Consider that what might feel like a "therapeutic impasse" can oftentimes lead to a "therapeutic breakthrough" (Edelwich & Brodsky, 1991, p. 137). Thus, overt or covert sexual advances clients make are not always roadblocks to therapeutic progress, but sometimes are opportunities for deeper therapeutic exploration. Also consider the possibility that a client who is referred because of perceived or overt sexual behavior may suffer from feelings of confusion and rejection. This is especially likely considering that sexual acting out in therapy may indicate a need for nonsexual nurturance on the part of the therapist (Edelwich & Brodsky, 1991). Thus, it is ethically appropriate for a therapist to attempt to delineate boundaries rather than automatically refer the client. Of course, there are always exceptions and instances in which a client is insistent on violating sexual boundaries. In such cases, therapists may need to take action to protect themselves both physically and professionally by referring the client. In a study of marriage and family therapists conducted by Harris and Hays (2008), comfort level in having these sexuality-related discussions increased when the therapist had both sexual education and adequate supervision in the topic.

Do Not Assume the Relationship is a Two-way Relationship

One mistake that therapists may make is to assume the therapeutic relationship is a mutual, two-way relationship. There is a power differential that does not allow this to be true. In addition, transference and countertransference occur on an unconscious or subconscious level, not allowing either the client or the therapist to have a level playing field in terms of a mutual relationship. It is a *therapeutic* relationship. Another mistake therapists may make is to think love can heal previous harm (Gabbard, 1997), thus taking on a role of rescuer while still in a position of power. Therapists need to stay in a professional role so as to not harm the client and to promote the client's well-being.

Sexual Intimacy with Current and Former Clients

Engaging in sexual relationships with present and former clients is prohibited by all major mental health professional associations, as is entering into a sexual relationship with a client's romantic partner or family members. A sexual and/or romantic relationship between therapist and client compromises the therapeutic process as well as the possibility for a future therapeutic relationship, damages the image of the profession as a whole, and causes corruption of the personal relationship by the privileged knowledge and inequality of the therapeutic relationship. The therapeutic relationship between therapist and client is inherently unbalanced in terms of power. Therapists are privileged and powerful in that they have access to the most vulnerable parts of a client's emotional life. This is not a reciprocal process, as the client does not have the same access to the vulnerable parts of the therapist (Edelwich & Brodsky, 1991). The relationship begins with a power imbalance making the transition to a romantic relationship an abuse of that power.

Reports of Unethical Conduct

> Megan's new client, Susan, is a married woman in her mid-30s. Susan is seeking therapy to decide whether she should stay married or divorce. Susan suspects her husband is having an affair. As the therapy progresses, Susan decides to hire a private detective and discovers that her husband is having an affair with his therapist, John. Megan does not know John, but knows of him. He has a good reputation in the community and Megan is shocked by the realization.

Discovering that another professional behaved in a sexually unethical manner is unfortunately a common event. Noel (2008) examined psychologists' attitudes toward reporting colleagues who were sexually intimate with a client. He found that 84% of the sample said that they had at some time been told of a colleague who had been sexually intimate with a client or clients. Of those, fewer than 20% confronted the colleague (either by mail or in person), only 35% encouraged the client to file a report with the ethics committee, and fewer than 10% assisted the client in filing a report. The proportion of psychologists encouraging (9%) or assisting (4%) a client in the use of the legal system was even lower.

Therapists may discover ethical violations of other therapists in a variety of ways. A client may inform the practitioner of a therapist's boundary breach, gossip from other clinicians, or the offending therapist may discuss it him- or herself. The steps that follow are recommended when a colleague is inappropriate.

Seek Supervision or Consultation

As with most ethical situations, it is useful to discuss and consult with another trusted professional. The supervisor/colleague can provide other questions to ask as well as other perspectives and give options on how to approach the situation. In addition, many therapists in Megan's situation may feel resentful, betrayed, humiliated, exploited and deidealized, especially if the violator was a mentor (Nicholsen, 2010). Seeking support from supervision and self-care from therapy can assist the therapist in processing difficult emotions surrounding knowing of the transgression. This not only aids the therapist in coping with the emotions surrounding the transgression, but also can help the therapist process the information for what it is and the role in addressing the situation. The therapist should be wary of seeking support in this matter from peers or colleagues who work with—or know of—the individual in question (Nicholsen, 2010).

Ask Legal Counsel

Most professional organizations provide free legal service for members. This service is useful to gain guidance especially in ethical areas that are not clear and/or if legal issues may be involved.

If It Is Appropriate, Approach the Colleague

There are situations in which a therapist may see a colleague be very friendly or even flirtatious with a client, or a colleague could be heard talking about an attraction to a client. Many ethical violations can be avoided or resolved by an informal discussion in which one concerned professional approaches another in a nonjudgmental manner. It should be addressed as an attempt to protect the client, colleague, and the profession (Ford, 2014).

Walk the Client Through the Complaint Process

If the client does not want to file a complaint, then the therapist's primary goal is to ensure that the client understands their options and the therapist supports the client in that decision. Megan's first priority was to ensure Susan's well-being. After processing the information with Susan, Megan informed Susan of her options and offered Susan time to think about what she would like to do, if anything. After session, Megan scheduled supervision with her former supervisor and also spoke with a couple of trusted colleagues. Megan was informed that without her client's consent, she would not be able or required to file a complaint against the perpetrating therapist because it would break her client's confidentiality and Megan did not have firsthand knowledge of the event.

Consequences for the Client

Several researchers documented the negative effects for clients of sexual exploitation in therapy (Barnett, 2013; Bates & Brodsky, 1989; Bouhoutsos, Holroyd, Lerman, Forer, & Greenberg, 1983; Disch & Avery, 2001; Gabbard & Peltz, 2001; Pope, 1988; Wallace, 2007). These effects are sometimes compared to the consequences commonly suffered by victims of incest (Barnhouse, 1978; Bates & Brodsky, 1989; Gabbard, 1989). The boundary crossed when engaging in sexual relations with a client is "symbolically incestuous" (Barnhouse, 1978) in that the therapeutic relationship is inherently intimate with a power differential that mirrors a parent–child relationship.

The symptoms of clients sexually exploited by professionals may include confusion, loss, emotional turmoil, shame, fear, self-blame, loss of trust, isolation, and rage (Disch & Avery, 2001). Shame, intense guilt, poor self-esteem, and suicidal or self-destructive behavior are also potential symptoms (Gabbard, 1989). Luepker (1999) surveyed 55 women who had been sexually exploited by mental health practitioners and found the clients suffered from posttraumatic stress disorder, major depressive disorder, suicidality, increased use of prescription drugs, disrupted relationships, and disruptions in their work or earning potential. In an earlier study by Bouhoutsos et al. (1983), 11% of clients who engaged in sex with a former therapist were hospitalized and 1% committed suicide.

Consequences for the Therapist

Clients are not the only individuals at risk of suffering often dire consequences stemming from the breach of sexual ethics in therapy. In many states, sex with a client (or former client) is a criminal action, punishable by imprisonment. Sexual misconduct is one of the most frequent reasons for malpractice lawsuits (Stromberg & Dellinger, 1993), though personal and financial relationships with clients also invite malpractice action (Tarvydas & Johnston, 2008). In addition to tort action for sexual abuse of clients, liability insurance policies typically exclude sexual relationships with clients, or the policies have much lower ceilings than for other malpractice actions. Additionally, therapists may find they encounter loss of their job, livelihood, and career (Edelwich & Brodsky, 1991). Other damages include liability for supervisors, consultants, and the agencies or organizations that employ the offending therapist; loss of respect from colleagues is a natural consequence (Keith-Spiegel, 2014; Nicholsen, 2010). Sexual misconduct also hinders the mental health fields because clients no longer trust the profession (Keith-Spiegel, 2014; Nicholsen, 2010).

Warning Signs for the Therapist

Some warning signs a therapist may be moving from attraction to an unethical boundary breach include:

- Lack of self-care. Therapists do not partake in self-care, which leaves them unable to effectively manage stressors in their life. They can seek therapy to manage feelings or to address personal or professional stressors.

- Clients meet therapists' needs. Therapist begins to share their personal problems with the client; therapy starts to meet the therapist's needs instead of the client's needs. To prevent this from occurring, therapists should not isolate professionally; they can be aware of their own feelings, thoughts, and needs (Anderson & Handelsman, 2010; Barnett, 2013; Keith-Spiegel, 2014).
- Making exceptions for some clients. Therapist who make exceptions to their usual therapy and office policies may be at risk for boundary crossing. For example, therapists do not see clients on weekends, but make an exception only for one client (Anderson & Handelsman, 2010; Barnett, 2013; Keith-Spiegel, 2014).
- Seeing a client as "special." A client may be seen as special for a myriad of reasons. Examples include beauty, youth, fame or community status, intellect, or therapeutic challenge (Norris, Guthell, & Strasburger, 2003).
- Personal and professional relationships become blurred. Examples include attending a client's birthday party or other social function, having coffee together, etc. Conversely, therapists may invite clients to functions or events that are not part of therapy (Anderson & Handelsman, 2010; Barnett, 2013; Keith-Spiegel, 2014).
- Problems with boundary setting and enmeshment. Limit setting for some therapists can be difficult. They may feel that limit setting may exacerbate a client's distress. Clients may express distress, discomfort, or frustration when encountering limits set by therapists, which may be difficult for therapists who feel compelled to meet client's demands or who are intimidated by not meeting client demands. Likewise, clients who seek therapy may be more accustomed dependency than autonomy. This may be particularly true for clients who come from enmeshed systems, making it difficult for the client to break away from therapists and push toward porous boundaries with them. When therapists do not set those boundaries and enmeshment occurs, risk for sexual boundary crossing increases (Norris et al., 2003).
- Life crises, illness, and transitions. These stressors all increase the chances of sexual boundary crossing (Norris et al., 2003).
- Role reversals. For example, therapists who are lonely may find relief in confiding to a client, thus corrupting the therapist–client relationship (Norris et al., 2003).
- Denial. Therapists who deny early problems can be more vulnerable to boundary violations later on in the therapeutic relationship. They may think the boundary problem is not serious or may be rationalize away the problematic boundary (Norris et al., 2003).

Discussing Sex and Sexuality in Therapy

Case Scenario 1

Gina is a couple and family therapist who specializes in sex therapy. She is currently seeing a couple, Danny and Caroline, who are worried that their sex life has become dull. The problem is that when Gina asks the couple questions pertaining to their sexual relationship, Danny and Caroline describe sexual details that make Gina uncomfortable. They talk explicitly about their intimate encounters for what seems like the entire hour, and even redirect the conversation back to their sex life when Gina asks unrelated questions. Frustrated, Gina says to herself, "You are a sex therapist! You are not supposed to be ruffled when people talk about sex!" Nevertheless, Gina sometimes wonders if Danny and Caroline are there for her help or for the excitement of sharing their sexual escapades with a relative stranger.

Case Scenario 2

Henry is seeing a couple, Zach and Terrance, who are having trouble with premature ejaculation. Henry has worked with many couples with the same problem, but Terrance and Zach are a particularly fun and attractive couple whom Henry enjoys working with very much. Soon Henry finds himself asking detailed questions about the couple's sex life that he is not sure he would ask other couples. Henry tries to tell himself that the purpose of his questions is to gather information, but in the back of his mind he wonders if he is more or less interested in the sexual details out of selfish curiosity. Henry cannot deny that hearing about peoples' sex lives is an exciting element of his job. As soon as the thought crosses his mind, however, he feels tremendous guilt. He worries that he has crossed an ethical boundary and refers Terrance and Zach to another therapist right away.

These case scenarios present two different dilemmas: in scenario one, the therapist worries how to proceed with clients she perceives to be exhibitionistic, as the clients seem to constantly and graphically share their sexual exploits, and in scenario two, the therapist worries that he is a voyeur when he catches himself enjoying a client's sexual details. Ethical matters involving the sharing of sexual information can be quite serious, uncomfortable, and possibly harmful for clients if not handled appropriately.

"Verbal exhibitionism" of clients, as demonstrated in the first vignette, can be handled in a similar manner as dealing with covert sexual advances of clients. Therapists may benefit from understanding that clients who seem to excessively and graphically recount sexual details may be doing so for a number of reasons. A client may be gauging the therapist's sexual interest in the activities described or simply evading a more intimate therapeutic conversation (Edelwich & Brodsky, 1991). Moreover, clients may feel they gain power by sharing shocking information with the therapist. Ideally, a therapist may integrate a conversation regarding how sharing graphic details may impact the therapeutic relationship. However, if this is implausible or fails, and if the explicit conversations seem to be impeding therapy, it is appropriate for the therapist to tactfully define the limitations of their role as a therapist. In the first vignette, Gina might say:

> I'm not sure if I'm making too much of the situation, but sometimes I feel like the two of you like to gauge my reaction to your sexual stories just for the sake of pushing my buttons! You should know that I need to gather important details about your sex life, but I don't want to cross a boundary and jeopardize our therapeutic relationship. So will it be okay if I put the brakes on some of your juicy stories in the future if I think it would be helpful to move on to something else?

In the previous statement, Gina is clearly establishing a therapeutic boundary without coming across as judgmental or rejecting. She also leaves room for the possibility that her perceptions are incorrect and asks for permission to set limits in the future. Also note that Gina's statement uses a sense of humor and playfulness as a tool to diffuse what could be an otherwise awkward conversation (as well as to match the style of her clients, Danny and Caroline). A therapist in a similar situation should use clinical judgment in determining the appropriate amount of humor that will be well received by clients.

Soliciting sexual information for therapeutic treatment is sometimes necessary; for example sexual history may relevant to certain treatment problems (e.g., dating issues, sexual concerns, sexual abuse history). Actively soliciting sexual information for one's own enjoyment, however, is unethical. A therapist's suspicion that they are behaving voyeuristically in therapy can be handled in a similar manner as dealing with sexual attraction and fantasy involving clients; supervision or consultation should be sought. It is when a therapist *chooses* to ask questions for the purpose of sexual gratification that an ethical boundary is crossed (Edelwich & Brodsky, 1991).

Much like the therapist who recognizes a sexual attraction to a client, the therapist (like Henry in the vignette) who realizes that they enjoy hearing the details of a client's sex life should (1) acknowledge to oneself that it is a natural human response and experience to enjoy and have interest in sexual information; (2) refrain from "giving" the problem to clients by refraining from discussing their feelings of enjoyment; (3) seek support from a supervisor, peer, or professional consultant; and (4) refer the client only when the therapist feels that the previous steps have not been successful in ensuring that enjoyment in hearing the sexual details does not impede the therapeutic process, or if the therapist feels that they cannot refrain from actively choosing to elicit sexual information for personal gratification.

In the second scenario, Henry may have been too quick to refer Terrance and Zach. If he had acknowledged the normalcy of his sexual feelings and sought supervision, Henry may have noticed a reduction in his anxiety and an increase in his ability to work effectively with the couple. However, if he continued to notice that he was actively asking sexual questions of Terrance and Zach that he would not ask other couples, it would be appropriate for Henry to make a referral.

Summary

Boundary violations, including sex with clients, are damaging to clients, therapists, and the mental health professions as a whole. Clients attend therapy for a protected space to explore their innermost lives, and we have a duty to protect them from sexual harassment and abuse (Keith-Spiegel, 2014).

However, the simple dictate to "not have sex with your clients" is insufficient to cover the range of boundary crossing and violations than can occur if therapists are not attentive to their own feelings and longings. Issues pertaining to sexual attraction, sexual fantasy, sexual advances of clients, sexual relations with former clients, and sexual discussions in therapy warrant consideration and further discussion. Although sexual attraction to a client can be a byproduct of our human, therapeutic relationship with them, much is at stake, making it vital for the therapist to learn productive ways to deal with this common issue. Likewise, clients' sexual attraction to therapists, if managed therapeutically, can be a source of therapeutic growth and understanding for them.

References

Anderson, S. K., & Handelsman, M. M. (2010). *The ethical culture of psychotherapy.* Hoboken, NJ: Wiley-Blackwell.

Barnett, J. E. (2013). Sexual feelings and behaviors in the psychotherapy relationship: An ethics perspective. *Journal of Clinical Psychology: In Session, 70*(2), 170–181. doi: 10.1002/jclp.22068.

Barnhouse, R. (1978). Sex between patient and therapist. *Journal of the American Academy of Psychoanalysis, 6*(4), 533–546.

Bates, C., & Brodsky, A. (1989). *Sex in the therapy hour: A case of professional incest.* New York, NY: Guilford.

Blonna, R. (2014). An acceptance commitment therapy approach to sexual attraction. In M. Luca (Ed.), *Sexual attraction in therapy: Clinical perspectives on moving beyond the taboo: A guide for training and practice* (pp. 80–96). West Sussex, England: Wiley-Blackwell.

Bouhoutsos, J., Holroyd, J., Lerman, H., Forer, B. R., & Greenberg, M. (1983). Sexual intimacy between psychotherapists and patients. *Professional Psychology: Research and Practice, 14*(2), 185–196. doi: 10.1037/0735-7028.14.2.185.

Brandenburg, J. B. (1997). *Confronting sexual harassment: What schools and colleges can do.* New York, NY: Teachers College Press.

Disch, E., & Avery, N. (2001). Sex in the consulting room, the examining room, and the sacristy: Survivors of sexual abuse by professionals. *American Journal of Orthopsychiatry, 71*(2), 204–217. doi: 10.1037/0002-9432.71.2.204.

Eddington, N., & Shuman, R. (2004). *Ethics.* Paper presented at the meeting of Continuing Psychology Education, Austin, TX.

Edelwich, J., & Brodsky, A. (1991). *Sexual dilemmas for the helping professional.* New York, NY: Brunner/Mazel.

Fisher, C. D. (2004). Ethical issues in therapy: Therapist self-disclosure of sexual feelings. *Ethics and Behavior, 14*(2), 105–121. doi: 10.1207/s15327019eb1402_2.

Ford, G. (2014). *Ethical reasoning for mental health professionals.* Thousand Oaks, CA: Sage.

Gabbard, G. O. (1989). *Sexual exploitation in professional relationships.* Washington, DC: American Psychiatric Press.

Gabbard, G. O. (1997). Lessons to be learned from the study of sexual boundary violations. *Australian and New Zealand Journal of Psychiatry, 31*(3), 321–327. doi: 10.3109/00048679709073839.

Gabbard, G. O., & Peltz, M. (2001). Speaking the unspeakable: Institutional reactions to boundary violations by training analysts. *Journal of the American Psychoanalytic Association, 49*(2), 659–673. doi: 10.1177/00030651010490020601.

Garrett, T. (2010). The prevalence of boundary violations between mental health practitioners and their clients. In F. Subotsky, S. Bewley, & M. Crowe (Eds.), *Abuse of the doctor-patient relationship* (pp. 51–63). London, England: RCPsych.

Harris, S. M. (1998). Sexual attraction in the therapeutic relationship. In American Association for Marriage and Family Therapy (Ed.), *A marriage and family therapist's guide to ethical and legal practice: Answers to questions on current ethical topics and legal considerations in MFT practice* (pp. 4–9). Alexandria, VA: American Association for Marriage and Family Therapy.

Harris, S. M., & Hays, K. W. (2008). Family therapist comfort and the willingness to discuss sexuality. *Journal of Marital and Family Therapy, 34*(2), 239–250. doi: 10.1111/j.1752-0606.2008.00066.x.

Keith-Spiegel, P. (2014). *Red flags in psychotherapy: Stories of ethics complaints and resolutions.* New York, NY: Routledge.

Kim, S., & Rutherford, A. (2015). From seduction to sexism: Feminists challenge the ethics of therapist-client sexual relations in 1970s America. *History of Psychology, 18*(3), 283–296. doi: 10.1037/a0039524.

Ladany, N., Klinger, R., & Kulp, L. (2011). Therapist shame: Implications for therapy and supervision. In R. Dearing & J. Tangney (Eds.), *Shame in the therapy hour* (pp. 307–322). Washington, DC: American Psychological Association. doi: 10.1037/12326-013.

Luepker, E. T. (1999). Effects of practitioners' sexual misconduct: A follow-up study. *Journal of the American Academy of Psychiatry and the Law, 27*(1), 51–63.

Nicholsen, S. W. (2010). Too close to home: Counter-transference dynamics in the wake of colleague's sexual boundary violation. *Canadian Journal of Psychoanalysis, 18*(2), 225–247.

Nickell, N. J., Hecker, L. L., Ray, R. E., & Bercik, J. (1995). Marriage and family therapists' sexual attraction to clients: An exploratory study. *The American Journal of Family Therapy, 23*(4), 315–327. doi: 10.1080/01926189508251362.

Noel, M. M. (2008). *Sexual misconduct by psychologists: Who reports it?* Dissertation Abstracts International: Section B: The Sciences and Engineering, 68(10-B).

Norris, D. M., Guthell, T. G., & Strasburger, L. H. (2003). This couldn't happen to me: Boundary problems and sexual misconduct in the psychotherapy relationship. *Psychiatric Services, 54*(4), 517–522. doi: 10.1176/appi.ps.54.4.517.

Plaut, S. M. (2008). Sexual and nonsexual boundaries in professional relationships: Principles and teaching guidelines. *Sexual and Relationship Therapy, 23*(1), 85–94. doi: 10.1080/14681990701616624.

Pope, K. (1988). How clients are harmed by sexual contact with mental health professionals: The syndrome and its prevalence. *Journal of Counseling and Development, 67*(4), 222–226. doi: 10.1002/j.1556-6676.1988.tb02587.x.

Pope, K. S., Sonne, J. L., & Greene, B. (2006). *What therapists don't talk about and why: Understanding taboos that hurt us and our clients.* Washington, DC: American Psychological Association.

Pope, K. S., Sonne, J. L., & Holroyd, J. (1993). *Sexual feelings in psychotherapy: Explorations for therapists and therapists-in-training.* Washington, DC: American Psychological Association.

Pope, K., Keith-Spiegel, P., & Tabachnick, B. (1986). Sexual attraction to clients: The human therapist and the (sometimes) inhuman training system. *American Psychologist, 41*(2), 147–158. doi: 10.1037/1931-3918.S.2.96.

Pope, K., Tabachnick, B., & Keith-Spiegel, P. (1987). Ethics of practice: The beliefs and behaviors of psychologists as therapists. *American Psychologist, 42*(11), 993–1006. doi: 10.1037/0003-066X.42.11.993.

Rutter, P. (1989). *Sex in the forbidden zone.* New York, NY: Fawcett Crest.

Strean, H. S. (1993). *Therapists who have sex with their patients.* New York, NY: Brunner/Mazel.

Stringer, D. M., Remick, H., Salisbury, J., & Ginorio, A. B. (1990). The power and reasons behind sexual harassment: An employer's guide to solutions. *Public Personnel Management, 19*(1), 43–52. doi: 10.1177/009102609001900105.

Stromberg, C., & Dellinger, A. (1993). A legal update on malpractice and other professional liability. *The Psychologist's Legal Update, 3*, 3–15.

Tarvydas, V. M., & Johnston, S. P. (2008). Managing risk in ethical and legal situations. In I. Marini & M. A. Stebnicki (Eds.), *The professional counselor's desk reference* (pp. 99–111). New York, NY: Springer.

Wallace, E. M. (2007). Losing a training analyst for ethical violations: A candidate's perspective. *International Journal of Psychoanalysis, 88*(5), 1275–1288. doi: 10.1516/ijpa.2007.1275].

8

Risk Management in Practice

Amber Sampson

James, a Caucasian male in his mid-40s, presented for therapy because of depression, substance use, marital separation, and recent work-related discipline received. He had a history of suicide attempts, violent behavior, and childhood trauma. James' therapist, Maria, took her time getting to know her new client while consistently and kindly discussing James' risk for suicide, and options to enhance his safety. Maria regularly sought consultation with her supervisor and she took meticulous notes of these discussions with her supervisor, as well as her communication attempts with James. She collaborated with James' psychiatrist and primary care physician, and continued to see James despite him losing his job and insurance. Despite Maria's efforts and alliance with James, he eventually stopped showing up for scheduled appointments. Maria provided resource information to his family if James' mental health deteriorated, providing the family with information regarding hospitalization for James. Despite Maria's conscientious efforts, some weeks later, James killed himself.

Suicide Risk

The fear of losing a client to suicide is a warranted concern for any therapist. In a survey of psychotherapists in the American Mental Health Counselors Association, 71% of responding psychotherapists reported managing at least one client who has attempted suicide, whereas 28% reported having had at least one client die by suicide (Rogers, Gueulette, Abbey-Hines, Carney, & Werth, 2001). According to the World Health Organization (WHO), someone dies by suicide every 40 seconds (WHO, 2014). Additionally, clients do not always welcome a therapist's efforts to decrease their suicide risk. Marsha Linehan, the founder of dialectical behavior therapy, is fond of saying "suicide is a solution for the client, and a problem for the therapist" (Jobes, Linehan, & Yanez, 2015, p. 38; Linehan, 2013). Suicide ideation or intent puts therapists in high vigilance mode, carefully therapeutically assessing and managing the client, potentially putting the client's goals and therapist's goals at odds.

The most recent statistics provided by the Center for Disease Control and Prevention (2015) about suicide attempts and completions are grim:

- Suicide is the tenth most prominent reason for deaths across all age groups,
- Women have suicidal thoughts more often than men, but men die by suicide more frequently,
- Suicide is the seventh leading cause of death in men, and the fourteenth leading cause of death for women,
- Men use firearms to suicide more than 50% of the time,
- People who have origins of two or more racial backgrounds are at the highest risk of suicide as adults, followed by American Indians/Alaska Natives, Native Hawaiians/Other Pacific Islanders, Whites, Hispanics, Asians, and Blacks,
- Suicide is the third leading cause of death for children from 10 to 14 years of age, and
- For those aged 15 to 34, suicide is the second most common reason for death.

How does a couple and family therapist go about decreasing risk of death of a client? First, knowing risk factors is important. Below is a list of risk factors of which couple and family therapists should be aware:

- Previous suicide attempts,
- Presence of a diagnosed mental illness,
- Strong suicide ideation,
- Reporting of hopelessness,
- Distress and anxiety,
- Evidence of impulsive or self-destructive actions,
- Access to lethal means/methods,
- Significant psychosocial stressors,
- Personal losses and exposure to other suicides,
- Childhood trauma,
- Substance abuse, and
- Identification within the lesbian, gay, bisexual, transgender, and queer community (Jacobs et al., 2010; WHO, 2006).

The risk factors for James, Maria's client in our case scenario, are not unusual, and actually may be common to see in practice. His various risk factors are important clues for a therapist to further discuss and assess how best to incorporate into a safety plan. Suicide prevention research is still in its infancy; research on how to specifically decrease suicide completion is forthcoming. Management of suicide ideation and behaviors is contingent upon appropriate assessment.

Assessment

It takes time, training, and appropriate guidance to become adept with the process of suicide assessment. Too often, clinicians expect that pointed questions to a client about their desire to die are enough to adequately assess for suicide potential. Jobes, Rudd, Overholser, and Joiner (2008) contend that in addition to a client's subjective responses to inquiry about suicidal ideation, it is important for clinicians to:

- Administer objective symptom measures,
- Seek out client records for historical information,
- Recognize the difference between chronic and acute risk for suicidal ideation, and
- Display awareness of the different warning signs and risk factors.

Those with chronic risk are clients demonstrating a history of multiple attempts and often require lower and lower stressor levels before attempting suicide each time. Clients with current acute risk have attempted suicide once, but must be considered at the start of a chronic path. Better understanding a client's thoughts regarding the first suicide attempt can lend awareness to further imminent or chronic risk. Jobes et al. (2008) relate the importance in assessing for a client's regret in surviving the attempt as a key clue in understanding potential for chronicity in risk. Additionally, it is important to understand the difference between assessment for warning signs and risk factors. Warning signs are considerations for immediate risk. For example, a client demonstrating increased hopelessness or recent release from the hospital is potentially at more immediate risk, showing warning signs of a suicide attempt in the very near future. Risk factors are more associated with long-standing concerns and previously identified concepts that could increase potential for suicide attempts along a client's lifespan.

Because there are no known treatment "cures," assessment for suicidal ideation and intent is an ongoing process throughout treatment. Clinicians are wise to employ the previously mentioned combination of assessment processes throughout the span of treatment and demonstrate such routines through comprehensive documentation. Even in the process of ending therapy, the client's needs are best served if a summary of current suicide risk is documented at the time of release from care. Clear documentation allows for continuity of care if a client reemerges for treatment, whether in the same therapist's care or in being treated by others. No client with a history of suicidal ideation is without risk at the time of discharge. One would be naïve and at risk of legal and ethical consequences to believe otherwise.

Intervention and Documentation

Once a clinician has become attuned to watching for potential risk factors outside a client's self-report of the desire/intent to die, it is important to have a plan for further assessment, appropriate documentation, and standard procedures for intervening to diminish risk of active suicidal behaviors. Clinicians are encouraged to consult with the policy and procedures of their employment settings when available, and seek out supervision—clinical or peer, depending on licensure status—each time a therapist encounters concern for suicide risk. Additionally, documentation of each step taken in the process of managing a case with the potential for death is highly advised. Documentation can provide a clinician with a record of steps taken, notes on advised interventions, and a sense of engagement with an issue that can bring clinical feelings of unease and fear. If documentation is absent, clinicians are in jeopardy of litigation for failing to provide the accepted appropriate standard of care, both topics discussed below.

When providing intervention for a suicidal client, Jacobs et al. (2010) advise the therapist use a combination of several components to effectively understand and help the client. What follows are themes meant to intertwine as the current status of the client's needs dictate and not as a list to be followed in linear fashion. Initially, as in any other case, it is advised a clinician attend to the therapeutic alliance so that trust can be fostered and used as the backbone for joining with the client in collaboration with the goal of decreasing their hopelessness, increasing desire to end pain, and minimizing active suicidal risk. Simultaneously, the therapist develops a plan to increase the immediate safety of the client. Through assessment questions about plans to kill oneself and standard questions regarding access to weapons, the therapist can determine if immediate action is needed to enhance the client's environmental safety. This might include employing family, friends, or other appropriate resources to assist in removing potential weapons from the client's possession or determining if a higher level of care is needed. When determining the level of care, it is important to keep the immediacy of the threat for suicide in mind. Generally, the health care system is based on employing lesser restrictions on clients when possible. If clients are not actively trying to, nor have recently tried to kill themselves, and deny intent at this time, it is possible they may not qualify for hospitalization. It is important to know the resources in the area that can still assist in managing treatment without relying on a hospital setting each time to keep a client safe.

Additionally, a good therapeutic alliance and comprehensive assessment of biopsychosocial concerns and protective factors can aid in a well-developed and easily documented treatment plan. Over time, because the goal is not likely feasible nor recommended to expect elimination of suicidal ideation, the treatment plan can provide a working record of overall safety and other goals to address underlying mental health concerns and daily living deficits.

As previously mentioned, it is important to remember the multiple ways documentation plays a part in the treatment process. Specifically, the treatment record not only provides the potential to assist the client in looking for patterns in mood and other biopsychosocial stressors impacting ideation, but it also aids in the portability of information pertaining to progress and barriers other clinicians involved with the client's care will need to know. Ongoing clinical collaboration is necessary to promote a client's engagement with the treatment plan and identify when the therapist can provide further psychoeducation to the client and their network of support to promote success. Finally, Jacobs et al. (2010) advise it is important to continually assess for suicide risk and safety needs as treatment progresses.

Appropriate Standard of Care

What constitutes, or better yet, who determines the definition to appropriate standard of care with regard to management of suicidal clients? Ideally, the appropriate standard of care would be absolute prevention of suicide through a clinician's care but as discussed previously, there can be no definitive end to the potential for suicide risk. So what can therapists look to for guidance on the appropriate standard of care in the therapy process? Simon (2002) takes the perspective that appropriate standard of care is addressed by documenting a comprehensive and evolving risk assessment process to specifically determine the foreseeability of suicide and demonstrate the influence on treatment planning thereafter. If a full assessment is undertaken and diligence is demonstrated in collaborating with previous and concurrent professionals in a client's life, foreseeability increases. When foreseeability increases, one has a better informed ability to judge the potential for suicide action and treatment options needed. Clinical judgment can be employed through interpretation of the acute, chronic, and protective factors reported in a client's life at any given time to enhance treatment and thus outcomes.

Therapists might benefit from looking at the suicide risk assessment process as a ripple in the water when a stone is thrown. The most constricted rings are the basic assessment tools—checklists, symptom inventories, etc.—providing first indication of concern. As the assessment process broadens, the clinician can use more specific individual factors such as knowledge of home and work stress to probe for the impact they are having on thoughts of dying. Finally, clinical collaboration with doctors and family members can provide valuable information regarding real-time changes to acute and chronic factors in the client's life.

Safety Planning

Safety planning can mean a variety of different concepts and interventions depending on the clinical setting. Fundamentally, safety planning is the process of creating a set of strategies designed to use the support and protective factors in a client's life. Specifically, safety plans are best designed to provide options and actions steps for care *before* a client becomes acutely suicidal.

Research reinforces the idea that the therapeutic alliance is critical in the development of the safety plan (Jacobs et al., 2010; Stanley & Brown, 2008). Plans are to be pragmatic, solution oriented, and easy to read. Use of a client's own words and providing them a copy when finished are encouraged. Sources agree there are consistent components important to a safety plan. Clinicians are prudent to include warning signs both common to clients in crisis and specific to the client in the room. Additionally, it is important to list personal coping strategies, places of comfort and activity, and people as supports to be contacted when coping has become too difficult alone. Finally, providing specific information to clients regarding professional community resources and how to contact the provider directly is advised (Sher & Labode, 2011).

No-suicide or "no-self-harm" contracts pose a specific legal and ethical risk for uninformed therapists as to their validity, protection, and purpose in working with suicidal clients. Jacobs et al. (2010) draw back to the concept of the value of the therapeutic alliance above all when considering a contract. If used as a way to strengthen awareness of the care and concern a clinician has for a client, within appropriate ethical boundaries, a suicide contract may be helpful. However, because it is a socially constructed concept such contracts do not have actual power to prevent clients from committing suicide or protect clinicians from legal claims for a client's death. Some studies have found no-suicide contracts to be detrimental because they do not prevent deaths and provide a false sense of security for clinicians (Edwards & Sachmann, 2010).

Confidentiality

The client's right to confidentiality in the therapy process is a cornerstone of the profession. Unfortunately, there are times when it is necessary for clinicians to break this inherent and expected dynamic to maintain the safety of a client who presents with suicidal ideation. It is the ethical duty of the therapist to inform clients of limits to confidentiality for concerns in emergency situations and obtain proper written authorization to exchange/release information when collaborating with others in the client's treatment team before acute suicidality. Emergency situations might entail concern for a client's welfare in the absence of scheduled appointments when past suicidal ideation was identified, leaving the office with active suicidal ideation and statements, or reports via phone or e-mail indicating suicidality. Each may require the contact of the client's designated emergency contact, the police for a welfare check, or other crisis services available in the community to prevent lethal action.

Clinicians are encouraged to spend time during the initial meeting to specifically address confidentiality and the exceptions to confidentiality. Best practice incorporates a statement regarding such exceptions in the clinician's informed consent document and specifying such exceptions are legal and ethical obligations and standard practice in therapy. When clients acknowledge a history or current suicidal thoughts, the process of collaborating to identify specific support and emergency contacts is a good way to actively incorporate clients in their own care and thus diminish unknown breaches of confidentiality by the clinician.

Litigation

The ability to know how to appropriately care for clients with thoughts of suicide is necessary both for the client's well-being and to protect the clinician from being blamed for wrongdoing. As previously discussed, engaging in a high appropriate standard of care procedure and documentation of such efforts are necessary to diminish successful lawsuits by demonstrating diligence in trying to determine foreseeability. Melonas (2011) expands on this, outlining three central themes to aid in diminishing chance for successful litigation. The first entails not only a full assessment and knowledge found within past treatment records, but expands to suggest the importance of staying current on available treatments. Second, communication is specified to include the patient, other professions, and the client's family. The third theme outlines the importance of what to document—both the findings of a thorough assessment and the decision-making process for how the clinician arrived at specific clinical judgments throughout the treatment process. If a therapist consistently assesses for and treats suicidal ideation and documents observations/actions of care, courts are likely to find the therapist has a sound legal defense against a negligence lawsuit (Simon, 2002). Therapists are encouraged to consult with their specific state codes for definitions of and codes pertaining to appropriate legal conduct in the therapy field.

Self-Harm

Self-Harm Versus Suicide

The concepts of self-harm and suicide can be confusing when trying to determine the differences between the two in speaking with clients and staying up to date on clinical literature. Generally, the terms are interchangeable and may increase confusion when clients present with non-suicidal self-injury (NSSI) behaviors. The following discussion focuses on NSSI because risk management practices associated with suicide was previously discussed in this chapter. The most relevant factor in distinguishing between suicidal action and NSSI is the specific intention of the act. Andover, Morris, Wren, and Bruzzese (2012) define NSSI as "deliberate, self-inflicted destruction of body tissue without suicidal intent and for purposes not socially sanctioned" (p. 2). A comprehensive assessment, as previously discussed, can help to clarify the client's purpose for inflicting self-injury. It should be noted that research indicates a moderate to high correlation between NSSI and suicidal ideation at various points in life (Andover et al., 2012). This correlation further drives the reinforcement for ongoing clinical assessment of intention for self-harming behaviors.

Cutting and Other Methods

Methods of self-injury are commonly used, despite being maladaptive, as a way to regulate significant negative emotions or engage physical awareness when emotionally numb, including to stop disassociation, to punish oneself, for attention, and as a way to fit in with self-injuring peers (Peterson, Freedenthal, Sheldon, & Andersen, 2008). Common methods include cutting, burning, scratching, head-banging, interfering with wounds healing, and breaking bones (Brown & Kimball, 2013).

Kerr, Muehlenkamp, and Turner (2010) report general prevalence of self-injury in adults is around 4%, with increased risk in adolescents and college students. No significant differences have been reported between men and women, although men are more likely to hit/burn themselves and women to cut/burn themselves. Common clinical disorders associated with self-injury are borderline personality disorder, eating disorders, dissociative disorders, alcohol dependence, and major depressive disorder. Recent family therapy research conducted by Halstead, Pavkov, Hecker, and Seliner (2014) determined a significant correlation exists between family dynamics and the severity, duration, and frequency of self-injury behaviors. Data regarding onset identifies clients most likely to begin self-injury activity to be between 14 and 24 years of age, thus making family therapy a viable option among other treatment approaches such as medication, cognitive behavioral therapy, and dialectical behavioral therapy (Kerr et al., 2010).

Trauma-based clinicians believe cutting and other self-injurious behaviors increase dopamine levels in the body (Levine & Kline, 2007). Such a response can lead to an addictive quality. Qualitative research conducted by Brown and Kimball (2013) identified three major themes emerging in clients with NSSI behaviors. The first theme included the concept of self-harm as addictive and therefore, misunderstood. Second, self-harm has a purpose. Whether it provides distraction, punishment, or release, it has a function in the client's coping mechanisms. The final theme provides narrative to clinicians about the need to be educated and less assumptive about NSSI behaviors. As discussed earlier in suicidal clients, the findings of this research encourage therapists to focus on a strong therapeutic alliance. Ethically, clinicians are obligated to stay current on research and only practice within one's professional scope.

Intimate Partner Violence

> Mary and Albert began conjoint couples therapy in the couples and family therapy clinic on campus where Mary attended college. They met with an intern therapist reporting intense communication issues resulting in multiple breakups and reunifications. The therapist followed clinic protocol in discussing basic goals, informed consent, and therapy process in the first session and spent time meeting with Mary and Albert separately in the second session to assess for domestic violence. Both Mary and Albert reported no physical violence. After several sessions, the therapist noted Mary and Albert had not returned for therapy and did not respond to the standard letter sent for clients assessing desire to return for services. They were discharged from services. Six months later, Mary called to request an individual session. She reported violence was in fact a large factor in the relationship and, after sessions, Albert would use the therapist's suggestions and homework assignments as reasons to belittle Mary if he felt she did not complete them appropriately. Mary left Albert, but continued to be fearful of him. Mary continued with individual therapy, constructed a safety plan, and safety resources were provided to assist Mary in managing fear of Albert.

Working with couples in therapy is a core element to the training in systemic therapy services. Couple and family therapy promotes a core value recognizing change becomes more sustained and effective when multiple parts of the system come together for a common process. What, then, does a therapist do when they learn of intimate partner violence (IPV), also called domestic violence, occurring in the client system? What are the steps that led them to learn about the IPV and were they purposefully assessed?

Assessment and Screening

The statistics concerning IPV are alarming. National Crime Victimization Survey data from between 2003 and 2012 found IPV to account for 21% of all violent crimes. Women were identified as the victim in 76% of IPV (Truman & Morgan, 2014). Equally alarming is the rate at which studies have found couples and family therapists do not integrate standard assessment and screening protocols into their practice when working with couples. Schacht, Dimidjian, George, and Berns (2009) found that less than 4% of therapists use all three standard assessment procedures recommended to detect IPV. To effectively minimize risk of adding to the potential for violent conflict and ethically serve the best interest of the clients it is important to incorporate three separate components to the IPV assessment process. Schacht et al. (2009) recognize standard best practice includes concurrent:

- Use of universal screenings,
- Engagement of each partner individually in an assessment, and
- Use of risk assessment measures to address concerns regarding IPV and other factors, such as assessing for weapons in the home and engagement of substance use.

The third measure is one of the less frequently used components found by the authors in their work. Such omission is concerning as statistics indicate the presence of a firearm increases likelihood of homicide for the victim of abuse by 500% (Campbell et al., 2003).

Universal screenings best practices mean every client/couple that begins therapy work is screened for the potential for IPV just as one would screen for mental health concerns, suicidal/homicidal ideation, and substance abuse issues. Todahl and Walters (2011) report benefits, in addition to uncovering the existence of IPV when present, of universal screens to include increased comfort level of the practitioner speaking about IPV when in routine practice, clients experiencing less likely feelings of being singled out/discriminated against for specific characteristics that promote assumption of IPV, and general opportunity provide psychoeducation on the serious matter of IPV.

In the process of assessing IPV, clinicians are wise to engage each partner in individual sessions. Doing so provides opportunity to discuss their perceptions of the violence when found to be present in an uninhibited environment. Power and gender dynamics have been found to influence perceptions and thought distortions regarding responsibility, and individual time to explore such perceptions is very important (Whiting, Oka, & Fife, 2012). Further, Bograd and Mederos (1999) identify seven goals for the individual interviews aiding in effective risk management:

- Learn whether there is any violence between the couple,
- Ascertain the nature, frequency, severity, and physical consequences of the physical aggression,

- Elicit detailed behavioral descriptions describing the sequence of events in context,
- Understand the intended function of the violence and its impact,
- Evaluate the degree of fear and intimidation present,
- Determine whether there is a broader pattern of coercion and domination, including psychological abuse and marital rape, and
- Lay the groundwork for an informed decision about the advisability of continued couples work.

Just as was discussed in the section on suicide, it is necessary to incorporate a full-risk assessment regarding access to lethal means, history of violence, etc. when assessing IPV. Information gathered from the risk assessment can provide opportunity to inform clinicians of the potential for future IPV to occur and inform the trajectory of therapy. The published research findings of Smith, Whiting, Karakurt, Oka, and Servino (2013) on the Self Assessment of Future Events Scale provide a guided measure to assist clinicians in discussing perceptions of risk for future violent incidents in addition to current and past violent experiences.

Individual Versus Conjoint Treatment

Modality of treatment when there is awareness of IPV has been a topic of debate for quite some time. Stith, McCollum, Amanor-Boadu, and Smith (2012) have provided updated findings to the ongoing research of what constitutes best practices in determining most appropriate modality of treatment upon completion of an IPV assessment. Earlier literature has relied heavily on individual, separate treatment for each partner in the relationship. Stith et al. (2012) report some movement away from this perspective in specific populations. Recent research acknowledges situational couple's violence often involves mutual use of violence between both partners. Therefore, the authors suggest there are potential benefits derived from conjoint treatment with high emphasis on safety planning, lowering other risk factor concerns, and mutual desire to cease violent behaviors in these couples.

One area that remains steadfast in contraindication to conjoint therapy is in the instances of intimate partner terrorism (Stith et al., 2012). Intimate partner terrorism is defined as multiple tactics of abuse to ensure power and control over a partner. Physical violence is only one form of abuse in a perpetrators arsenal of control tactics. Those who most often engage in intimate partner terrorism also use significant psychological and emotional abuse tactics to incite dominance over a partner. Albert, introduced in the case scenario, demonstrated actions inherent in the definition of intimate partner terrorism. His use of the therapist's homework assignments and therapy discussions to belittle Mary displayed elements of a quest for dominance without singular use of physical violence to be in control.

Individual sessions held after the initial general assessment intake are a good time to assess for intimate partner terrorism without heightened concern for a client's safety and allows for discussion with each partner as discussed before regarding perceptions of responsibility if violence has been acknowledged (Whiting et al., 2012). It is very important to observe the potential areas of practice in which an intimate terrorism perpetrator might influence the therapy process. If a partner rejects the idea of a universal screening/assessment materials/separate interviews there may be early red flags to manage. Checking to see that each partner filled out inventories and couple's questionnaires individually may also provide information for power and control dynamics.

No-Violence Contracts

No-violence contracts are similar to safety plans in that they are created for the purpose of providing common ground for shared goals of safety at all times and agreement to disrupt the current conflict cycle through alternative behaviors. Rosen, Matheson, Stith, McCollum, and Locke (2003) assert that in couples displaying situational/mutual violence, specific work can be done to create new means of coping that promotes shared understanding of each person's actions. Rosen et al. (2003) encourage the creation of a negotiated time-out process as part of a no-violence contract. The seven steps provide in-the-moment guidance to accompany statements of commitment to cease any IPV behaviors.

It is necessary to note that no-violence contracts are not binding in any legal sense. They should not replace sound risk assessment, be reinforced if violence continues without first assessing current dynamics and fit of conjoint therapy, nor used as the only intervention to actively address IPV when conjoint therapy is indicated. Safety should always be a primary goal. Additionally, it may be important to discuss the lack of legal status such a contract possesses with clients to provide adequate informed consent regarding the purpose of the intervention.

Potentially Dangerous Clients

Duty to Warn/Protect

The ethical and legal expectations surrounding a therapist's duty to warn and protect the public from potentially dangerous clients has been part of clinical practice for close to 40 years now. The pivotal case of *Tarasoff v. Regents of the University of California* has set the stage for clinicians as gatekeepers for the safety of others when a client has specifically expressed intent to harm another person. For further understanding of the history of this important event in mental health history, please refer to Chapter 3.

Common questions to arise about the duty to warn are surrounding the privilege of confidentiality inherent to the patient-practitioner privilege rights of state legal codes. A cornerstone of the Tarasoff case is associated with the idea that "the protective privilege ends where the public peril begins," a well-known quote by Justice Tobriner of the California Supreme Court. In other words, most states now accept significant risk of harm to the public as a reasonable and protected reason to break confidentiality. Each state code is different and clinicians are prudent to know the facts about duty to warn/protect in their practicing state. Most states have mandatory duty to warn/protect laws, though some have permissive laws, and a few have none at all. The National Conference of State Legislatures is a good resource to learn more about the state laws in which a clinician resides.

Client Risk Factors

Several factors associated with potential for violence are important for clinicians to know. Friedman (2006) reports that clients with co-occurring major mental illness diagnoses and substance abuse are at highest risk for violence at 43.6% prevalence, followed by clients with substance or alcohol issues only, clients experiencing schizophrenia or other major affective disorders, and finally those clients with no major diagnoses at a prevalence rate of 7.3%. It is important to note that the diagnoses themselves are not overall predictors of potential for dangerousness or violence, but rather the experience of active symptomology that raises concern. Additionally, Monahan et al. (2001) identified the following factors to be clinically significant risk concerns: male gender, historical violence, adverse childhood experiences such as abuse, and living in disadvantaged neighborhoods. The authors reported more specific definitions of active symptomology to include psychopathy, suspiciousness, anger, violent thoughts, and hallucinations commanding violent acts.

Assessment

Similar to the assessment process for suicidal ideation, it is the responsibility of the clinician to complete a thorough risk assessment that includes use of professional judgement when concerned that a client may be at risk for violent behaviors. Many assessment tools exist as an aid to the clinician, but should only be seen as a starting point for the ongoing monitoring of potential for violence. Singh, Grann, and Fazel (2011) found, during a meta-analysis review of common assessment tools, that the more specific an assessment is to a population, for example the Structured Assessment of Violence Risk in Youth, the higher the validity. Clinicians are urged to consult with their employment setting to determine assessment protocols or adopt a standard practice of assessment procedures. The Center for Disease Control and Prevention provides online basic tools to guide the assessment process. The resources address the immediacy of a client's dangerousness, basic triage questions for emergency settings, and tools to assist in assessing nonverbal cues of potential for more immediate violence.

Decision-making

Due to the nature of fear that violent clients can bring out in a therapist it is very important to seek supervision or consultation quickly when concerned about a client committing a violent act. Decisions regarding actions to take when a client reports threats of harm to others may include consideration of state legal mandates, need for a client to be hospitalized or involuntarily committed, who in particular requires notification, and safety measures necessary in the immediate moment for the clinician/staff. Commonly, ethical decision-making processes often incorporate consultation of legal and ethical code mandates and may be helpful to reference when documenting the process of creating a well-thought-out plan for engaging in one's action associated with duty to warn. Documentation in this respect is crucial and important to do in quick succession of meeting with someone presenting concern for violence.

Ideally, while a duty to warn is difficult to face, clinicians have already informed clients at the beginning of treatment of the procedure for handling imminent violent behaviors. Clients can be made aware that violent threats falls outside the topics kept confidential. Additionally, identifying the duty to warn as an ethical and (most often) legal requirement of the profession opens space for an increased therapeutic alliance through trust and honesty. If a client needs hospitalization and a strong therapeutic alliance is present, it may be more productive to encourage the client to go to a facility for observation rather than call the police for a client to be transported.

Safety Plans and Hospitalization

Similar to suicide safety planning, clients with a history of violence, thoughts of harming others, or other specific risk factors associated with dangerousness can benefit from creating a safety plan early in the therapy process. Identifying initial warning signs, triggers, and resources as a first step can assist clients in increased self-regulation. Additionally, it is wise to document who they can utilize as support in an informal and formal context, as well as discuss the importance of removing means of violence such as firearms from one's possession.

Hospitalization in the case of imminent harm to others can occur in two ways. Clients can be hospitalized voluntarily or through involuntary (civil) commitment. Every state has differing procedures for commitment, length of stay, etc. and clinicians are advised to consult their local resources to learn more about this process. Many states have adopted hospitalization procedures according to the concepts of "parens patriae," which allows a state to protect a citizen that is unable to care for themselves as they would if impairment were absent and "police power" directing authority for the state to act in ways that protects the general welfare of citizens (Menninger, 2001).

There is ethical controversy to take note of in the expectations of a client's hospitalization due to violent threats. As one cannot expect a hospitalization, voluntary or otherwise, to "inoculate" a client from becoming violent in the future, there is still the question remaining regarding duty to warn the intended victim. Some resources suggest by hospitalizing a client confidentiality can be maintained because the client is not accessible to the public to cause harm, but this is a dangerous assumption (Richards, 2011). Thinking back to the concept of foreseeability in reference to suicidal risks, there is continued diligence necessary to anticipate/assess for the potential of future violent action.

Danger to Therapist

Therapists are not immune to the unwanted advances and attention of clients. It is necessary to maintain vigilance when assessing a client's awareness and care to observe boundaries set forth in the therapeutic relationship. Informed consent documents are a good way to open discussion of the boundaries of the professional relationship, ethical implications of multiple relationships, and under what circumstances clients may be referred to other therapy resources. Informed consent, however, is not a prevention of a client's unwanted attention. Galeazzi, Elkins, and Curci (2005) reported study findings that 34% of professional mental health clinicians have experienced harassment from a client and eleven percent met the criteria for an official stalking definition. Ninety percent of stalkers were clients being directly treated by the victims. Common experiences for the victims were phone calls, physical presence near the clinician, sending letters and other unwanted materials, spreading rumors, following, and property violation.

There are five categories found to identify general stalking typology: "rejected, intimacy-seeking, incompetent, resentful, and predatory types" (Mullen, Pathe, Purcell, & Stuart, 1999, p. 1246). Each stalking type requires different type of intervention to diminish negative activity. Miller (2014) suggests therapists are more prone to victimization by rejected, intimacy-seeking, and resentful clients due to the nature of the professional duties performed. Empathy and recommendations adverse to a client's favor have potential to be precursors to stalking activity.

In addition to the dangers of stalking behaviors, it is prudent for clinicians to maintain awareness of potential for imminent harm to themselves when working with dangerous clients during sessions. Therapists employed by inpatient programs and violent offender programs may be more susceptible to assault, but private practice clinicians are wise to maintain alertness and safety protocols in the event a client becomes agitated, threatening, or violent.

Protective Measures for Clinical Practice

Protective measures to ensure therapist safety should involve both emergency protocols and environmental considerations. Therapists are wise to schedule new clients, when feasible, at a time when help is more accessible as history of violence is not yet known. Arranging offices in a way that the therapist can easily exit the room without clients obstructing the path and minimizing objects providing potential for use in harm are also important security measures. Security systems and cameras are more cost effective and easy to use to monitor the office setting today while offering encryption for confidentiality. Informed consent documents and signage can provide awareness to clients of the prohibited nature of weapons and intoxication during sessions. Therapists are sensible to probe about a client's firearms and other permits. It is recommended, in addition to the use of clear verbiage in informed consent documents, for clinicians to keep colleagues or peer professional supports abreast of concerns associated with unwanted or excessive client intrusions as a safety measure (Galeazzi et al., 2005).

Therapy conducted in the client's home requires its own set of protective measures. Initial intakes can be performed at an office or confidential setting in public spaces such as a library study room to assess risk for violence.

Therapists can provide initial assessment in the home with a second professional accompanying or checking in part way through the session via phone. Requiring sessions in the home in a space with easy access to an exit is also recommended.

Summary

Risk management is a concept applicable to all clinicians in every setting of client care. Understanding the responsibilities, prudent actions, and resources necessary to minimize risk in practice is a career-long process of inquiry and adaptation. Whether managing risk of suicidal ideation, self-harm, intimate partner violence, or potentially dangerous clients, the sage clinician remains current through understanding and action. Understanding is observed through the awareness and discussion of risk factors identified in most recent research. Action is demonstrated by maintaining a mindful approach to managing client risks with a combination of using consultation in supervision/peer groups, documenting all decision-making processes, and attending to, rather than denying, the potential for both ethical and legal repercussions. Clinicians are in a field too acquainted with risk; it is a professional hazard. Rather than deny this discomfort, it is crucial practitioners arm themselves with understanding, a knowledgeable network, and realistic awareness of risk to appropriately manage clinical action and protect their ability to practice in the future.

References

Andover, M. S., Morris, B. W., Wren, A., & Bruzzese, M. E. (2012). The co-occurrence of non-suicidal self-injury and attempted suicide among adolescents: Distinguishing risk factors and psychosocial correlates. *Child and Adolescent Psychiatry and Mental Health, 6*(11), 1–7. doi: 10.1186/1753-2000-6-11.

Bograd, M., & Mederos, F. (1999). Battering and couples therapy: Universal screening and selection of treatment modality. *Journal of Marital and Family Therapy, 25*(3), 291–312. doi: 10.1111/j.1752-0606.1999.tb00249.x.

Brown, T. B., & Kimball, T. (2013). Cutting to live: A phenomenology of self-harm. *Journal of Marital and Family Therapy, 39*(2), 195–208. doi: 10.1111/j.1752-0606.2011.00270.x.

Campbell, J. C., Webster, D., Koziol-McLain, J., Block, C., Campbell, D., Curry, M. A., … Laughon, K. (2003). Risk factors for femicide in abusive relationships: Results from a multisite case control study. *American Journal of Public Health, 93*(7), 1089–1097. doi: 10.2105/AJPH.93.7.1089.

Center for Disease Control and Prevention: National Center for Injury Prevention and Control Division of Violence Prevention. (2015). *Suicide facts at a glance*. Retrieved from http://www.cdc.gov/violenceprevention/pdf/suicide-datasheet-a.pdf.

Edwards, S. J., & Sachmann, M. D. (2010). No-suicide contracts, no-suicide agreements, and no suicide assurances: A study of their nature, utilization, perceived effectiveness, and potential to cause harm. *Crisis, 31*(6), 290–302. doi: 10.1027/0227-5910/a000048.

Friedman, R. A. (2006). Violence and mental illness – How strong is the link? *New England Journal of Medicine, 355*(20), 2064–2066. doi: 10.1056/NEJMp068229.

Galeazzi, G. M., Elkins, K., & Curci, P. (2005). Emergency psychiatry: The stalking of mental health professionals by patients. *Psychiatric Services, 56*(2), 137–138. doi: 10.1176/appi.ps.56.2.137.

Halstead, R. O., Pavkov, T. W., Hecker, L. L., & Seliner, M. M. (2014). Family dynamics and self injury behaviors: A correlation analysis. *Journal of Marital and Family Therapy, 40*(2), 246–259. doi: 10.1111/j.1752-0606.2012.00336.x.

Jacobs, D. G., Baldessarini, R. J., Conwell, Y., Fawcett, J. A., Horton, L., Meltzer, H., ... Simon, R. I. (2010). *Practice guidelines for the assessment and treatment of patients with suicidal behaviors*. Retrieved from http://psychiatryonline.org/pb/assets/raw/sitewide/practice_guidelines/guidelines/suicide.pdf.

Jobes, D., Linehan, M., & Yanez, D. C. (2015) *Principles of effective suicide care: Evidence-based treatments* [PowerPoint Slides]. Retrieved from http://zerosuicide.sprc.org/sites/zerosuicide.actionallianceforsuicideprevention.org/files/Principles%20of%20Effective%20Suicide%20Care%202-10-15%20slides.pdf.

Jobes, D., Rudd, M., Overholser, J., & Joiner, T. (2008). Ethical and competent care of suicidal patients: Contemporary challenges, new developments, and considerations for clinical practice. *Professional Psychology: Research and Practice, 39*(4), 405–413. doi: 10.1037/a0012896.

Kerr, P. L., Muehlenkamp, J. J., & Turner, J. M. (2010). Non-suicidal self-injury: A review of current research for family medicine and primary care physicians. *Journal of the American Board of Family Medicine, 23*(2), 240–259. doi: 10.3122/jabfm.2010.02.090110.

Levine, P. A., & Kline, M. (2007). *Trauma through a child's eyes*. Berkley, CA: North Atlantic Books.

Linehan, M. [UWTV]. (2013, November 26). Suicidal individuals: Evaluation, therapies, and ethics – Part 2 – 2007 [video file]. Retrieved from https://www.youtube.com/watch?v=BN_2rP5ldoQ.

Melonas, J. M. (2011). Patients at risk for suicide: Risk management and patient safety considerations to protect the patient and the physician. *Innovations in Clinical Neuroscience, 8*(3), 45–49. doi: 10.1176/pn.39.8.0024.

Menninger, J. A. (2001). *Involuntary treatment: Hospitalization and medications*. Retrieved from http://www.brown.edu/Courses/BI_278/Other/Clerkship/Didactics/Readings/INVOLUNTARY%20TREATMENT.pdf.

Miller, A. [Newsletter Article] (2014). Dealing with improper contact. *Monitor, 45*(9), 72. Retrieved from http://www.apa.org/monitor/2014/10/improper-contact.aspx.

Monahan, J., Steadman, H., Silver, E., Appelbaum, P., Robbins, P., Mulvey, E., Banks, S. (2001). *Rethinking risk assessment: The MacArthur study of mental disorder and violence.* New York, NY: Oxford University Press.

Mullen, P. E., Pathe, M., Purcell, R., & Stuart, G. W. (1999). Study of stalkers. *American Journal of Psychiatry, 156*(8), 1244–1249. doi: 10.1176/ajp.156.8.1244.

Peterson, J., Freedenthal, S., Sheldon, C., & Andersen, R. (2008). Non-suicidal self-injury in adolescents. *Psychiatry, 5*(11), 20–26. Retrieved from http://innovationscns.com/nonsuicidal-self-injury-in-adolescents/.

Richards, L. (2011, April). The dangerous patient. *Avoiding Liability Bulletin.* Retrieved from www.cphins.com/legalresources/bulletin/dangerous-patient.

Rogers, J. R., Gueulette, C. M., Abbey-Hines, J., Carney, J. V., & Werth, J. L. (2001). Rational suicide: An empirical investigation of counselor attitudes. *Journal of Counseling and Development, 79*(3), 365–372. doi: 10.1002/j.1556-6676.2001.tb01982.x.

Rosen, K. H., Matheson, J. L., Stith, S. M., McCollum, E. E., & Locke, L. D. (2003). Negotiated time-out: A de-escalation tool for couples. *Journal of Marital and Family Therapy, 29*(3), 291–298. doi 10.1111/j.1752-0606.2003.tb01207.x.

Schacht, R. L., Dimidjian, S., George, W. H., & Berns, S. B. (2009). Domestic violence assessment procedures among couple therapists. *Journal of Marital and Family Therapy, 35*(1), 47–59. doi: 10.1111/j.1752-0606.2008.00095.x.

Sher, L., & Labode, V. (2011). Teaching health care professionals about suicide safety planning. *Psychiatria Danubina, 23*(4), 396–397.

Simon, R. I. (2002). Suicide risk assessment: What is the standard of care? *Journal of the American Academy of Psychiatry and the Law, 30*, 340–344.

Singh, J. P., Grann, M., & Fazel, S. (2011). A comparative study of risk assessment tools: A systematic review and metaregression analysis of 68 studies involving 25,980 participants. *Clinical Psychology Review, 31*(3), 499–513. doi: 10.1016/j.cpr.2010.11.009.

Smith, D. B., Whiting, J. B., Karakurt, G., Oka, M., & Servino, D. (2013). The self assessment of future events scale (SAFE): Assessing perceptions of risk for future violence in intimate partner relationships. *Journal of Marital and Family Therapy, 39*(3), 314–329. doi: 10.1111/j.1752-0606.2012.00319.x.

Stanley, B., & Brown, G. K. (2008). *Safety plan treatment manual to reduce suicide risk: Veterans version.* Retrieved from http://www.mentalhealth.va.gov/docs/va_safety_planning_manual.pdf.

Stith, S. M., McCollum, E. E., Amanor-Boadu, Y., & Smith, D. (2012). Systemic perspectives on intimate partner violence treatment. *Journal of Marital and Family Therapy, 38*(1), 220–240. doi: 10.1111/j.1752-0606.2011.00245.x.

Todahl, J., & Walters, E. (2011). Universal screening for intimate partner violence: A systematic review. *Journal of Marital and Family Therapy, 37*(3), 355–369. doi: 10.1111/j.1752-0606.2009.00179.x.

Truman, J. L., & Morgan, R. E. [Special Report]. (2014). Nonfatal domestic violence, 2003-2012. *U.S. Department of Justice, Office of Justice Programs, Bureau of Justice Statistics*. Retrieved from http://www.bjs.gov/content/pub/pdf/ndv0312.pdf.

Whiting, J. B., Oka, M., & Fife, S. T. (2012). Appraisal distortions and intimate partner violence: Gender, power, and interaction. *Journal of Marital and Family Therapy, 38*(supplement s1), 133–149. doi: 10.1111/j.1752-0606.2011.00285.x.

World Health Organization. (2014). *Preventing suicide: A global imperative*. Retrieved from http://apps.who.int/iris/bitstream/10665/131056/1/9789241564779_eng.pdf?ua=1&ua=1.

9

Spirituality and Religion

Rebecca A. Cobb, Jacob B. Priest, and Taimyr B. Strachan

> Marcella and her husband, Micah, attend family therapy with their 17-year-old son, Jeremiah. Marcella reports that she and her husband are concerned about Jeremiah. For the past 3 months, Jeremiah has been depressed, his grades have been getting worse, and he has been distancing himself from his friends at school and church. During the course of therapy, Jeremiah tells the therapist in confidence that he thinks he is gay. He believes that homosexuality is a sin and is fearful of his feelings toward one of his best friends. Jeremiah says that he is also afraid that if his parents knew, they would kick him out of the house or never speak to him again. He tells the therapist that he has asked God to change him, but his feelings remain.

Introduction

Spirituality and religion play a dynamic role in family life. Family therapists are likely to encounter situations in which spirituality and religion intersect with family dynamics and the process of therapy (Wolf & Stevens, 2001). Often, spirituality and religion are strengths and resources that can be used to reach therapeutic goals. Other times, spirituality and religion may relate to conflict and distress within families.

The therapist's spiritual and religious values also affect the process of therapy. The therapist's values may influence aspects of family dynamics that are emphasized or deemphasized, or may impact selected treatment modalities (Haug, 1998a, 1998b). Additionally, therapists may work with families whose spiritual and religious values are dissimilar to their own. Though this dissimilarity may serve to benefit both the therapist and the family, value-based conflicts may negatively affect the therapeutic process (Priest & Wickel, 2011).

Until recently, the couple and family therapy (CFT) field lacked literature addressing the impact of spirituality and religion. However, within the past 15 to 20 years, the CFT field has experienced an increase in the number of journal articles that address spirituality and religion. Research on CFT clinicians (Carlson, Kirkpatrick, Hecker, & Killmer, 2002), educators (Carlson, McGeorge, & Anderson, 2011; Grams, Carlson, & McGeorge, 2007), and students (McNeil, Pavkov, Hecker, & Killmer, 2012; Prest, Russel, & D'Souza, 1999) document the essential role of incorporating the spiritual and religious aspects of clients' lives into CFT. Given the role of spirituality and religion in CFT, the question is not *whether* to address issues of the sacred with spiritual and religious clients, but when and how to address these issues (Post & Wade, 2009) in the most ethical and culturally competent way possible.

In this chapter, we aim to help family therapists navigate ethical issues related to spirituality and religion in CFT, as in our case scenario presented previously. We begin with a definition of spirituality and religion and an overview of the prevalence of religious beliefs in the United States. We then provide a discussion of how couple and family therapists can develop spiritual and religious competence; specifically, we discuss five ways in which therapists can gain a greater understanding of their clients' spiritual and religious values and effectively apply this knowledge to treatment. Next, we discuss ways in which therapists may gain awareness of their own spiritual and religious values and discuss ways in which therapists may use this awareness to avoid imposing values on clients in family therapy. Additionally, we provide a conceptualization of value-based conflicts in therapy and present a five-step decision-making model (Kocet & Herlihy, 2014) to assess and resolve value-based conflicts. Then, we provide a brief overview of ethical considerations for agency practice. Finally, we return to the case example provided at the beginning of the chapter and discuss the aforementioned topics as they relate to the intersection of clients' spirituality, religion, and sexual orientation in therapy.

Spirituality and Religion

To address issues of spirituality and religion in CFT, it is first important to distinguish between the two (Carlson et al., 2002). Spirituality has been defined as "the feelings, thoughts, experiences and behaviors that arise from a search for the sacred" (Hill et al., 2000, p. 66). The definition of religion encompasses the definition of spirituality, but also includes "a setting or context that is designed to foster the search for the sacred" (p. 66). Though both spirituality and religion encompass a search for the sacred, religion is typically understood as an organized social entity with defined boundaries and is associated with particular rituals and practices. Alternatively, spirituality contains less clearly defined boundaries and is viewed as a more personal attribute that is concerned with subjective experience (Berkel, Constantine, & Olson, 2007).

More than 80% of American adults say that they are absolutely certain or fairly certain there is as God (Pew Research Center, 2015a) and 53% say that religion is very important in their lives (Pew Research Center, 2015b). Although the numbers of religiously unaffiliated, agnostic, or atheist have grown substantially within the past few years, approximately 36% of American adults report attending religious services at least once a week, and 33% report attending once or twice a month (Pew Research Center, 2015c). Moreover, 52% of American adults think that religion can answer all or most of today's problems (Gallup, 2015).

For many, religion provides a framework that reinforces the importance of spirituality, marriage, and family life (Cornwall, 2013). Religious rituals often mark family events including births, weddings, and deaths. Religion can help to support the creation of family identity, provide a source of hope and optimism, and is linked to many other positive family outcomes (Cornwall, 2013). For example, Petts (2014) found that youth who attend religious services with their parents in late childhood have better psychological well-being throughout adolescence. Additionally, the reported strength of a person's relationship with God is associated with religious communication between partners, and increased religious communication is associated with better marital quality (David & Stafford, 2014). Overall, religion in the home is frequently associated with better outcomes for both children and parents (Mahoney, Pargament, Tarakeshwar, & Swank, 2001).

Although religion is frequently associated with positive family outcomes, definitions of marriage and family have been restricted in the name of religion. For example, throughout much of the 20th century, many religious denominations in the United States have strongly opposed interracial marriage. The political power of religious institutions helped keep interracial marriage illegal until 1967 when the U.S. Supreme Court deemed antimiscegenation laws unconstitutional. Similarly, although the U.S. Supreme Court recently ruled that state-level bans of same-sex marriage are unconstitutional, many religious institutions and individuals continue their opposition to same-sex marriage (Pew Research Center, 2015d). This may result in conflict for many families.

For example, lesbian and gay youth whose parents' religious views are against lesbian, gay, bisexual, and transgender (LGBT) orientations are at greater risk for chronic suicidal thoughts and suicide attempts (Gibbs & Goldbach, 2015). In the case scenario at the beginning of this chapter, we highlight this conflict. In situations similar to Jeremiah's, parents' religious views may create an oppressive atmosphere in which children feel that their sexual orientation is wrong or immoral. Furthermore, feelings of estrangement could result in internalizing or externalizing behaviors such as suicidal thoughts or attempts (Gibbs & Goldbach, 2015). Given the impact of spirituality and religion on individual, couple, and family functioning, it is imperative that CFTs maintain competence and a willingness to address topics related to spirituality and religion.

Spiritual and Religious Competence in Therapy

Most mental health professional codes of ethics require clinicians to remain educated about new developments within the field, as well as mandate that clinicians maintain competence through trainings and supervised experience (e.g., American Association for Marriage and Family Therapy [AAMFT], 2015; American Counseling Association [ACA], 2014; American Psychological Association [APA], 2010; National Association of Social Workers [NASW], 2008). In addition, accredited mental health training programs require students to demonstrate a commitment to diversity and the wide range of elements it encompasses. Furthermore, all mental health professional codes of ethics include aspirational or direct statements about diversity, nondiscrimination, and cultural competence.

An array of literature supports the need for spiritual and religious competence among therapists (e.g., Prest et al., 1999), with spirituality and religion integrated within training, curriculum, and supervision. McNeil et al. (2012) found that, among a sample of 135 graduate students from programs accredited by the Commission on Accreditation for Marriage and Family Therapy Education, 81.4% indicated that they were not offered a course on spirituality and religion, 35.7% indicated that they wanted to learn more about integrating religion into family therapy, and 46% indicated the desire to learn more about integrating spirituality with assessment and interventions. Similarly, others have raised concern that there "is a lack of accredited [CFT] training programs for therapists in the use of spirituality in therapy" (Rusu & Turliuc, 2011, p. 89). If therapists are not trained to address spirituality and religion, they risk avoiding the topic because of discomfort, or addressing spiritual and religious issues in an ineffective or even potentially harmful manner (Ahn & Miller, 2010).

To provide competent, ethical care of clients, it is recommend that family therapists seek education, training, and/or supervised experience specifically regarding the integration of client spirituality and religion in family therapy. Lack of familiarity with the particular spiritual and/or religious beliefs and traditions of clients may heighten couple and family therapists' need to seek opportunities to gain competence (Duba & Watts, 2009). Next, we discuss five ways couple and family therapists can learn about the religious traditions of their clients.

Understand Clients' Spiritual and Religious Beliefs

First, it is important that couple and family therapists understand spiritual and religious beliefs from a client-centered perspective (Duba & Watts, 2009). In accordance with a client-centered approach, couple and family therapists must avoid making assumptions, but instead maintain a stance of curiosity about the spiritual and religious beliefs and practices of individuals and the collective family system. Understanding family system dynamics through lenses of spirituality and religion can aid in treatment endeavors. Spiritual and religious assessments (verbal and written) may aid in this process (e.g., Anderson & Worthen, 1997; Ellison, 1983; Genia, 1991; Hall & Edwards, 1996; Hodge, 2005, 2013; Watson, 1997).

Explore Diverse Religious and Spiritual Cultural Contexts

Second, gaining knowledge of diverse faith traditions using available professional literature is important. Although couple and family therapists learn from clients, we also have a responsibility to educate ourselves on cultural contexts. A 2014 issue of *Family Therapy Magazine* titled "Spirituality and Faith: Reflections for Family Therapists" supports this goal by exploring how diverse spiritual and religious beliefs impact the lives of clients and family therapy. These types of resources help expand knowledge of different religious backgrounds by exploring important world religions such as Buddhism, Christianity, and Islam (AAMFT, 2014). Additionally, Walsh's (2008) text *Spiritual Resources in Family Therapy* provides an overview of ways in which spiritual resources may be used in family therapy with multifaith and culturally diverse clients.

Gain Advanced Training to Increase Competency

Third, couple and family therapists should seek opportunities to gain formal education or training to further their religious competence. Family therapists may find presentations on the integration of spirituality and religion in family studies and CFT practice at state, national, and international conferences. Additionally, many universities offer courses specifically on theology and religious studies, with some focusing on the integration of spirituality and religion. CFT training programs may also offer this type of course. Couple and family therapists can pursue continuing education opportunities that focus on the topic via seminars and workshops.

Seek Consultation or Supervision

Fourth, when formal education and trainings are not available, couple and family therapists should seek consultation or supervision from knowledgeable colleagues (Duba & Watts, 2009), particularly if needed in relation to clients the couple and family therapist is seeing. Preferably, the colleague or supervisor should have knowledge and experience with the faith tradition(s) of the clients with which the therapist is working. Many agency settings, for example, have an identified cultural consultant available for assistance in matters related to client diversity. Ideally, these consultants should also be knowledgeable of various faith traditions.

Use Community Resources

Finally, to gain spiritual and religious competence, Berkel et al. (2007) express the need to use community resources. For example, they encourage CFT faculty members in training programs to invite leaders from diverse spiritual and religious traditions (e.g., pastors, priests, rabbis) to participate on panels in which different presenting issues (e.g., abortion, divorce, same-sex marriage) are discussed from the perspectives of different faith traditions. Couple and family therapists are also encouraged to seek consultation and collaboration with religious leaders (Duba & Watts,

2009; Weaver, Koenig, & Larson, 1997) for informational (not supervisory) purposes, while maintaining client confidences.

Therapist Values

To provide care that addresses the spirituality and religion of clients, couple and family therapists must also maintain an awareness of their own assumptions, values, and biases as related to spirituality and religion (Berkel et al., 2007). Many values originate from—or are closely related to—spiritual and religious beliefs and practices. Haug (1998a, 1998b) proposes that therapists' spiritual and religious beliefs and values organize the ways in which therapists interact with clients, conceptualize pathology, interpret presenting problems, and ultimately make treatment decisions. Similarly, those who do not identify as religious, or who identify as agnostic or atheist, also need to examine how the values associated with these stances affect their interactions with clients.

Therapists' spiritual and religious values, or the lack thereof, can also create conflict between therapists and clients. Examples of religious-based value conflicts include

> (a) a Catholic counselor and a client considering an abortion, (b) a Mormon counselor and a client whose lifestyle includes smoking cigarettes and drinking alcohol … [and (c)] a Jewish counselor and a bigoted client who uses offensive and anti-Semitic language to describe Jews (Kocet & Herlihy, 2014, p. 183).

Priest and Wickel (2011) used Bowen's family systems theory (Kerr & Bowen, 1988) to conceptualize value conflicts in therapy. They suggest that when clients and therapist's values differ, anxiety is introduced into the therapeutic system. As anxiety increases, the need for togetherness also increases (Kerr & Bowen, 1988). This togetherness need may lead the therapist to fuse with their values (Priest & Wickel, 2011), which can result in inflexible stances in therapy that create a myopic view of the situation, leading to decrease options available to the therapist (Kerr & Bowen, 1998). "Instead of seeking options that are most beneficial for the client and therapeutic relationship, a therapist may engage in patterned behavior in an attempt to reduce anxiety" (Priest & Wickel, 2011, pp. 142–143). If the therapist cannot effectively manage this anxiety, they may do harm to clients by actively discriminating against or imposing their own values on clients.

Examples of this process are evident in recent legal cases that document significant challenges related to values conflicts in therapy. In *Keeton v.*

Anderson-Wiley (2010), a graduate student attending Augusta State University expressed that she preferred not to engage in therapy with LGBT clients unless it involved conversion therapy. Similarly, in *Ward v. Wilbanks* (2010, 2012), graduate student Julea Ward adamantly refused to work with a gay client. In both cases, the students asserted that counseling LGBT clients conflicted with their religious beliefs; they were ultimately dismissed from their respective counselor education programs because of that refusal. These cases highlight the difficulty that some clinicians experience when there is a need to integrate personal religious beliefs and values with codes of ethics and general professional values. Regarding LGBT issues, professional values have evolved significantly since homosexuality was removed as a psychological disorder from the *Diagnostic and Statistical Manual of Mental Disorders* in 1973. Modern treatment now focuses on the effects of being a stigmatized sexual minority, instead focusing on LGBT affirmative practices (Johnson, 2012). Even so, there are continued political movements to introduce bills to provide for exemptions to providing services for LGBT individuals (America Civil Liberties Union, 2015).

Imposition of Values in Therapy

In addition, professional associations such as AAMFT and ACA assert that family therapists and counselors must actively avoid the imposition of their own spiritual and religious values on clients throughout the therapeutic process (Gonsiorek, Richards, Pargament, & McMinn, 2009; Haug, 1998a, 1998b). The AAMFT Code of Ethics states,

> [Couple and family therapists] respect the rights of clients to make decisions and help them to understand the consequences of these decisions. Therapists clearly advise clients that clients have the responsibility to make decisions regarding relationships such as cohabitation, marriage, divorce, separation, reconciliation, custody, and visitation (AAMFT, 2015, 1.8).

Similarly, the ACA Code of Ethics states that counselors must be "aware of—and avoid imposing—their own values, attitudes, beliefs, and behaviors" (ACA, 2014, A.4.b). For example, if a therapist's religious belief suggests that cohabitation before marriage is immoral, the therapist must allow client autonomy regarding the decision to cohabitate regardless of the therapist's religious belief.

Often, the imposition of values can go unrecognized by therapists due to good intentions for client well-being. For example, when exploring the pros and cons of making the decision to have an abortion, a devout Catholic therapist may sway conversation toward focus on the cons of abortion out of fear of the client ultimately experiencing moral guilt, shame, and humiliation. Likewise, a devout Muslim therapist may outwardly or inadvertently encourage clients to avoid conforming to American standards, such as encouraging a Muslim woman to wear her hijab and stay true to her beliefs, in spite of her wishes. In both cases, although the therapist may have the best of intentions for the client, the imposition of one's own values into the therapy process directly violates client autonomy in decision-making. If family therapists impose their own values on clients, the clinician is responsible for seeking supervision and/or their own therapy to address the source of the problem. Ideally, the therapist should seek supervisors and therapists who are skilled in working with religious clientele (Whitman & Bidell, 2014).

Therapists must not only be aware of imposing their values on the couples and families they work with, but they must also possess tools to navigate situations in which the spiritual and religious beliefs of the therapist may conflict with their clients' values. To navigate value conflicts in therapy and avoid the imposition of values on clients, Kocet and Herlihy (2014) developed a five-step decision-making model. These steps include: (1) determine the nature of the value-based conflict, (2) explore core issues and potential barriers to providing the appropriate standard of care, (3) seek remediation and assistance to any blocks to providing the appropriate standard of care, (4) determine and evaluate possible courses of action, and (5) ensure that therapy promotes client welfare.

Determine the Nature of the Value-Based Conflict

According to Kocet and Herlihy's model (2014), when a value conflict arises in therapy, couple and family therapists should first determine the nature of the value-based conflict. Specifically, they suggest examining whether the value-based conflict is personal or professional. A personal value conflict occurs when one's own values impede the counseling relationship. A professional value conflict occurs when there is a deficit in skills or training to provide the appropriate standard of care to the client.

Explore Core Issues and Potential Barriers to Providing the Appropriate Standard of Care

Once the type of conflict is identified, the second step is to examine the core of the value-based conflict; this is accomplished by exploring core issues and possible obstacles to providing the appropriate standard of care. Personal value-based conflicts can be addressed by seeking opportunities to increase therapist self-awareness and seeking external help from colleagues, supervisors, or the literature. When there is a personal value conflict between therapist and client values, Kocet and Herlihy (2014) urge exploration of the therapist's personal, moral, and/or religious biases, as well as the impact of their personal experiences. This examination can aid the therapist in identifying potential barriers to therapy as well as understanding how personal values may impede the therapeutic relationship. A professional value conflict may stem from lack of skill or training necessary for competent practice or conflicts from countertransference. For couple and family therapists, countertransference can arise from several sources: the therapist's relationship with the system, in reaction to the dynamics of the system, or the culture, values, or other characteristics of the family system (Kocet & Herlihy, 2014).

Seek Remediation and Assistance to Any Blocks to Providing the Appropriate Standard of Care

In this third step, the therapist focuses on receiving the assistance necessary to provide the appropriate standard of care. If the value-based conflict is personal, the therapist may consult colleagues or supervisors in order to identify ways to maintain spiritual/religious beliefs while providing effective counseling. If the value-based conflict is due to professional knowledge-based deficits, the therapist may need to create a remediation plan to increase skill and expertise.

Determine and Evaluate Possible Courses of Action

If the conflict is personal, the therapist needs to examine the rationale and basis for a potential referral and examine if a referral from personal bias is ethical or unethical. Additionally, the therapist should create a plan to work through personal biases that prevent them from resolving the conflict to continue working with the client(s). If the conflict is due to a professional skill deficit, the therapist must consider the ethical implications of a referral and assess the effectiveness of their remediation plan.

Ensure that Therapy Promotes Client Welfare

At this fifth and last step, the couple and family therapist's professional and personal values should have been sufficiently explored to forge a clear treatment path. The therapist must then ensure that proposed actions promote client welfare.

Therapist Self-Awareness of Spiritual and Religious Values

Because values can affect the course of therapy and value conflicts have consequences for both therapists and clients, therapists need to be aware of their spiritual and religious values and understand how these values can affect the process of therapy (Berkel et al., 2007; McNeil et al., 2012; Rusu & Turluic, 2011). By maintaining self-awareness, clinicians may prevent countertransference issues from negatively affecting the therapeutic process and avoid ethical mishaps associated with the integration of spirituality and religion in family therapy (Haug, 1998a, 1998b).

One way for therapists to increase awareness of spiritual and religious values is with a spiritual genogram (Frame, 2000). Though originally designed for use with families in therapy, the spiritual genogram is also a useful tool for family therapists to explore their beliefs. Frame (2000) outlines four steps for the creation and use of the spiritual genogram, which begins with drawing a three-generation genogram. This genogram should include information regarding significant family events (e.g., births, deaths, marriages, divorces). Additionally, the genogram should include important religious events including dates of baptisms, bar and bat mitzvahs, confirmations, samskaras, or other religious ceremonies. Religious or spiritual affiliation can be designated with various colors. The genogram can also include indictors of religious closeness or religious conflict. If there has been conflict based on a member of the family leaving a religious tradition, this could be noted as well.

After the completion of the genogram, the therapist can use it to probe the role and function that religion and spirituality play in the therapist's family of origin (Frame, 2000). The therapist should reflect on questions such as,

> When you were growing up, what role, if any, did religion/spirituality play in your life? What role does it play now? What does your religious/spiritual tradition say about gender? About ethnicity? About sexual orientation [and identity]? How have these beliefs affected you and your extended family? What patterns of behavior and relationships resulting from religion/spirituality emerge for you as your study your genogram? How are you currently maintaining or diverting from those patterns? (Frame, 2000, p. 213)

The therapist may choose to reflect on this individually or as part a supervision experience.

After the therapist has reflected individually on these questions, the next step is to contact members of the therapist's family of origin and discuss the spiritual genogram with them. By reaching out and asking members of the family of origin about patterns identified in the genogram, the therapist can gain information about the past and renegotiate current relationships that are tied to spirituality and religion. The therapist may want to ask the family members questions such as

> How do you perceive the importance of religion/spirituality in our family? How do you think that your experience of the religious/spiritual climate was similar or different from mine? How difficult do you think it has been or would be for family members to seek a different spiritual or religious path than the one that in which we were raised? Who in our family would be supportive and why? Who would not be supportive and why? (Frame, 2000, p. 214)

This new information is then added to the genogram originally constructed by the therapist.

Once the therapist has fully constructed the genogram, the final step is to tie it into the therapist's work with couples and families. The therapist can use this reflection to make connections between past beliefs, experience, and family of origin issues and how this may affect a therapist's work (Frame, 2000). The hope is that as therapists increase awareness of their own spiritual and religious values and how they connect with their family of origin, they will move toward increased understanding and appreciation for the ways in which these values shape their therapeutic practice. Additionally, this practice may assist in increasing awareness of potential blind spots that may inhibit therapeutic work with families (Haug, 1998a, 1998b).

Spiritual and Religious Issues in Agency Settings

The discussion in this chapter thus far has focused on the spiritual and religious values of clients and therapists and the ways in which these values interact. In this section, we briefly discuss how therapists can ethically address issues of spirituality and religion in agency settings. Many practitioners work in agency settings; some therapists work in publically funded agencies; others work in agencies that have ties to a particular religion. Although different agencies place differing emphasis on aspects of spirituality and religion, the following recommendations can help therapists navigate issues of spirituality and religion in agency settings, regardless of affiliation.

First, before implementing spiritual interventions in agency settings, a therapist must assess if clients are open to the topic of discussion

(Ahn & Miller, 2010). This process begins with informed consent. Though many agencies have uniform informed consent documents, many do not address the role of spirituality and religion in the therapeutic process. When possible, therapists may wish to add to the informed consent document a disclosure of openness to the exploration of spiritual and religious values in therapy (Haug, 1998a, 1998b). Moreover, if a therapist is open to using spiritual interventions in therapy, this should also be included in the informed consent document. In so doing, therapists allow clients to make choices regarding treatment options that are in their best interest.

Second, Ahn and Miller (2010) suggest that therapists give attention to language when creating outcome goals and writing progress notes when integrating spirituality and religion into therapy. For example, many agencies require treatment plans with measurable objectives. Words such as "spirituality" or interventions, such as prayer or reading scriptures, may not be measurable or may not fit into the mission of the agency. They suggest using terms such as "relaxation skills" that can encompass the meaning of the spiritual intervention and provide an accurate and measureable outcome.

Finally, couple and family therapists have an ethical mandate to avoid discrimination. Although this is applicable to all therapists, it is particularly salient for those practicing in state-funded agencies to avoid violating laws regarding the separation of church and state. All professional codes of ethics contain a nondiscrimination statement that prevents discrimination on the basis of client characteristics or attributes such as race, age, ethnicity, socioeconomic status, disability, gender, health status, religion, national origin, etc. Some states may legally allow for the discrimination by way of refusal to counsel particular populations (e.g., LGBT) or certain presenting problems (e.g., death with dignity) based on grounds of religious freedom. There will continue to be tensions to navigate between religious and ethical values, and legal dictates. Ultimately, therapists must respect client autonomy and manage their own value-based conflicts to best benefit the therapeutic process.

Spirituality, Religion, and Sexual Orientation

At the beginning of the chapter, we introduced you to three members of a family who were struggling with issues related to spirituality, religion, and sexual orientation. As you may recall, Jeremiah's parents reported that he had been depressed, his grades had been falling, and he had been socially isolating himself. During the course of therapy, Jeremiah confided to the therapist that he thinks he is gay, has feelings for his best friend, and is worried that if his parents find out, he may be kicked out of the house. Although there may be many issues related to the case example that could be addressed, for the purposes of this chapter, we focus specifically on the spiritual and religious values that may be present in family therapy and how they could serve as a benefit or a determent to the therapeutic process.

In the case scenario, it is imperative that the therapist first notice client language that indicates the importance of spiritual and religious beliefs. The clients make mention of church, sin, and asking God for help. These are key topics of discussion with the family as they relate to the presenting problem.

Next, it is important that the therapist seek to understand spiritual and religious beliefs regarding sexual orientation from a client-centered perspective. Specifically, it may be necessary for the therapist to talk with each member of the family regarding its spiritual beliefs and how these relate to sexual orientation. If a therapist knows the religious background of the family, but does not understand how the family practices its beliefs, the therapist may mistakenly make assumptions that could hinder the process of the therapy. It may be that Jeremiah's religious belief informs his views about sexual orientation, leading him to believe that it is a sin. However, it may be that one or both of Jeremiah's parents do not hold the same views. The parents may hold a religious belief that God loves everyone, including those who identify as LGBT. Only by taking a client-centered approach can the therapist avoid making erroneous assumptions regarding the family's religious beliefs. In the case scenario, it would be important to discuss the differing belief systems of each member of the family and the ways in which these differences impact family structure and functioning as related to the presenting problem.

Although the family may hold a set of beliefs that may or may not be in line with its religious affiliation, it would also be important for the therapist to gain an understanding of the doctrinal stance of the family's religion(s) on sexual orientation. This doctrinal stance may affect the religious standing or social support the family receives. For example, Jeremiah's family may face excommunication if his family is Islamic, Mormon, or a member of the Southern Baptist Convention should he come out and/or pursue a same-sex relationship. On the other hand, Jeremiah and his family may find support and acceptance if family members are Quakers or are members of the Episcopal or Unitarian Universalist church, where homosexuality is tolerated and/or accepted. When working with spiritual and religious clients, it is important that therapists understand the doctrinal stances of the religion(s) with which clients are affiliated and how these stances may affect family functioning and the course of therapy.

In addition to understanding the family's religious beliefs and affiliation, clinicians must have a clear understanding of how their own values may affect the therapeutic process. If therapists have a clear understanding of their own values, they may be more likely to avoid imposing values on clients and making harmful treatment decisions. In this case, example, if the therapist believes, as Jeremiah has expressed, that homosexuality is a sin, and they have not worked to examine this belief and how it affects the therapeutic process, the therapist may develop a treatment plan that could result in harm.

For example, if the therapist believes, as does Jeremiah, that homosexuality is a sin; this belief may lead the therapist to work to try to change Jeremiah's sexual orientation. However, this could result in serious harm. Sexual reorientation therapy, or therapy aimed to change the sexual orientation of an individual, leads to "serious psychological and interpersonal problems during the therapy and after its termination" (Shidlo & Schroeder, 2002, p. 254), including depression and suicide attempts. Recently Bradshaw, Dehlin, Crowell, Galliher, and Bradshaw (2015) studied a sample of 1,612 former and current Mormons who engaged in therapy aimed to change their sexual orientation. They found that less than 4% of their sample reported any change in sexual attraction and 37% reported that the therapy was moderately or severely harmful. As previously stated, the stance from all of the major mental health professions is that homosexuality is not a disorder does not require treatment; this is based on considerable research and clinical evidence. Additionally, sexual reorientation therapy for minors is now illegal in four states and the District of Columbia. Although Jeremiah's and the therapist's beliefs may be congruent, if therapists are not aware of their own spiritual and religious values, they may use treatments that could worsen Jeremiah's depression and/or his social isolation.

If the therapist working with Jeremiah and his family has different beliefs regarding sexual orientation, this could also result in harm if not carefully addressed. For example, the therapist may come from a religious tradition that accepts and supports same-sex relationships. On the other hand, the therapist may be agnostic or atheist and not agree with the religious assumption that homosexuality is a sin. In either case, if the therapist reacts to Jeremiah's belief in a way that tries to get him to change his belief regarding homosexuality or God, this could result in Jeremiah feeling alienated, the family feeling disrespected, and/or the therapist providing treatment that does not respect the family's autonomy. Regardless of the values or belief system of the therapist, the therapist must help the family to explore its own values and beliefs as they relate to the presenting problem. This task may involve an exploration of the root of each member's beliefs regarding sexuality and a discussion of the ways in which particular beliefs are valued over other available options. All decisions in therapy include both personal and professional values; it is incumbent upon the couple and family therapist to explore any issues of their own that may be impediments to treatment.

Conclusion

Ethically addressing spirituality and religion in therapy can be complex. Couple and family therapists have a responsibility to inform clients of their openness and willingness to engage in discussion of spirituality and religion in therapy. In addition, couple and family therapists must follow codes of ethics that prohibit the imposition of values on clients and discrimination based on religious belief. To competently deal with this complexity, it is important that family therapists actively seek to understand clients' spiritual and religious beliefs through client-centered conversation and assessment, while seeking knowledge, training, and consultation about varied spiritual beliefs and religious traditions. Similar to other areas of cultural competence, the expectation is not that clinicians have knowledge of all that there is to know about all faith traditions. Rather, the expectation is that family therapists maintain a sense of openness and the desire to learn more about the role of spirituality and religion in family life and clinical practice.

Additionally, clinicians must actively examine their own spiritual and religious beliefs and the ways in which these beliefs impact the therapeutic process; the therapist may consider the use of the previously mentioned spiritual genogram (Frame, 2000) or other techniques or activities to aid in this process specifically as it relates to beliefs regarding sexuality. By increasing knowledge and self-awareness of spiritual and religious beliefs, couple and family therapists can better navigate value-based conflicts, avoid ethical mishaps, and provide competent care to the individuals, couples, and families they serve.

References

Ahn, Y. J., & Miller, M. M. (2010). Can MFTs address spirituality with clients in publically funded agencies? *Contemporary Family Therapy, 32*(2), 102–116. doi: 10.1007/s10591-009-9107-5.

American Association for Marriage and Family Therapy. (AAMFT). (2014, January/February). Spirituality & faith: Reflections for family therapists. *Family Therapy Magazine, 13.*

American Association for Marriage and Family Therapy (AAMFT). (2015). *American Association for Marriage and Family Therapy: Code of ethics.* Alexandria, VA: Author.

American Civil Liberties Union. (2015). *Anti-LGBT religious exemption legislation across the country.* Retrieved from https://www.aclu.org/anti-lgbt-religious-exemption-legislation-across-country#rfra16.

American Counseling Association. (ACA). (2014). *ACA code of ethics: As approved by the ACA Governing Council, 2014.* Retrieved from https://www.counseling.org/resources/aca-code-of-ethics.pdf.

American Psychological Association. (APA). (2010). *Ethical principles of psychologists and code of conduct.* Retrieved from http://www.apa.org/ethics/code/principles.pdf.

Anderson, D. A., & Worthen, D. (1997). Exploring a fourth dimension: Spirituality as a resource for the couple therapist. *Journal of Marriage and Family Therapy, 23*(1), 3–12. doi: 10.1111/j.1752-0606.1997.tb00227.x.

Berkel, L. A., Constantine, M. G., & Olson, E. A. (2007). Supervisor multicultural competence: Addressing religious and spiritual issues with counseling students in supervision. *The Clinical Supervisor, 26*(1-2), 3–15. doi: 10.1300/J001v26n01_02.

Bradshaw, K., Dehlin, J. P., Crowell, K. A., Galliher, R. V., & Bradshaw, W. S. (2015). Sexual orientation change efforts through psychotherapy for LGBQ individuals affiliated with the Church of Jesus Christ of Latter-day Saints. *Journal of Sex & Marital Therapy, 41*(4), 391–412. doi: 10.1080/0092623X.2014.915907.

Carlson, T. D., Kirkpatrick, K., Hecker, L., & Killmer, M. (2002). Religion, spirituality, and marriage and family therapy: A study of family therapists' beliefs about the appropriateness of addressing religious and spiritual issues in therapy. *The American Journal of Family Therapy, 30*(2), 157–171. doi: 10.1080/019261802753573867.

Carlson, T. S., McGeorge, C. R., & Anderson, A. (2011). The importance of spirituality in couple and family therapy: A comparative study of therapists' and educators' beliefs. *Contemporary Family Therapy, 33*(1), 3–16. doi: 10.1007/s10591-010-9136-0.

Cornwall, M. (2013). Religion and family research in the twenty-first century. In G. W. Peterson & K. R. Bush (Eds.), *Handbook of marriage and the family* (3rd ed., pp. 637–655). New York, NY: Springer.

David, P., & Stafford, L. (2014). A relational approach to religion and spirituality in marriage: The role of couples' religious communication in marital satisfaction. *Journal of Family Issues, 36*(2), 232–249. doi: 10.1177/0192513X13485922.

Duba, J. D., & Watts, R. E. (2009). Therapy with religious couples. *Journal of Clinical Psychology: In Session, 62*(2), 210–223. doi: 10.1002/jclp.20567.

Ellison, C. (1983). Spiritual well-being: Conceptualization and measurement. *Journal of Psychology and Theology, 11*(4), 330–340.

Frame, M. W. (2000). The spiritual genogram in family therapy. *Journal of Marital and Family Therapy, 26*(2), 211–216. doi: 10.1111/j.1752-0606.2000.tb00290.x.

Gallup. (2015). *Religion.* [Data file]. Retrieved from http://www.gallup.com/poll/1690/religion.aspx.

Genia, V. (1991). The Spiritual Experience Index: A measure of spiritual maturity. *Journal of Religion and Health, 30*(4), 337–347. doi: 10.1007/BF00986905.

Gibbs, J. J., & Goldbach, J. (2015). Religious conflict, sexual identity, and suicidal behaviors among LGBT young adults. *Archives of Suicide Research, 19*(3), 472–488. doi: 10.1037/sgd0000124.

Gonsiorek, J. C., Richards, P. S., Pargament, K. I., & McMinn, M. R. (2009). Ethical challenges and opportunities at the edge: Incorporating spirituality and religion into psychotherapy. *Professional Psychology: Research and Practice, 40*(4), 385–389. doi: 10.1037/a0016488.

Grams, W. A., Carlson, T. S., & McGeorge, C. R. (2007). Integrating spirituality into family therapy training: An exploration of faculty members' beliefs. *Contemporary Family Therapy, 29*(3), 147–161. doi: 10.1007/s10591-007-9042-2.

Hall, T. W., & Edwards, K. J. (1996). The initial development and factor analysis of the Spiritual Assessment Inventory. *Journal of Psychology and Theology, 24*(3), 233–246.

Haug, I. (1998a). Including a spiritual dimension in family therapy: Ethical considerations. *Contemporary Family Therapy, 20*(2), 181–194. doi: 10.1023/A:1025077425777.

Haug, I. E. (1998b). Spirituality as a dimension of family therapists' clinical training. *Contemporary Family Therapy, 20*(4), 471–483. doi: 10.1023/A:1021628132514.

Hill, P. C., Pargament, K. I., Hood, R. W., McCullough, M. E., Swyers, J. P., … Zinnbauer, B. J. (2000). Conceptualizing religion and spirituality: Points of commonality, points of departure. *Journal for the Theory of Social Behaviour, 30*(1), 51–77. doi: 10.1111/1468-5914.00119.

Hodge, D. R. (2005). Developing a spiritual assessment toolbox: A discussion of the strengths and limitations of five different assessment methods. *Health & Social Work, 30*(4), 314–323. doi: 10.1093/hsw/30.4.314.

Hodge, D. R. (2013). Implicit spiritual assessment: An alternative approach for assessing client spirituality. *Social Work, 58*(3), 223–230. doi: 10.1093/sw/swt019.

Johnson, S. (2012). Gay affirmative psychotherapy with lesbian, gay, and bisexual individuals: implications for contemporary psychotherapy research. *American Journal of Orthopsychiatry, 82*(4), 516–522. doi: 10.1111/j.1939-0025.2012.01180.x.

Keeton v. Anderson-Wiley, No. 1:10-CV-00099-JRH-WLB, 733 F. Supp. 2d 1368 (S.D. Ga., Aug. 20, 2010).

Kerr, M. E., & Bowen, M. (1988). *Family evaluation*. New York, NY: Norton.

Kocet, M. M., & Herlihy, B. J. (2014). Addressing value-based conflicts within the counseling relationship: A decision-making model. *Journal of Counseling & Development, 92*(2), 180–186. doi: 10.1002/j.1556-6676.2014.00146.x.

Mahoney, A., Pargament, K. I., Tarakeshwar, N., & Swank, A. B. (2001). Religion in the home in the 1980s and 1990s: A meta-analytic review and conceptual analysis of links between religion, marriage, and parenting. *Journal of Family Psychology, 15*(4), 559–596. doi: 10.1037/1941-1022.S.1.63.

McNeil, S. N., Pavkov, T. W., Hecker, L. L., & Killmer, J. M. (2012). Marriage and family therapy graduate students' satisfaction with training regarding religion and spirituality. *Contemporary Family Therapy, 34*(4), 468–480. doi: 10.1007/s10591-012-9205-7.

National Association of Social Workers. (NASW). (2008). *Code of ethics of the National Association of Social Workers* (as approved by the 1996 NASW delegate assembly and revised by the 2008 NASW delegate Assembly). Retrieved from https://www.socialworkers.org/pubs/code/code.asp.

Petts, R. J. (2014). Family, religious attendance, and trajectories of psychological well-being among youth. *Journal of Family Psychology, 28*(6), 759–768. doi: 10.1037/a0036892.

Pew Research Center. (2015a). *Belief in God*. Retrieved from http://www.pewforum.org/religious-landscape-study/belief-in-god/.

Pew Research Center. (2015b). *Importance of religion in one's life*. Retrieved from http://www.pewforum.org/religious-landscape-study/importance-of-religion-in-ones-life/.

Pew Research Center. (2015c). *Attendance at religious service*. Retrieved from http://www.pewforum.org/religious-landscape-study/attendance-at-religious-services/.

Pew Research Center. (2015d). *Changing attitudes on gay marriage*. Retrieved from http://www.pewforum.org/2015/07/29/graphics-slideshow-changing-attitudes-on-gay-marriage/.

Post, B. C., & Wade, N. G. (2009). Religion and spirituality in psychotherapy: A practice-friendly review of research. *Journal of Clinical Psychology, 65*(2), 131–146. doi: 10.1002/jclp.20563.

Prest, L. A., Russel, R., & D'Souza, H. (1999). Spirituality and religion in training, practice and personal development. *Journal of Family Therapy, 21*(1), 60–77. doi: 10.1111/1467-6427.00104.

Priest, J. B., & Wickel, K. (2011). Religious therapists and clients in same-sex relationships: Lessons from the court case of Bruff v. North Mississippi Health Service, Inc. *The American Journal of Family Therapy, 39*(2), 139–148. doi: 10.1080/01926187.2010.530196.

Rusu, P., P., & Turliuc, M. N. (2011). Ethical issues of integrating spirituality and religion in couple and family therapy. *Romanian Journal of Bioethics, 9*(1), 83–95.

Shidlo, A., & Schroeder, M. (2002). Changing sexual orientation: A consumers' report. *Professional Psychology: Research and Practice, 33*(3), 249–259. doi: 10.1037/0735-7028.33.3.249.

Walsh, F. (2008). *Spiritual resources in family therapy* (2nd ed.). New York, NY: Guilford.

Ward v. Wilbanks, No. 09-CV-11237, Doc. 139 (E.D. Mich., Jul. 26, 2010).

Ward v. Wilbanks, No. 10–2100/2145 (6th Cir. Court of Appeals, Jan. 27, 2012).

Watson, W. H. (1997). Soul and system: The integrative possibilities of family therapy. *Journal of Psychology and Theology, 25*(1), 123–135.

Weaver, A. J., Koenig, H. G., & Larson, D. B. (1997). Marriage and family therapists and the clergy: A need for clinical collaboration, training, and research. *Journal of Marital and Family Therapy, 23*(1), 13–25. doi: 10.1111/j.1752-0606.1997.tb00228.x.

Whitman, J. S., & Bidell, M. P. (2014). Affirmative lesbian, gay, and bisexual counselor education and religious beliefs: How do we bridge the gap? *Journal of Counseling & Development, 92*(2), 162–169. doi: 10.1002/j.1556-6676.2014.00144.x.

Wolf, C. T., & Stevens, P. (2001). Integrating religion and spirituality in marriage and family counseling. *Counseling and Values, 46*(1), 66–75. doi: 10.1002/j.2161-007X.2001.tb00207.x.

10

Ethics in Therapy with Children in Families

Lorna Hecker and Catherine Ford Sori

> Elisa Madison and her children, David, age 13, Matt, age 8, and Mitzy, age 5, attend an intake session with Ms. Tuttle, a licensed marriage and family therapist. The family appears to be unorganized and arrives late to session. At the intake, Ms. Madison discusses that the reason they are there is that Matt was diagnosed with attention deficit disorder (ADD). Matt interrupts to say it is actually attention-deficit/hyperactivity disorder (ADHD). The school referred them because of Matt's continued disruptions at school. Ms. Madison is refusing to medicate Matt for the ADHD, and the school is at a loss for how to deal with Matt. Matt is failing several of his subjects, but the school also appears not to be following his Individualized Education Plan (IEP). Ms. Madison appears unsure of how to navigate the school system and get Matt the help he needs. David appears sullen and withdrawn during the session. Mitzy often tries to capture the therapist's attention by dancing throughout the session.

Who is the client in this scenario? Is it Matt, all the children, or the family unit? What impact will Matt's diagnosis have on him? How was he diagnosed? How does couple and family therapy work successfully with the parent, the child, and the school system? What does the couple and family therapist do regarding the issue of empirical evidence in the treatment of ADHD, conflicting values, and medication and the treatment of Matt's ADHD? If the couple and family therapist focuses on Matt, what happens to the needs of the other children or of the family unit? Are they to be assessed as well?

In family therapy, it is often difficult to balance the needs of individuals with those of the family (see discussion in Bailey & Sori, 2000; Sori, Dermer, & Wesolowski, 2006); it is even more difficult when some voices are those of minors. What is distinct in family therapy and child therapy is that children are seldom voluntary clients (Berg & Steiner, 2003). A child is brought for therapy at the request of the parents, school, clergy, the courts, or other sources involved in the child's life. Children do not have the same cognitive capacities as adults, so treatment types and agendas differ from adult clients. Diagnostic labels can affect how the child is treated and can even shape how the child is viewed into adulthood.

There are potentially conflicting guidelines regarding various state laws and regulations, ethical guidelines and professional standards, and the ethical conundrum of balancing family versus individual needs (Keller, 1999). Couple and family therapists who must make decisions about child welfare inevitably rely on a web of views, values, and morality. The question is *whose* values and morality should guide decisions regarding children's best interests? This decision-making must take into account the values, beliefs, and sociocultural context of all the stakeholders in the treatment dilemma (Hill, Glaser, & Harden, 1995; Keller, 1999), although it is ultimately the parents who make the majority of the choices for the child based on those values (Buchanan & Brock, 1989).

Who Is the Client?

Couple and family therapists who work with children can encounter challenges in determining the identity of the client (Koocher & Keith-Spiegel, 1990). When parents bring a child to therapy, the couple and family therapist must evaluate the extent of a child's individual problem versus the problem arising from issues within the family system, or the interactional problem therein. The treatment unit must then be identified. What decisions are made regarding whom to involve in therapy? Families can be part of a child's problem, as when parents blame one another for poor parenting or they are at odds as to how to proceed. In our case scenario, it is unclear if Ms. Madison is a single parent, widow, or if the children's father is not involved for some other reason (e.g., he is estranged from the family, he may have to work during session time). Couple and family therapists are seeing more same-sex parents as well. The couple and family therapist, Ms. Tuttle, is tasked with determining who the client is, who has custody, who to work with, who is involved in parental decision-making, and what therapeutic modality to use (e.g., individual, parental, family).

Inevitably, parents will be some part of the solution to the problem. Yet, a child may need to have the sanctuary of individual therapy to find relief from symptoms. Likewise, parents may need sessions without the children to share their frustrations and attempted solutions, and help them work together to plan strategies to address the child's problems. See Sori et al. (2006) for a more in-depth discussion of this decision-making process.

The choice of therapeutic goals can reflect the conflict couple and family therapists have in identifying who the client is. Is the couple and family therapist guided by their own goals, the child's goals, the school's goals, or the parents' goals for the child (Koocher & Keith-Spiegel, 1990)? If the child has no stated goals, does treatment continue? When and how are the parents and family integrated into treatment? How does the couple and family therapist avoid labeling the child and not aiding a family in scapegoating the child as an "identified patient?" There is a struggle to maintain integrity in the treatment of the family, as well as in the treatment of a child who may be at risk (Keller, 1999). Split loyalties may occur when the couple and family therapist faces the need to balance the interests of the family and manage the risk of harm to the child or children (Keller, 1999, p. 118). When external agencies are involved, such as the courts or child protection services, the loyalty concerns may be even more exaggerated.

Likewise, the exclusion of children from therapy can be problematic. One study that explored children's views of family sessions found that although often excluded, children overwhelmingly wanted to participate in family sessions, *even when they were not the focus of treatment* (Stith, Rosen, McCollum, Coleman, & Herman, 1996). Another study found that even when children were physically present in therapy, they were not actively engaged in therapy, and they spoke only 3.5% of the total words spoken (Cederborg, 1997). Unfortunately, children are largely excluded from family therapy sessions oftentimes because of inadequate training and therapists' lack of comfort in working with children in therapy (Johnson & Thomas, 1999; Korner & Brown, 1990). Couple and family therapists have an ethical responsibility to obtain the necessary training to successfully engage and treat children in a family context (Sori, 2006; Sori & Hecker, 2006; Sori & Sprenkle, 2004), including family play therapy and child therapy approaches (Gil, 2015).

Determining the client treatment unit has ripple effects throughout treatment and case management. Assessments must include whether to treat from an individual child perspective or from a family perspective. Assessment instruments, treatment modality, treatment interventions, and diagnostic labeling vary depending upon the couple and family therapist's perspective with regard to whom to treat; the child, the family system, the parental executive system, and various iterations all change the course of treatment and record keeping. Some recommend a multimodal approach that assesses and may treat several or all of these components of the family (including individuals), based on the needs of the clients (see Bailey & Sori, 2000; Sori et al., 2006). Labeling a child can have lifelong consequences, and couple and family therapy competency and conceptualization of the case can have long-term consequences.

Conversely, family systems therapists often advocate seeing the entire family and may even believe that seeing a child or adolescent alone, depending upon their theoretical orientation, is countertherapeutic. Many child problems can be alleviated by family therapy, given that symptoms may arise as a function of family system dynamics. However, children can remain symptomatic even after family therapy has been a success (Sori et al., 2006; Wachtel, 1991). Even one's treatment modality can bring unique ethical and clinical concerns. For example, in the 1996 Fort Bragg Evaluation Project (Helfinger, Nixon, & Hamner, 1999), the majority of disclosures of suicide ideation were revealed only when couple and family therapists saw children individually without their parents. In the Fort Bragg project, 84% of suicidal intent by children or adolescents was disclosed by the child or adolescent to the interviewer *when the parent was not present.* This punctuates the need for couple and family therapists to be skillful in building relationships with children and adolescents, in creating a climate where they feel safe enough to disclose such information, knowing how to gently encourage young clients to share this information with parents, and how to execute an effective safety plan.

Consent to Treatment

When working with minors, depending upon state law, parental consent is typically needed to commence treatment. Generally, either parent has the right to obtain mental health treatment for their child. However, it is strongly recommended to get consent to treat from *both parents* (Koocher & Keith-Spiegel, 1990) to avoid any potential pitfalls. There are several benefits to including both parents in the treatment of a minor. First, change is more likely to occur when both parents are working to institute modifications in the child's life. Second, if the couple and family therapist fears the parents may disagree about consent, they can quickly detriangulate from potential conflict by requiring both parents to sign the treatment consent.

In divorce or custody issues, the (legal) custodial parent may bring the child to therapy without the other parent's consent. Both parents can have joint legal custody. If a couple is not yet divorced, joint custody is assumed, and unless stated otherwise in the provisional divorce decree, either parent may present the child for therapy. It is recommended that the couple and family therapist ask the parent to bring a copy of the most recent divorce or custody decree, or a provisional order if the couple is not yet divorced. Couple and family therapists are wise to include the alternate parent in treatment, which makes sense clinically; inevitably if one does not, the couple and family therapist will likely receive an angry phone call demanding to know why the parent was not contacted regarding their child receiving services.

Minors' access to mental health outpatient treatment varies from state to state (for a summary, see Guttmacher Institute, 2000). In regard to outpatient mental health treatment, children generally may be seen without parental consent when the child presents with an emergency (e.g., suicide, homicide) or when it would be in the minor's best interest, such as in cases of abuse, neglect, or endangerment. When minors receive treatment for these legal exceptions to parental consent, the records are kept confidential from parents. However, if a child is not seen under one of these exceptions, parents are generally privy to the records.

An exception to parental consent is when the minor is emancipated; emancipated minors may give their own consent to treatment. Emancipated status occurs at age 18, or when an individual joins the military, but state law governs specific emancipation requirements (Lane & Kohlenberg, 2012). State statutes typically specify that when individuals can support themselves independently from parent or guardians, they can petition the state for emancipation. An unemancipated minor is a person who has not reached the age of majority, which in all states but four, is 18. As of 2003, the American Civil Liberties Union reported that in Alabama and Nebraska, the age of majority is 19. In Pennsylvania and Mississippi, the age of majority is 21 (though in Mississippi the age of consent for health care is 18; American Civil Liberties Union, 2003).

Although some states regulate who can give consent to treatment, children's rights to consent to treatment are largely ignored. However, research indicates that minors may be capable of providing it (Hall & Lin, 1995). A child's lack of consent can seriously impair the therapeutic relationship and inhibit therapy's effectiveness (Levine, Anderson, Ferretti, & Steinberg, 1993). The child's development of self-determination is largely nonexistent. Couple and family therapists must mediate between the best interests of the child and the intention of the parents, which is sometimes played out in the courtroom (Keith-Spiegel & Koocher, 1985).

A child should be provided with the option to have some decisional influence in therapy, whenever possible. This gives the child some control in therapy and can therapeutically increase the child's capacity for self-determination (Levine et al., 1993). Minors may be able to give *assent* to treatment (Lawrence & Kurpius, 2000). Assent is when minors are encouraged to be involved in their treatment decisions in a developmentally appropriate way (Kuther, 2003). Generally, the social science literature states that the decision-making process of children older than age 13 is virtually indistinguishable from adults with regard to medical procedures (Tremper & Kelly, 1987). Yet, even young children can make decisions to contribute to their own welfare and treatment. Margolin (1982) suggests a child older than age 7 provide assent. The couple and family therapist's language in explaining assent should be appropriate to the client's level of understanding.

Despite the virtuous intentions of assent, none of the literature reviewed provided suggestions for placating a child who refuses to provide assent. In such a case, the clinician may be deemed untrustworthy by the client because the child will be required to continue in therapy despite dissent. This dilemma in itself raises ethical questions. The couple and family therapist must balance the needs of the child, the wishes and needs of the parents, and the law. The courts have largely placed responsibility upon the mental health professionals to mediate between the best interest of the child and the intentions of the parents (Keith-Spiegel & Koocher, 1985). In cases where treatment is mandatory, couple and family therapists may work collaboratively with young clients to identify what has to happen for them *not* to have to attend therapy.

Minors and Confidentiality and Privilege

> Mrs. Smith brought her 9-year-old son, Tommy, to Dr. Ray because she and Tommy's father were going through a divorce and she was concerned about the effects of the divorce on Tommy. Mrs. Smith wanted Dr. Ray to see Tommy so he would have a "neutral place" to discuss the divorce, and wanted to make sure Tommy was coping adequately with the family changes. Dr. Ray explained to Tommy that what would be said in their sessions together would be shared just between them, unless there was an emergency or something very important about which his mother or father needed to know. Tommy agreed and several sessions were held in which Tommy expressed both positive and negative feelings about both of his parents and the difficulties of the divorce. A few months later, Mrs. Smith called Dr. Ray requesting a copy of Tommy's records for the custody hearing. Dr. Ray was in a difficult spot, because legally in their state, Mrs. Smith had access to Tommy's records, but ethically, he had promised Tommy confidentiality.

As covered in Chapter 3, *confidentiality* is the ethical obligation to keep a client's personal information in therapy private; confidentiality can also be codified into state statute. As our case scenario illustrates, confidentiality of a minor can become complex. State law typically denotes when minors have the right to independently access treatment and keep health information private, and often depends upon the type of services received (e.g., mental health, substance abuse, sexually transmitted diseases). Even in cases where state law allows a minor to seek therapy independently, parents may be privy to a minor's records. If state law is silent regarding minor confidentiality, the Health Insurance Portability and Accountability Act (HIPAA) allows parents or guardians to have access to the minor's health care information, with some legal exceptions (Hecker, 2016).

When state statute does not allow a minor to keep therapy information private, confidentiality should be defined and agreed upon before treatment with parent(s) and child. Although some professional ethical codes state the couple and family therapist must make confidentiality arrangements at the outset of therapy or as circumstances change (e.g., American Psychological Association), others require written permission to share information (e.g., American Association for Marriage and Family Therapy). Arrangements can range from complete confidentiality for the child to no confidentiality, based on information and preferences from the involved stakeholders: the child, parents, couple and family therapist, ethical codes, etc. Most couple and family therapists arrange for limited confidentiality for a minor, where there is a caveat for issues when the child may be in peril, or when the couple and family therapist is a mandated reporter. When possible, it is best practice to have both parents integrated into the treatment in order to transfer changes made in therapy into the child's home(s). If a child is to be seen alone, apart from their family, it is best to engage all members in a discussion of how to preserve confidentiality when seeing the child or adolescent individually.

If the child's information is not protected by state statute, there may be cases in which, ethically, a couple and family therapist may wish to advocate for a child's right to privacy of some therapy information, depending upon the nature of the information disclosed. This example is not uncommon and brings ethical issues to the forefront when parents indicate to a couple and family therapist that they want their child to be able to discuss feelings about a divorce in therapy on neutral ground. It is often therapeutic to allow a child to disengage from parental conflict or to have a forum to discuss issues that they feel may burden a parent. It would not be unusual in such a situation for a child to unburden any negative feelings about the divorce or the behavior of one or both parents.

Couple and family therapists have a responsibility, in conjunction with the child's needs and wishes, to inform the parents of ways in which the parent may be helpful with the child's transitions within the divorce.

Parents may, however, subsequently ask for access to the child's therapy records. Intentions for this action vary; a parent may genuinely want to know all they can about the child to help the child, or the parent may be excessively intrusive in the child's life, or the parent may request copies of the records to "prove" in a custody evaluation or court proceeding that they have been a good parent to the child and have accessed professional services to alleviate distress. In more difficult situations, the parent may be requesting records to "show" the court how the other parent has negatively affected the child. The couple and family therapist is now in the crux of a legal and ethical conundrum. Sans state law to the contrary, the parent has access to the child's therapy records, but ethically both the parent and the couple and family therapist have indicated to the child that therapy is to be a neutral environment, free from reprisals and conflict. It would be unethical to make this promise and subsequently release records for others to review. The couple and family therapist needs to advocate for child privacy in these and other similar situations. Just because a client is a minor does not mean that they lose the right to privacy, especially when adults have promised this privacy. In some cases, parents who request records are satisfied with a written statement from the couple and family therapist that therapy has been sought for the child; the statement may include dates of service. In other cases, parents may wish the records to be released to the court, despite the couple and family therapist's objections. It should not be assumed that a child can freely give assent to release records in this type of pressured situation. If need be, couple and family therapists can petition the judge not to release the records, and explain to the court or custody evaluator the need to protect the child's privacy in situations such as these. Another option is the judge can do an "in camera review," in which the judge reviews the notes in chambers and then renders a decision about whether or not this information is relevant to court proceedings.

To address the dilemma of a minor's treatment information being part of divorce litigation, some couple and family therapists add a statement to their informed consent such as:

> It is important that you agree not to call me as a witness or to attempt to subpoena records in the event you choose to pursue a divorce. Although a judge may overrule this agreement and issue a court order for information, your signature below reflects your agreement not to call me as a witness or attempt to subpoena therapeutic records.

This type of statement is controversial because at times couple and family therapists are needed in the legal arena to protect children. An alternative is to have a separate informed consent for clients who are intending to use the couple and family therapist in legal proceedings, so that expectations, confidentiality issues, and payment for services can be clearly detailed. It is recommended that all forms be reviewed by the couple and family therapist's attorney before use.

Custody Issues

Presently, the terms *custody* and *visitation* are being replaced with more amicable terms such as *parenting agreements* and *parenting time.* Hopefully, the outdated legal terms *physical custody* and *legal custody* will follow. According to Hecker and Sori (2006), "*physical custody* refers to the residence and daily care of the child. *Legal custody* refers to who makes decisions for the child such as education, health care and religious training" (p. 181). Noncustodial parents are granted *visitation,* though many courts now use the preferable term *parenting time.*

The following is a list of custody configurations that may occur (Hecker & Sori, 2006, p. 181):

1. Sole legal custody with one parent; sole physical custody with the same parent,
2. Joint legal custody with both parents; sole physical custody with one parent,
3. Joint legal and joint physical custody,
4. Sole legal custody with one parent; joint physical custody with both parents, or
5. Sole legal custody with one parent; sole physical custody with the other parent.

The most common parenting arrangement is joint legal and sole physical custody. One unconventional arrangement is referred to as *split custody,* which occurs when the children are split up between two homes. Each parent has custody of one or more children. According to Hodges (1991), approximately 5% of parents use a split custody arrangement.

Issues Related to Custody Evaluations and Custody Decisions

Custody evaluations aid judges in deciding which parent should gain custody. Psychologists or other mental health professionals typically conduct the evaluations (Hecker & Sori, 2006). Custody evaluation guidelines have been prepared by the American Psychological Association (APA, 2010), including a focus on parenting capacity, the psychological and developmental needs of the child, and the resulting fit between the parent and child (Hecker & Sori, 2006). Those who wish to provide custody evaluations must receive specialized training. Most judges incorporate custody evaluations as one criterion in determining custody. However, some use the custody evaluation as the principal criteria in making decisions regarding child custody issues. If a couple and family therapist is providing therapy to a family, or a family member, it is considered *unethical* to provide the family with the custody evaluation (Sori & Hecker, 2006).

Sometimes a couple and family therapist may be contacted by a custody evaluator or be subpoenaed to testify as a witness in a custody hearing (Sori & Hecker, 2006). This puts couple and family therapists who work with children and their parents in a different type of working relationship than what was originally contracted. Because therapy is to aid the family in increasing their functioning and is concerned with the child's best interests, how is the therapy process changed when parents think they may influence the couple and family therapist's testimony? If a couple and family therapist does not want to go to court (or one of the parents forbids it by invoking privilege), is the couple and family therapist denying the court relevant information that may have a direct bearing on the case at hand? Might a child be done a disservice if the couple and family therapist does not want to be involved in the custody considerations? If the couple and family therapist has promised the child confidentiality, but then a judge orders the couple and family therapist to court, what does the couple and family therapist then tell the child? In addition, what if one parent wishes for the CFT to release information to the court, but the other parent prohibits the couple and family therapist from releasing information? Couple and family therapists are advised to have the consultation services of a reputable attorney available in the event any such issues arise.

Because of the reliance on psychological testing, couple and family therapists have tended not to perform custody evaluations. Others use a team approach that includes either having a psychologist as part of the team, or contracting with a psychologist for the testing and interpretation used as part of the evaluation. Yet, family therapists may be missing the opportunity to provide a service that they are uniquely qualified to offer.

A child or family therapist should remember the limitations of what they can attest to as a *fact witness*. A fact witness (as opposed to expert witnesses) can only testify to what they have witnessed in therapy sessions. It is important to remember that the treating couple and family therapist has *not* done a custody evaluation and should *never give a recommendation for custody based on having been a therapist in the case.* This is up to the custody evaluator, who has gathered information from multiple sources. To form a custody decision simply based on therapy sessions would result in the couple and family therapist's conduct falling significantly below "the appropriate standard of care," thus opening up the therapist to a lawsuit. One of the most litigious areas in therapy practice involves issues emanating from child custody conflicts.

When couple and family therapists have been seeing parents before their decision to divorce, the couple and family therapist may be of great help to the couple in establishing a cooperative parenting relationship with each other. Yet, couple and family therapists must be careful not to give legal advice, because this is clearly outside the therapist's scope of practice. Couple and family therapists need to know when to refer a client to an attorney. Although many states are moving toward providing families with *parenting arrangements* instead of *custody*, it is naïve to think that the legal system has strayed far from the adversarial system on which it was built. This system may give the couple and family therapist quite a challenge to keep the couple in a collegial stance with regard to parenting arrangements. Chapter 11, *Ethical, Legal, and Professional Issues in Mediation and Parent Coordination*, explores options such as mediation and parent coordination, which are promising alternatives.

If a child's interests diverge significantly from that of the parents' interests, the court may appoint a guardian ad litem. A guardian ad litem represents the child's best interests, and may be an attorney, therapist, or another mental health professional, whose role is, at times, defined by state law. Guardian ad litem are not always necessary, even in conflictual divorces. They are appointed only if one or both parents do not have the child's best interest in mind. If couples are conflictual, but keep the majority of their conflict from the child, and both have the child's best interests in mind, a guardian ad litem is typically not needed.

Parent Alienation

Increasingly, couple and family therapists are seeing cases where children are becoming victims of parent alienation tactics in the context of contentious divorces or separations. Children are triangled into the divorce process, as one parent aims to turn a child (or children) against the alternate parent, or what Kelly and Johnston (2001) call the "target parent." This is a process that includes legal, ethical, and clinical issues and couple and family therapists find these cases referred to them from courts that are ill equipped to deal with the complex dynamics.

Parental alienation differs from normative divorce. In normative divorce, there is more of a systemic process whereby the conflict cycle of the parents is escalated by the adversarial legal system. So when one parent makes a move using a lawyer, the other parent (and their lawyer) responds with an escalated conflict cycle in which systemically the output of one party becomes the input of another and vice versa. Although normative divorces are not always completely resolved, they may not be particularly toxic to the children, and resolve to tolerable levels over time. Parental alienation cases are quite different.

Parental alienation differs from normative divorce situations; typically with parental alienation, there is one parent who is attempting to turn the child(ren) against the target parent. Typically, the target parent is blocked access to the child(ren) at every turn. Although couple and family therapists may consider this couple conflict, without the parent who is blocking access, the escalation would have little fuel. Although the parents appear to be locked in conflict, the reality is that the target parent may simply be fighting for access and the ability to parent their children. The alienating parents typically suffer from borderline, narcissistic, or histrionic personality disorders (Eddy & Kreger, 2011), or they may evidence significant psychopathology or sociopathy (Friedlander & Walters, 2010).

Ethical and clinical issues arise when a couple and family therapist adopts a misapplied systemic viewpoint, believing that the parents are locked in a circular, mutually reinforcing conflict pattern, as discussed previously. In the more entrenched, nonnormative divorces, however, the target parent may simply be fighting for the right to be involved with their child(ren). The smaller, intrapsychic system is overlooked, with individual pathology instead viewed as a function of the interactional cycle. This is dangerous. Judges, by action or inaction, can exacerbate the process. Therapists who do not understand this dynamic can inadvertently add to the alienation when they conceptualize and operate from a place where both parents are contributing to the conflict. The reality is, in these cases, the pathology of one parent is the driver of the conflict; the other parent is responding to the alienating parent's attempts to remove them from their child(ren)'s lives. This requires the couple and family therapist to use a wider lens and evaluate the macro-socio-political context (including the legal system), the parent's microsystem (their mental health), as well as the conflict cycle itself. Although there are dregs of the couple system at hand, this conflict rises to a much higher, sophisticated level, with significant long-term psychological associations in the lives of children and subsequently adults who experienced parental alienation as children, creating vulnerability in future relationships as well as future generations. Research has been clear about the negative effects of parental alienation on the emotional and behavioral development of children (Baker & Verrocchio, 2015; Fidler & Bala, 2010). They include:

- Problems with intrapersonal thoughts, feelings and behaviors, resulting in depression, self-hatred, low self-esteem and suicide ideation, poor reality testing, illogical cognitive operations, and simplistic and rigid information processing,
- Emotional problems such as emotional instability, impulse control problems, substance abuse, emotional constriction, passivity or dependency, lack of remorse, and guilt,
- Disturbed and compromised interpersonal functioning, including poor definition of self as evidenced by enmeshment,
- Social competency issues, antisocial functioning including self-isolating behaviors, pseudo maturity, social phobias, aggression and violent behaviors, disregard for social norms and authority, and
- Health problems such as asthma, hypertension, and somatic complaints.

Sadly, 80% of adults who were alienated as children wished someone had stopped the alienation (Fidler & Bala, 2010) and that they had more time with their noncustodial parent.

This alienation is child abuse, which couple and family therapists often miss, in part because of their systemic viewpoint. Couple and family therapists emphasize context, but Friedman (2004) notes this "does not mean that we understand and explain any behavior only by its context, rather that we enrich our understanding of the behavior by considering its context" (p. 103). Couple and family therapists then can wittingly or unwittingly contribute to the alienation dynamic, along with attorneys, guardians ad litem, and custody evaluators. Couple and family therapists must learn to recognize this dynamic as to not get triangled into this process, not provide support for stances that can further damage the child(ren)'s relationship with the target parent, and not treat allegations as objective facts (Kelly & Johnston, 2001). Couple and family therapists have an obligation to understand how individual factors (microsystem) can affect the family (system) as well as legal system (macrosystem). This dynamic is more complex than a "conflictual couple" formulation, and couple and family therapists must obtain training to help children in these abusive situations that have devastating developmental consequences. In some situations, the target parent finally gives up, leaving the child to deal with feelings of abandonment. We also need additional research on parental alienation dynamics; Kelly and Johnston (2001) note that although many parents engage in alienating behaviors, only a small percentage of children become alienated.

Child Maltreatment

All 50 states have some sort of reporting requirement following the 1974 creation of the Child Abuse Prevention and Treatment Act. Reporting laws have been adopted under the authority of *parent's patriae*. Parent's patriae is the state's right to assume the role of a parent when a child is abused or neglected. Therapists must consult state statutes regarding reporting abuse or neglect because they differ in terms, and who is a mandatory reporter, as well as how and under what conditions reports must be filed (Wagner, 2003). Parents generally may care for their children without interference from the state, as long as their parenting behavior falls within social norms and is not outside of state law. What is considered abuse and neglect varies from state to state (Stein, 1998). Therapists working with children are only to *report* suspected abuse, not investigate it. Child protection agencies and law enforcement are required to investigate reported allegations or suspicions. A study entitled the *National Incidence Study by the Department of Health and Human Services* (U.S. Department of Health and Human Services, 2010) found that only about one third of the cases known to professionals were reported to child protective agencies. There is no statute of limitations on reporting child sexual abuse (Berman, 1997).

Definitions of child abuse include physical abuse, sexual abuse, and neglect, but what become ethical quagmires for some therapists include the less obvious forms of abuse. These less obvious forms of abuse listed by the *National Incidence Study of the Department of Health and Human Services* (U.S. Department of Health and Human Services, 2010) include:

- Extreme or habitual verbal abuse or other overtly hostile, rejecting, or punitive treatment,
- Abandonment or other refusal to maintain custody, such as desertion, expulsion from home, or refusal to accept custody of a returned runaway,
- Permitting of or encouragement of chronic maladaptive behavior, such as truancy, delinquency, serious drug or alcohol abuse, and so on; "permitted" means that the child's caregiver had reason to be aware of the existence and seriousness of the problem (such as by having been informed of previous incidents), but made no reasonable attempt to prevent further occurrences,
- Refusal to allow needed treatment for a professionally diagnosed physical, educational, emotional, or behavioral problem, or failure to follow

the advice of a competent professional who recommended that the caregiver obtain or provide the child with such treatment, if the child's primary caregiver was physically and financially able to do so,
- Failure to seek or unwarranted delay in seeking competent medical care for a serious injury, illness, or impairment, if the need for professional care should have been apparent to a responsible caregiver without special medical training,
- Consistent or extreme inattention to the child's physical or emotional needs, including needs for food, clothing, supervision, safety, affection, and reasonably hygienic living conditions, if the child's primary caregivers were physically and financially able to provide the needed care, and
- Failure to register or enroll the child in school (or homeschool), as required by state law.

Some states also require that abuse of emancipated minors be reported, but others do not. Some states require written reports; others require a telephone report, or both. In spite of mandatory reporting laws, some therapists hesitate to report (Beck & Ogloff, 1995), presumably for fear of losing the therapeutic alliance with clients.

Use of Touch in Therapy

It is natural to embrace children; hugs can be therapeutic and rewarding in and of themselves. In fact, it is difficult to counsel children without using some form of touch, even if it only involves helping or restraining a child (see McNeil-Haber, 2004). Practical and ethical considerations include boundary considerations, cross-gender touch, history of trauma for the child, power differentials, and consent by parents (and the child) (Hecker & Sori, 2006). Cultural considerations may also come into play. Using touch with children in therapy, however, can be fraught with ethical issues. Does the parent approve of the touch? Has the child had any negative experiences with touch from an adult? Ethical and professional issues that emanate from touch include:

- *Boundaries*—How do therapists know when they are broaching improper boundaries, compared to increasing intimacy by providing therapeutic touch? What cultural norms should be considered? If a child uses inappropriate touch (e.g., sexual) with the therapist, how does the therapist set gentle yet firm boundaries?
- *Gender*—Cross-gender touch may be viewed more as a boundary violation than same-gender touch.

- *Client Background*—Children who have been abused (especially sexual abuse) may misinterpret touch, and experience it much differently than those who have not been abused. The therapist certainly does not want to create further damage to a child who may see touch as threatening.
- *Consent*—The therapist should respect children's boundaries as they do adult boundaries, and ask if they may hug or touch a child. In addition, it is wise to ask the parent's position on therapeutic touch, and explain what types of touch might be used (e.g., pat on the back), when (e.g., after child has worked hard on a drawing), and why (e.g., to show encouragement and compliment the effort).
- *Therapist self-protection*—In this litigious era, there are times when the therapist must think about how the touch would be interpreted in a legal arena.
- *Power differentials*—The therapist must be cognizant of the power differentials with children and be sure to guard against exploitation of any sort.

Although therapist-initiated touch appears to be widespread, therapists should carefully consider the following before initiating any touch with children (McNeil-Haber, 2004):

- How might the child benefit from being touched? For example, might touch help to calm the child, serve as reinforcement, or be an expression of acceptance?
- How might this particular child interpret being touched? Would this child be empowered enough to comment?
- Has this child experienced any abuse or safety issues that might make touch feel inappropriate or alarming?

Before touching a child, therapists should always check themselves to determine whose needs are being served—those of the child or those of the therapist (Holub & Lee, 1990). The needs of the child should always be foremost, and therapists should be alert to any countertransference issues that might impair their judgment. It is also important to consider the cultural and ethnic background of the child and family, as there are cultural differences in how touch can be used with children, or as a means of emotional expression (McNeil-Haber, 2004).

Because of the power differential between adults and children, and because we live in a litigious society, touch should be used sparingly with children. A child could have an undisclosed history of abuse that could lead them to sexualize or misinterpret any therapist-initiated touch. In working with sexually abused children, therapists must be gentle but firm in setting boundaries regarding inappropriate child-initiated touch (Gil, 2006).

Yet touch is vital to children (and adults), and we can sidestep the potential pitfalls of therapist-child touch by facilitating nurturing, gentle touch between parents and children. Theraplay is highly recommended by Dr. Bruce Perry and Eliana Gil in promoting brain development and treating childhood trauma (Sori & Schnur, 2014). Therapists can model nurturing Theraplay activities with the parent, and then coach the parent to do them with the child. Parent–child touch can promote strong attachment and brain development, and reduce behavior problems.

Therapists should discuss the potential use of touch with parents at the outset of therapy, explain when it might occur (e.g., returning a child-initiated hug, to keep a child from harm), and ask permission to use appropriate touch (Sori & Hecker, 2006).

Conclusion

Children are almost never voluntary clients in therapy and bring unique ethical issues to the forefront for couple and family therapists to consider. First, the therapist must decide who the client is—the child, the family unit, or subsystems within the family unit. Couple and family therapists ultimately must decide if family needs are emphasized, or if the individual needs of the child are paramount. Confidentiality concerns are unique when a minor is involved in therapy; minors may be mentally capable of giving consent, but not legally able to do so. Children who are unable to give consent may be able to give assent, and the therapist must take special consideration to use language that is accessible to this client population. Because of the power and privilege held by adults over children, the therapist must be ever aware of how children can be hurt by abuse of power by adults, with special attention paid to issues such as child maltreatment and potential issues of oppression. These issues may surface in the therapy room with the simple issue of the use of touch in therapy. Boundaries, a child's history with abuse, consent, and power are all issues to consider in the use of touch in therapy.

Of special consideration in working with children are custody considerations. Couple and family therapists need to consider issues of who can give consent to the child's therapy, who has access to records, and making therapy a respite for a child from parental conflict while working with the parents and legal system. Of note is the seeming increase of children who are alienated from parents within a divorce. These can be difficult issues for couple and family therapists to navigate, but the children placed in these sometimes acrimonious situations have the most to benefit from the services of a child-focused family therapist who can decrease the conflict and increase the functioning of the family system that nurtures the child's development. Couple and family therapists are well advised to gain specialized training in working with children and to stay current on legal and ethical issues emanating from working with children and their families.

References

American Civil Liberties Union. (ACLU). (2003). *Protecting minors' heath information under the federal medical privacy regulations.* New York, NY: Author.

American Psychological Association. (APA). (2010). Guidelines for child custody evaluations in family law proceedings. *American Psychologist, 65*(9), 863–867. doi: 10.1037/a0021250.

Bailey, C. E., & Sori, C. E. F. (2000). Involving parents in children's therapy. In C. E. Bailey (Ed.), *Children in therapy: Using the family as a resource* (pp. 475–502). New York, NY: Norton.

Baker, A. J. L., & Verrocchio, M. C. (2015). Parental bonding and parental alienation as correlates of psychological maltreatment in adults in intact and non-intact families. *Journal of Child and Family Studies, 24*(10), 3047–3057. doi: 10.1007/s10826-014-0108-0.

Beck, K. A., & Ogloff, R. P. (1995). Child abuse reporting in British Columbia: Psychologists' knowledge of and compliance with the reporting law. *Professional Psychology: Research and Practice, 26*(3), 245–251. doi: 10.1037/0735-7028.26.3.245.

Berg, I. K., & Steiner, T. (2003). *Children's solution work.* New York, NY: Norton.

Berman, P. S. (1997). Ethical issues in child maltreatment. In D. T. Marsh & R. D. Magee (Eds.), *Ethical and legal issues in professional practice with families* (pp. 183–196). New York, NY: Wiley.

Buchanan, A. E., & Brock, D. W. (1989). *Deciding for others: The ethics of surrogate decision making.* New York, NY: Cambridge University Press.

Cederborg, A. D. (1997). Young children's participation in family therapy talk. *American Journal of Family Therapy, 25*(1), 28–38. doi: 10.1080/01926189708251052.

Eddy, B., & Kreger, R. (2011). *Splitting: Protecting yourself while divorcing someone with borderline or narcissistic personality disorder.* Oakland, CA: New Harbinger Publications.

Fidler, B. J., & Bala, N. (2010). Children resisting postseparation contact with a parent: Concepts, controversies, and conundrums. *Family Court Review, 48*(1), 10–47. doi: 10.1111/j.1744-1617.2009.01287.x.

Friedlander, S., & Walters, M. G. (2010). When a child rejects a parent: Tailoring the intervention to fit the problem. *Family Court Review, 48*(1), 98–111. doi: 10.1111/j.1744-1617.2009.01291.x.

Friedman, M. (2004). The so-called high-conflict couple: A closer look. *The American Journal of Family Therapy, 32*(2), 101–117. doi: 10.1080/001926180490424217.

Gil, E. (2006). *Sand therapy integrated with play therapy: Theory and application.* Training provided by Starbright Training Institute for Child and Family Play Therapy, Fairfax, VA.

Gil, E. (2015). *Play in family therapy* (2nd ed.). New York, NY: Guilford.

Guttmacher Institute. (2000). Minors and the right to consent to health care. *The Guttmacher Report on Public Policy, 3*(4), 4–7. Retrieved from www.guttmacher.org/pubs/tgr/03/4/gr030404.html.

Hall, A. S., & Lin, M. J. (1995). Theory and practice of children's rights: Implications for mental health counselors. *Journal of Mental Health Counseling, 17*(1), 63–80.

Hecker, L. (2016). *HIPAA demystified: HIPAA compliance for mental health professionals.* Crown Point, IN: Loger Press.

Hecker, L. L., & Sori, C. F. (2006). Divorce and stepfamily issues. In C. F. Sori (Ed.), *Engaging children in family therapy: Creative approaches to integrating theory and research in clinical practice* (pp. 177–204). New York, NY: Routledge.

Heflinger, C. A., Nixon, C. T., & Hamner, K. (1999). Handling confidentiality and disclosure in the evaluation of client outcomes in managed mental health services for children and adolescents. *Education and Program Planning, 19*(2), 175–182. doi: 10.1016/0149-7189(96)00008-0.

Hill, M., Glaser, K., & Harden, J. (1995). A feminist model for ethical decision making. In E. J. Rave & C. C. Larsen (Eds.), *Ethical decision-making in therapy* (pp. 18–37). New York, NY: Guilford.

Hodges, W. (1991). *Interventions for children of divorce: Custody, access and psychotherapy.* New York, NY: Wiley.

Holub, E. A., & Lee, S. S. (1990). Therapists' use of nonerotic physical contact: Ethical concerns. *Professional Psychology, Research, and Practice, 21*(2), 115–117. doi: 10.1037/0735-7028.21.2.115 .

Johnson, L., & Thomas, V. (1999). Influences on the inclusion of children in family therapy. *Journal of Marital and Family Therapy, 25*(1), 117–123. doi: 10.1111/j.1752-0606.1999.tb01114.x.

Keith-Spiegel, P., & Koocher, G. P. (1985). *Ethics in psychology: Professional standards and cases.* Hillsdale, NJ: Lawrence Erlbaum Associates.

Keller, S. A. (1999). Split loyalties: The conflicting demands of individual treatment goals and parental responsibility. *Women and Therapy, 22*(2), 117–133. doi: 10.1300/J015v22n02_09.

Kelly, J. B., & Johnston, J. R. (2001). The alienated children: A reformulation of parental alienation syndrome. *Family Court Review, 39*(3), 249–266. doi: 10.1111/j.174-1617.2001.tb00609.x.

Koocher, G. P., & Keith-Spiegel, P. C. (1990). *Children, ethics, and the law: Professional issues and cases.* Lincoln, NE: University of Nebraska Press.

Korner, S., & Brown, G. (1990). Exclusion of children from family psychotherapy: Family therapists' beliefs and practices. *Journal of Family Psychology, 3*(4), 420–430. doi: 10.1037/h0080555.

Kuther, T. L. (2003). Medical decision-making and minors: Issues of consent and assent. *Adolescence, 38*(150), 343–358.

Lane, S. H., & Kohlenberg, E. (2012). Emancipated minors: Health policy and implications for nursing. *Journal of Pediatric Nursing, 27*(5), 533–548. doi: 10.1016/j.pedn.2011.07.014.

Lawrence, G., & Kurpius, S. E. R. (2000). Legal and ethical issues involved when counseling minors in nonschool settings. *Journal of Counseling and Development, 78*(2), 130–136. doi: 10.1002/j.1556-6676.2000.tb02570.x.

Levine, M., Anderson, E., Ferretti, L., & Steinberg, K. (1993). Legal and ethical issues affecting clinical child psychology. In T. H. Ollendick & R. J. Prinz (Eds.), *Advances in clinical child psychology* (Vol. 15, pp. 81–117). New York, NY: Springer.

Margolin, G. (1982). Ethical and legal considerations in marital and family therapy. *American Psychologist, 37*(7), 788–801. doi: 10.1037/0003-066X.37.7.788.

McNeil-Haber, F. M. (2004). Ethical considerations in the use of nonerotic touch in psychotherapy with children. *Ethics and Behavior, 14*(2), 123–140. doi: 10.1207/s15327019eb1402_3.

Sori, C. F. (2006). On counseling children and families: Recommendations from the experts. In C. F. Sori (Ed.), *Engaging children in family therapy: Creative approaches to integrating theory and research in clinical practice* (pp. 3–20). New York, NY: Routledge.

Sori, C. F., Dermer, S., & Wesolowski, G. (2006). Involving children in family counseling and involving parents in children's counseling: Theoretical and practical guidelines. In C. F. Sori (Ed.), *Engaging children in family therapy: Creative approaches to integrating theory and research in clinical practice* (pp. 139–158). New York, NY: Routledge.

Sori, C. F., & Hecker, L. L. (2006). Ethical and legal considerations when counseling children and families. In C. F. Sori (Ed.), *Engaging children in family therapy: Creative approaches to integrating theory and research in clinical practice* (pp. 159–176). New York, NY: Routledge.

Sori, C. F., & Schnur, S. (2014). Integrating a neurosequential approach in the treatment of traumatized children: An interview with Eliana Gil, Part II. *The Family Journal, 22*(2), 251–257.

Sori, C. F., & Sprenkle, D. H. (2004). Training family therapists to work with children and families: A modified Delphi study. *Journal of Marital and Family Therapy, 30*(4), 479–495. doi: 10.1177/1066480713514945.

Stein, T. J. (1998). *Child welfare and the law* (rev. ed.). Washington, DC: CWLA Press.

Stith, S. M., Rosen, K. H., McCollum, E. E., Coleman, J. U., & Herman, S. A. (1996). The voices of children: Preadolescent children's experiences in family therapy. *Journal of Marital and Family Therapy, 22*(1), 69–86. doi: 10.1111/j.1752-0606.1996.tb00188.x.

Tremper, C. R., & Kelly, M. P. (1987). Mental health rationale for policies fostering minor's autonomy. *International Journal of Law and Psychiatry, 10*(2), 111–123. doi: 10.1016/0160-2527(87)90003-3.

U.S. Department of Health and Human Services. (2010). *Fourth national incidence study of the Department of Health and Human Services: Definitions of abuse and neglect.* Retrieved from https://www.nis4.org/DefAbuse.asp.

Wachtel, E. F. (1991). How to listen to kids. *Networker, 15*(4), 46–47.

Wagner, W. G. (2003). *Counseling, psychology and children: A multidimensional approach to intervention.* Upper Saddle River, NJ: Pearson Education.

11

Ethical, Legal, and Professional Issues in Mediation and Parent Coordination

Julia M. Bernard, Nicole Manick, and Maike Klein

> Two divorcing parents, Pat and Joe, have been ordered by a family court judge to seek mediation before they return for their court date in 2 months. The domestic relations office of the family court assigns them a mediator, Jane, a local family therapist. When Jane receives the case, she notices that she knows Pat's attorney from prior business dealings—she bought her office from him some years back. She calls Pat's attorney, as well as Joe's attorney, so that they can advise their clients of her past business relationship with the attorney. In addition to the call, Jane writes both clients an introduction letter, in which she specifies the past business relationship. Both Pat and Joe agree to continue with the mediation in Jane's office. Once this conflict of interest is disclosed, the parties continue with the informed consent process.

Parents such as Pat and Joe, who must encounter the legal system to end the legal status of their relationship, can consequently transfer their relational life into an adversarial arena in which conflicts between the can last for years. Continued parental conflict after a divorce negatively affects children (Amato, 2001, 2010; Ayoub, Deutsch, & Maraganorr, 1999; Kelly, 2000), and can also be harmful to the parent–child relationship (Amato & Booth, 1996; Amato & Cheadle, 2008). Therapists can, and should, respond to the need to move families from an adversarial stance to one of healing with a successful transition to a post-conflict family life, where both adults and children can thrive.

Couple and family therapists have applicable skills that can aid these family transitions. For example, Miller and Rose (2009) and Morris and Halford (2014) suggest that evidence-based practices therapists are trained in (such as motivational interviewing and coparenting education) are likely to enhance outcomes for families in transitions such as divorce. Emery,

Rowen, and Dinescu (2014) note that the coparenting relationship never ends, but must be renegotiated in a divorce. Couple and family therapists can aid in this transition, with skills that can help families limit or reduce exposure to the adversarial legal system.

Alternative dispute resolution (ADR) is a service typically offered through the legal system but can be offered by a couple and family therapist with appropriate training. ADR is commonly seen in business practices as mediation or arbitration and has long been seen as a more amicable and cost-effective way to settle disputes. In this chapter, two methods of ADR in which couple and family therapists can engage are discussed. Mediation and parent coordination are two areas that show promise for the practice and profession of couple and family therapist.

Mediation

Mediation is a process whereby dispute resolution is facilitated by a neutral third person who is selected by the two disputing parties, such as those with contested issues such as in divorce or custody litigation. Mediation provides a neutral third party who facilitates the negotiation process, giving individuals a nonadversarial alternative to family court. The mediator has no authority to settle the dispute, if parties fail to reach their own agreement (Emery et al., 2014). Sullivan (2004) noted that, in the best interest of the child, judges delegate their decision-making power to an expert, the mediator.

The mediation process involves joint and separate meetings between the mediator and the parties to emphasize the strengths and weaknesses of the case and to reach a compromise. Once an agreement is reached by both parties, it results in a legally enforceable contract, which often includes a parenting plan. The benefits of mediation can include the following:

- Participants can avoid taking adversarial positions or "battling" issues in court,
- Clients are saving time and money by avoiding litigation, thereby gaining an economic advantage,
- Clients learn to communicate such that it sets the tone for further dispute resolution (Saposnek, 1998),
- Parents formulate a joint set of parenting rules,
- Parents model positive adult behavior for their children,
- The two parties maintain decision-making power over their own circumstances (Gilchrist & Marshall, 1999),

- Parents experience a decrease in conflict, which can take children out of the middle of conflict, and
- Clients experience an emotional advantage of compromise versus conflict.

Mediation begins with two disputing parties selecting a mediator for the facilitation of a resolution to their case. Often, a judge will order mediation to attempt to resolve the dispute, or if both parties' attorneys know the judge will order this, they may suggest it themselves. Parties are usually at least somewhat willing to participate, as legal fees and missed work time for litigation readily accrue.

The first consideration the mediator should make, as Jane did in our case scenario, is whether or not the mediator has had past contact with the parties. Neutrality, including avoiding dual relationships, is essential to the ethical practice of mediation. As Jane modeled in our case study, if the therapist has had social or professional contact with either party, it should be disclosed in writing to both parties (Goodman, 2004). This does not indicate that the therapist could not act as the mediator, but both parties must have knowledge of the prior contact and still agree that this mediator is appropriate. The mediator should then disclose their qualifications, how the process occurs, fees, and any other necessary arrangements that the mediator would need to facilitate a resolution of the dispute. The parties then sign a contract and usually pay a retainer for the mediator to begin to work on the dispute. Informed consent must be obtained from both parties to proceed with mediation, as with therapy.

Attorneys may or may not be present at the mediation. If one party has informed the mediator of the presence of an attorney, the mediator should let the other party know before the first session; this balances the power equally in the session. Mediation, unlike arbitration, is nonbinding, and *ex parte* (contact with only one party) is permitted. A mediator may ask for a caucus and speak confidentially with one party at a time to try to reach a settlement. It must be understood that the mediator can ask to speak to either party with or without an attorney, or with an attorney alone to help reach a settlement or break an impasse.

Process of Mediation

The mediation begins with the mediator's opening statements and those of the parties on their positions with regard to the conflict at hand (e.g., custody, parenting time). All necessary paperwork (e.g., custody evaluation results, provisional custody order, divorce decree) is reviewed in advance, but may also be reviewed during the session as needed (Emery, 1994). Every part of the mediation should be brief; summaries of documents are usually best. Both parties should be informed that they will be charged for time the mediator must spend reviewing documents.

Usually, the mediator then goes on to list the important issues of the case that require compromise. The needs of the child, the custody (referred to as parenting time within mediation), child support, and legal custody (referred to as academic decisions, religious decisions, and health decisions in mediation) must all be discussed within the family mediation process. Each issue must be explored from multiple angles so that both parties know and understand the settlement they are agreeing to in session.

The process of mediation ends when the couple agrees that no further decisions can be made. This happens in one of three ways. The couple may have reached a solution to all important issues. The couple may have partial agreement on some of the issues, but cannot agree on others. Finally, no resolutions may have been made and the mediator calls an impasse. Whatever the conclusion, the mediator writes the outcome down and has all parties sign that this is what was agreed upon in the meeting, even if that was no agreement was reached. This could be a handwritten, numbered list of the resolved issues that includes payment by one party or the other, return of goods, restitution of funds, promises to perform certain conduct, and issues that were discussed and are no longer at issue. The mediator does not sign the agreement, as only the parties involved sign the document. This agreement document will suffice, but the parties may request that their attorney draft a more detailed document that is then signed by both parties (Goodman, 2004). If the couple has been court ordered, the judge will then receive a copy of the mediator's report and settle any issues that were unresolved in the mediation process.

Requirements for Mediators

Every state has mediation as an ADR. It is widely used as an alternative to litigation; in some states, it is mandated before a judge will hear a case. In many states, it is often used for those high-conflict cases that continually appear before the same judge. It can also be a viable alternative to litigation for the modification of a custody arrangement. Many states allow the ADR rules, the American Bar Association Section of Dispute Resolution, and the Academy of Family Mediators to set the guidelines for ethical mediation practices. Some states, such as Florida, New York, and California, have Mediator Ethics Advisory Committees to set and ensure the ethical and moral standards to which the mediator complies. Other states use their standing Ethics Advisory Committees of their state Bar Association as the authority in maintaining standards of practice.

In mediation, authority is earned through the appointment of the mediator, who also has to have many of the same qualities as a couple and family therapist, such as listening skills, general communication skills, conflict management skills, and a desire to help others. Ideally, the mediator should be a licensed professional, have at least a master's degree, be trained in family issues and conflict management, and possess an understanding of child development, which all closely mirror the training of couple and family therapists. There are mediation training programs available on a state-by-state basis, which usually run between three and seven days. Standards are set by rule or statute (Welsh, 2004), although there is no required certification at this time (Milne, Folberg, & Salem, 2004).

Couple and family therapists are well qualified to serve post-decree families in reducing conflict and aiding parents in coming together for the sake of the children. As a mediator, the therapist has experience necessary in decreasing tension in the room, the ability to help in reaching a compromise, and familiarity with the general discussion format that both roles require.

Ethical Issues

First, "the mediator has an ethical obligation to ascertain whether mediation is appropriate, whether it is safe, whether parties should be brought together in the same room, and who ought to be at the table" (Mayer, 2004, p. 40). As discussed previously, the first order of business, before mediation, is to disclose any conflicts of interest. A contract that includes informed consent should be reviewed and signed.

When tensions rise or a party feels uncomfortable, it may be necessary to caucus and meet separately with each party to explore possible settlements. When couple and family therapists see conflictual couples separately, they are often in the position to negotiate or facilitate the agreement of positions on issues. These discussions are also confidential, and information shared within caucus must not be shared with the other party or the other party's lawyer. The mediator must ask the party exactly what settlement offer or issue can be communicated to the other party. The mediator also needs to make sure that they do not provide counseling or give legal advice during mediation.

Within the context of mediation, one of the most important ethical considerations is confidentiality. Confidentiality should be described within the couple and family therapist's written disclosure or discussed in the explanation of the process. Any limitations to confidentiality must be disclosed to the clients. Like therapist–client and attorney–client privilege, everything that is said within the session remains confidential. Only the parties and their attorneys are allowed to be present. If another person is necessary (e.g., a guardian ad litem), that person may also attend. Another alternative form of mediation, child-inclusive mediation, allows for the child to be interviewed by an expert and their perspective to be shared with the parents and mediator (Emery et al., 2014). The child's perspective is also to remain confidential. Whether a mediator allows anyone else (a friend or stepparent) to be present is at the discretion of the mediator.

Another important ethical and legal consideration is that of noncoercion, or the right of the client to self-determination. It is important to educate clients and allow them to make their own choices, free from pressure from the mediator (Welsh, 2004). Even though a settlement is optimal, it should not be made at the expense of free will of the clients. Mediator bias is also a significant issue that can get in the way of a fair and ethical mediation. Mediators who find themselves unable to be neutral or bias free must excuse themselves from the case and make necessary referrals. Mediation proceedings are confidential by state statute with some exceptions. In jurisdictions where mediators must testify, the mediator is allowed more influence in aiding parties to come to an agreement; they may advise the parties that their recommendations are generally followed by the court. However, the parties are never required to reach an agreement in mediation, but allowed their day in court if needed or preferred (Emery et al., 2014).

The mediator should be conscious of coparents who have had violence in their relationship, as coercion or intimidation may be present, but never overtly stated. Again, caucus can be used to ensure that these problems do not interfere with the process. The mediation process is voluntary, and no one can be forced to participate. Rules of the mediation sessions should also be explained during the initial session, and those clients who cannot adhere to the rules (no shouting, throwing things, and so forth) should also be asked to caucus. Mediation may be terminated in these instances. In any instance in which a client is emotionally unable to effectively participate in mediation, it is the ethical responsibility of the mediator to suspend or terminate mediation (Welsh, 2004).

Aside from violence, there are other power imbalances of which the mediator needs to be aware to facilitate a fair settlement; the mediator has to walk a thin line between protecting a disempowered party from an unfair settlement and staying neutral. These include tangible disparities such as education and income differences, but also intangible factors such as "status, dominance, depression, self-esteem, reward expectation, fear of achievement, and sex role ideology" (Walther, 2000, p. 95).

At times, parents will make agreements on issues that may not be in the child's best interests—for example, the parents want to fly a 3-year-old across country alone for summer and holiday visits with the alternate parent. Most mediators ask questions to help parents understand the implications of their decision making (Mayer, 2004). This tends to be an effective way to get parents to understand the effects of their decision on the child and reconsider their options for a more child-focused solution. How the mediator raises concerns will affect the mediation relationship that should be bias free.

The mediator is there to control the process and suggest solutions or compromises that may be agreeable to both parties. A mediator is facilitating a settlement discussion and should know that anything said during the process is inadmissible in court. The mediator may ask permission to take notes but may also communicate that those notes will leave with that mediator and be destroyed after the session (Goodman, 2004). Malpractice insurance is available through the Academy of Family Mediators, the Society of Professionals in Dispute Resolutions, and Association of Family and Conciliation Courts.

Parent Coordination

Parent coordination is another ADR process available to facilitate the resolution of family issues; it is a child-focused process that is performed by a mental health professional or an attorney. The parent coordinator assists high-conflict parents in implementing their parenting plan by facilitating resolution to their disputes, educating parents about their children's needs, and making decisions within the scope of the court or appointment contract (Association of Family and Conciliation Courts [AFCC] Task Force on Parenting Coordination, 2006). Parent coordinators (also called *special masters* and *custody commissioners*), are a third party selected to act as arbitrators to settle the dispute for the parties when agreement cannot be reached. They can also be appointed before the divorce to help set up the parenting plan, or can be appointed years after the divorce to help execute the parenting plan and facilitate other decisions or day-to-day conflicts or trouble spots. Parent coordinators are usually used for those high-conflict parents who demonstrated their longer-term inability or unwillingness to make parenting decisions on their own, to comply with parenting agreements and orders, to reduce their child-related conflicts, and to protect their children from the impact of the conflict (AFCC Task Force on Parenting Coordination, 2006).

Process of Parent Coordination

Parenting coordinators can be seen as peacemakers as well as peacebuilders as they try to resolve disagreement between parents and facilitate clear and honest communication by exploring possibilities for compromise, developing methods of compromise, identifying the most important concerns, and maintaining compliance with court guidelines, similar to the mediation process (Coates, 2015). First, the parenting coordinator makes every attempt to mediate decisions between both parents; however, if neither or both parties are able to make a decision, the coordinator is allowed legal jurisdiction to make a decision for them. Typically parents are court referred. Parent coordinators have an assessment function (they gather information from all referring sources), they have an education function (they educate parents about child development and the impact of parental conflict), they perform a case management function between all involved parties, they provide conflict management, and if the parents cannot agree on a decision, they have the legal authority to make the decision for them (AFCC Task Force on Parenting Coordination, 2006).

A parenting coordinator is helpful for families because they have the opportunity to make the decisions about the living arrangements of their children and are able to have a voice in these decisions. Other benefits of having a parenting coordinator:

- It is less expensive to use a parenting coordinator than to go through the process in the court system. The court fees and the costs for attorneys are much more than the cost of hiring one parenting coordinator,
- For situations in which the parenting coordinator must make a decision, that person will have a greater understanding about the case than a judge

due to the close contact with both parents. The coordinator can, therefore, make a more informed decision,

- Parent coordination is timelier than the potential drawn-out process in a divorce in which many delays may take place due to extensions or modifications in child custody,
- A successfully parent–coordinator-mediated case will be less likely to return to the courtroom for revisions at a later date, unlike the divorce litigation,
- Parent coordinators can help with day-to-day details in parenting conflict that courts are unable to litigate on an ongoing basis,
- Children may fare better in a parent–coordinator-mediated situation because parents may be less likely to continue to carry on destructive behavior as a result of coming to joint decisions together, and
- There can be regular contact with someone who is monitoring the family situation, and the family does not need to wait for court dates for intervention to occur.

Requirements for Parent Coordinators

Currently, in more than 30 states as well as some Canadian provinces, parent coordination is used (Sullivan, 2013). The legal requirements of a parent coordinator differ from state to state; it is important to find out what the requirements are in one's jurisdiction and if there are any statutes used to appoint parent coordinators (Boyan & Termini, 2005). Parent coordinators in California are either special masters or parent coordinators. Special masters are attorneys, whereas parent coordinators are typically therapists (Boyan, 2000). Parent coordinators in Hawaii are called custody commissioners (Sullivan, 2004). Most states require applicants to go through a training program along with other various requirements. According to Kirkland and Sullivan (2008), parent coordinators usually have an academic background in social work, the mental health professions, or law. Furthermore, most parent coordinators must undergo extensive training and gather experience in mediation before they can actively practice parent coordination (Barsky, 2011).

The AFCC Task Force on Parenting Coordination (2006) suggests one should become a qualified mediator and receive training on the parent coordination process, family dynamics in separation and divorce, parent coordination techniques and issues, the court-specific parent coordination process, as well as domestic violence training. Some states require that parent coordinators have considerable training in the effects of abuse on victims to take on cases such as these (Bartlett, 2004). However, in other states, such as Pennsylvania (Supreme Court of Pennsylvania Domestic Relations Procedural Rules Committee, 2013), parenting coordination is no longer practiced because it was ruled that only judges should have decision-making power in child custody cases (Emery et al., 2014). Other states have shifted to allowing parents the right to delegate the decision-making authority to a parent coordinator themselves, without the intercession of a judge (Emery & Emery, 2014).

The AFCC is committed to providing an interdisciplinary means for exchanging ideas and to the improvement of procedures in aiding families in disputes. More information can be found on their website at www.afccnet.org. AFCC can be a helpful resource for networking with other professionals to exchange information, expertise, and support. Seeking support is recommended to reduce burnout by communicating and networking with other parent coordinators (Boyan, 2000). Parent coordinators must protect themselves from professional burnout in order to keep efficacy. The work can be very rewarding but also tremendously challenging.

Roles of the Parent Coordinator

There are several roles of a parent coordinator. They are:

- Required to assess a family's dynamics and to refer parents who may need mental health assistance to an appropriate professional for care,
- Expected to educate parents on co-parenting techniques, the effects of parental conflict on children, and appropriate developmental issues (Bartlett, 2004),
- Expected to connect with other professionals, including the children's school, therapists, attorneys, social services, extended family, and others (Boyan & Termini, 2005), and
- Expected to create a plan to resolve parental conflicts.

Parent coordinators model empathy and respect for both parents to mimic in a parallel parenting relationship. Therapists in this role must also be certain not to act as a therapist as well as a parent coordinator (Boyan, 2000), instead referring parents to a therapist if psychotherapy is needed. Parent coordinators will find that they cannot be as effusive as they might be in their role as a therapist, instead sticking to the more limited role of problem-solving between the parents. To this end, parent coordinators must occasionally be authoritative, and direct the structure of the session, in addition to limiting what parents discuss for progress to occur. Parent coordinators have the authority to recommend additional services, send updates to counsel, make temporary visitation modifications, and, when legally allowed, they may be able to temporarily arbitrate parenting matters when an impasse is reached. In some cases, mental illness or substance abuse issues may preclude a parent coordinator from productively and ethically seeing a case.

Parent coordinators are expected to expertly manage conflict. It is suggested to use separate waiting areas, stagger arrival and departure times for both parties, consider the use of a caucus model, and take security precautions (Doty & Berman, 2004). In domestic violence cases, it may be less productive or inappropriate to meet with both individuals together to make conjoint decisions. The abuse victim may feel too threatened in conjoint sessions to suggest or make decisions that could upset their coparent.

Ethical Issues

Informed Consent

An informed consent document is especially important to outline the role that the parent coordinator plays for the parents. This process is not confidential, because the clients are court mandated to participate; the parent coordinator will often be required to share information with the court. The limits of confidentiality need to be clearly outlined. There is no confidentiality for communications between the parents and their children, and the parent coordinator. Likewise, there is no confidentiality for communications between the parent coordinator and other relevant parties to the parent coordination process (e.g., guardian ad litem; attorneys) or for communication to the court (American Psychological Association, 2012). Any conflicts of interests need to be explained. Fees (for in-session and out-of-session time spent) need to be divulged. Mandatory reporting guidelines also apply.

Clarity of Role

The role of the parent coordinator can be easily confusing for both the client and, at times, the coordinator. The coordinator must be careful to not perform therapy, but to facilitate parenting to remain child-focused. Referrals should be made for any additional services needed, and never to any professional from which the therapist profits in some way (Boyan & Termini, 2005). According to the American Psychological Association Guidelines (2012), the parent coordinator must refrain from implementing clinical, forensic, or legal practices as this would be beyond the scope of the parent coordinator's role. Additionally, the coordinator should not serve in sequential roles, such as becoming one party's therapist after parent coordination has terminated (AFCC Task Force on Parenting Coordination, 2006).

Neutrality and Decision-making

As in mediation, the parent coordinator must take care to remain impartial and provide effective parent coordination services to the dyad. They need to be aware of any values or biases that may interfere with their ability to perform duties, maintaining a neutral stance, or being committed to assisting all parties (AFCC Task Force on Parenting Coordination, 2006). If the parent coordinator is unable to do this, they should make a referral to a new parent coordinator, making sure to facilitate the transition to the new coordinator (Boyan & Termini, 2005). Although parents should be free to determine their parenting stances, when they choose options that are not in the best interests of the child, a parent coordinator may adjust parenting plans or take an arbitrator position and make a decision for the family. The parents always retain the right to appeal the decisions made by the parenting coordinator in court (Emery et al., 2014).

Communication with the Court

Even though the parent coordinator regularly communicates with others involved in the case, the parent coordinator *must not* engage in ex parte communication with the judge. Ex parte communication is communication with the judge without involving the attorneys of the involved parties; this includes communication by e-mail, fax, or in person (Coates, 2015). If it is specified in writing in the order of appointment, parent coordination agreement, or stipulation, the coordinator may communicate with each of the parties or their attorneys (AFCC Task Force on Parenting Coordination, 2006).

Parent coordinators may be ordered to provide status reports to the court. It is also not unusual for parent coordinators to be subpoenaed if the case were to go to court, and they have no immunity from such situations. Therefore, they must be prepared to testify in cases involving their clients. Additionally, in allegations of child abuse, a parent coordinator has a duty to protect or warn (see Chapter 3), and parent coordination may not be appropriate in these situations (Doty & Berman, 2004).

Comparing and Contrasting the Mediator and Parenting Coordinator Roles

The most pronounced difference between the mediator and the parent coordinator is the decision-making authority. In mediation, the two disputing parties maintain the choice to select what is appropriate for them. In the parenting coordinator's session, the parenting coordinator acts as an arbitrator and can make judgments if the two parties do not reach agreement. Mediators not only mediate child custody, but are also certified to mediate property settlements.

Mediators help parents resolve disputes that arise during separation and after the divorce, and parent coordinators help divorcing parents implement parenting plans and make day-to-day decisions about the children (Jessani & James, 2006). Parent coordinators have legal jurisdiction, whereas mediators must call an impasse if final decisions cannot be reached. They may also make minor adjustments to temporary departures from the parenting plan. Parenting coordinators often determine when children are ready for increased visitation and can make sure that children receive items from one parent when with another in high-conflict cases. They are also able to speak with the child's therapist and the courts.

Anything shared in the mediation session is inadmissible in court, so there is no written record of the session (Goodman, 2004). The mediator may choose to use a dry-erase board, chalkboard, notepad, or large sketchpad to take notes on those topics that have been agreed upon, but nothing written in session, with the exception of the final settlement, is ever kept after the mediation. Goodman (2004) suggested that all notes from a mediation session be destroyed. It is important to note that one should only keep documents that support the mediator's fees and should maintain confidentiality in storing those documents. Confidentiality should be considered in the process of destroying documents. It is also important to inform the parties that the mediator will not testify in court and that the mediator's documents may not be subpoenaed. In most states, the mediator has the same immunity as a judge from testifying in further proceedings (Gilchrist & Marshall, 1999). As previously stated, all documents and parenting coordination proceedings are admissible in court. A summary of differences between mediation and parent coordination is provided in Table 11.1.

TABLE 11.1 Mediation and Parent Coordination

Mediators	Parent Coordinators
Resolve disputes that arise during separation and after divorce.[a]	Help divorcing and divorced parents implement parenting plans and make daily decisions about children.[a]
Often voluntary process at all stages in divorce process; usually occurs in beginning of divorce process.[a]	Self-referral, attorney referral, court referral. Usually last resort.[a]
Confidential process.[a]	Not confidential.[a]
Must call impasse if parents do not agree.	Can make decisions if parents do not agree.
No contact with judge.[a]	Typically referrals from court and can inform judge of recommendations.[a]
Nothing admissible in court.	Everything admissible in court.
No documentation.	Documentation.

[a] Adapted from Jessani & James (2006).

Toward a National Standard

The American Bar Association Section of Dispute Resolution, the Academy of Family Mediators, and the AFCC all work to ensure that mediation and parent coordination sessions are working to resolve disputes in a fair and ethical way. Many state legislating bodies are also aware of mediators and parent coordinators and are working to get immunity rights for those who decide to practice in these fields if they do not already hold them (that is, protection from civil liability). A national standard would be a benefit to those states still litigating all domestic relations cases. The courts would be less inundated with familial issues that can be negotiated outside of the costly litigation process. Children could avoid having to testify or speak to a judge, and their interests could be more readily served.

Summary

Couple and family therapists are increasingly called upon to stretch beyond the realm of therapy to best serve families in need. Mediation and parent coordination are two areas in which family therapists, with additional training, can make a valuable contribution to parents and children suffering the ill effects of protracted parental conflict. Even when conflict is minor or nonexistent, therapists acting as mediators can help parents establish parenting plans and help parents stay out of the conflictual roles that can inadvertently develop out of the adversarial nature of the U.S. court system. Couple and family therapists can use the skills they have in managing conflictual situations as a resource in parent coordination and their systems training is immensely valuable in understanding the contextual underpinnings of the conflict at hand. Along with marital dissolution and child custody, couple and family therapists are trained to manage parent/child disputes, sibling disputes, and cases involving older adults and their families. couple and family therapists are well positioned to give families a foundation of agreement on which to build relationships extending into the future. It is incumbent upon couple and family therapists to stretch outside of the therapy office into areas in which families are experiencing anxiety, transitional stress, and duress, to help them navigate the pain ensconced in such conflicts.

References

Amato, P. R. (2001). Children and divorce in the 1990's: An update of the Amato and Keith (1991) meta-analysis. *Journal of Family Psychology, 15*(3), 355–370. doi: 10.1037/0893-3200.15.3.355.

Amato, P. R. (2010). Research on divorce: Continuing trends and new developments. *Journal of Marriage and Family, 72*(3), 650–666. doi: 10.1111/j.1741-3737.2010.00723.x.

Amato, P. R., & Booth, A. (1996). A prospective study of divorce and parent–child relationships. *Journal of Marriage and the Family, 58*(2), 356–365. doi: 10.2307/353501.

Amato, P. R., & Cheadle, J. E. (2008). Parental divorce, marital conflict and children's behaviour problems: A comparison of adopted and biological children. *Social Forces, 86*(3), 1139–1161. doi: 10.1353/sof.0.0025.

American Psychological Association. (2012). Guidelines for the practice of parenting coordination. *American Psychologist, 67*(1), 63–71. doi: 10.1037/a0024646.

Association of Family and Conciliation Courts (AFCC) Task Force on Parenting Coordination. (2006). Guidelines for parenting coordination. *Family Court Review, 44*(1), 164–181. doi: 10.1111/j.1744-1617.2006.00074.x.

Ayoub, C. C., Deutsch, R. M., & Maraganorr, A. (1999). Emotional distress in children of high-conflict divorce: The impact of marital conflict and violence. *Family Conciliation Courts Review, 37*(3), 297–314. doi: 10.1111/j.174-1617.1999.tb01307.x.

Barsky, A. E. (2011). Parenting coordination: The risks of a hybrid conflict resolution process. *Negotiation Journal, 27*(1), 7–27. doi: 10.1111/j.1571-9979.2010.00290.x.

Bartlett, B. A. (2004). Parenting coordination: A new tool for assisting high conflict families. *The Oklahoma Bar Journal, 75*(6), 453.

Boyan, S. (2000). What is a parenting coordinator? Specialized therapists and mandated high conflict families. *Family Therapy News, AAMFT,* (June/July), 28–30.

Boyan, S. M., & Termini, A. M. (2005). *The psychotherapist as parent coordinator in high conflict divorce: Strategies and techniques.* New York, NY: Haworth.

Coates, C. (2015). The parenting coordinator as peacemaker and peacebuilder. *Family Court Review, 53*(3), 398–406. doi: 10.1111/fcre.12161.

Doty, D. R., & Berman, W. B. (2004). *Divorce transition services.* Tulsa, OK: Parenting Coordination.

Emery, R. E. (1994). *Renegotiating family relationships: Divorce, child custody, and mediation.* New York, NY: Guilford.

Emery, R. E., & Emery, D. C. (2014). Who knows what's best for children? Honoring agreements and contracts between parents who live apart. *Law and Contemporary Problems, 77*(1), 151–176. Retrieved from http://scholarship.law.duke.edu/lcp/vol77/iss1/6.

Emery, R. E., Rowen, J., & Dinescu, D. (2014). New roles for family therapists in the courts: An overview with a focus on custody dispute resolution. *Family Process, 53*(3), 500–515. doi: 10.1111/famp.12077.

Gilchrist, C. A., & Marshall, C. L. (1999). Indiana family mediation. *Indiana Continuing Legal Education Forum.* Indianapolis, IN.

Goodman, A. H. (2004). *Basic skills for the new mediator* (2nd ed.). Rockville, MD: Solomon Publications.

Jessani, A. D., & James, L. (2006). Mediators and parent coordinators: 20 questions/40 answers. *American Journal of Family Law, 2*(3), 180–187.

Kelly, J. (2000). Children's adjustment in conflicted marriages and divorce: A decade review of research. *Journal of the American Academy of Child and Adolescent Psychiatry, 39*(8), 963–973. doi: 10.1097/00004583-200008000-00007.

Kirkland, K., & Sullivan, M. (2008). Parenting coordination (PC) practice: A survey of experienced professionals. *Family Court Review, 46*(4), 622–636. doi: 10.1111/j.1744-1617.2008.00228.x.

Mayer, B. (2004). Facilitative mediation. In J. Folberg, A. L. Milne, & P. Salem (Eds.), *Divorce and family mediation: Models, techniques, and applications* (pp. 29–52). New York, NY: Guilford.

Miller, W. R., & Rose, G. S. (2009). Towards a theory of motivational interviewing. *American Psychologist, 64*(6), 527–537. doi: 10.1037/a0016830.

Milne, A. L., Folberg, J., & Salem, P. (2004). The evolution of divorce and family mediation: An overview. In J. Folberg, A. L. Milne, & P. Salem (Eds.), *Divorce and family mediation: Models, techniques, and applications* (pp. 3–25). New York, NY: Guilford.

Morris, M., & Halford, W. K. (2014). Family mediation: A guide for family therapists. *Australian and New Zealand Journal of Family Therapy, 35*(4), 479–492. doi: 10.1002/anzf.1078.

Saposnek, D. T. (1998). *Mediating child custody disputes: A strategic approach* (2nd ed.). San Francisco, CA: Jossey-Bass.

Sullivan, M. J. (2004). Ethical, legal, and professional practice issues involved as acting as a psychologist parenting coordinator in child custody cases. *Family Court Review, 42*(3), 576–582. doi: 10.1111/j.174-1617.2004.tb00670.x.

Sullivan, M. J. (2013). Parenting coordination: Coming of age? *Family Court Review, 51*(1), 56–62. doi: 10.1111/fcre.12008.

Supreme Court of Pennsylvania Domestic Relations Procedural Rules Committee. (2013). *Rule 1915 11-1. Elimination of parent coordination.* Retrieved from http://www.pacode.com/secure/data/231/chapter1915/chap1915toc.html.

Walther, G. M. (2000). Power imbalances in divorce mediation. *American Journal of Family Law, 14*(2), 93–101.

Welsh, N. A. (2004). Reconciling self-determination, coercion, and settlement in court-connected mediation. In J. Folberg, A. L. Milne, & P. Salem (Eds.), *Divorce and family mediation* (pp. 420–446). New York, NY: Guilford.

12

Ethical Issues in Clinical Practice

Z. Seda Sahin and Julie Ramisch

> Mary was excited to receive the keys to her new office, where she was to begin seeing clients at her very own practice. As she hung her license on the wall, she reflected on the years of work that brought her to this point. She recalled all of the classes, supervisions, presentations, clinical hours, as well as the many other requirements that led to this day. These all contributed to and helped her realize her goal of opening her own private practice. However, she realized that, for all of her education and experience, she lacked knowledge of the business aspect of running a practice and the ethical considerations that must be taken into account. She realized that she was unaware of how to get on insurance panels, how to market her company, and how to build a business. She was overwhelmed with where to begin.

Although graduate programs focusing on couple and family therapy offer extensive training on providing therapy services to individuals, couples, and families, the business of building and maintaining a practice is rarely covered in the curriculum. Starting a private practice requires legal and ethical knowledge and a sound business plan. The goal of this chapter is to provide information that facilitates the process of starting and sustaining a successful private practice.

Building a Practice

When thinking about starting to practice, there are many different areas that couple and family therapists must consider. This process has many layers including, but not limited to, maintaining a valid license and malpractice insurance, choosing a location for the practice, learning about the legal requirements of opening a business, and getting on insurance panels. Following is a summary of the different areas and some guidelines to aid couple and family therapists in managing different circumstances that may arise during the course of practice.

Licensure or Certification Laws and Malpractice (Professional Liability) Insurance

Each state has its own summary of guidelines that include educational requirements, supervision, and clinical hours that must be obtained before a therapist can be licensed. Information regarding state certification or licensure requirements can be found on the websites of each of organization (American Association for Marriage and Family Therapy, 2016; American Counseling Association, 2016; American Psychological Association, 2016; National Association of Social Workers, 2016).

Obtaining malpractice insurance is the next step before starting clinical work (Barnett & Musewicz, 2013). There are multiple malpractice insurance carriers for different mental health professionals. Professional organizations typically provide discounted rates for coverage. More information can be found at each professional organization's website.

Office Space

When considering office space, choosing a convenient location is vital. An office that is easily accessible with enough parking spaces makes the practice convenient for clients. Also, a location that offers accommodations for all clients is very important because many insurance companies will request information regarding disability accessibility. Budget, demographics, traffic patterns, and signage are all important considerations. If you intend to specialize in a particular market area, consider location to the consumer. For example, if you wish to do Employee Assistance Program work, it is wise to place your office near the employers.

When establishing a practice in an office building or a home that was not originally designed to be used as therapy offices, it is imperative that therapists spend the necessary money to guarantee client confidentiality by soundproofing the offices. Sessions should not be heard in hallways, waiting rooms, or reception areas (Pope & Vasquez, 2001). Therapists should make every effort to keep private not only what the client says, but also that the person is a client (Congress, 1999). This can be optimally accomplished by having one door for an entrance and a separate exit door that allows clients to exit a therapy session without being seen by clients waiting in the waiting room.

Common Requirements for Opening a Business

Although it is not a requirement, forming a business as a limited liability company (LLC) or corporation (Inc.) separates personal assets from professional assets. This helps protect your personal finances from liability issues or lawsuits and also provides legitimacy to your business. The U.S. Small Business Administration offers detailed information to assist with choosing a business structure. This information can be found on the Small Business Administration website at www.sba.gov.

Next, you need to obtain an employer identification number (EIN) from the Internal Revenue Service, commonly known as your tax ID number. Using this number allows you to avoid using your Social Security number when filling out any type of paperwork, such as credentialing forms for insurance companies. To apply for an EIN, visit www.irs.gov.

Finally, therapists need to obtain a National Provider Identification Number, known as an NPI, allowing you to seek reimbursement as a mental health provider. Therapists may apply as an individual or group practice through the National Plan and Provider Enumeration System available through the Department of Health and Human Services website.

Working With Managed Care Organizations

Managed health care and managed care organizations (MCOs) have drastically changed the landscape of clinical practice of couple and family therapy. The development of preferred provider organizations (PPOs), health maintenance organizations (HMOs), and exclusive provider organizations (EPOs) has made payment for health care a complicated maze to navigate. Getting paid for therapeutic services is no longer between the couple and family therapist and the client, but is between the therapist, the third-party payer, and the client. For therapists, being part of a panel, or being a preferred provider for an MCO typically means that they provide therapeutic services for clients who belong to that specific organization at a reduced rate. Theoretically, a therapist would benefit from being part of an MCO in exchange for seeing clients at a reduced rate, as presumably client volume would increase.

First, therapists should fill out an application with the Council for Affordable Quality Healthcare (CAQH). The CAQH is the online application system used by the majority of insurance companies to obtain professional information of therapists. Therapists can set an account for themselves prior to applying to insurance panels (Council for Affordable Quality Healthcare, 2016). Then, the insurance panels contact CAQH to receive the required information.

In addition to completing a CAQH application, therapists must complete individual applications with each MCO to become a provider and begin accepting clients using insurance from various MCOs. In order to become a provider for most MCOs, therapists must select which MCOs they would like to provide for and then contact the provider relations division of the company directly to ask for the proper application forms. Often, the applications can be found on the company websites. Sometimes companies are closed to new members and do not allow any therapists to join. If denied access to the panels, clients who are members of the MCO can contact the organization (usually done by letter) or can ask their professional association to ask that the panel be opened. When granted application forms, therapists will be asked to provide information such as relevant education, experience, curriculum vita, copies of degrees, copies of license and certification, and a copy of liability insurance (Christensen & Miller, 2001).

Getting paid from MCOs presents an ethical dilemma in that companies require therapists to give a *Diagnostic and Statistical Manual of Mental Disorders (DSM)* diagnosis in order to demonstrate medical necessity and receive reimbursement. Kielbasa, Pomerantz, Krohn, and Sullivan (2004) reported that clinicians were 10 times more likely to not assign a diagnosis when the client paid out of pocket versus when managed care paid for the client. For couple and family therapists who give relational diagnoses (V-codes), it might be beneficial to investigate MCOs that accept these diagnoses before becoming a preferred provider. If no MCO in an area accepts relational diagnoses, therapists may prefer to accept only clients who are willing to pay out of pocket rather than going through insurance companies that do not accept relational diagnoses. Some therapists use the International Classification of Diseases (ICD), instead of the DSM, because of demands by insurance companies and/or because the ICD is preferred by social service agencies. Further, information regarding ethical issues involved in diagnosing can be found in Chapter 13.

Finally, it is unethical and also considered fraud by many MCOs to use a sliding fee scale that is different than a scale used for payment by MCOs. To avoid this, therapists who accept payments from insurance companies might want to consider setting standard session fees rather than sliding fees that are determined by a client's financial condition.

In the realm of managed care and insurance companies, the therapist must always remember that in the case of third-party payment sources, the primary allegiance of the therapist should be with the person receiving the services. Therapists should always explain to clients about the nature of having a third-party payer and the type of information that might be shared with the insurance company for billing purposes. It ultimately should be up to clients if they would like to use their MCO. Just because the client and the therapist belong to the same organization does not mean that the client cannot choose to pay out of pocket to preserve privacy. Additionally, if clients who pay out of pocket ask you to not share their treatment information with a third-party payer, and the law does not require disclosure, Health Insurance Portability and Accountability Act (HIPAA) regulations require that the provider not share the information with the third-party payer.

Documentation, Marketing, and Legal Issues

It is imperative that therapists be knowledgeable about HIPAA regulations as well as state law to maintain client privacy as completely as possible (see Chapter 4 for more information on HIPAA). Developing and maintaining forms for an ethical clinical practice are essential to record keeping. In addition to the documentation process, marketing efforts play a very important role in growing the practice. This following section also discusses when to hire an attorney and the development of a professional will.

Informed Consent Process

A crucial part of clinical practice is preparing the necessary documents that need to be discussed with clients before treatment. First is informed consent, which needs to, in clear language, explain the risks and benefits of therapy and give the client the option to decide whether or not to continue with therapy. Please see Appendix 12.1 for an example of an informed consent document. Informed consent, however, is not simply one document or conversation; it is a *process* that occurs throughout therapy is argued that it is not possible for it to happen in just one session (Pomerantz, 2005).

For clients to make an informed decision about participating in therapy, they need to know to what they are agreeing (Hudgins, Rose, Fifield, & Arnault, 2013). Many states require *disclosure statements* that typically require disclosure of the therapist's education and qualifications, though they may legislate other disclosures as well (Hecker, 2015). It is important that therapists be specific in these descriptions. For example, it is important to note any specific licenses and degrees of the therapist (Moline, Williams, & Austin, 1998).

In addition, if therapists have a specific certification, such as eye movement desensitization and reprocessing (EMDR) certification, it is important to specify that information in the disclosure statements.

The first section of an informed consent should introduce the therapist and include information about the therapist's credentials, theoretical orientation, procedures surrounding observation, any recording, consulting or supervision of the sessions, the limits of confidentiality, and when confidentiality must be legally broken (Caudill, 2001).

Second, the rights of each client should be described. The informed consent should state that the client has access to their records, the right to choose the therapist and to be active in the treatment planning, the right to refuse counseling, the implication of refusing treatment, the right to ask additional questions about therapy, and the right to have questions answered in understandable language (Welfel, 2002). Third, the logistics section of the document should include the fees and billing practices, an estimate of the length of therapeutic services, procedures surrounding making and rescheduling appointments, what to do in an emergency, information about how long appointments will last, and how clients should address any grievances that may arise (Welfel, 2002). Fourth, risks and benefits of therapy should be clearly described. Risks to treatment, such as symptoms not improving or in some cases getting worse, should be noted. Clients should be notified that therapy does not necessarily work for each person. The risks and benefits of procedures, such as the use of cell phone communication should also be fully described and discussed with the client. Special consent is needed if the therapist is going to use any controversial or experimental techniques. Controversial techniques are those that are often unusual, and experimental techniques are newer without much empirical support (Caudill, 2001). Some mental health associations prescribe written informed consent; others do not specify that a written informed consent is required.

Couple and family therapists also need to remember that a written document is not to replace a discussion about the contents of the document. Beahrs and Gutheil (2001) suggested that a compromise to the customized oral agreement and a written document would be a personalized written informed consent form that may also help to increase clinical rapport. Couple and family therapists should periodically update informed consents when there are material (e.g., changes to the agreement) or operational changes (e.g., changes to your business) or when the modality of therapy changes (e.g., individual to couple therapy).

Finally, per HIPAA regulations, a client must receive a Notice of Privacy Practices (NPP). Most professional associations provide a sample NPP on their website; if state law provides clients with more confidentiality than HIPAA, state law must be integrated in the NPP. The couple and family therapist must attempt to get acknowledgment that clients have received the NPP, although services may not be denied should they refuse to sign the acknowledgment. Acknowledgment of receipt of the NPP can be included as part of the informed consent.

In the case of minor children, the level of consent varies by state statute. Many times children and/or people with disabilities are not often legally required to participate in the informed consent process; ethically, they should be involved by therapists to the fullest extent possible (Ramisch & Franklin, 2008; Sori & Hecker, 2006), and give assent to therapy. Assent means that clients are involved in decisions about therapy and agree to engage in therapy. Obtaining assent is not only an ethical matter, but also creates collaboration and accountability (Welfel, 2002). In cases of divorce or separation of parents, the therapist should make sure that consent is given by the legal custodial parent(s). See Chapter 10 for more information on minor clients.

Record-Keeping

Solid record-keeping not only benefits clients, but also the therapist in the event that person must show evidence of treatment. Professional code of ethics typically provides some guidance or standards regarding record-keeping; state mental health statutes may also prescribe required contents of mental health records. Much like the research regarding the informed consent process, research regarding what constitutes adequate records is not explicit. The following are suggested guidelines for adequate, accurate, and ethical record-keeping. This list has been compiled from marriage and family therapy literature as well as traditional psychotherapy and social work literature (Cameron & turtle-song, 2002; Caudill, 2001; Moline et al., 1998).

Identifying Information

Records should include basic information about the client such that anyone who might have access to the file can easily identify the client. This section should include the client's name, phone number, date of birth and age, marital status, occupation, school or education, people living in the same house, mental health insurance company, and policy number. It should be specific about how the therapist is to contact the client. Some clients choose to keep the fact that they are seeking therapy private from the other people that they live with; thus, the therapist should be respectful of that. During the informed consent process, therapists should ask clients how they should introduce themselves when calling on the telephone. Additionally, therapists should ask clients about leaving messages, and if therapists should leave a message, how they should address themselves on the answering service.

Diagnostic Testing and Assessment/Interview

This section should include the presenting complaints, results of the mental status evaluation (oriented to date, location, and who the client is), and any significant history (past suicide attempts, substance use, or abuse).

Background and Historical Data

Information regarding the client's medical history, current problems (symptoms), social or personal history, developmental history, marital history, physical health, psychiatric and psychological history (inpatient services), medication history, family history, work history, sexual history, indication of a danger to self and others, and history of abuse should be kept. In case of any present suicidal or homicidal ideation, the therapist should make a detailed record of how the situation was handled.

Progress Notes and Treatment Plan

Progress notes should include a descriptive summary of all contacts, observable data (appearance, behavior, mood), reactions of clients, reactions of parents/guardians, and significant events. Note the type of therapy (individual, group, couple, marital, or family) and the progress or lack of progress in relation to the treatment plan. Progress notes are proof that sessions are being held and that sessions are continuing in the best interest of the client. They should include the date and the start and stop time of the session. Therapists should also keep in mind that clients have the right to see their own records; therefore, therapists must take special care to write only what they are comfortable with the client reading.

Subjective, objective, assessment, and plan, abbreviated as SOAP, notes were developed by Weed (1964) and are meant to help clinicians effectively communicate with each other as well as provide information about the continuation of the therapy process. When writing a case note, if an error is made, Cameron and turtle-song (2002) recommend not erasing the error, but rather drawing a single strike line through the word or verbiage, with the word "error" next to it, and initialing it with date and time of the correction. Black ink is standard for written notations as well as printed records, although there are typically not statutory requirements in this regard.

The treatment plan section should include an ongoing assessment of the client's progress and treatment success. Progress toward treatment goals is important to note and keep up to date for reasons important to third-party payers. This documentation may be also be helpful for clients who are involved in litigation to show that they are meeting any legal requirements deemed necessary by a court. All of the possible strategies and interventions to be used in therapy to help clients meet their short- and long-term goals should be described. It is recommended that the therapist note all directives or homework assignments that were given and what the client's response was to those directions or assignments. If there is a lack of progress in therapy, this should also be noted. It is particularly important to record instances in which the client failed to follow through with directions, recommendations, or assignments.

A summary of any discussion of the material should be noted in the progress notes. Therapists should also record all no-shows to sessions as well as cancellations (on both the client's and therapist's end); late arrivals should also be noted. Clients may also send the therapist a greeting card or a letter in the mail, or give therapists a copy of what they wrote in their journal, diaries, or even poetry related to their therapy endeavors. A copy of this material should be dated and included in the file.

Collaboration with Other Professionals

There may be specific areas in which both the client and the therapist could benefit from a second opinion by another professional. Supervision is a formal arrangement and the supervisor assumes liability as well as the therapist. Even in informal consultations with colleagues, the consultant could also be held liable in the event of litigation. If a therapist asks for a consultation from another therapist, the name of the therapist consulted, date of consultation, rationale for the consult, and what was stated should be noted. If a therapist is using supervision, they should also keep track of when they were supervised, what the supervisor requested of the therapist, and what suggestions the supervisor made regarding each case. It is best to have the supervisor sign their name to the record after each supervision session. Results of these consultations should be noted in the client's file. Record-keeping for both supervision and consultations is essential for both the therapist and the consulted party.

When consulting with colleagues, it is important that therapists discuss only the minimum necessary information (see Chapter 4 for more information on the "minimum necessary" requirement). Precautions should be taken to ensure privacy and to keep the identity of the client private (Pope & Vasquez, 2001), or a release form is needed.

Current Medications

This section should include the name, dose, prescribing doctor, and possible side effects of all medications as stated by the client. If the therapist is unsure about any details, quick research can be done with the aid of the latest *Physician's Desk Reference* (2016), or through consultation with a psychiatrist. Any materials about the medications can be printed out and kept in clients' files for easy reference.

Diagnosis

Because diagnoses are typically used for billing and insurance purposes, this section must be accurate and up-to-date. It is wise for therapists to work collaboratively with the client about the diagnosis, as other third parties such as a probation officer, employer, or future employer may gain access to diagnoses, as will insurers.

Correspondence and Phone Calls

Any time that a client is contacted or an attempt at contact is made, a record should be kept about the date, time, reasons for the contact, and what transpired during these conversations. Therapists should also keep copies of all signed letters that were mailed to the client or others, along with mailing dates. Reports to authorities should also be documented (e.g., child or dependent adult protective services).

Release of Information

It is standard practice for the current therapist to obtain previous treatment records. This aids therapy in several ways: the therapist can avoid making the same recommendations that were unsuccessful, understand what types of interventions contributed to client progress, find out about any previous suicidal or homicidal ideation, intent, or attempts, diagnoses, and reasons for prior therapy terminations. A release of information (ROI) document should be constructed by the therapist and typically includes date, the name and address of the agency providing the information, the name and address of the agency receiving the information, information about what specific information is to be released, the time period of treatment covered by the release, and the length of time the release is to be in effect. State statute typically mandates what is to be included in an ROI. Likewise, HIPAA regulations require an authorization for release of information for psychotherapy notes, as well as any other treatment information when it is not required for treatment or insurance purposes. The couple and family therapist must integrate the requirements of both state statute and HIPAA regulations. If there is overlap between the requirements, the stricter provision applies. Generally, therapists should not rerelease records they obtained from another provider, but instead require the requestor obtain release of documents from the original provider. State and federal laws may be applicable to rerelease of records. For example, if psychotherapy notes are released, they are not afforded the same level of federal privacy protection granted by HIPAA regulations when they are in the hands of another party.

Family/Marital/Couple and Group Therapy

When starting a case file for a family, couple, or group, therapists should think about who the "client" is they are treating. If the "client" is the family, that needs to be documented to protect the privilege of all family members. In the case of divorce, in conjoint therapy moving to individual therapy, or in any legal matters, the files can be easily separated. Information that is about the entire family can be copied and placed in each person's file (Moline et al., 1998).

Even if separate progress notes are kept for each family member, if an individual's case records are requested to be released, it is imperative for the therapist to obtain written permission from *all* legal adult clients or guardians of clients (in a release form) to release the records. The reason for this is that most likely information about all involved parties was documented on that individual's case notes when that individual was involved in family sessions.

If a family case file is split into individual case files and an individual's case records are requested to be released, it is imperative for the therapist to obtain an ROI from *all* family members to release the records. The reason for this is that most likely information about all involved parties was documented on that individual's case notes when that individual was involved in family sessions.

If group members are always seen together, one record may be kept for the whole group provided that measures are taken to protect confidentiality of all group members (Congress, 1999). Using a coding system instead of using client names can do this. If group members are ever seen individually, therapists should keep individual files for each member (Moline et al., 1998).

Termination Notes

This section should include a brief note about how the decision to terminate therapy was made, what goals were attained that led to the termination, suggested referrals, the client's diagnosis at the time of termination, and the client's mental status. It is important to note any rationale for termination if the therapist made the decision to terminate.

Confidentiality and Digital Concerns

With the increased usage of digital technology with regard to record-keeping or between sessions, communication confidentiality is at more risk than ever. It is important for therapists to be knowledgeable about technology and also have conversations with the clients about the usage of technology in treatment (Zilberstein, 2015). Refer to Chapter 14 for more information on e-therapy.

Therapists should always make every effort to ensure that faxes or e-mails sent and received keep confidential information protected. "Confidential or sensitive information should be faxed or e-mailed *only* if both sender and recipient have sufficient reason to be confident that the data will be protected both during transmission and once it arrives" (Pope & Vasquez, 2001, p. 239). Couple and family therapists can verify that an authorized person is able to receive the fax. A cover page should include a clear statement about the following confidential pages (Welfel, 2002). A way to guard confidentiality is for therapists to make telephone contact before and after sending a fax when sending confidential information; having preset numbers for parties who regularly receive faxes (e.g., probation officers) can help assure confidentiality.

Clients may, of their own accord, request these alternate forms of communication in a nonencrypted format. Therapists can oblige this request, but should have written documentation that the client expressly consented to the alternate communication means (e.g., e-mail, text).

Therapists need to guard client confidentiality by being mindful about where files are placed and how files are labeled. When making files for clients, instead of using the client's name to label the file, a numbering or coding system can be used (Pope & Vasquez, 2001). These files should also never be left unattended and should be locked away when not in possession of the therapist. Additionally, if a computer is used to write case notes or store information about clients, the information should be coded so that no identifying information is revealed. All computers maintaining client information should be encrypted. Automatic log-offs for inactive screens should be set. For more information on the impact of HIPAA regulations on privacy and electronic security of confidential information, please refer to Chapter 4.

Retention of Records

For therapists to determine the exact number of years that full records or summary of records need to be kept, they should look into the regulations for the state in which they practice because state laws vary. For example, some states require that records be kept for 3 years after the last appointment, and other states mandate that a summary be kept for 12 years (Pope & Vasquez, 2001). HIPAA is silent on the number of years records must be maintained. Proper disposal of records in a confidential manner is also imperative (Moline et al., 1998).

Marketing

Once a therapist opens a practice and establishes an ethical system of documentation, marketing will enable therapists to build their practices. Creating a strong online presence with a website and additional social media resources (e.g., Facebook, Twitter, LinkedIn) is beneficial for a private practice. Therapists often place their ads on different websites (e.g., psychologytoday.com, goodtherapy.org, yelp.com) to attract clients.

Typically therapists can add information to their professional organization's directory as well.

In addition to a solid online presence, marketing efforts should also be spent on building a community where the practice is located. Sending introduction letters or flyers to other local professionals, such as doctors, lawyers, schools, and churches can help therapists build their caseloads (Barnett & Musewicz, 2013). Taking the extra step of setting up introductory meetings may also be beneficial. Specific thank you letters to referral sources should be avoided to maintain client confidentiality.

Joining the local chamber of commerce and attending professional networking groups may also prove helpful in establishing a successful practice. Marketing the business requires ongoing efforts, such as leaving business cards in visible places for the public to see, and listing contact information in the local yellow pages or newspapers. In addition to all of these strategies, having an open house will allow therapists to present their services to the community and local professionals.

Hiring an Attorney and Developing a Professional Will

It is recommended that therapists consult with and hire local attorneys to assist with concerns such as state and local laws, assistance with documents, and representation against third parties (see Chapter 3 for additional legal information). Some professional organizations provide free legal consultations for members so therapists should check with their organizations for more information.

An attorney also can assist in the development of a professional will. Unless the therapist works in a location that already has policies in place to manage record-keeping issues in the instance of sudden incapacity or death, a professional will is essential. An efficient professional will outlines, step by step, the process of accessing information regarding the location of confidential client data, keys, or passwords to access this data; the procedure for retrieving the therapist's weekly schedule; and any other information required that may assist during this stressful circumstance (Pope & Vasquez, 2005).

Conclusion

This chapter provided therapists with fundamental knowledge of ethical and legal considerations when starting and sustaining a successful private practice. When first building a practice, common concerns arise such as getting licensed, obtaining and maintaining malpractice insurance, acquiring office space, filing as a business, and obtaining an NPI number. This chapter also provided guidance about working with MCOs, from becoming a provider with local organizations to getting paid. To maintain an ethical practice in line with state and federal laws, it is essential that therapists maintain knowledge of standards of practice and continually update policies and procedures in their office. Informed consent, record-keeping, and confidentiality are all areas about which therapists want to remain meticulous to maintain ethical practice and protect one's practice as much as possible from litigious interference. In addition to these standards, therapists who desire to operate a successful private practice must have knowledge about starting and maintaining a business. As always, confidentiality of client information is paramount.

References

American Association for Marriage and Family Therapy (AAMFT). (2016). *Directory of MFT licensure and certification boards.* Retrieved from http://www.aamft.org/imis15/AAMFT/Content/Directories/MFT_Licensing_Boards.aspx.

American Counseling Association (ACA). (2016). Licensure and certification. Retrieved from https://www.counseling.org/knowledge-center/licensure-requirements.

American Psychological Association (APA). (2016). State licensure. Retrieved from http://www.apapracticecentral.org/ce/state/.

Barnett, J. E., & Musewicz, E. (2013). Training to begin a private practice. In M. J. Prinstein (Ed.), *The portable mentor: Expert guide to a successful career in psychology* (pp. 203–214). New York, NY: Springer Science+Business Media.

Beahrs, J. O., & Gutheil, T. G. (2001). Informed consent in psychotherapy. *The American Journal of Psychiatry, 158*(1), 4–10. doi: 10.1176/appi.ajp.158.1.4.

Cameron, S., & turtle-song, i. (2002). Learning to write case notes using the SOAP format. *Journal of Counseling and Development, 80*(3), 286–292. doi: 10.1002/j.1556-6678.2002.tb00193.x.

Caudill, O. B. (2001). Practice management: Integrating ethics into business. In R. H. Woody & J. D. Woody (Eds.), *Ethics in marriage and family therapy* (pp. 169–195). Alexandria, VA: American Association for Marriage and Family Therapy.

Christensen, L. L., & Miller, R. B. (2001). The practice of marriage and family therapists with managed care clients. *Contemporary Family Therapy, 23*(2), 169–180. doi: 10.1023/A:1011146202371.

Congress, E. P. (1999). *Social work values and ethics: Identifying and resolving professional dilemmas*. Belmont, CA: Wadsworth Group.

Council for Affordable Quality Healthcare. (2016). *Getting started*. Retrieved from https://proview.caqh.org/PR/Registration.

Hecker, L. L. (2015). Ethical, legal, and professional issues in marriage and family therapy. In J. L. Wetchler & L. L. Hecker (Eds.), *An introduction to marriage and family therapy* (pp. 505–524). Binghamton, NY: Haworth.

Hudgins, C., Rose, S., Fifield, P. Y., & Arnault, S. (2013). Navigating the legal and ethical foundations of informed consent and confidentiality in integrated primary care. *Families, Systems, & Health, 31*(1), 9–19. doi: 10.1037/a0031974.

Kielbasa, A. M., Pomerantz, A. M., Krohn, E. J., & Sullivan, B. F. (2004). How does clients' method of payment influence psychologists' diagnostic decisions? *Ethics and Behavior, 14*(2), 187–195. doi: 10.1080/10508420701310141.

Moline, M. E., Williams, G. T., & Austin, K. M. (1998). *Documenting psychotherapy: Essentials for mental health practitioners*. Thousand Oaks, CA: Sage.

National Association of Social Workers (NASW). (2016). *Association of social work boards*. Retrieved from https://www.socialworkers.org/nasw/ethics/boards.asp.

Physician's Desk Reference. (70th ed.). (2016). Montvale, NY: PDR Network.

Pomerantz, A. M. (2005). Increasingly informed consent: Discussing distinct aspects of psychotherapy at different points in time. *Ethics and Behavior, 15*(4), 351–360. doi: 10.1207/s15327019eb1504_6.

Pope, K. S., & Vasquez, M. J. T. (2001). *Ethics in psychotherapy and counseling*. San Francisco, CA: Jossey-Bass.

Pope, K. S., & Vasquez, M. J. T. (2005). *How to survive and thrive as a therapist: Information, ideas, and resources for psychologists in practice*. Washington, DC: American Psychological Association.

Ramisch, J. R., & Franklin, D. (2008). Families with a member with mental retardation and the ethical implications of therapeutic treatment by marriage and family therapists. *The American Journal of Family Therapy, 36*(4), 1–11. doi: 10.1080/01926180701647439.

Sori, C. F., & Hecker, L. L. (2006). Ethical and legal considerations when counseling children and families. In C. F. Sori (Ed.), *Engaging children in family therapy* (pp. 159–174). New York, NY: Routledge.

Weed, L. L. (1964). Medical records, patient care and medical education. *Irish Journal of Medical Education, 39*(6), 271–282. doi: 10.1007/BF02945791.

Welfel, E. R. (2002). *Ethics in counseling and psychotherapy: Standards, research, and emerging issues*. Pacific Grove, CA: Wadsworth Group.

Zilberstein, K. (2015). Technology, relationships and culture: Clinical and theoretical implications. *Clinical Social Work Journal, 43*(2), 151–158. doi: 10.1007/s10615-013-0461-2.

Appendix 12.1

*Informed Consent for Treatment**

Office of Mary F. Jones, LMFT

Please read the following information carefully. If you have questions regarding the content, please ask Ms. Jones for an explanation for your questions before signing the consent for treatment.

Information about Your Therapist and Therapy

Mary F. Jones graduated with her master's of science in marriage and family therapy from Purdue University Northwest. She is currently licensed to practice as a marriage and family therapist in the state of Indiana. She is dedicated to the treatment of family systems, including families, couples, children, and adult individuals. She primarily uses solution-focused therapy in her work with families and individuals; this type of therapy focuses on the resiliencies and strengths of people to aid them in solving the concerns they bring to therapy. Therapy will be held in sessions that typically last for 50 minutes, once a week. These may occur more or less frequently depending on the situation and availability of the therapist. It is important that all therapy sessions be held in the therapy office. Because wireless systems are easily accessible by third parties, therapy sessions will not be held over the phone or the computer.

The therapist is available for sessions Monday through Friday from 10:30 am to 9:00 pm. Outside of these hours, or if the therapist or office staff is unable to answer the phone, a confidential voicemail box is available for messages. If you need *immediate* emergency services, please seek out your nearest hospital emergency room. If it is determined in our work that you need services beyond the capabilities of this office, a referral will be made.

Confidentiality

All information about clients is kept strictly confidential. Case notes and records are kept on a computer that is password protected by the therapist. In most cases, clients must give written consent for the release of any information. There are, however, a few legal exceptions to the therapist keeping therapy information confidential. Therapists are legally required to break confidentiality when the following situations occur:

1. If a client threatens to harm themselves, the therapist may be obligated to seek hospitalization for them, or to contact family members who can provide them protection.
2. If a client threatens physical violence against another party, and has both the means and intent to commit violence, the therapist may have to disclose information in order to take protective action.

3. If the therapist has reasonable cause to suspect child abuse or neglect or elder/dependent adult abuse or neglect, the therapist is required to report this information to the proper authorities.
4. If a client files a lawsuit against a therapist, the therapist may disclose relevant information in order to defend themselves.
5. If a judge orders release of therapy information, or state or federal law requires it, the therapist is required to provide them with the information, although therapists will attempt as best as they can to protect clients' confidentiality.
6. For purposes of insurance billing if the client wishes to bill an insurance company to pay for services.

If individual family members choose to share secrets with the therapist, the therapist may ask the individual to share this information if it is important for therapy to progress. The therapist will discuss with the individual this information and how it is important for therapy first before it is brought up in family sessions.

Sometimes the therapist will need to consult with other professionals to ensure that they are providing the best therapy possible. In the case that identifying information needs to be revealed, you will have the opportunity to sign a statement agreeing to a release of your confidential information.

Cost

The fee for 50 minutes of therapy in the office with the therapist is $150 due at the end of each session. If the therapist is required to attend a court hearing or other proceedings, you will be billed $200 an hour, including any waiting and travel time. A retainer is expected in these cases. If you are not able to attend your scheduled session, please call within 1 business day before your session. Please call the office to speak to the office staff or leave a message after business hours. If you do not call, the therapist reserves the right to charge you for your missed session. All phone calls lasting longer than 20 minutes will also be billed to you at the hourly rate. The therapist accepts all forms of payment including cash, check, and credit, and your payment is due at the time of service. There is a $35 fee for any returned checks.

Risks and Rights

Therapy is a highly collaborative process that involves both you and your therapist. At times, therapy may feel like it is challenging you and the way that you think or believe. Therapeutic work can be intensive and stressful. It may also be uncomfortable if it is necessary to bring up specific memories or feelings. Resolutions of the issues that brought you into therapy may result in some changes that you never thought possible or intended to happen. These changes may happen quickly or slowly, and to one family member or to all family members. What is viewed as a positive change for one family member may be viewed negatively by another family member. There are no guarantees that therapy will have the results that you wish it to have.

You have the right to ask questions about your treatment at any time. You have the right to have input and say into your treatment goals and treatment plan. You have the right to ask about alternative treatments. If you wish to end therapy, you have the right to do so, although this decision is typically best made between you and the therapist together.

Minors

Minors (children younger than 18 who are not emancipated) will not be seen in therapy unless there is permission from both parents, the court, or the legal guardian. In cases where minor children are seen individually, confidentiality will be maintained unless the therapist is required to break confidentiality (see previous). However, the therapist may share general treatment themes and progress with the guardian. In cases when the minor child is seen individually with the therapist but is part of a client-family, the therapist may ask the child to share information with the parents or significant others in the family if it important for therapy to progress.

By signing below, I agree that I have read and understood the above information. My signature indicates that I give Mary Jones, LMFT, consent to treat myself and any minor children that I may bring into therapy. If I have any questions, comments, or grievances, I agree to discuss these with my therapist.

By signing below, I acknowledge that I have received the Notice of Privacy Practices for the office of Mary F. Jones.

______________________________ __________________

Signature Date

______________________________ __________________

Signature Date

______________________________ __________________

Signature Date

______________________________ __________________

Witness Signature Date

*Each state may have specific therapist requirements regarding disclosures, age of consent, and limitations of confidentiality. Couple and family therapists should check their own specific state laws.

13

Ethical Issues with Systemic and Social Constructionist Family Therapies

Joseph L. Wetchler and Rachel M. Moore

> John has just received his master's degree in marriage and family therapy and has started his first job providing home-based therapy for a community social service agency. He finds himself struggling to align his systems and social constructionist family therapy training with his new charge to find a Diagnostic and Statistical Manual for Mental Disorders (DSM) diagnosis for the identified patient in the family. He feels this is not in keeping with his family therapy beliefs and finds himself conflicted about being true to his field of thought. Also, he finds himself feeling resentful about the role that others involved with his cases (e.g., case workers, psychiatrists, judges) have in directing how he is supposed to treat his clients. They prescribe medications, require behavioral treatment plans, and have him write progress reports to the court. John believes that many of these requirements are antithetical to the family therapy models he learned in graduate school. How does he proceed? Does he give up family therapy to fit in with his job? Does he quit his job in hopes of finding a family therapy-friendly agency? How does he deal ethically with these seemingly polar opposites that appear to be pulling him in different directions?

John's problem is not unique. In fact, many family therapists have found themselves dealing with the supposed boundary between systemic and social constructionist models, and the individual linear, cause and effect, models of traditional mental health treatment. If we examine the history of marriage and family therapy, we see that the field started as a revolution within mental health to depathologize the individual (Broderick & Schrader, 1991; McGeorge, Carlson, & Wetchler, 2015). Family therapists moved away from viewing the problem as residing in the individual and placing it instead within the interactional system of the family (e.g., Haley, 1987; Minuchin, 1974; Watzlawick, Weakland, & Fisch, 1974). Bowen

(1978) went so far as to hospitalize entire families to study how family interactional patterns impacted psychotic behavior in young adults.

The social constructionist revolution evolved within family therapy during the late 1980s and early 1990s. Social constructionists believed that systemic family therapists had merely moved the label of pathology from the individual to the family (e.g., Anderson, 1997; White & Epston, 1990). They moved away from the systems metaphor, which they saw as inherently pathologizing as the idea of individual emotional problems. Instead, they focused on how problems reside in the social construction of language, and how reality exists less as an objectifiable construct, but rather within the conversations of societies, cultures, and even closely aligned groups (White, 2007).

With this focus in family therapy on viewing problems as existing within family interactions or socially constructed labels, many ethical issues may arise for students and practicing clinicians. This chapter focuses on three of these issues: the relationship of family therapy to issues of the *DSM* (American Psychiatric Association, 2013), the ethical responsibility of the therapist in family therapy, and the role of the client in treatment. This chapter addresses these issues through the theoretical lenses of systems-based and social constructionist family therapies by focusing on the perspectives of several of our field's founders. In doing so, we hope to bridge the duality that exists for some therapists between family therapy and traditional mental health through a more collaborative conversation (Anderson, 1997).

Integrating Family Therapy with DSM Diagnosis

> Elisa was directed by her supervisor to conduct a depression assessment on an adolescent whose parents expressed concerned that she was not sleeping at night, seemed constantly down, and had decreased appetite. The adolescent felt she did not have a problem and was concerned that her parents did not listen to her. Elisa was concerned that by conducting the assessment, she would pathologize the girl and place a disempowering label on her. She further felt she would not be able to assess potential family patterns that maintained her status as the identified patient; she also wanted to externalize the label from the girl.

This is a situation that many family therapists have faced. Systems-based family therapies and social constructionist family therapies attempt to depathologize the individual by assessing and treating family interactions and externalizing diagnostic labels (White & Epston, 1990). Because of this,

DSM diagnosis may lead to many ethical issues for family therapists. For example, Lebow (2015) argues that the DSM focuses on individual pathology, often within an individual brain, with little regard to more contextual factors. He further expresses concern that individual diagnosis and subsequent medication may move family therapy to an adjunctive treatment. Hoyt and Gurman (2012) worry that family therapists may have to rely on an individual diagnosis as a way to ensure their treatment families receive insurance reimbursement. This practice has been referred to as "insurance diagnosis" (Packer, 1988, p. 19). The concern is that this will create a false diagnosis for the individual to simply gain reimbursement, but the more theoretical concern is that it may solidify the family's belief that the identified patient (IP) is the problem, and the IP must be the sole person to change. In an attempt at theoretical purity, some have called for an inclusion in the DSM of relational diagnoses for reimbursement (Kaslow, 1996; Lebow, 2015). Although this movement gained some initial support within the larger mental health community in the early to mid-1990s, it has not received much support outside the couple and family therapy field.

On the other hand, Benson, Long, and Sporakowski (1992) argue that an individual diagnosis does not necessitate individual treatment. Couple and family therapists can continue to apply a systemic framework to these cases. Yet, although DSM diagnosis may be troubling for many couple and family therapists, Denton and Bell (2013) advise that "sometimes these assignments are necessary" (p. 153) either for insurance purposes or the need to assess for pathology. For example, when working with a couple in which one of the members is exhibiting depressive symptoms, the couple and family therapist needs to be able to adequately assess the severity of the depression, potential for suicidality, and, if necessary, appropriately refer the individual for medication management or hospitalization. Failure to do so places the client at risk, and in the event of a suicide attempt, puts the couple and family therapist at risk for malpractice action.

Therefore, it is crucial that couple and family therapists receive training on DSM diagnoses, keeping up this sphere of confidence with updated training upon DSM changes. It is incumbent upon the couple and family therapist to refer clients out to appropriately qualified providers for assessment and treatment areas outside of their scope of competence. When medication management is needed, a referral list of qualified and trusted psychiatrists should be available; working relationships with area psychiatrists should be established.

In the following section, we address the use of DSM diagnosis and medication within the systems-based and social constructionist family therapies.

We will focus on the writings of key theorists in how they addressed these issues. We provide this in hopes of resolving some of the arguments regarding the use of individual diagnosis and medication in couple and family therapy.

The Relationship Between Systems-Based and Social Constructionist Family Therapy and DSM Diagnosis

Systems-based Family Therapy and Individual Diagnosis

Early systems-based family therapists did not prohibit individual diagnosis; rather they were focused on studying systemic patterns that maintained psychosis (e.g., Bateson, 1972; Bowen, 1978) and juvenile delinquency (Minuchin, 1974), and providing interactional treatments. Although the clinician focused on relational sequences, the family and other mental health professionals often focused on the diagnosis/problem. In fact, Haley (1987) cautioned therapists against presenting systemic diagnoses as they may promote family resistance to treatment. If the family believes that the problem is due to one individual, it is easier to leverage family change by keeping their focus on this individual, the IP.

In other words, maintaining an individual diagnosis does not preclude doing family therapy. In fact, it may enhance it. A focus on the diagnosis allows the development of clear clinical goals and outcomes. A family with a member with depression is more likely to participate in identifying changes in symptomatic behaviors (e.g., sleeping more hours a night, returning to regular eating patterns, engaging in more activities) and is more likely to engage in activities to help that person than they would if the focus is on the family.

The Relationship Between Social Constructionist Treatment, Individual Diagnosis, Medication, and Referral

If systems-based family therapy sought to depathologize clients by incorporating their families in treatment, social constructionist therapists sought to avoid pathology by recognizing the role of society and culture in creating labels that limit individuals' abilities to resolve problems in their lives (White, 2007). Plus, narrative therapists believe in not solely focusing on the objective stance of a psychiatric label and allowing clients a say in how they define their problem (White, 1995). This has led some couple and family therapists to assume that to do narrative therapy they must avoid the use of psychiatric labels and require their clients to create their own labels. Yet, on the issue of DSM labels, White (1995) focuses more on the usefulness of the label for the client. Allowing a client to define how they view their problem allows them the freedom to use their diagnosis or describe it differently. He clearly does not prohibit diagnosis (White, 1995).

Similarly, Wetchler (1999) posits that DSM diagnoses are as easily externalized as any other labels. The early narrative concern that people's identity becomes synonymous with their label (White & Epston, 1990) does not preclude diagnosis. For example, people rarely say "I am cancer," but rather "I have cancer." And with that language, people look at their treatment as "fighting cancer." In many cases it is relatively easy to stay within the scope of the diagnosis and utilize similar medical language to externalize the diagnosis (Wetchler, 1999).

Related to the issue of diagnosis, narrative therapists do not take an antimedication stance. White (1995) shows more interest in helping individuals assess the importance of medication in their lives. Although he expresses his concern with overmedication, he also states, "I have witnessed drugs being used in way that have a profound effect in opening up the horizons of people's lives, in ways that bring a range of new possibilities for action" (pp. 117–118). White's stance reflects the belief that DSM diagnosis and medication do not preclude doing narrative therapy but may, in fact, enhance it.

Larger Systems Issues and Individual Diagnosis

The mental health profession is a large and multifaceted system. It comprises an array of institutions including outpatient treatment, inpatient psychiatric services, court-mandated treatment, day treatment, home-based services, child protective services, insurance providers, employee assistance programs, and medical services, to name a few. Plus, there are a host of treatment providers and associated professionals comprising family therapists, psychologists, psychiatrists, judges, lawyers, probations officers, mental health counselors, social workers, physicians, and nurses, among many others. Negotiating this large interconnected system requires that family therapists assess beyond the family and respect the depth and complexity of the entire mental health system. To focus solely on the family poses in itself ethical problems. For example, if a couple and family therapist focuses solely on the treatment family while ignoring the prescription of a consulting psychiatrist, the family may become caught in a triangle (Kerr & Bowen, 1988; Minuchin, 1974) in which the client's complete treatment needs become second to the ongoing battle between therapist and psychiatrist.

The Milan Associates (Boscolo, Cecchin, Hoffman, & Penn, 1987) discovered that although their trainees in Milan were successful in learning their model and treating client families, they often failed when they went back to their own treatment agencies. They realized that although a pure Milan approach could work at the Milan training center, other agencies provided different contexts with different rules. For their approach to work within other contexts, trainees needed to assess these systems and shift their approach to fit their host agencies. To not incorporate DSM diagnosis appropriately into one's practice fails to take into account the larger systemic mental health service issues that impinge on a family.

The Integration of Family Therapy Treatment with Substance Abuse Diagnosis

A good example of how family therapy has successfully interacted with diagnosis and medication management has been the substance-abuse field. Stanton and Todd (1982) were among the first to integrate the fields. They provided structural/strategic family therapy with young adult heroin addicts receiving methadone treatment. They found that those receiving family therapy and individual treatment fared better than those receiving individual treatment alone (Stanton & Todd, 1982). Since that time, numerous studies have shown several systems-based couple and family therapy models to be effective with adolescent and adult drug addiction (Rowe, 2012) and alcoholism (O'Farrell & Clements, 2012). The preponderance of evidence supporting the efficacy of family therapy with drug addiction led Rowe (2012) to state "family-based models are not only viable treatment alternatives for the treatment of drug abuse, but are now consistently recognized among the most effective approaches for treating both adults and adolescents with drug problems" (p. 59). Although most of the studies have focused on systems-based family therapy models, Smock et al. (2008) found that level one substance abusers did better in a solution-focused brief therapy group than those in a traditional substance abuse group. This is an encouraging finding, but clearly more research is necessary to support the social constructionist models as being effective with substance abuse.

With the rise in family substance abuse models, Whittinghill (2002) expressed concern that many substance abuse therapists were not properly trained in family therapy and misused it in treatment. He decried the demand that the entire family must be seen for treatment to proceed as many substance abusers are homeless and often family members may refuse to participate in treatment. Plus, many traditional substance abuse counselors have carried over the individual "disease" concept to the entire family. The "family disease" model has not been supported (O'Farrell,

1994). "Although the family disease model of substance abuse treatment in and of itself is not necessarily unethical, counseling limited exclusively to the disease model without giving proper consideration and attention to more critical familial issues is not beneficial" (Whittinghill, 2002, p. 76).

Therapist Responsibility in Systemic-Based and Social Constructionist Family Therapies

When I (JW) was a doctoral family therapy student, my professor (Fred Piercy) challenged the class: if we were all systems thinkers (an interactional construct), how did we incorporate the role of personal responsibility (a linear/cause-and-effect construct)? If we exist in an interactional world, do we never have agency over our own behaviors? If social constructionism views reality as related to the conversation in which it exists, are *all* solutions viable, as long as they work? The following sections address both therapist and client responsibility related to system-based and social constructionist family therapies. Although the roles are separated for reasons of clarity, in reality, they tend to be highly interactive.

Therapist Responsibility in Systems-Based Family Therapies

Traditional individual psychology models placed the role of change within the control of the client. For example, Freud (1953) viewed the therapist as a blank slate, allowing the client to free associate whatever thoughts or feelings came up. The therapist sat quietly behind the client who discussed whatever came to their mind. It was only in this free association that the client's unconscious issues could emerge. Later, Rogers (1961) taught that clients had all the answers they needed within themselves and could access them if the therapist provided a warm and accepting environment.

Systems-based family therapists felt this placed an undue burden on the individual and missed key contextual factors that impacted the client (Broderick & Schrader, 1991; McGeorge et al., 2015). Individuals, although aware of their own thoughts and feelings, were unable to totally grasp how they impacted and were impacted by the interactional sequences in which they existed (Watzlawick et al., 1974). They feared that simply waiting for client insight to emerge could lead to interminable therapies that were costly and took advantage of the client (Watzlawick et al., 1974). Haley (1987) placed responsibility for client change directly on the therapist. He saw this as the therapist's ethical mandate to provide competent, effective, clinical service. He further believed that therapists could not chalk up failures to client resistance. They must learn the skills to deal with an array of clients (Haley, 1987).

This emphasis on family therapist responsibility is reflected in the general principle that therapists only continue therapeutic relationships in which clients are benefiting from treatment. This clearly places the responsibility on therapists to regularly assess whether therapy is resolving client concerns, and if not, then the therapist should suggest termination of therapy or referral to another therapist. If referral is necessary, therapists are advised to assist clients in obtaining competent and appropriate therapeutic services.

Therapist Responsibility in Social Constructionist Family Therapies

Social constructionist family therapists see a problem associated with all responsibility for change lying in the hands of the therapist because it places the client in a passive disempowered role (Anderson, 1997; de Shazer, 1994; White; 2007). Social constructionist family therapies view client change as a co-constructed process in which the therapist and client jointly share responsibility for the process of therapy (Anderson, 1997; White & Epston, 1990). Unfortunately, some therapists confuse this to place all responsibility on the client. For example, some have questioned if Anderson's (1997) not-knowing approach to therapy places so much responsibility on the client that it compromises the therapist's usefulness (Guilfoyle, 2003; Rober, 2002). Many times, family therapy trainees complain that in an attempt to work in a social constructionist framework, they are forced to support a client in doing something they find morally questionable. Yet, this confusion is not in keeping with the stance of co-construction in which both therapist and client play an important role. Real (1990) believes that a constructionist conversation demands that the therapist play an active and ethical role. Therapy is a two-sided conversation and not solely within the domain of the client.

Therapist responsibility and maintaining an ethical compass becomes crucial to the practice of social constructionist family therapy (Rober, 2005). Anderson (1997) views the shared discussion as leveling the playing field between therapist and client in which the client is the expert on their life, whereas the therapist is the expert on conducting therapeutic conversations in which they are responsible for the questions they ask. White (2007) views the therapeutic conversation as one in which the therapist helps clients to discover their subjugated stories. This does not mean an "anything goes" attitude takes place with what the client deems a useful solution. In fact, White (1995) sees the therapist as being morally responsible within the co-construction of subjugated stories.

Social constructionist therapists must always be aware how their values both shape and impact the therapeutic conversation. Laird (1995) reminds us:

> Our theories are *never* neutral or value-free; indeed, science itself is value-laden. We can never fully distinguish between facts and values, and the values of everyone concerned are relevant to the mutual change endeavor. As researcher or practitioner, we cannot participate without influencing or being influenced by what we are observing. Therefore, our values must be identified, reexamined, made transparent, and brought into the therapeutic conversation (p. 152).

Management of Therapist/Client Boundaries

Therapist/client boundaries exist to protect the integrity of the therapeutic relationship (Reilly, 2003). Issues may arise when there is a crossing of professional and personal boundaries between therapists and clients (Reamer, 2003). Nickel (2004) believes that the crossing of therapeutic boundaries opens the door to financial, emotional, or sexual relationships with clients.

The purpose of a therapeutic relationship is for the therapist to provide support to the client within the confines of that relationship. This creates a necessary power imbalance in which the therapist serves as guide, nurturer, and confidant to the client. Because of this heightened position of power, it is possible for the therapist to exploit the client when other relationships are involved (Kitchner, 2000); therefore, therapists avoid getting involved in business deals with clients or developing friendships with clients after therapy has ended. For example, clients might later feel they were exploited due to the therapist's power within the relationship or be concerned with therapist violation of confidentiality in later friendship relationships (Sommers-Flanagan, 2012). Finally, multiple relationships run the risk of impairing therapist judgment in relation to client treatment (Kitchner, 2000). A therapist might find it difficult to clinically confront a client who also is a business partner for fear of ruining the business relationship.

An even more damaging multiple relationship is when therapists become involved romantically or sexually with their clients or former clients (Sommers-Flanagan, 2012). For example, *Eric saw a single-parent family for behavior problems with a teenage son. The therapy went exceptionally well, but as the therapy neared completion, the single mother invited him to go on a date with her after the therapy was over.* Imagine the damage dating this client could do if her asking him out was based on a pattern of sexualizing relationships due to her having been abused as a child? Might she eventually feel Eric used his power as her therapist to seduce her? Even if the client solicits the therapist, this is still considered exploitation because of the power the therapist holds within the therapeutic relationship, even after therapy ends. Eric needs to be aware that it is unethical for therapists to engage in sexual relationships with their present or former clients (Sommers-Flanagan, 2012), as well as with a client's spouse or romantic partner, and the client's family. Other consequences for therapists engaging in sexual relationships with clients include (imprisonable) criminal charges, civil action, and licensing board sanctions. Malpractice insurance typically exempts sexual improprieties from coverage. Based on these potential issues, Eric should thank her for the invitation, but explain the prohibitions of therapist/client romantic relationships, and discuss how these prohibitions exist for her protection as a client.

The Systems-Based Therapy Perspective on Multiple Therapist/Client Relationships

The structural and strategic schools of family therapy have been exceptionally adamant against clinicians crossing therapeutic boundaries with clients. The idea of the therapist as the temporary leader of the therapy system (Haley, 1987; Minuchin, 1974) was designed to create order in a hierarchically confused family. Violating those clear boundaries exacerbates the confusion and exploitation that exists when boundaries are inappropriately crossed in families. It is possible that clients who come from families with boundary problems may be especially vulnerable to being victimized in therapist/client boundary violations.

The Social Constructionist Therapy Perspective on Multiple Therapist/Client Relationships

Although social constructionist family therapists have not written about multiple therapist/client relationships from a boundary perspective, they are especially sensitive to the issue of empowering clients within the therapy relationship (Anderson, 1997; White, 1995). Exploitive dual relationships undermine client power and replicate the dominant narratives that leave them in powerless positions (White, 2007).

In the following section, we discuss family therapists' management of client secrets. As the stances of systems-based and social constructionist family therapists are essentially the same for secrets as their rationale for the avoidance of multiple relationships, we will omit this distinction from the following section.

Management of Client Secrets

> Ashley is seeing a couple for marital issues. During a session in which she saw each alone to get their honest feelings about the relationship, the wife informed her that she is having an affair with a colleague at work. She states that she does not want this revealed in therapy.

It is an ethical violation for Ashley to reveal the wife's confidence to her husband without her written approval (Bass & Quimby, 2006). Now what should she do? Situations like this are relatively common in couple therapy. In a study of therapists' views on maintaining secrets in couple therapy, Butler, Rodriguez, Roper, and Feinauer (2010) discovered that the majority recommended facilitated disclosure, which means a process by which a therapist works with the individual to disclose the secret, with the appropriate signing of written authorization. Still, some therapists choose to keep client confidentiality and not reveal the secret (Negash & Hecker, 2010). Regardless of the therapist's policy on revealing secrets, it is recommended that they include their no-secrets policy in their informed consent and present this to clients at the beginning of therapy and explain it in a way that facilitates trust and openness (Butler et al., 2010).

Therapists must be aware that the revealing of a secret is the prerogative of the client. A therapist cannot force facilitated disclosure on a client as this violates the client's right to confidentiality. Some therapists will then reveal that there is a secret that impedes couple therapy and offer individual treatment until it is revealed, or if they feel they lack sufficient maneuverability in the case, decide to terminate therapy (Negash & Hecker, 2010).

Client Responsibility in Systems-Based and Social Constructionist Family Therapies

Although most of the clinical literature, and surely the ethics literature, has focused on the responsibilities of the therapist, the client also shares responsibilities in the development of change. Although client agency has been largely discussed within the social constructionist family therapies (e.g., Anderson, 1997; de Shazer, 1994; White, 2007), client responsibility is also important within the systems-based family therapies (e.g., Boscolo et al., 1987; Boszormenyi-Nagy & Krasner, 1986; Kerr & Bowen, 1988).

The Role of Client Responsibility in Systems-Based Family Therapies

Although systems thinkers have tended to focus on the role of context in maintaining problems, that does not mean that a client is without agency. In fact, not only is the client problem maintained within an interactional system, but the therapeutic relationship is also an interactional system in which both the family and therapist impact each other (Boscolo et al., 1987). Although strategic (Watzlawick et al., 1974) and structural (Minuchin, 1974) family therapists saw the role of the therapist as a leader and outside observer of the family in therapy, they also understood the interactional nature of the therapy relationship. Haley (1987) openly questioned whether the therapist derived an intervention or whether the family led the therapist to come up with the intervention. For Minuchin (1974) the idea of joining involved the therapist adapting to the family. The therapist must be open to learning from the family. Most important is the realization that families and individuals are competent beings who have the inherent ability to solve their problems as new structures emerge (Simon, 1995). It is when therapists become so involved with the system that they overlook client agency that ethical issues emerge.

For the transgenerational family therapist, it is crucial to *promote* client agency to resolve intergenerational issues. For Bowen (1978), therapy involved helping clients assume responsibility for their own behavior in relationship to others. His preference was to work with individual clients, help them identify the interactional pattern in which they participate, and promote their exploration of ways to change to alter their behavior. It is only when that individual could take responsibility for self in relation to others could the pattern shift and differentiation develop (Bowen, 1978). The problem the individual must wrestle with is understanding that their view of the family system is also part of the interactional system that maintains the problem. The individual must interact with the family and develop a clearer view of self, which subsequently leads to a clearer view of the other family members (Kerr & Bowen, 1988). Williamson (1991) refers to this as the intimacy paradox.

For Boszormenyi-Nagy and Krasner (1986), clients have an ethical mandate to understand their role in the intergenerational pattern. This means recognizing how they were impacted by the pattern, separating themselves from the pattern, and taking ethical responsibility to not continue the pattern with intimate others. Although family members have an existential right to bear a grudge for what had been done to them from preceding generations, they lose their sense of self and intimacy with others if they pass these behaviors on to them (Boszormenyi-Nagy & Spark, 1973). Passing on these patterns negatively impacts self and others. For example, Boszormenyi-Nagy and Krasner (1986) state:

> A person's desire to use a relationship for self-validation is not reliable *per se*. Genuine care about the due needs and rights of others does contribute to one's own worth and entitlement… Recurrent tendencies to scapegoat "bad" family members constitute an exploitative and destructive use of relationships. At an ethical level, inauthentic attempts at self-justification actually diminish the self's ethical worth (p. 79).

To resolve this destructive pattern, the client must take a realistic appraisal of self. This is an ethical mandate that helps the client develop self-worth and give intimate others their just due.

The Role of Client Responsibility in Social Constructionist Family Therapies

Social constructionist family therapists have championed the responsibility of the client as a contributing member of therapy with agency and competence. For Anderson (1997), the therapist's role in therapy is to be the expert on facilitating conversations. The client's role is to be the expert on their life. For White (2007), it is the therapist's use of questions that facilitates the client's sense of personal agency. As the client separates the problem from self, the client gains in agency and responsibility. This leads to the question are all client solutions acceptable? Similar to transgenerational therapists, must social-constructionist therapists hold clients morally responsible for the alternate stories they develop?

For White (1995), part of the moral responsibility of the narrative therapist is to hold clients accountable for their actions. For example, in his work with male abusers, he focuses on helping the male take responsibility for perpetuating the abuse, develop empathy for those he abused, and the acknowledge impact of the abuse on those he abused (White, 1995).

To facilitate these tasks, he specifically helps the male examine the impact of male power on his own life. Even in social constructionist family therapies therapists must hold clients accountable for their moral behavior.

Who Does the Family Therapist Invite to Therapy?

This question has plagued the field since its founding. To do family therapy effectively, must one include the whole family and if not, should service be withheld? Some have questioned if it is ethically valid to withhold service to committed clients when some of their family members refuse treatment (Huber, 1994; Margolin, 1982). Rather than focus on the issue of whether to see entire families or not, we present an alternative to this dialectic. We focus on client motivation—thus the inclusion of this question in this section.

For many of the founders of our field, family therapy was a theory for understanding how problems were maintained and resolved. Family therapy was not related to the number of people in the room, but rather involved working to understand the context in which the problem was embedded and altering that context. Members of the Mental Research Institute believed it was best to not include unmotivated family members from therapy. Instead, they focused treatment on the most interested family members (Fisch, Weakland, & Segal, 1983). The most interested family member, or customer, would be most compliant with helping to understand the problem-maintaining sequence and most invested in trying directives to disrupt it. Bowen (1978) felt it best to work with the individual client in a relaxed, anxiety free atmosphere. Including other family members would drive up the anxiety in the room and impede the ability to reflect on the potential transgenerational sequences. He preferred this person be the one most motivated to resolve the problem.

Anderson (1997) moved beyond the question of including the entire family in therapy by focusing on the problem-determined system. For her, the problem-determined system was comprised of those concerned about the problem. The problem determined those who were concerned about it (Anderson, 1997). This could include the family, certain members of the family, or the network of those providing service to resolve the problem. In other words, the problem-determined system could be as small as one individual or all of the members in a care network. The issue for inclusion was concern over the problem.

Perhaps de Shazer (1988, 1994) comes as close as anyone to answering the question regarding who to include in therapy as he discusses the clinical relationships with clients as visitors, complainants, and customers. Visitors tend to be those clients with no recognition of a problem and no interest in making changes in their lives. Complainants are those who recognize the existence of a problem, but have not identified what to do about it. Customers are those who recognize a problem are open to developing solutions. He recommended that unless mandated to therapy, therapists exclude visitors from therapy and work with complainants and customers (de Shazer, 1988). They are the ones most motivated to participate.

Summary

Although family therapy arose as an antidote for pathologizing individuals, a whole array of ethical issues emerged as therapists adopted a systems-based or social constructionist viewpoint. This chapter highlighted some of the key ethical issues that have arisen for the field of family therapy as a result. We have attempted to show that many of these issues arose due to therapists reifying the ideas in the field. Further, we have shown, through focusing on the stances our founders actually took, how many of these issues could be handled.

References

American Psychiatric Association. (2013). *DSM 5: Diagnostic and statistical manual of mental disorders* (5th ed.). Washington, DC: Author.

Anderson, H. (1997). *Conversation, language, and possibilities: A postmodern approach to therapy*. New York, NY: Basic Books.

Bass, B. A., & Quimby, J. L. (2006). Addressing secrets in couples counseling: An alternative approach to informed consent. *The Family Journal, 14*(1), 77–80. doi: 10.1177/1066480705282060.

Bateson, G. (1972). *Steps to an ecology of mind*. New York, NY: Ballantine Books.

Benson, M. J., Long, J. K., & Sporakowski, M. J. (1992). Teaching psychopathology and the DSM-III-R from a family systems perspective. *Family Relations, 41*(2), 135–140. doi: 10.2307/584824.

Boscolo, L., Cecchin, G., Hoffman, L., & Penn, P. (1987). *Milan systemic family therapy*. New York, NY: Basic Books.

Boszormenyi-Nagy, I., & Krasner, B. R. (1986). *Between give & take: A clinical guide to contextual therapy*. New York, NY: Brunner/Mazel.

Boszormenyi-Nagy, I., & Spark, G. M. (1973). *Invisible loyalties*. New York, NY: Harper & Row.

Bowen, M. (1978). *Family therapy in clinical practice*. Northvale, NJ: Aronson.

Broderick, C. B., & Schrader, S. S. (1991). The history of professional marriage and family therapy. In A. Gurman & D. Kniskern (Eds.), *Handbook of family therapy* (Vol. II, pp. 3–40). New York, NY: Brunner/Mazel.

Butler, M. H., Rodriguez, M. A., Roper, S. O., & Feinauer L. L. (2010). Infidelity secrets in couple therapy: Therapists' views on the collision of competing ethics around relationship-relevant secrets. *Sexual Addiction & Compulsivity: The Journal of Treatment & Prevention, 17*(2), 82–105. doi: 10.1080/10720161003772041.

Denton, W. H., & Bell, C. (2013). DSM-5 and the family therapist: First-order change in a new millennium. *Australian and New Zealand Journal of Family Therapy, 34*(2), 147–155. doi: 10.1002/anzf.1010.

de Shazer, S. (1988). *Clues: Investigating solutions in brief therapy*. New York, NY: Norton.

de Shazer, S. (1994). *Words were originally magic*. New York, NY: Norton.

Fisch, R., Weakland, J. H., & Segal, L. (1983). *Tactics of change*. New York, NY: Norton.

Freud, S. (1953). *A general introduction to psychoanalysis*. New York, NY: Pocket Books.

Guilfoyle, M. (2003). Dialogue and power: A critical analysis of power in dialogical therapy. *Family Process, 42*(3), 331–343. doi: 10.1111/j.1545-5300.2003.00331.x.

Haley, J. (1987). *Problem-solving therapy*. San Francisco, CA: Jossey-Bass.

Hoyt, M. F., & Gurman, A. S. (2012). Wither couple/family therapy? *The Family Journal, 20*(1), 13–17. doi: 10.1177/1066480711420050.

Huber, C. H. (1994). *Ethical, legal, and professional issues in the practice of marriage and family therapy*. Upper Saddle River, NJ: Merrill.

Kaslow, F. (Ed). (1996). *Handbook of relational diagnosis and dysfunctional family patterns*. New York, NY: Wiley.

Kerr, M. E., & Bowen, M. (1988). *Family evaluation*. New York, NY: Norton.

Kitchner, K. S. (2000). *Foundations of ethical practice, research, and teaching in psychology*. Upper Saddle River, NJ: Lawrence Erlbaum.

Laird, J. (1995). Family-centered practice in the postmodern era. *Families in Society: The Journal of Contemporary Human Services, 76*(3), 150–162. Retrieved from http://familiesinsocietyjournal.org.

Lebow, J. (2015). Editorial DSM-V and family therapy. *Family Process, 52*(2), 155–160. doi: 10.1111/famp.12035.

Margolin, G. (1982). Ethical and legal considerations in marital and family therapy. *American Psychologist, 37*(7), 788–794. doi: 10.1037/0003-066x.37.7.788.

McGeorge, C. R., Carlson, T. S., & Wetchler, J. L. (2015). The history of marriage and family therapy. In J. L. Wetchler & L. L. Hecker (Eds.), *An introduction to marriage and family therapy* (2nd ed., pp. 3–42). New York, NY: Routledge.

Minuchin, S. (1974). *Families and family therapy.* Cambridge, MA: Harvard University Press.

Negash, S. M., & Hecker, L. L. (2010). Ethical issues endemic to couple and family therapy. In L. Hecker (Ed.), *Ethics and professional issues in couple and family therapy* (pp. 225–241). New York, NY: Routledge.

Nickel, M. B. (2004). Professional boundaries: The dilemma of dual & multiple relationships in rural clinical practice. *Counseling and Clinical Psychology Journal, 1*(1), 17–22. Retrieved from http://web.b.ebscohost.com.

O'Farrell, T. J. (1994). Marital therapy and spouse-involved treatment with alcoholic patients. *Behavioral Therapy, 23*(3), 391–406. doi: 10.1016/S00005-7894(05)80154-6.

O'Farrell, T. J., & Clements, K. (2012). Review of outcome research on marital and family therapy in treatment for alcoholism. *Journal of Marital & Family Therapy, 28*(1), 122–144. doi: 10.1111/j.175-06062011.00242.x.

Packer, P. (1988). Let's put a stop to the "insurance diagnosis." *Medical Economics, 28,* 19–28. Retrieved from http://medicaleconomics.modernmedicine.com.

Real, T. (1990). The therapeutic use of self in constructionist/systemic therapy. *Family Process, 29*(3), 255–272. doi: 10.1111/j.1545-5300.1990.00255.x.

Reamer, F. G. (2003). Boundary issues in social work: Managing dual relationships. *Social Work, 48*(1), 121–134. doi: 10.1093/sw/48.1.121.

Reilly, D. R. (2003). Not just a patient: The dangers of dual relationships. *Canadian Journal of Rural Medicine, 8*(1), 51–53. Retrieved from danreilly.ca.

Rober, P. (2002). Constructive hypothesizing, dialogic understanding and the therapist's inner conversation: Some ideas about knowing and not knowing in the family therapy session. *Journal of Marital and Family Therapy, 28*(4), 467–478. doi: 10.1111/j.1752-0606.2002.tb00371.x.

Rober, P. (2005). The therapist's self in dialogical family therapy: Some ideas about not-knowing and the therapist's inner conversation. *Family Process, 44*(4), 477–495. doi: 10.1111/j.1545-5300.1999.00209.x.

Rogers, C. (1961). *On becoming a person.* Boston, MA: Houghton Mifflin.

Rowe, C. L. (2012). Family therapy for drug abuse: Review and updates 2003–2010. *Journal of Marital and Family Therapy, 38*(1), 59–81. doi: 10.1111/j.1752-0606.2011.00280.x.

Simon, G. M. (1995). A revisionist rendering of structural family therapy. *Journal of Marital and Family Therapy, 21*(1), 17–26. doi: 10.1111/j.1752-0606.1995.tb00135.x.

Smock, S. A., Trepper, T. S., Wetchler, J. L., McCollum, E. E., Ray, R., & Pierce, K. (2008). Solution-focused group therapy for level 1 substance abusers. *Journal of Marital and Family Therapy, 34*(1), 107–120. doi: 10.1111/j.1752-0606.2008.00056.x.

Sommers-Flanagan, R. (2012). Boundaries, multiple roles, and the professional relationship. In T. Knapp (Ed.), *APA handbook of ethics in psychology: Moral foundations and common themes* (Vol. 1, pp. 241–277). Washington, DC: American Psychological Association.

Stanton, M. D., & Todd, T. C. (1982). *The family therapy of drug abuse and addiction*. New York, NY: Guilford.

Watzlawick, P., Weakland, J. H., & Fisch, R. (1974). *Change: Principles of problem formation and problem resolution*. New York, NY: Norton.

Wetchler, J. L. (1999). Narrative treatment of a woman with panic disorder. *Journal of Family Psychotherapy, 10*(2), 17–30. doi: 10.1300/j085v10n02_02.

White, M. (1995). *Reauthoring lives: Interviews & essays*. Adelaide, Australia: Dulwich Centre.

White, M. (2007). *Maps of narrative practice*. New York, NY: Norton.

White, M., & Epston, D. (1990). *Narrative means to therapeutic ends*. New York, NY: Norton.

Whittinghill, D. (2002). Ethical considerations for the use of family therapy in substance abuse treatment. *The Family Journal: Counseling and Therapy for Couples and Families, 10*(1), 75–78. doi: 10.1177/1066480702101012.

Williamson, D. (1991). *The intimacy paradox: personal authority in the family system*. New York, NY: Guilford.

14

Ethical Couple and Family E-Therapy

Markie L. C. Twist and Katherine M. Hertlein

> Dr. Stellar holds a small private practice in a suburb of a large city. She has, on average, 15 clients per week and shares office space with two other family therapists. Because the office space she rents does not come with a landline phone, she and her co-renters have their clients contact them via each therapist's smartphone. Although several of her clients use the phone to make a call to confirm or schedule an appointment, eight well-established clients on her caseload routinely communicate scheduling with her via text message. Of those that schedule via text, about half of them also routinely communicate with her between sessions through e-mail and texts about what has happened since the last session, as well as ask questions about how to proceed. Her e-mail and text messaging practices with her clients have grown over time, and she has not really thought of them as e-therapy and consequently has not implemented an online communication agreement with her clients. Last month, Dr. Stellar conducted a session via Skype with one of her most well-established clients with whom she felt comfortable, because the client and his wife were desperately needing services while they were traveling out of state. Even though she recognized the video session as a form of e-therapy, because of the extenuating circumstances, her joined relationship, and the session going so smoothly, she does not recognize any potential ethical and/or legal problems.

Our case scenario with Dr. Stellar raises several questions. What constitutes e-therapy? What are the benefits and risks related to e-therapy? What are the legal and ethical issues of electronic practices? The purpose of this chapter is to address these questions, and provide guidelines to help couple and family therapists (CFTs) attend to common and potential ethical issues that arise in e-therapy. CFTs are integrating technology in their practices at a rapid pace, with an increasing number of articles and books on the topic (e.g., Dewan, Luo, & Lorez, 2015; Turvey & Myers, 2013). It is not uncommon for CFTs to use videoconferencing for treatment or supervision; they may have even participated in their own personal therapy via videoconferencing. There are, however, subtle ways in which technology enters treatment, such as text messages and e-mails between clients and therapists. CFTs may be unknowingly engaging in online practices, with minimal to no thought to potential ethical issues that arise when using these digital medium (Hertlein, Blumer, & Smith, 2014).

We consider e-therapy as *any professional interaction between clients, therapists, and/or supervisors that utilizes Internet and electronic media* (i.e., chatting, video calling, discussion boards, e-mailing, texting, websites, social network sites, etc.) (Blumer & Hertlein, 2012). Technologies are constantly changing, necessitating CFTs to understand how to work ethically within the dynamic framework of e-therapy. To that end, we propose guidelines to aid systemic therapists in e-therapy—termed the Couple and Family Therapy Technology Framework—which is an evolving framework that can be used by CFTs as a guide in working with individual, couple, and family systems in online clinical contexts (Figure 14.1) (Blumer, 2014, 2015; Hertlein & Twist, 2015).

The Couple and Family Technology Framework captures the interaction between technology and couple and family relationships (Hertlein & Blumer, 2013). Because technologies evolve at such a rapid pace, the strategies to for e-therapy practices presented in this chapter provide guidelines for the CFT, rather than specific practice suggestions, using the Couple and Family Therapy Technology Framework.

Couple and Family Therapy Technology Framework

The Couple and Family Therapy Technology Framework aids the CFT in understanding human–technology relationships directly applicable to e-therapy practices (Blumer, 2014, 2015; Hertlein & Twist, 2015). The framework explores how the ecological elements of the Internet (anonymity, approximation, accessibility, affordability, ambiguity, accommodation, and acceptability; Table 14.1) affect both the structure (roles, rules, boundaries) and process (phase of e-therapy, relationship between therapist and client) of one's practice. Additionally, as the components of new technologies change over time, therapists must revisit how these components affect the structure and process of their treatment so as to provide the same standard of care as they would in offline treatment. In this chapter we discuss ethical and clinical elements of e-therapy; readers are referred to Figure 14.1 and Table 14.1 for additional information.

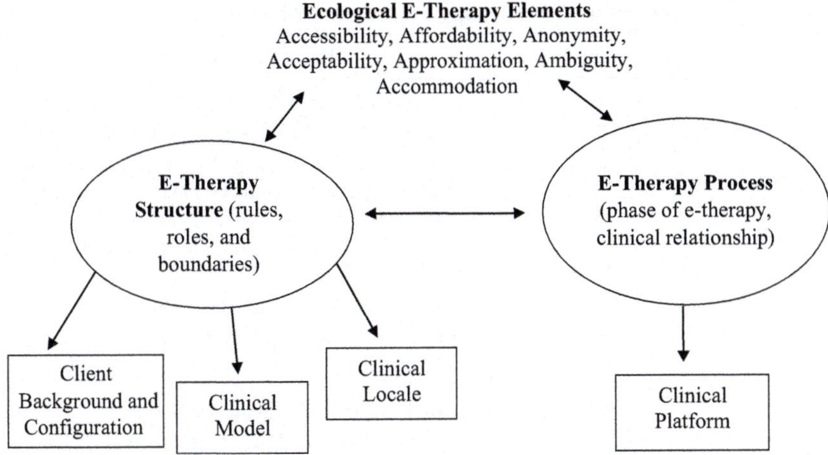

Figure 14.1 Couple and Family Therapy Technology Framework.

*Adapted from The CFT Framework (Hertlein & Blumer, 2013).

TABLE 14.1 Ecological E-Therapy Elements

Ecological Elements[a]	Recommendations[b]
Approximation – quality with which the Internet approximates offline, real-world clinical practices (Ross & Kauth, 2002)	**Closing the Approximation Gap** – Review similarities and differences between face-to-face therapy and e-therapy – Minimize the gap between face-to-face therapy and e-therapy by enhancing the online fields through measures such as ensuring technological clarity and quality
Affordability – degree to which the Internet and new media are widely available and affordable in clinical contexts (Cooper, 2002)	**Checking Affordability** – Consider financial costs of e-therapy for all relevant parties – Online payment transactions need to be secure and encrypted – Informed consent document needs to include payment information, specifically if occurs through provider or third-party platform and if the latter provide the merchant information
Ambiguity – lack of clarity and related difficulties in defining e-therapy technologically and relationally (Blumer & Hertlein, 2012; Hertlein & Stevenson, 2010)	**Reconciling Relational Ambiguity** – Agree on definition of e-therapy – Consider relational appropriateness (i.e., fit of population, presenting problem, platform, etc.) of relevant parties (e.g., clients, clinicians, supervisors) for engagement in e-therapy

(Continued)

TABLE 14.1 Ecological E-Therapy Elements (continued)

Ecological Elements[a]	Recommendations[b]
	- Informed consent document that includes risks and benefits of e-therapy, geographical jurisdiction information, plans during technological breaks, management of emergencies, payment information, and management of boundaries around dual relationships online and offline (Anthony & Nagel, 2010) - Review and have parties sign contractual agreements around participation in e-therapy
	Reconciling Technological Ambiguity - Review the technological requirements (e.g., encryption, back-up systems, password protections, firewalls, back up protections, hardware, software, and use of third-party systems) for e-therapy participation - Consider technological appropriateness (i.e., technological literacy level, level of education and training, intergenerational experiences with technology, etc.) of relevant parties for participation in e-therapy
Accessibility – ease with which one has the opportunity and capability to access the Internet and new media on a daily and unlimited basis from an array of locations (Cooper, 2002)	**Managing Accessibility** - Management of boundaries with relevant parties is necessary, because with technology: one is virtually always accessible and visible, there is an expectation of availability being equated with this accessibility (Wilcoxon, 2015), there are differences on the experiencing of the therapeutic relationship based on phase of e-therapy and platform utilized, there is a high potential for work–family spillover (Chelsey, 2005) - Adhere to current state licensure regulations concerning e-therapy while in the same/different place as one's client - Include information about accessibility with regard to the handling of emergencies, expectations around frequency and timing of online communications, etc. in informed consent document - Scheduling and record keeping needs to be through secure and encrypted means

(Continued)

TABLE 14.1 Ecological E-Therapy Elements (continued)

Ecological Elements[a]	Recommendations[b]
Anonymity - online users can present themselves in any manner, and in the context of being protected from being identified (Hertlein & Sendak, 2007)	**Managing Anonymity** - To ensure the relevant party is agreeing to participate in e-therapy, have them review and sign informed consent and contractual agreements in person or via videoconferencing - Do not search for clients via search engines or social media - E-therapy services need to be HIPAA-compliant - Attend to safety, and security around confidentiality in e-therapy practices, meaning for: • online practices: encryption measures, recognizing therapist as owner of online records, providing information on security of file storage, and having privacy policies in informed consent and on website (Anthony & Nagel, 2010) • face-to-face practices: keep smartphones out of sessions or if in session remove battery, and password protect phones
Accommodation - differences between the ways one presents in their offline therapy practices versus their e-therapy practices (Hertlein & Stevenson, 2010)	**Aligning Accommodation** - Presentation of one sense of self in offline environments and another sense of self (i.e., an electronic self or e-self) in online environments (Michikyan, Subrahmanyam, & Dennis, 2014) - Reconciliation of self and e-self is needed for all relevant parties and can be accomplished by focusing on: self-reflection, attainment of congruence between self and ideal self, ceasing to compare oneself online with others online, and being authentic and consistent across online and offline contexts **Acknowledging E-Visibility Management** - Visibility management is the degree to which minority identity individuals are "out" in varied contexts (Iwasaki & Ristock, 2007) - E-visibility management is the degree to which one's minoritized identity/ies is visible in online environments (Blumer, Bergdall, & Ullman, 2014) - Acknowledging visibility and e-visibility management practices is important in terms of monitoring the ability to protect relevant parties from cyberbullies, trolls, and other online predators

(Continued)

TABLE 14.1 Ecological E-Therapy Elements (continued)

Ecological Elements[a]	Recommendations[b]
Acceptability – degree to which a multitude of functions once deemed inappropriate offline and/or online have now become accepted e-therapy practices (Blumer & Hertlein, 2011; King, 1999)	**Determining Acceptability** – Determine what is acceptable for online versus offline therapy. For example: for clients online practices are acceptable after completion of an assessment that involves gathering client identification, signing informed consent, completion of thorough mental, medical, and relational health history, and gathering information about daily health, hygiene, and living skills (Anthony & Nagel, 2010) – Determine the current state standards, ethics codes, and insurance regulations to follow – Display education and credentials, crisis intervention information, provider information, terms of use and privacy policy, ensuring of encrypted transmission, and a reflection of sensitivity to people of diverse backgrounds in one's online space (Anthony & Nagel, 2010) – Use acceptable e-therapy models and platforms

[a]Definitions of ecological elements adapted from Hertlein and Blumer (2013) and Blumer (2014).
[b]Summary of recommendations adapted from Blumer (2015).

Guidelines for the Structural Components of E-Therapy

There are many features of technology that are changing CFT practice. In addition to the effect of the ecological elements on the structure of e-therapy practices, it is important that therapists consider other structural elements such as client background and configuration, the clinical model, and the clinical locale (Godleski et al., 2008; Kramer, Mishkind, Luxton, & Shore, 2013). Clinical locale refers to the degree to which both the client(s) and the clinician have privacy, safety, and security while engaging in e-therapeutic practices. Because of the accessibility of e-therapy, CFTs facilitating e-therapy also need to consider management of e-therapy practices in relation to geographical location for both the client(s) and the clinician because interstate therapy is typically not supported by state licensing laws. A CFT practicing outside of the state(s) in which they are licensed is considered practicing without a license, which can bring misdemeanor and felony charges as well as substantial fines. Thus, a CFT must examine applicable state and federal laws and board regulations.

An essential step in structuring e-therapy is deciding who the client is, and who will be included in e-therapy, as is required in offline therapy. This means considering whether the e-therapy will be with an individual, couple, and/or family client system, or some combination therein. Much of this can be managed with clear and appropriate paperwork (e.g., informed consent), describing who is to participate in therapy, rules about the structure of sessions, and both how and under what circumstances crises will be managed. Informed consent should address any and all electronic communications, no matter how insignificant that communication may seem (e.g., texts). In addition, therapists should implement a screening process to determine a client's fit for e-services. Akin to offline therapy, therapists need to evaluate the evidence for specific approaches on presenting problems seen in treatment and decide which clinical model is the best fit for the clients.

Guidelines for Process Components of E-Therapy

Establishing guidelines for the process of e-therapy is equally important to establishing structural guidelines. In terms of the process components of e-therapy it important to consider, once again, the effect of the ecological elements (i.e., anonymity, approximation, accessibility, affordability, ambiguity, accommodation, and acceptability) and the clinical platform, the relationship between the therapist and client(s), and the phase of e-therapy. For example, the clinical platform that the therapist works through in engaging online with the client(s) may vary based on the stage of the therapy, and the nature of the clinical relationship/therapeutic alliance. Thus, understanding the effect of communication platforms on the therapeutic alliance is essential. For instance, early on in a relationship, asynchronous and primarily text-based communications (e.g., e-mail) (Suler, 2000) tend to promote interactions characterized by higher amounts of self-disclosure, which in turn tends to build intimacy (in this case, intimacy in the form of a therapeutic alliance) more rapidly than other forms of online communication (Jiang, Bazarova, & Hancock, 2013; Twist & Hertlein, 2015). Asynchronous, text-based online communications, however, tend to create emotional distance in the therapeutic relationship over time, as the communications become shorter in length and more sporadic (Twist & Hertlein, 2015; Wilding, 2006). Thus, in terms of the maintenance stage of e-therapy, it might be more effective to make use of synchronous and interpersonal platforms. In addition, the ability for videoconferencing to approximate a real-time therapy session may be advantageous compared to other forms of media (such as e-mail), which do not as closely approximate an offline therapeutic situation.

Types of E-Therapy

The types of e-therapy that currently exist are typically conceptualized in two ways: (1) modalities of online therapy and (2) platforms used to engage in online therapy. Viewing e-therapy modalities and platforms through the lens of the Couple and Family Therapy Technology Framework, it is evident that the modalities one uses involve the structure of e-therapy, whereas the platform involves the process. Through both, the clinician is addressing the ecological e-therapy element of approximation (Ross & Kauth, 2002)—or the ability of the e-therapy experience to approximate the offline face-to-face experience.

Clinical Modalities

Common treatment modalities dispensed electronically include cognitive-behavioral therapy (CBT), integrative behavioral couple therapy (IBCT), structural therapy, support groups, self-help practices, and psychoeducation. Of these, the modalities that have received the most attention for use in online environments are CBT and psychoeducational programming (Blumer, Hertlein, Smith, & Allen, 2013).

Communication Platforms

There are several platforms available to conduct treatment or interact with clients online. The characteristics of these platforms include five overlapping dimensions: (1) synchronous/asynchronous, (2) text/sensory, (3) imaginary/real, (4) automated/interpersonal, and (5) invisible/present (Suler, 2000). The first dimension—synchronous/asynchronous—refers to timing. Synchronous online communication occurs between participants simultaneously, whereas asynchronous communications occur between participants at different times—in other words, there is a time lag (Suler, 2000). Examples of synchronous platforms include texting, chatting, videoconferencing, instant messaging, short-messaging systems, and telephony. Examples of asynchronous platforms include e-mail, discussion boards, weblogs, message boards, listservs, and recorded video and/or audio playback. This dimension has implications for therapists because clients may mistakenly believe that having accessibility (one of the ecological e-therapy elements) to the Internet makes all interactions synchronous and their therapist can and will respond immediately to any concerns raised through electronic platforms (Wilcoxon, 2015).

The text/sensory dimension breaks down into text communications (occurring via the Internet/media that are typed text only), and sensory communications (sight and sound) (Suler, 2000). Examples of text-only communication include: e-mail, message boards, discussion boards, newsgroups, short-messaging services, websites, and weblogs. Sensory communications include videoconferencing, telephony, sending pictures via the Internet, social media, avatars, virtual reality, and websites. The imaginary/real environment is the third dimension of the online and computer-mediated psychotherapy model. How closely the online environment can approximate (another of the ecological e-therapy elements) the offline environment is the degree of the realness of that online context. The closest we can get to offering encounters that approximate in-person interactions at present is through videoconferencing (Suler, 2000), through which most e-therapy is conducted.

The degree to which the online exchanges are with a computer or a human is the focus of the automated/interpersonal dimension (Suler, 2000). When a human is the primary entity that one interacts with online, then this interaction is thought to be interpersonal in nature (Suler, 2000). The bulk of e-therapy that is occurring at the moment is still in the form of interpersonal communications, primarily in the forms of virtual reality, videoconferencing, and personalized e-mails. Interactions are described as automated when a computer or a bot is the primary entity that interacts with one online. In clinical applications, programs can scan e-mails to determine one's mood, score inventories, and distribute e-mails automatically (Suler, 2000).

The fifth and final dimension is the degree to which users are visible versus present in online environments (Suler, 2000). When clients believe they are only talking with a computer, then the therapist is thought to be invisible. This can happen when a therapist watches clients interact in online messaging or discussion boards, or via an e-mail listserv. Clinicians can also hold office hours via instant messaging or chatting for clients who want to have brief check-ins; in this way, a therapist can be interacting with several clients simultaneously without them being aware of each other's presence. Clients may also appear to be invisible online because they can be in online support groups, discussion boards, and/or listservs without directly interacting with other participants, but instead just observing (Suler, 2000).

Clinical and Ethical Issues

Benefits of E-Therapy

Effective Treatment for Specific Problems

The benefits of e-therapy within the context of the Couple and Family Therapy Technology Framework are both a reflection and perpetuation of the growing acceptance of e-therapy practices. At one time, e-therapy was thought to be ineffective, unhelpful, inappropriate, and even unethical. Yet as the technology grows and changes and a growing body of empirical evidence mounts, suggesting that there are distinct benefits to e-therapy, the clinical community's acceptance of e-therapy practices propagates (Hertlein, Blumer, & Mihaloliakos, 2015; Hertlein et al., 2014). E-therapy is now an effective delivery method for a host of presenting problems such as anxiety and panic disorders (Rees & Maclaine, 2015), mood disorders, and posttraumatic stress disorder (Fortney et al., 2015), depression, maternal depression, long-term medical problems, childhood and adolescent anxiety (Eells, Barrett, Wright, & Thase, 2014; Hesser et al., 2012; Sheeber, Seeley, Feil, Sorensen, Kosty, & Lewinsohn, 2012), and eating disorders (Loucas et al., 2014). Early evidence suggests that treatment therapy has the same effectiveness as face-to-face therapy and, in some cases, demonstrates higher levels of efficacy (Fortney et al., 2015; Frueh, 2015; Morland et al., 2010).

Children and families also benefit from e-therapy, although with limited integration with family therapy theories. Families and children are more likely to adopt teleconferencing procedures than clinicians, potentially because it is easier for families to be coordinated to be together for the session (Goldstein & Myers, 2014). In the treatment of childhood depression, CBT delivered via videoconference fared the same as treatment delivered face-to-face (Nelson, Barnard, & Cain, 2006). CBT-based e-therapy has also been found to be effective for teaching parents the skills they need to better manage attention-deficit/hyperactivity disorder (Palmer, Myers, Vander Stoep, McCarty, Geyer, & DeSalvo, 2010; Xie et al., 2013). Systemic therapists have relied on using IBCT in online service delivery. For example, Doss and colleagues (2013) have developed a web-based version of the systemic-based model, IBCT, for use with couples experiencing relationship distress and who may be at risk of divorcing.

Bridging the Gap Between Service Needs and Delivery

In the context of the Couple and Family Therapy Framework, the ability to bridge the gap between mental and relational health service needs and therapeutic delivery at a distance is helpful to consider via the ecological e-therapy element of accessibility. Accessibility, or the ability to access others via technologies from virtually anywhere (Cooper, 2002), is another key benefit because it enables clinicians to provide services to people who would not be able to otherwise receive services, especially a rural population (Hertlein et al., 2014; Morland et al., 2010; Simms, Gibson, & O'Donnell, 2011). Early evidence shows great need for mental health services (Frueh, 2015) in rural locales, but the ability of e-therapy to reach those regions was far below what one would expect, thereby not closing the gap. The lack of use of e-therapy for bridging this gap is especially problematic considering other research has suggested that those in rural communities may be more likely to use mental health services if they were available (Harwood & L'Abate, 2009). E-therapy is also a timely way to get practitioners to provide services to those in areas affected by disaster (Augusterfer, 2013).

Offering therapeutic services online may also reduce costs for both clients and therapists compared to offering them solely face-to-face, which addresses the ecological e-therapy element of affordability (Cooper, 2002), or the degree to which e-therapeutic technologies are available and affordable in clinical contexts. Cost savings occur when the need for office space decreases, practitioners do not have to rent a specific office space, there is decreased travel time for clinicians, and when clinicians are able to see a greater number of clients (Glueck, 2013a). Likewise, clients also experience a cost-benefit via e-therapy services because they are able to take less time off from work for traveling to appointments and they spend less money on child care and other expenses associated with travel such as gas, car insurance, and mechanical maintenance (Glueck, 2013b). Cost savings also get passed on to clients in decreased treatment costs. For example, in a controlled study, Crow and colleagues (2009) found the average cost of the treatment of bulimia electronically was $7,300 compared to $9,325 for face-to-face treatment.

Risks (and Perceptions of Risk) in E-Therapy

CFTs who were asked to clarify their perceptions about issues that might arise in their technology practices listed five issues for consideration, which included: confidentiality, the perceived damage to the therapeutic relationship, liability and licensing issues, concerns around how to handle emergency situations, and training issues (Hertlein et al., 2015). With regard to informed consent, CFTs expressed that codes of other health professional organizations were helpful in making decisions about how to obtain informed consent in an ethical manner (Hertlein et al., 2015).

Confidentiality

CFTs are concerned about confidentiality in e-therapy (Hertlein et al., 2015). Specifically, there is concern as to who is on the other end of the computer and that security online is not guaranteed. First, there are any number of people who might have access to one's electronic accounts and passwords. In one case, a patient's husband gained access to her passwords online by installing a key logging system on her computer. He logged into her e-mail accounts and was attempting to log in to her secure patient account where she journaled for her therapist. Upon discovery of the keylogging system and his disclosure of information that was only in her e-mail accounts, her therapist advised her to stop journaling in case he might also gain access to her secure patient account and cease any e-mail connection until such a time when she felt safe and was no longer being observed.

In other cases, confidentiality may be violated on the therapist's end, because e-mail addresses can be auto-populated with relative ease (Gamble, Boyle, & Morris, 2015). Additionally, it is impossible to guarantee confidentiality because clients open their e-mail on their phone, and mobile phones can be lost or stolen (Gamble et al., 2015). When considering confidentiality in e-therapeutic contexts via the Couple and Family Therapy Technology Framework, it is helpful to consider the ecological e-therapy element of anonymity, or the extent to which a client(s) can be protected from being identified in online contexts (Hertlein & Sendak, 2007).

Perceived Risk to the Therapeutic Alliance

The therapeutic alliance is one area in which practitioners' perceived risk in e-therapy situations is greater than the research on therapeutic alliance and e-therapy supports. Therapeutic alliance is a key concept in psychotherapy, as well as in the process of e-therapy. It drives, to some degree, client disclosures to the therapist, client responsiveness and execution of interventions, and the therapist's ability to accurately hypothesize and design interventions. Many perceive that the practice of e-therapy impairs the joining process; the therapist can be more likely to structure the session so it focuses more on tasks and less on process, which disrupts the therapeutic alliance (Simms et al., 2011). However, the consensus in the literature is that there are few differences, if any, in the therapeutic alliance when service delivery is performed online (Germain, Marchand, Bouchard, Guay, & Drouin, 2010; Glueck, 2013b; Morgan, Patrick, & Magaletta, 2008). These results seem to be consistently independent of presenting problem (Jenkins-Guarnieri, Pruitt, Luxton, & Johnson, 2015).

In some instances, the challenges of developing a solid therapeutic alliance can be even greater in online service delivery than face-to-face (e.g., Knaevelsrud & Maercker, 2006). For example, when there is insufficient bandwidth, there may be transmission issues such as delay in transmission of pictures or jagged movements or other technical issues (Jenkins-Guarnieri et al., 2015), which may affect the therapeutic alliance. In addition, therapists and clients need to have camera software that allows for the clinician to view the pertinent parts of the physical setting (e.g., other individuals in the session, client's setting) (Glueck, 2013b). Eye contact may be a challenge as cameras are often mounted in a place that does not allow for direct eye contact with the person on the other end of the camera; rather, cameras are mounted at the top of a screen and give the impression of the other person looking away. This might be viewed as a risk or a challenge to gain the same level of alliance for those participating in e-therapy in comparison to those in face-to-face therapy sessions.

In reviewing studies on the impact to the therapeutic alliance in e-therapeutic treatments, one of the primary findings was the attitude of the clinician toward e-therapy may be a key factor in polluting the alliance findings (Simpson & Reid, 2014). Specifically, therapeutic bond is a key factor in the therapeutic alliance, which includes the therapist's attitude, abilities, and therapist anxiety. Therefore, therapists who are apprehensive or mistrustful of using videoconferencing technologies may communicate that apprehension through the technology, thus negatively impacting the bond, and relatedly the alliance (Simpson & Reid, 2014).

Perceived Risk of Increased Symptomatic Behavior

One area of risk sometimes introduced by the therapist is the inability to conduct a proper assessment without the person being face-to-face, such as when evaluating for psychosis. Part of this concern may be rooted in the ecological e-therapy element of accommodation, or the differences between the ways a client may present themselves offline versus online (Hertlein & Stevenson, 2010). Others are concerned that e-therapy enables those fearful of traveling or leaving their homes. However, researchers thus far have indicated that symptoms do not tend to increase because of service modality in these populations (Turvey & Myers, 2013).

Emergency Situations

Equally important is the issue related to potential risk of suicidality and self-harm in clients participating in online therapy (Kramer et al., 2013). Suicide assessments conducted via e-therapy have three main associated legal and ethical issues: licensing, involuntary commitment, and liability (Godleski et al., 2008). Licensing and involuntary commitment overlap when there is a need to detain a client with suicidal ideation or intent to harm self or others, but an inability to do so when the clinician is not licensed to practice in the state in which the client resides. This can be particularly problematic for veteran's administration practitioners who are only required to be licensed in one state to work agency-wide, but may encounter detainment issues when engaging in e-therapy practices (Godleski et al., 2008). Finally, liability is generally discussed as falling in two categories: abandonment (characterized by technology failing resulting in an inability to "meet" with the client) and negligence (characterized by a failure to provide medical attention to a suicidal client). Each state differs in its definition of what constitutes a client who is in danger of harming oneself, thus introducing more confusion for interstate practitioners.

Training Issues

Because CFTs are increasing their adoption of e-therapy practices, they are interested in receiving adequate training on how to provide the appropriate standard of care in their couple and family therapy technology practices (Blumer, Hertlein, & VandenBosch, 2015). Sunderji, Crawford, and Jovanovic (2015) conducted a literature review of telepsychiatry competencies and found that competencies to be included in training are those that address technical aspects of telehealth, ideas on collaboration, and competencies on how to perform specific administrative tasks. Alternatively, Nelson, Bui, and Sharp (2011) identified competencies as falling into two categories: clinical and outreach. Several states are working on developing and adopting core competencies of training for those who conduct telemental health (e.g., Areas of Competence for Psychologists in Telepsychology, 2013). Outside of the states, there are also professional organizations such as Association of Marital and Family Therapy Regulatory Boards (AMFTRB), American Psychological Association (APA), American Telemedicine Association (ATA), and National Association of Social Workers (NASW) who are working to develop core competencies and guidelines for their respective organization(s) (Blumer et al., 2015). One of the main challenges, however, is the lack of coordination on the part of the organizations in these efforts, which makes the development of a coherent frame for therapists difficult.

Privacy, Security, and Confidentiality

Security is such an issue that many of the e-therapy guidelines speak directly to the necessity for practitioners to understand the nuances about the system they use to provide the best security for clients. Security refers to the ways in which the practitioner would safeguard the information to prevent unauthorized disclosure. This differs from privacy, which refers to how one manages and distributes their personal information. Finally, confidentiality refers the ethical responsibility of the therapist to not share personal information shared. Therapists working in online environments need to ensure their client's electronic information is safeguarded—from the security provided by the system to the client during sessions to the way in which personal information and data is protected. The main point of both the issues of malpractice and protecting client information is that the standard of care "does not change with technology" (Vanderpool, 2015, p. 172). The Health Insurance Portability and Accountability Act (HIPAA) security regulations are of particular import here, and are discussed further in Chapter 4.

Informed Consent

It is essential that the ecological e-therapy element of ambiguity be addressed before and while engaging in online therapy. In the context of the Couple and Family Therapy Technology Framework, ambiguity is described as the lack of clarity and related difficulties associated with defining e-therapy, both technologically and relationally (Blumer & Hertlein, 2012; Hertlein & Stevenson, 2010). There are myriad authors who pose several independent considerations for managing such ambiguities in one's digital practice, with most advocating for thorough informed consent regarding the risks and benefits of e-therapy. Informed consent should address why e-therapy is being used, what to do when technological issues happen that may interfere with having a session, the basic nuts and bolts of the process of treatment (Glueck, 2013b), and assist clients in understanding how to promote the confidentiality and privacy of their therapeutic information (Sabin & Skimming, 2015). Wilcoxon (2015) also suggests therapists think critically and with forethought about any potential technology-related issues, clarify meanings of terms, develop policies around electronic communication and explain them to the client, keep updated on literature related to e-practices, identify whether e-therapy is covered by one's insurance, and avoid social networking with clients. The HIPAA security risk assessment as discussed in Chapter 4 will aid in this process. Cyber-insurance is also available.

Legal Issues

Licensing and Credentialing

As previously mentioned, a significant advantage to e-therapy is the ability to serve populations who are at a geographical disadvantage for receiving services (Hertlein et al., 2014; Koocher, 2007). One of the primary challenges of e-therapy is that of licensure. Historically, the regulations regarding licensure dictated that mental and relational health professionals could only practice e-therapy in the states in which they were licensed (Vanderpool, 2015). As opportunities arose for practitioners to expand practices beyond their state lines, such as when clients resided in another state, legislation is being introduced that will enable therapists to participate in service delivery across state lines. At present, this is not the case, though some states will allow mental health professionals to obtain a temporary license to practice within their state for a maximum number of days or sessions per year (Kramer et al., 2013).

Malpractice

As previously mentioned, interstate practice without appropriate licenses can lead to misdemeanors, felonies, and fines. If harm has been generated when therapists practice outside of the purview of their license, they may find themselves facing malpractice suits. For many practitioners, their malpractice insurance covers to face-to-face interactions and says little about what happens when that contact is over the Internet. CFTs should look closely at their policy; for example, CPH and Associates Professional Liability Insurance does cover online therapy in those states that allow it, and encourages therapists to contact their state board to ensure they are practicing lawfully An additional malpractice risk to consider is that because e-therapists must expand their informed consent to cover e-therapy contingencies, they inadvertently have also expanded their scope of practice, and consequently their liability risks.

Application of the Couple and Family Therapy Technology Framework

Knowledge of ethical issues surrounding the structure and process of e-therapy is important as CFTs use technology to address client needs. Using the Couple and Family Therapy Technology Framework, CFTs can make more informed decisions regarding e-therapeutic practices. Returning to our case scenario at the beginning of this chapter, Dr. Stellar would likely alter her choices in terms of CFT technology practices. For instance, if she attended to the ecological e-therapy element of ambiguity and its effect on the structure and process of e-therapeutic practices, she would recognize the importance of agreeing with her clients on a definition of e-therapy for the sake of clarifying their online interactions. In addition, she would likely recognize the need for having the clients review and sign a detailed informed consent document related to e-therapeutic treatment, aiding her in addressing safety and security issues, and other legal and ethical issues. Additionally, she would also be better informed as to which technological platform would be most appropriate to use with which clients, and during which phase of treatment, rather than just using various platforms for clinical work in what seems to be a haphazard and/or urgency-based manner.

Conclusion

CFTs face a myriad of issues in practicing e-therapy. E-therapy is evolving at a rapid pace, and we recognize that because of that, aspects of e-therapy that are not clear now will be clarified as technology practices become standardized. However, what becomes standardized can quickly become outdated, requiring the CFT to stay current how both therapeutic and technology issues advance. For ethical practice, we advise CFTs to continue to check with their state laws regarding the current standards of care, to stay up-to-date with the relevant scholarly literature, utilize knowledgeable attorneys as resources to e-practice, and participate in continuing education opportunities that are related to online therapy.

References

Anthony, K., & Nagel, D. M. (2010). *Therapy online: A practical guide*. Thousand Oaks, CA: Sage.

Areas of Competence for Psychologists in Telepsychology. (2013). *Areas of competence for psychologists in telepsychology*. Retrieved from: http://www.ohpsych.org/about/files/2012/03/FINAL_COMPETENCY_DRAFT.pdf.

Augusterfer, E. F. (2013). Clinically informed telemental health in post-disaster areas. In K. M. L. Turvey (Ed.), *Telemental health* (pp. 347–366). Oxford, England: Elsevier.

Blumer, M. L. C. (2014). Ecological elements in couple and family therapy technological practice. *MFT Courier*, *28*(2), 2–5.

Blumer, M. L. C. (2015). Couple and family therapy technology practices: A framework for ethical engagement. *Family Therapy Magazine*, 40–45.

Blumer, M. L. C., Bergdall, M., & Ullman, K. (2014, November). *E-visibility management of LGB identities*. Poster, Scientific Society for Sexuality Studies Annual Conference. Omaha, NE.

Blumer, M. L. C., & Hertlein, K. M. (2011). "Twitter, and texting, and YouTube, oh my!" MFT networking via new media. *Family Therapy Magazine*, 24–25.

Blumer, M. L. C., & Hertlein, K. M. (2012). Addressing ambiguity in e-practice management: Family therapy and supervision in a digital age. *Family Therapy Magazine*, 16–18.

Blumer, M. L. C., Hertlein, K. M., Smith, J. M., & Allen, H. (2013). How many bytes does it take? A content analysis of cyber issues in couple and family therapy journals. *Journal of Marital and Family Therapy, 39*(S3). doi: 10.1111/j.1752-0606.2012.00332.x/full.

Blumer, M., Hertlein, K. M., & VandenBosch, M. (2015). Towards the development of educational core competencies for couple and family therapy technology practices. *Contemporary Family Therapy, 37*, 113–121. doi: 10.1007/s10591-015-9330-1.

Chelsey, N. (2005). Blurring boundaries: Linking technology use, spillover, individual distress, and family satisfaction. *Journal of Marriage and the Family, 67*, 1237–1248.

Cooper, A. (2002). *Sex and the Internet: A guidebook for clinicians*. New York, NY: Brunner-Routledge.

Crow, S. J., Mitchell, J. E., Crosby, R. D., Swanson, S. A., Wonderlich, S., & Lancanster, K. (2009). The cost effectiveness of cognitive behavioral therapy for bulimia nervosa delivered via telemedicine versus face-to-face. *Behaviour Research and Therapy, 47*(6), 451–453. doi: 10.1016/j.brat.2009.02.006.

Dewan, N. A., Luo, J. S., & Lorez, N. M. (2015). (Eds.). *Mental health practice in a digital world: A clinician's guide*. New York, NY: Springer.

Doss, B. D., Benson, L. A., Georgia, E. J., & Christensen, A. (2013). Translation of integrative behavioral couple therapy to a web-based intervention. *Family Process, 52*(1), 139–153. doi: 10.1111/famp.12020.

Eells, T. D., Barrett, M. S., Wright, J. H., & Thase, M. (2014). Computer-assisted cognitive-behavior therapy for depression. *Psychotherapy, 51*(2), 191–197. doi: 10.1037/a0032406.

Fortney J. C., Pyne, J. M., Kimbrell, T. A, Hudson, T. J., Robinson, D. E. … Schnurr, P. P. (2015). Telemedicine-based collaborative care for posttraumatic stress disorder: A randomized clinical trial. *JAMA Psychiatry, 72*(1), 58–67. doi: 10.1001/jamapsychiatry.2014.1575.

Frueh, B. C. (2015). Solving mental healthcare access problems in the twenty-first century. *Australian Psychologist, 50*(4), 304–306. doi: 10.1111/ap.12140.

Gamble, N., Boyle, C., & Morris, Z. A. (2015). Ethical practice in telepsychology. *Australian Psychologist, 50*(4), 292–298. doi: 10.1111/ap.12133.

Germain, V., Marchand, A., Bouchard, S., Guay, S., & Drouin, M. (2010). Assessment of the therapeutic alliance in face-to-face or videoconference treatment for posttraumatic stress disorder. *Cyberpsychology, Behavior, and Social Networking, 13*(1), 29–35. doi: 10.1089/cyber.2009.0139.

Glueck, D. (2013a). Business aspects of telemental health in private practice. In K. M. L. Turvey (Ed.), *Telemental health* (pp. 111–133). Oxford, England: Elsevier.

Glueck, D. (2013b). Establishing therapeutic rapport in telemental health. In K. M. L. Turvey (Ed.), *Telemental Health* (pp. 29–46). Oxford, England: Elsevier.

Godleski, L., Nieves, J. E., Darkins, A., & Lehmann, L. (2008). VA telemental health: Suicide assessment. *Behavioral Sciences & the Law, 26*(3), 271–286. doi: 10.1002/bsl.811.

Goldstein, F., & Myers, K. (2014). Telemental health: A new collaboration for pediatricians and child psychiatrists. *Pediatric Annals, 43*(2), 79–84. doi: 10.3928/00904481-20140127-12.

Harwood, T. M., & L'Abate, L. (2009). *Self-help in mental health: A critical review*. New York, NY: Springer.

Hertlein, K. M., & Blumer, M. L. C. (2013). *The couple and family technology framework: Intimate relationships in a digital age*. New York, NY: Routledge.

Hertlein, K. M., Blumer, M., & Mihaloliakos, J. (2015). Marriage and family therapists' perceptions of the ethical considerations of online therapy. *The Family Journal, 23*(1), 5–12. doi: 10.1177/1066480714547184.

Hertlein, K. M., Blumer, M. L. C., & Smith, J. (2014). Marriage and family therapists' use and comfort with online communication with clients. *Contemporary Family Therapy, 36*, 58–69. doi: 10.1007/s10591-013-9284-0.

Hertlein, K. M., & Sendak, S. (2007). *Love bytes: Intimacy in computer-mediated relationships*. Retrieved from: http://www.persons.org.uk/ptb/persons/pil/pil1/hertleinsendak%20paper.pdf.

Hertlein, K. M., & Stevenson, A. J. (2010). The seven "As" contributing to Internet-related intimacy problems: A literature review. *Cyberpsychology: Journal of Psychosocial Research on Cyberspace, 4*(1), article 1. Retrieved from: http://www.cyberpsychology.eu/view.php?cisloclanku=2010050202.

Hertlein, K. M., & Twist, M. L. C. (2015, September). *Core competencies of technology for couple and family therapists.* Workshop, American Association for Marriage and Family Therapy Annual Conference, Austin, TX.

Hesser, H., Gustafsson, T., Lunden, C., Henrikson, O., Fattahi, K., … Andersson, G. (2012). A randomized controlled trial of Internet-delivered cognitive behavior therapy and acceptance and commitment therapy in the treatment of tinnitus. *Journal of Consulting and Clinical Psychology, 80*(4), 649–661. doi: 10.1037/a0027021.

Iwasaki, Y., & Ristock, J. (2007). The nature of stress experienced by lesbians and gay men. *Anxiety, Stress, & Coping, 20,* 299–319. doi: 10.1080/10615800701303264.

Jenkins-Guarnieri, M. A., Pruitt, L. D., Luxton, D. D., & Johnson, K. (2015). Patient perceptions of telemental health: Systematic review of direct comparisons to in-person psychotherapeutic treatments. *Telemedicine and E-Health, 21*(8), 652–660. doi: 10.1089/tmj.2014.0165.

Jiang, L., Bazarova, N. N., & Hancock, J. T. (2013). From perception to behavior: Disclosure reciprocity in computer-mediated and face-to-face interactions. *Communication Research, 40,* 125–143. doi: 10.1177/0093650211405313.

King, S. A. (1999). Internet gambling and pornography: Illustrative examples of psychological consequences of communication anarchy. *Cyberpsychology & Behavior, 2,* 175–193. doi: 10.1089/cpb.1999.2.175.

Knaevelsrud, C., & Maercker, A. (2006). Does the quality of the working alliance predict treatment outcome in online psychotherapy for traumatized patients? *Journal of Medical Internet Research, 8*(4), e31. doi: 10.2196/jmir.8.4.e31.

Koocher, G. P. (2007). Twenty-first century ethical challenges for psychology. *American Psychologist, 62*(5), 375–384. doi: 10.1037/0003-066X.62.5.375.

Kramer, G. M., Mishkind, M. C., Luxton, D. D., & Shore, J. H. (2013). Managing risk and protecting privacy in telemental health: An overview of legal, regulatory, and risk-management issues. In K. M. L. Turvey (Ed.), *Telemental health* (pp. 83–107). Oxford, England: Elsevier.

Loucas, C. E., Fairburn, C. G., Whittington, C., Stockton, Pennant, M. E., Stockton, S., & Kendall, T. (2014). E-therapy in the treatment and prevention of eating disorders: A systematic review and meta-analysis. *Behavior Therapy and Research, 63,* 122–131. doi: 10.1016/j.brat.2014.09.011.

Michikyan, M., Subrahmanyam, K., & Dennis, J. (2014). Can you tell me who I am? Neuroticism, extraversion, and online self-presentation among young adults. *Computers in Human Behavior, 33,* 179–183. doi: 10.1016/j.chb.2014.01.010.

Morgan, R. D., Patrick, A. R., & Magaletta, P. R. (2008). Does the use of telemental health alter the treatment experience? Inmates' perceptions of telemental health versus face-to-face treatment modalities. *Journal of Consulting and Clinical Psychology, 76*(1), 158–162. doi: 10.1037/0022-006X.76.1.158.

Morland, L. A., Greene, C. J., Rosen, C., Foy, D., Reilly, P., … Frueh, C. (2010). Telemedicine for anger management therapy in a rural population of combat veterans with posttraumatic stress disorder: A randomized noninferiority trial. *Journal of Clinical Psychiatry, 71*(7), 855–863. doi: 10.4088/JCP.09m05604blu.

Nelson, E., Barnard, M., & Cain, S. (2006). Feasibility of telemedicine intervention for childhood depression. *Counselling and Psychotherapy Research, 6*(3), 191–195. doi: 10.1080/14733140600862303.

Nelson, E., Bui, T., & Sharp, S. (2011). Telemental health competencies: Training examples from a youth depression telemedicine clinic. In M. B. Gregerson (Ed.), *Technology innovations for behavioral education* (pp. 41–47). New York, NY: Springer.

O'Reilly, R., Bishop, J., Maddox, K., Hutchinson, L., Fisman, M., & Takhar, J. (2007). Is telepsychiatry equivalent to face-to-face psychiatry? Results from a randomized controlled equivalence trial. *Psychiatric Services, 58*(6), 836–843. doi: 10.1176/appi.ps.58.6.836.

Palmer, N. B., Myers, K. M., Vander Stoep, A., McCarty, C. A., Geyer, J. R., & DeSalvo, A. (2010). Attention-deficit/hyperactivity disorder and telemental health. *Current Psychiatry Reports, 12*(5), 409–417. doi: 10.1007/s11920-010-0132-8.

Rees, C. S., & Maclaine, E. (2015). A systematic review of videoconference-delivered psychological treatment for anxiety disorders. *Australian Psychologist, 50*(4), 259–264. doi: 10.1111/ap.12122.

Ross, M. W., & Kauth, M. R. (2002). Men who have sex with men, and the Internet: Emerging clinical issues and their management. In A. Cooper (Ed.), *Sex and the Internet: A guidebook for clinicians* (pp. 47–69). New York, NY: Brunner-Routledge.

Sabin, J. E., & Skimming, K. (2015). A framework for ethics for telepsychiatry practice. *International Review of Psychiatry, 27*(6), 490–495. doi: 10.3109/09540261.2015.1094034.

Sheeber, L. B., Seeley, J. R., Feil, E.G., Sorensen, E., Kosty, D. B, & Lewinsohn, P. M. (2012). Development and pilot evaluation of an Internet-facilitated cognitive-behavioral intervention for maternal depression. *Journal of Consulting and Clinical Psychology, 80*(5), 739–749. doi: 10.1037/a0028820.

Simms, D. C., Gibson, K., & O'Donnell, S. (2011). To use or not to use: Clinicians' perceptions of telemental health. *Canadian Psychology, 52*(1), 41–51. doi: 10.1037/a0022275.

Simpson, S. G., & Reid, C. L. (2014). Therapeutic alliance in videoconferencing psychotherapy: A review. *Australian Journal of Rural Health, 22*(6), 280–299. doi: 10.1111/ajr.12149.

Suler, J. R. (2000). Psychotherapy in cyberspace: A 5-dimension model of online and computer-mediated psychotherapy. *CyberPsychology and Behavior, 3*, 151–160. doi: 10.1089/109493100315996.

Sunderji, N., Crawford, A., & Jovanovic, M. (2015). Telepsychiatry in graduate medical education: A narrative review. *Academic Psychiatry, 39*(1), 55–62. doi: 10.1007/s40596-014-0176-x.

Turvey, C. L., & Myers, K. (2013). Research in telemental health: Review and synthesis. In K. M. L. Turvey (Ed.), *Telemental health* (pp. 397–419). Oxford, England: Elsevier.

Twist, M. L. C., & Hertlein, K. M. (2015). Tweet me, follow me, friend me: Prevalence of online professional networking between family therapists. *Journal of Feminist Family Therapy: An International Forum, 27*(3/4), 116–133. doi: 10.1080/08952833.2015.1065651.

Vanderpool, D. (2015). An overview of practicing high quality telepsychiatry. In N. A. Dewan, J. S. Luo, & N. M. Lorez (Eds.), *Mental health practice in a digital world: A clinician's guide* (pp. 159–182). New York, NY: Springer.

Wilcoxon, S. A. (2015). Technology and client care: Therapy considerations in a digital society. *Australian and New Zealand Journal of Family Therapy, 36*, 480–491. doi: 10.1002/anzf.1128.

Wilding, R. (2006). 'Virtual' intimacies? Families communicating across transnational contexts. *Global Networks, 6*(2), 125–142. doi: 10.1111/j.1471-0374.2006.00137.x.

Xie, Y., Dixon, J. F., Yee, O., M., Zhang, J., Chen, Y. A., … Schweitzer, J. B. (2013). A study on the effectiveness of videoconferencing on teaching parent training skills to parents of children with ADHD. *Telemedicine and E-Health, 19*(3), 192–199. doi: 10.1089/tmj.2012.0108.

15

Ethical and Clinical Considerations for Home-Based Family Therapy

Kiran M. Hussain, M. Evan Thomas, Shannon Polezoes, and Léa El Helou

Ben, a couple and family therapist, conducted in-home family therapy with the Smith family, which included two parents and three children. During the intake call, Ben explained the therapy process, answered the family's questions, and set up their first appointment. During the first session, Ben noticed that the house seemed to be cluttered, and there was minimal seating available. He was seated on a small couch and was joined by both parents. Ben felt discomfort in the close proximity resulting from unintentional physical touch with Mrs. Smith because the couch was not large enough to comfortably seat three people. Later, the children and their large dog joined the session. Ben became uncomfortable as he was afraid of large animals since he was once bitten by a dog. The session was also interrupted several times by neighbors and relatives. They inquired about Ben's presence and noticed that he wore a badge listing his name and agency, which revealed information about his work. Ben became concerned about possibly violating client confidentiality as neighbors and relatives asked why Ben was present in the Smith's home. Despite the discomfort and interruptions, Ben continued the session. Upon the end of the session, Ben was invited to stay for dinner, but he respectfully declined. The family insisted he take dinner with him, and packed a container to go. Ben accepted the gift so as not to offend the family.

Introduction

Providing family therapy services in the client's home substantially changes the dynamics of therapy (Waisbrod, Buchbinder, & Possick, 2012). The difference in setting creates new ethical challenges for the therapist that traditional ethical decision-making models may not address. In this chapter, we provide ways to address ethical dilemmas pertaining to home-based family therapy. These suggestions include: collaboratively developing boundaries with clients, adhering to confidentiality regulations, focusing on self-care, and seeking supervision and guidance to deal with the challenges inherent to home-based family therapy.

Overview and Future of Home-Based Family Therapy

Although traditional mental health therapy is typically conducted in an office setting, an alternate modality such as home-based therapy can be substituted (Waisbrod et al., 2012). This unique modality of therapy can provide the client with a familiar environment where therapeutic interventions are administered; home-based therapy may be particularly useful when working with clients who have not been responding well to traditional therapeutic processes (Waisbrod et al., 2012). In-home family therapy dates back to the 1970s with Salvador Minuchin (1974), who began to see at-risk families in their homes. Later, other programs such as multisystemic therapy (MST) and multidimensional family therapy were established and recognized as home-based programs effective in treating families, especially with regard to drug abuse (McWey, Humphreys, & Pazdera, 2011).

Effectiveness of the home-based approach has been established by several research studies. Lietz (2009) found that 71% of the families that participated in the project reported experiencing improvements in their family after receiving home-based services. Eighty-three percent of those families attributed this feeling in particular to the home-based setting. Seeling, Goldman-Hall, and Jerell (1992) found that home-based therapy as an alternative to hospitalization in families with adolescents contributed to the family feeling empowered when dealing with crisis. Home-based therapy also allowed the family to utilize their resources when coping with crisis (Seeling et al., 1992).

The lack of response to office-based interventions can be partially attributed to clients leaving their comfortable environment and entering an unfamiliar setting (Waisbrod et al., 2012). Allowing the therapist to enter the client's home changes this dynamic; it leads to a reversal of roles in that the client remains in known territory, whereas the therapist enters the unknown. Boyd-Franklin and Bry (2001) argue that remaining within the family's home allows for cultivation of new relationships, and increases the family's incentive to make shifts.

Home-based family therapy provides another avenue of therapy for clients who experience difficulties with conventional office-based therapy. Low-income families unable to access transportation and/or locate appropriate childcare can benefit from the therapist conducting sessions in the home (Mattek, Jorgenson, & Fox, 2010). Home-based therapy can also provide assistance to the home-bound elderly and the physically disabled (Waisbrod et al., 2012). Home visiting programs in the United States of America already serve more than 500,000 mothers and their children (Ammerman, Putnam, Altaye, Teeters, Stevens, & Van Ginkel, 2013). Given the convenience and assistance offered through home-based therapy, as well as a decrease in overhead costs for couple and family therapists, home-based therapy is becoming a more accepted way to deliver treatment.

Furthermore, home-based therapy is more accessible to families and easier to coordinate since the therapist is accommodating to the family's needs (Lawson, 2005). This method of therapy also tends to be more intensive as therapists are readily available to meet clients (Bagdasaryan, 2004). Therapists have reported being more knowledgeable about their clients in this intimate setting, and noticed important client characteristics such as the religiosity of the family and the rituals they practice. Interns also reported increased friendliness and hospitality from the family because of the simple act of visiting their home and the "social expectation" tied to these visitations (Thomas, McCollum, & Snyder, 1999, p. 180). Finally, the gesture demonstrated by the therapist taking time to drive to meet clients highlights the commitment to the therapy process and strengthens the therapeutic alliance (Thomas et al., 1999).

The medical field has already paved the way for other disciplines to visit clients' homes through the use of concierge medicine. This form of a medical system, also known as retainer-based medicine, allows patients to pay an additional annual fee for more timely and comprehensive services (Gavirneni & Kulkarni, 2014). Mental health professionals can take advantage of such a health care system, extending their practice outside of their office and traveling to clients' homes. Along with an elevated quality of care, once the client becomes accustomed to this therapeutic design, a decrease in the number of cancellations and "no shows" is likely (Weber, 2003).

Challenges for Home-Based Therapists

Although home-based family therapy is shown to be beneficial for clients, it poses many ethical and logistical challenges for therapists, with limited access to therapeutic resources such as colleagues and co-therapists

(Christensen, 1995; Lauka, Remley, & Ward, 2013). Challenges encountered by home-based therapists include distractions such as visitors in the home and poor living conditions, which may interfere with the therapeutic process (Christensen, 1995). Concerns regarding therapist and client safety are also present in home-based settings (Christensen, 1995).

Additional challenges in home-based therapy include preserving appropriate boundaries and effectively dealing with issues regarding confidentiality (Scarborough, Taylor, & Tuttle, 2013). Therapists are not always granted sufficient space in which to practice, raising issues of client confidentiality and privacy in sessions (Scarborough et al., 2013; Thomas et al., 1999). The presence of neighbors and friends often obstructs client confidentiality in the home-based setting (Thomas et al., 1999). Concerns regarding confidentiality also arise when clients share information during session, which may result in difficulties for the family by creating a crisis within the system (Christensen, 1995; Scarborough et al., 2013). For example, children or adolescents may disclose information regarding pregnancy, use of substance, or a general chaotic environment that was intended to be discussed under confidential circumstances, but may need to be addressed and shared with other members of the system. To respond effectively in these circumstances, therapists may need to get family members involved in creating awareness of issues, or in reporting the issue as mandated and necessary (Scarborough et al., 2013). Moreover, therapist and client roles may not be clearly established, raising issues regarding boundaries in home-based therapy settings (Scarborough et al., 2013). Maintaining professional boundaries is often a difficult task when providing home-based therapy as therapists may be offered gifts, or be expected to disclose information about themselves. Boundaries and roles may shift depending on how therapists respond to such requests (Scarborough et al., 2013).

Providing services in the client's home and being part of their physical space raises concerns regarding power imbalances in the therapeutic relationship. Differences in cultural values also impact ways in which professionals create structure in home-based therapy sessions (Thomas et al., 1999). Other challenges include unqualified therapists providing home-based therapy services, and providing services which are outside the range of the counselor's capabilities. Insufficient supervision has also been recognized as an ethical issue for home-based therapy as therapists felt that the supervisors were not qualified, prepared, or trained to provide adequate support (Lauka et al., 2013). Although the literature recognizes various dilemmas encountered in home-based settings, few guidelines or suggestions are provided for resolution of these ethical issues.

Addressing Ethical Dilemmas in Home-Based Family Therapy

It is imperative to address ethical issues commonly experienced by home-based family therapists, in part staying abreast of pertinent and current literature regarding standards for ethical practice (Hecker, 2010; Pope & Vasquez, 2011), as well as applicable legal regulations (Cottone, 2001; Hecker, 2010; Pope & Vasquez, 2011). The following recommendations address ethical issues encountered during home-based family therapy.

Developing Boundaries

Couple and family therapists are responsible for maintaining appropriate boundaries, regardless of whether therapy takes place in the office or in-home. Home-based family therapists must maintain boundaries through engaging in professional behavior. Boundaries preserve the therapeutic relationship (Scarborough et al., 2013), and are particularly important with home-based work as the environment is more personal and intimate.

For example, therapists should be mindful of the time limit per session, arrive to session on time, and should avoid staying after the session is over to socialize. Therapists must also practice within their role. For example, therapists may be asked to check for cleanliness of the home and report back to case workers. Therapists must direct such requests to the appropriate service providers (i.e., case managers) and remind themselves and clients of what is expected within a family therapy session.

Boundaries and professionalism can be conveyed through subtle means in the home of the client; the way a therapist dresses and maintains personal space helps ensure that the therapist is practicing within the therapist role and therapist capabilities. It is advised that therapists discuss their expectations regarding professionalism within the home. Measures must also be taken to establish a firm beginning and end to each session. This may be more difficult in a home-based setting, and a discussion regarding the specific length of the session may be necessary. The family should be ready for the session by the time the therapist arrives to prevent any unwanted delays. It can be difficult to enforce such rules in chaotic environments, thus a firm reestablishment of these expectations may be needed, at times on a weekly basis. It is important to remember that basic steps, such as obtaining an informed consent, are still fundamental and can aid in establishing therapeutic boundaries. During the informed consent discussion, the therapist can explain policies and procedures, their qualifications, and expectations regarding therapy in the client's home. These expectations should be discussed with the clients in detail, and provide an excellent opportunity to clarify the nature of the relationship between the therapist and the client, as well as its limitations as applicable to the home-based setting.

Therapists must also be mindful of space within the home to conduct sessions while maintaining privacy. Specific seating arrangements may be necessary so as not to invade the family's personal space. The therapist may prefer to sit on a chair to be able to address all family members comfortably. The therapist can also be ready to direct clients to alter their seating arrangements as necessary. In addition, if there is not enough seating, the therapist can ask if additional chairs can be brought in from another room. Overall, the therapist can work to structure the session as needed, even if therapy is conducted in the client's home.

Home-based family therapists must also be cognizant of the myriad cultural values present in therapy, and collaborate with the client to create the expected culture of therapy specific to the client's home. Values can emerge in hospitality such as in our case scenario when Ben struggled to decide if he should stay for dinner. Ben may come from a culture that is less comfortable with close physical proximity, whereas his clients may more readily sit closer to others. Similarly, the family may demonstrate hospitality by offering Ben dinner (and insisting on a box "to go"), whereas Ben may feel that staying for dinner crosses a professional boundary. Setting boundaries around values can be a difficult task. In Ben's instance, he was presented with many challenges. To maintain the integrity of his relationship with the Smith family, Ben must continually work to establish and sustain boundaries while considering the client's cultural values. Setting boundaries can begin with the intake phone call. For example, Ben could have asked the family if there were any pets in the home, if he needed to park his car in the driveway or on the street, and/or if any friends or other visitors were expected to stop by during the session.

During Ben's first session, boundaries around hospitality may include a more in-depth discussion around respecting the client's home culture. This could include the seating arrangements for each session, the room that each session will take place in, and/or role expectations for Ben as the therapist and the Smith family as the clients. Ben will likely consider scheduling appointments that will not interfere with the families' dinner time, religious activities, extracurricular activities, and/or family functions. Many times, therapists are invited to participate in whatever activity the family typically has scheduled for the time slot of the therapy session.

By Ben discussing these expectations beforehand, it is more likely to eliminate Ben's declining to join in as an affront to the therapeutic relationship. Additionally, Ben may ask the family members if they are comfortable with him wearing his name badge while visiting the home or ask how the family would like him to react if company unexpectedly arrives. Establishing such guidelines helps to create a strong therapeutic alliance.

It is imperative that therapists discuss their rationale behind their decisions and make every attempt to try to understand the family's perspectives. Furthermore, therapists can demonstrate sensitivity by adapting their clothing to match the home they are visiting while remaining professional. For instance, wearing designer labels and specific brands may emphasize possible socioeconomic discrepancies between clients and therapist, which can then impact the therapeutic relationship. By dressing more casually and in a modest manner, therapists can seem more approachable.

Guidelines pertaining to multiple relationships and intimacy must also be established. Multiple relationships refer to whenever a therapist functions in more than one professional relationship or role, such as in the realm of social, personal, or business relationships (Sonne, 1994). When conducting therapy in the home of the client, therapists must be particularly cognizant of the possibility of multiple relationships because of the more personal nature of the setting. When assessing for risk in engaging in multiple relationships, three factors are usually evaluated: "harm to the professional relationship, loss of therapist objectivity, and risk of exploitation" (Campbell & Gordon, 2003, p. 433). Seeking supervision is crucial to ensure that the therapist remains objective and aware of the potential blurring of boundaries. Another fundamental rule to keep in mind is the rule of "abstinence," meaning the therapist must refrain from any exchange that leads to personal gratification (Simon & Williams, 1999), instead evaluating the impact of decisions both on the family and themselves. The rule of abstinence can help therapists navigate difficult situations in which boundaries have the potential to be breached. Being asked to help with a certain problem in the home that is unrelated to therapy can blur those professional boundaries and create confusion for the client. For example, if the therapist's car breaks down, and the client is a mechanic, does he allow the client to examine his car for the problem, or even fix it? If an elderly client needs a lightbulb changed, is it acceptable for the therapist to change the bulb? These are dilemmas that can occur in this type of therapy setting; therapists should bear in mind that the setting does not change the nature or limits of the therapeutic relationship.

Confidentiality

Confidentiality is an important dimension to consider when conducting home-based family therapy. Couple and family therapists are responsible for explaining and maintaining confidentiality with respect to each client involved in the therapeutic process. Because of the nature of the setting, many factors may be out of the therapist's control. The first thing to consider is the neighborhood and surrounding area. Neighbors and friends may often be present in home-based therapy setting (Thomas et al., 1999). It is also possible that neighbors will eventually notice the therapist coming in regularly, and may begin inquiring about the therapist's presence. Home-based family therapists must help the clients understand that having the therapist come to their home may arouse curiosity from others in the surrounding areas, raising concerns for privacy and violations of confidentiality. Reflections of the therapist's agency, such as nametags, car stickers, and other items can give away to neighbors the purpose of the therapist's visit, and by doing so breach the client's confidentiality. Discussing this possibility ahead of time, and brainstorming ideas with clients regarding how they might respond to curious neighbors is a good way of demonstrating respect for the client's confidentiality and being collaborative in the process.

Furthermore, therapy may be conducted in a neutral, open space such as the main living area, making it possible for members outside of the treatment unit to obtain confidential information. Overhearing can be a problem for both the client and the therapist. This can be especially challenging if therapy will not include all family members, if the home is very small, or if visitors such as neighbors or the children's friends will be roaming freely around the house and may overhear the conversation. Home-based family therapists must discuss the possibility of involuntary disclosure of confidential information resulting from such interference, and its impact on therapy and the therapeutic relationship. It is also crucial to keep in mind that clients of different cultures and socioeconomic statuses may have different expectations of confidentiality, and may be more or less concerned about such issues. The therapist's judgment comes into play here, both in balancing adherence to one's code of ethics and respecting the family's wishes and preferences. In-home therapy requires significant flexibility on the part of the therapist.

To further address this issue, additional measures can be taken, such as minimizing the amount of outside interruptions by having the family tell friends and neighbors that they are busy, and if possible, practicing within small private spaces to maintain confidentiality during session. White noise machines can be used, as can music, to minimize the likelihood of accidental overhearing. "Do not disturb" or "Session in progress" signs can help to avoid interruptions and maintain confidentiality as much as possible.

This can be especially helpful when therapy is conducted with smaller units of the family and information needs to be concealed from others, such as if the therapist is seeing the parents without their children. Additionally, the therapist may want to see children individually for some or parts of sessions, and if so, will sometimes have no choice but to see the child in their bedroom, which may be seen as inappropriate and ethically questionable. In this case, it may be necessary for the door to be left slightly open. Parents should be consulted for advice and permissions.

In home settings, therapists have much more information about the family available to them, and they may gain more information than what the client wishes to share. In such situations, therapists may be required to report issues such as abuse and neglect, especially when client and therapist safety are a concern. Each state has mandatory reporting laws; failure to comply with these laws constitutes a crime. It is important to remember that therapists are responsible for explaining to clients when disclosure of information may be necessary or legally mandated.

HIPAA brings major concerns for therapists who are practicing home-based family therapy for multiple reasons. The first reason is that therapists are constantly traveling between the office and the client's home. This makes it likely that the therapist is carrying protected health information (PHI), such as progress notes, case files, geographic information, and identification numbers with them on their travels. PHI left in the therapist's car can open the door for breach of PHI. Therapists have had records lost, stolen, or even cars with records in them stolen, in addition to electronic media housing therapy information. The HIPAA requirement of "physical safeguards" requires home-based therapists to secure their files in some manner such as a locked briefcase or locked file box when transporting records (Hecker, 2016).

Another dilemma for home-based family therapists is the use of their cell phones as a way to communicate with clients. With PHI including telephone numbers and e-mail addresses, the therapist's cell phone is prone to contain PHI. If the cell phone were to be stolen or lost, this would be considered a violation of HIPAA (Hecker, 2016). To remain compliant with HIPAA guidelines, home-based family therapists should not store clients' PHI in their phones. Even phone numbers can lead to identifying the client. In one case, a couple and family therapist lost the phone, and the finder called the first number on the phone to try to return the phone; it happened to be the name of a client. Alternatively, the couple and family therapist can encrypt the phone and meet the requirements of the regulations. Any media that is encrypted is considered "safe harbor" and the couple and family therapist will not be required to report the loss of encrypted media devices to the Department of Health and Human Services, as they would for other types of loss of PHI (Hecker, 2016; Hecker & Edwards, 2014). This can ease some stress and concern when transporting sensitive client information.

Home-Based Therapy Hazards

Boyd-Franklin and Bry (2001) describe how multiproblematic families usually cope with issues such as poverty, substance abuse, family violence, and physical and mental health distress. Low-income neighborhoods typically have a higher level of crime (Hammond & Czyszczon, 2014). These family stressors can lead to issues of safety for the clients and therapist. Home-based family therapists must exercise additional precautions to ensure safety in an unfamiliar and nontraditional therapeutic setting. Therapists must determine the level of potential danger within the unfamiliar neighborhood and arrange for any safety precautions. The steps below may be implemented to ensure client and therapist safety.

First, the therapist should only make daytime home visits, when possible, if the family resides in an unsafe neighborhood. It is recommended that therapists avoid scheduling appointments later than 5:00 pm or after dusk. If it is not feasible to visit clients during the daytime, then a second therapist or supervisor should also be present. Therapists should also park their cars in well-lit areas when visiting their clients at night. Second, the therapist must inform a secretary, colleague, or members of the agency of the residence of the family in treatment, as well as the date and time of the session. The therapist should then notify the chosen member of the agency upon the completion of the home-based session. Third, the therapist must have a cell phone available in case of an emergency.

Fourth, the therapist must be able to implement crisis management interventions when necessary. This begins as the therapist remains aware of the surroundings and is ready to take action if something unsafe is noticed. For example, if the clients live in an unsafe neighborhood, the therapists may not want to be on the phone while walking from the car to the client's home. The presence of the phone may bring attention to the therapist by residents of the neighborhood. If the therapist begins to feel uncomfortable or threatened within the environment, the therapist may consult with a supervisor or reschedule the session for a later date. Because of limited control within the environment, it is recommended that their supervisor or cotherapist accompany primary therapists. Supervisors might notice potential safety dilemmas more readily than the therapist, especially if the therapist is in training. This is especially applicable during the beginning phase of therapy when the therapist is less familiar with the area and the family.

Problems may arise while attempting to follow the previous steps; for example, the therapist and client may not be able to schedule during the daytime or a supervisor may not be able to accompany the primary therapist. When faced with these situations, the therapist must follow the remaining steps as closely as possible. Ensuring that another member of the agency is well-informed of the therapist's location and duration of the time in that location is vital. Mostly, it is important the therapist is mentally prepared for the dangers of the environment, leading to the therapist being able to react in a swift fashion.

Physically dangerous environments are not the only concern for home-based family therapists. Health issues also pose a potential challenge. Christensen (1995) discusses how cigarette smoking in the home has been described as an issue. Along with the dangers of cigarette smoking, other potentially harmful circumstances include parasitic infestation. For example, if the furniture and floor are infested with bugs, the therapist is left with the dilemma of where to conduct therapy and how the conditions could affect the therapist and client's health. Pets are another area of possible concern because of the risk of allergies or the possibility of an attack, as seen in Ben's case. It is imperative for the therapist to communicate expectations and ground rules regarding ecological concerns to ensure that the atmosphere is conducive for successful therapy. It is important to explain the possibility of termination or relocation because of health risks while keeping in mind that home-based family therapists must not abandon nor neglect their clients and provide appropriate referrals when unable to provide services.

Recommendations for Agencies and Therapists

Therapist Self-Care

Therapists have complained of many overwhelming, inadequate feelings while seeing home-based clients (Adams & Maynard, 2000). Burnout in the therapeutic setting may stem from the attributes of the client, the therapist, and the context in which therapy is provided (Durtschi & McClellan, 2010). The variety of problems that the family is experiencing will likely be more visible to the therapist while practicing in the client's home. Adams and Maynard (2000) mention that home-based therapy is typically used with families experiencing multiple problems that are severe in nature.

Home-based family therapy permits practitioners to serve diverse populations. Through home-based family therapy, therapists often learn about the challenges family members encounter, their personal values, and the rituals and practices most revered within the family's culture. It is important for home-based therapists to understand how the differences in setting and the relationships they create with clients impact their ability to provide appropriate services. It is possible that the therapist's values may not align with those receiving care. Under these circumstances, home-based family therapists are encouraged to keep in mind that they must provide appropriate services and value clients' rights in the therapeutic process. Home-based family therapists must also remember their obligation to provide services without discrimination based on characteristics such as gender, age, and religion. Thus, therapists are encouraged to reflect on their self and determine whether any identified differences help or hinder the therapeutic relationship.

In-home therapists can experience a sense of isolation, given that they are away from colleagues and others in the office. Supervision is necessary when the therapist is experiencing feelings of distance from the agency; discussing cases with a supervisor creates a sense of connectedness and provides the therapist with comfort. Ideally, consistent supervision will build the therapist's level of confidence and patience, so that better decision-making can take place. A supervisor can assist the therapist in determining appropriate courses of intervention for these families and deal with the pressures of confronting difficult situations. Staying in touch electronically can also alleviate some isolation.

Training and Supervision

To cope with the previously mentioned obstacles and counsel families effectively, adequate training and supervision is required. Mattek, Jorgenson, and Fox (2010) developed a training program for interns that would offer in-home therapy to young children with emotional and behavioral difficulties.

The authors provided their students information on poverty, diversity of cultures, normal and abnormal early childhood development, child management therapy procedures and training videotapes of experienced clinicians. Mattek et al. (2010) explained that supervisors kept records of how the students adhered to a specific treatment that illustrated the clinical skills needed to function as an independent therapist. Such methods of training can prove beneficial for the home-based therapy process.

For home-based family therapists, training should begin with education about this form of therapy. Training should also include ethical considerations in terms of poverty, culture, boundary management, therapist self-care, decision-making, and family abuse, among other pertinent topics. Shadowing clinicians in the home of the family is the next step for a beginning home-based therapist. The level of interaction between the trainee and the family should increase as treatment progresses. After obtaining relevant education and supervision, the trainee can transition into the role of lead therapist. Finally, ongoing communication with a supervisor is recommended for home-based family therapists—and maybe be a requirement for therapists working toward licensure. Finally, a strong alliance between therapists and supervisors ensures best clinical practice for home-based therapy.

Summary

Home-based family therapy can bring unique challenges and change the dynamics of traditional therapy. It is important to develop ethical sensitivity and practices applicable to these challenges (Waisbrod et al., 2012). This chapter explored potential home-based family therapy ethical issues. Suggestions to address issues have included: collaboratively developing boundaries between with therapist and clients, adhering to confidentiality regulations, focusing on self-care, and seeking supervision and guidance to cope with the obstacles present during home-based family therapy. The authors encourage home-based couple and family therapists to use recommendations suggested here, and flexibly adjust suggestions to their own unique circumstances. Because of issues such as cost and convenience, home-based therapy is likely grow as an acceptable and reimbursable therapeutic modality. Couple and family therapists will need to adapt and gain additional expertise in handling the unique challenges of home-based therapy.

References

Adams, J. F., & Maynard, P. E. (2000). Evaluating training needs for home-based family therapy: A focus group approach. *The American Journal of Family Therapy, 28*(1), 41–52. doi: 10.1080/019261800261806.

Ammerman, R. T., Putnam, F. W., Altaye, M., Teeters, A. R., Stevens, J., & Van Ginkel, J. B. (2013). Treatment of depressed mothers in home visiting: Impact on psychological distress and social functioning. *Child Abuse and Neglect, 37,* 544–554. doi: 10.1016/j.chiabu.2013.03.003.

Bagdasaryan, S. (2004). Evaluating preservation services: Reframing the question of effectiveness. *Children and Youth Services Review, 27,* 615–635. doi: 10.1016/j.childyouth.2004.11.014.

Boyd-Franklin, N., & Bry, B. H. (2001). *Reaching out in family therapy: Home-based, school, and community interventions.* New York, NY: Guilford.

Campbell, C. D., & Gordon, M. C. (2003). Acknowledging the inevitable: Understanding multiple relationships in rural practice. *Professional Psychology, 34*(4), 430–434. doi: 10.1037/0735-7028.34.4.430.

Christensen, L. L. (1995). Therapists' perspectives on home-based family therapy. *The American Journal of Family Therapy, 23*(4), 306–314. doi: 10.1080/01926189508251361.

Cottone, R. (2001). A social constructivism model of ethical decision making in counseling. *Journal of Counseling & Development, 79*(1), 39–45. doi: 10.1002/j.1556-6676.2001.tb01941.x.

Durtschi, J. A., & McClellan, M. K. (2010). The self of the therapist. In L. L. Hecker (Ed.), *Ethics and professional issues in couple and family therapy* (pp. 155–169). New York, NY: Taylor & Francis.

Gavirneni, S., & Kulkarni, V. (2014). Concierge medicine: Applying rational economics to health care queuing. *Cornell Hospitality Quarterly, 55,* 314–325. doi: 10.1177/1938965514537113.

Hammond, C., & Czyszczon, G. (2014). Home-based family counseling: An emerging field in need of professionalization. *The Family Journal, 22*(1), 56–61. doi: 10.1177/1066480713505055.

Hecker, L. L. (2010). Ethical decision making. In L. L. Hecker (Ed.), *Ethics and professional issues in couple and family therapy* (pp. 13–28). New York, NY: Taylor & Francis.

Hecker L. L., & Edwards, A. B. (2014). The impact of HIPAA and HITECH: New standards for confidentiality, security, and documentation for marriage and family therapists. *The American Journal of Family Therapy, 42*(2), 95–113. doi: 10.1080/01926187.2013.792711.

Hecker, L. (2016). *HIPAA demystified: HIPAA compliance for the mental health professional.* Crown Point, IN: Loger Press.

Lauka, J. D., Remley, P. T., & Ward, C. (2013). Attitudes of counselors regarding ethical situations encountered by in-home counselors. *The Family Journal, 21*(2), 129–135. doi: 10.1177/1066480712465822.

Lawson, G. (2005). Special considerations for the supervision of home-based counselors. *The Family Journal, 13*(4), 437–444. doi: 10.1177/10664807042 71189.

Lietz, C. A. (2009). Examining families' perceptions of intensive in-home services: A mixed methods study. *Children and Youth Services Review, 31*(12), 1337–1 345. doi: 10.1016/j.childyouth.2009.06.007.

Mattek, R. J., Jorgenson, E. T., & Fox, R. A. (2010). Home-based therapy for young children in low-income families: A student training program. *The Family Journal, 18*(2), 189–194. doi: 10.1177/1066480710364316.

McWey, L. M., Humphreys, J., & Pazdera, A. L. (2011). Action-oriented evaluation of an in-home family therapy program for families at risk in foster care placement. *Journal of Marital and Family Therapy, 37*(2), 137–152. doi: 10.1111/j.1752-0606.2009.00165.x.

Minuchin, S. (1974). Structural family therapy. In S. Arieti (Ed.), *The American handbook of psychiatry* (pp. 178–192). New York, NY: Basic Books.

Pope, K. S., & Vasquez, M. J. T. (2011). *Ethics in psychotherapy and counseling: A practical guide.* Hoboken, NJ: Wiley.

Scarborough, N., Taylor, B., & Tuttle, A. (2013). Collaborative home-based therapy (CHBT): A culturally responsive model for treating children and adolescents involved in child protective service systems. *Contemporary Family Therapy: An International Journal, 35*(3), 465–477. doi: 10.1007/s10591-012-9223-5.

Seeling, W. R., Goldman-Hall, B. J., & Jerell, J. M. (1992). In-home treatment of families with seriously disturbed adolescents in crisis. *Family Process, 31*(2), 135–149. doi: 10.1111/j.1545-5300.1992.00135.x.

Simon, R. I., & Williams, I. C. (1999). Maintaining treatment boundaries in small communities and rural areas. *Psychiatric Services, 50,* 1440–1446. doi: 10.1176/ps.50.11.1440.

Sonne, J. L. (1994). Multiple relationships: Does the new ethics code answer the right questions? *Professional Psychology, 25*(4), 336–343. doi: 10.1037// 0735-7028.25.4.336.

Thomas, V., McCollum, E. E., & Snyder, W. (1999). Beyond the clinic: In-home therapy with head start families. *Journal of Marital and Family Therapy, 25*(2), 177–189. doi: 10.1111/j.1752-0606.1999.tb01121.x.

Waisbrod, N., Buchbinder, E., & Possick, C. (2012). In-home intervention with families in distress: Changing places to promote change. *Social Work, 57*(2), 121–132.

Weber, D. (2003). Health care trends. *The Physician Executive, 29*(1), 6–14.

16

Ethics of Professionalism

Megan J. Murphy and Amber Sampson

Amelia, a newly licensed marital and family therapist in private practice, takes pride in her professional online presence. She consistently adds new content to her professional page and takes care to put relevant and interesting material on her social media site. She has found these efforts enhance potential and current clients' engagement in her practice. Amelia also maintains a personal social media account where she regularly posts pictures of her weekends out and family gatherings. Recently, she took to her private social media account to complain about a bad day at work and the stress of being subpoenaed by a client's lawyer. Amelia took care not to provide identifying information that would break confidentiality. Nonetheless, she saw a drop in the number of her referrals from other professionals she was personally connected with on social media.

Professionalism

When you think of professionalism, what comes to mind? Professionalism is a broad concept that can pose ethical challenges for therapists. The concept of professionalism includes publicly identifying oneself as a professional marriage and family therapist, embracing the identity of being a marriage and family therapist, and representing the profession of marriage and family therapy. Consistent with the idea of relational ethics, being professional, in part, means considering the impact that one has on others (Shaw, 2011), including clients (potential, current, future, and past), colleagues, employers, and the profession as a whole. Along with identifying as a marriage and family therapist comes the responsibility to manage power found within professionalism, and to be aware of the impact one has on others at all times. A relational ethics stance also suggests that our ethical actions reside in all the small decisions we make in our role as CFTs.

Presentation of Self

In the workplace, it may be more evident that we are to present ourselves in a professional manner. Professional presentation of self includes how we appear to others—how we dress, how we relate to others, having respect for others' space and time, completing paperwork on time, etc. Each of these behaviors seems like something small, but can quickly add up to contribute to others' perspectives of us as professional therapists. To start—what does it mean to dress professionally? The answer depends partly on context—what are the agency policies for appropriate attire? How does a therapist decide what is appropriate attire in the absence of specific agency policy? It is important for therapists to develop a sense of how others would view them—say a client or an employer. What is the difference between dressing for therapy and dressing for a night out on the town? Values clearly come into play, which can create ethical dilemmas in the moment. For example, must a woman avoid wearing a low-cut top overall and/or should this be a consideration when, for example, the therapist knows she will be working with a couple in which one issue for the wife is the husband who has a wandering eye? Overall, a conservative approach to attire for conducting sessions may be the best option.

Time and Space

Professionalism also involves having respect for others' space and time. Therapists frequently share space when working within an agency or in practice-shared offices; access to therapy rooms or desk space may be limited. Again, therapists are encouraged to consider others' perspectives and needs when sharing resources, meaning being sure to communicate about room usage, picking up after oneself, or finishing a task promptly so the next person can use the copier or computer. Being mindful of use of time, although abstract, is another important piece to professionalism. Arriving on time for meetings and sessions is sending a message of respect for others' time as well. In some cultures, time is more fluid, and arrival on time is less important than everyone gathering together. In some contexts, such as when conducting in-home family therapy, this fluidity of time will allow for flexibility in starting sessions or meetings. Therapists can be aware of the context in which they are practicing, considering the needs of those around them when making decisions.

Documentation

Typically, therapists in training acquire many hours of practice in writing and completing case notes and other treatment documentation. The timeliness of completion of case notes is a professionalism issue for several reasons. First, when completing case notes in a timely fashion, therapists are more likely to retain and document important information that is shared in the session. Second, failure to complete case notes or other paperwork in a timely fashion can result in an agency needing to "pay back" monies, as the result of an audit in which lack of documentation of sessions was found. Third, failure to complete paperwork may contribute to a lack of continuity of care for clients, for example, if a new therapist needs to take over a case and is unable to learn what work a previous therapist has done with a client. Fourth, files may be subpoenaed; incomplete files can put a therapist at a distinct disadvantage, ethically and legally speaking. Finally, in most states, clients are legally entitled to have access to their records; failure to complete paperwork or failure to maintain appropriate file organization can lead to a poor view of the profession of marriage and family therapy through a single therapist's actions. If hand written, case notes should be legible to others. Having the organizational skills related to managing paperwork can be crucial in warding off ethical issues related to documentation (Brennan, 2013).

Respect for Others

Therapists who embrace an ethic of professionalism also are always aware of how they treat others. Demonstrating respect in the workplace goes a long way, including working collaboratively with others, regardless of one's place in the "hierarchy" of the workplace. It may help therapists to think about what they consider to be healthy relationship dynamics and enact those in the workplace. Everyone is deserving of respect—regardless of role—including employers, supervisors, secretaries, custodial staff, etc. Respect includes treating each person as a valuable human being, worthy of consideration. In these days of technology, nearly everyone seems to need to be reminded that texting on the phone while in a meeting or talking with others is an example of unprofessional behavior. In that moment, we are deciding to "be elsewhere" instead of being fully engaged and present in interactions with others. Professional behavior includes putting the cell phone away when working with others.

Boundaries and Social Media

Another set of ethical issues arises when considering therapist boundaries between personal and professional. Maintaining professionalism at the office makes sense; how much professionalism is called for when one is not at the office? Therapists should consider how the public views them, keeping in mind that members of the public may only know the person as a therapist. For example, therapists often maintain Facebook pages; some maintain a professional page while also maintaining a personal page, as Amelia did in our initial case scenario. Clients who search out a therapist could see both types of Facebook pages. Therapists are strongly encouraged to maintain strict privacy settings for all Facebook accounts. Still, clients can see therapists' profile pictures. For this reason, therapists are strongly urged to consider the image they use to present themselves in this forum. Images that include inappropriate attire, use of alcohol or drugs, and engaging in otherwise unprofessional behavior are likely to be seen as unprofessional by the public, even if this appears on a therapist's personal Facebook page. In addition, therapists often have colleagues and current, past, and perhaps future employers as friends on Facebook. How might an employer view Amelia should they see her openly speaking about a case? Amelia took care not to mention identifying features of the client, which was good, but the larger issue of professionalism surfaces when Amelia complains about the actions of a client's lawyer. Additionally, how might the client feel if she could recognize herself in the post? Therapists should think carefully before posting anything about clients to their newsfeed. Perhaps something to consider before posting anything online is whether it might cause concern if clients came across the opinion/statement on their own. Indeed, some clients will Google search their therapists (Zur, 2012). Additionally, therapists might consider how representing oneself online as less than competent because of alcohol or other substance impairment has the potential to influence the public's perception of professional integrity. Will postings and pictures impact whether a therapist may be viewed as impaired and thus call into question their ability to practice competently? Therapists can learn about how to self-disclose online in an ethical way that maintains professionalism (Taylor, 2012). Posting confidential client information is unethical; however, even posting about a bad day in vague terms—for example, having challenging clients, as Amelia did in the scenario—can be seen as unprofessional by colleagues. Therapists should consider that anything posted online is potentially accessible to anyone at any time—and is a permanent record of one's activity.

Having access to information via the Internet can be very tempting for therapists as well as clients. Just as clients may Google search their therapists, therapists—out of curiosity—Google search their clients. Therapists who think systemically may decide that it is unethical to search for information about their clients online. A question arises about what the therapist would do with information found online about a client—and whether or how that information will be revealed to a client. Clients may feel a sense of violation if they learn that a therapist has a piece of information about them that was not revealed in the course of therapy, which can then damage the therapeutic relationship. Clients may be entitled to a sense of privacy about their personal lives, even if part of their lives appear online. Controversy remains about the ethics of therapists searching for client information online (Devi, 2011).

Therapists can remember professionalism also applies to any sort of communication about clients with other professionals. Information sent via e-mail or text needs to be professional—that is, written in complete sentences in a way that addresses a professional audience. Therapists must be mindful about how other professionals will receive their correspondence. Holding oneself out as professional applies to all domains of interaction! Seemingly small "slights" can be seen as very unprofessional by others, including use of slang, emoticons, informal greetings, and forwarding offensive jokes. In addition, therapists must never use information that could identify clients, such as name, initials, family details, or presenting problem. Even identifying clients by their problem is unprofessional, such as "my borderline client" or "the divorcing family." Therapists should be aware of photos attached to e-mails that are sent out. Some e-mail providers, such as Google, allow users to have a photo appear next to one's name in the e-mail header; therapists are encouraged to be mindful of the image that is sent with their e-mails. Finally, therapists can consider the ethics of using personal versus professional e-mail addresses in communications with others. If working for an agency or educational institution (or even if working in private practice), it is important to use professional e-mail addresses because it helps remind others (as well as the therapist) what role is being occupied when the e-mail is sent. Therapists who use personal e-mail for professional reasons must keep in mind how others may view the e-mail user name—for example, "flirtytherapist@email.com" is not appropriate when corresponding about professional matters.

Boundaries in Public

Having to think about social media and its intersection with the personal and professional is an added dimension to what therapists must consider already: presentation of self in public settings. It is not uncommon to see clients (past and current) while out in public—at grocery stores, concert venues, small parties, or at restaurants and bars, especially in smaller communities. In a sense, therapists are potentially always "on the clock." Therapists may have to make quick decisions about how to respond to a variety of in-person scenarios—for example, going grocery shopping with family and running into a client. Certainly, therapists are not expected to dress professionally at all times for the possibility of seeing a client in public. However, ethical responsibility to maintain confidentiality is definitely in play when seeing a client in public. Therapists can think ahead of time about maintaining client confidentiality when faced with situations in which clients come face-to-face with their friends or family. Alerting clients to their policy about seeing them in public settings during the first session can assist the client in understanding the therapist is in fact protecting their confidentiality if the therapist does not acknowledge the client in public. Such efforts to discuss public encounters early on can help to protect the therapeutic alliance with the client. Further, therapists can attempt to extract themselves from therapeutic conversations that clients initiate in public.

Ethical dilemmas regarding professionalism can rise to a higher level when therapists are in certain situations when out in public—for example, when a therapist is drinking at a bar and sees a client at the same bar. Are therapists entitled to personal lives that are completely separate from their professional life? In reality, the line between personal and professional is always blurred; it could be argued that the question is more of extent of the line between personal and professional rather than whether the line exists. In the bar scenario, the therapist must consider their own level of intoxication as well as that of the client, in addition to myriad other factors, such as the client's level of functioning, presenting problem, and the relationship between therapist and client. The therapist already has knowledge of the client's activities that evening, which is information that contributes to the therapist's understanding of the client's behaviors in session. The therapist may need to make a decision about leaving the bar for another venue and having to explain this decision to friends/family in a way that maintains client confidentiality.

Self-Care

One other common factor for consideration is the therapist's need and desire for a vacation, or time away from clients. Therapists must always consider the balance between their own needs and client needs. Again, the line can be quite fuzzy, and is dependent on contextual factors. For therapists, self-care is critical in preventing burnout; time away from clients is a necessity for maintaining therapists' own relationships. Therapists still need to ask themselves what provisions they have made for client care in their absence, and are these provisions adequate given the problems clients are currently experiencing? Furthermore, therapists can ask themselves how long is too long to be away? Therapists have a responsibility to make reasonable arrangements so as not to abandon or neglect clients. Consulting with colleagues and employers is essential in differentiating between therapist needs and wants. Therapists' decisions about personal time can impact clients in significant ways.

Professional Identity

A therapist's professional identity may be defined as a product of professionalism and is built upon what is and is not intentionally put forth into the community. Intentional efforts may include choosing to interact with media sources, establishing a social media presence online, maintaining awareness of how much access the public has to personal information (i.e., nonprofessional social media pages, photos, tweets), and how a therapist might go about maintaining professional interactions with colleagues and other referral sources.

Social Media

Interacting with the media has the potential benefit to one's practice through increased exposure of one's profession and skills but care must be taken to maintain ethical awareness when providing recommendations or opinion statements made available to the public. Ethical discretion cautions against making statements of opinion when one has not directly interacted with the person(s) discussed. Because therapists have the ability to influence how others think and act, it is important to manage such power with care.

It is especially important to remember a therapist does not have complete influence on how the material provided is presented, interpreted, or reproduced. Further, therapists may want to be selective in who they choose to engage with as representatives of the media. Media representatives have potential, by means of agenda or purpose, to influence the process of one's media exposure (Kilgore, 1979). When being interviewed by the media, therapists have a responsibility to review written articles prior to publication to check for accuracy in statements made for public consumption.

The proliferation of online engagement has most certainly touched the world of therapy. It is no longer a question of whether a therapist can benefit from an online presence but rather is a question of how much and in what forms are good practice for online marketing, presence, and service delivery. Social media in particular has the potential to quickly and consistently impact one's professional identity. A therapist's online presence through Facebook, Twitter, Instagram, and so on can enhance the platform for marketing and professional engagement, but some ethical cautions are in order. According to Jordan et al. (2014), ethical considerations to be addressed regarding use of social media include confidentiality, informed consent, potential for perception of dual relationships, professional competence and integrity (maintaining up to date training on use of technology and social media), and responsibility to students, supervisees, and research participants. Overall, because a therapist's duty is to the protection and best interest of the client, it is important to weigh the means of how one uses and benefits from use of social media against the potential for blurred boundaries, weakening of a client's confidentiality, and one's willingness to stay on top of new developments and safeguards when using social media sites for professional purposes. Therapists can consider how others may publicly view a client's connection to their social media pages, how much they know about keeping professional and personal social sites separate and "private," and how clients might interpret an acceptance or rejection of a social media connection.

Peer Supervision Networks

At each stage of professional development, therapists can benefit from growing and maintaining a peer supervision network. In the beginning stages of training and practice, peers are not appropriate for supervision guidance, but they do provide support and professional connection. Once a therapist is fully licensed and not required to receive consistent supervision, professional peers are often one of the only resources for community and feedback. Such a network helps to provide clarity, challenge, and support for one's professional identity. A peer supervision group not only provides feedback on challenging cases and options for referral resources, but also a sounding board for networking, resources, professional conduct off- and online, and perhaps the best support to understand what it means to maintain awareness of the intricacies of personal and professional therapeutic boundaries. For example, therapists might consider the specific contexts of a professional social connection, such as employment relationships, as well as what type of boundaries and connections to have with individuals in the peer supervision network outside professional support needs. A therapist might ask whether it is appropriate to go for drinks, engage in romantic relationships, etc. with those they rely on for impartial feedback about professional and clinical issues and concerns.

Licensure

Students graduating with a master's degree typically need to practice for a minimum of 2 years and accrue client contact and supervision hours before being eligible to apply for a full license. Therapists need to be careful with terminology they use to describe themselves before licensure and should examine their state licensing law for guidance. Various types of terms may be protected by state statutes and rules, such as "family therapist" or "marriage and family therapist." Therapists must avoid placing these terms on business cards, business stationary, e-mail signatures, Facebook pages, resumes, or curriculum vitae before licensure. It is important to follow state laws and ethics codes on this matter, regardless of what an employer or licensing agency staff member says. Similarly, some states offer temporary or associate licenses. Therapists who hold one of these licenses must clearly state so on materials identifying themselves as therapists who hold a license.

Clinical and Supervisory Hours

A common area that brings forth ethical dilemmas is in counting hours, particularly client contact hours. Training programs and state licensure statutes typically require a number of overall client contact hours as well as a certain number or percentage of relational hours in which a couple or family is seen by the therapist. This can place pressure on the therapist to act in a number of unethical ways, including seeing couples and families beyond what is clinically indicated; turning individual clients into couple/family clients without a clear clinical rationale; holding sessions for longer than is typical for the benefit of the therapist instead of the client; or outright falsifying hours. It is imperative for therapists to consider the needs of the client first before considering one's own needs. Therapists who put their needs first when making clinical decisions can end up justifying or rationalizing actions taken as a means to benefit clients, when in reality the benefit is more for the therapist. Therapists who cut corners regarding clinical hours not only cheat themselves, but also shortchange the profession by holding themselves out as having more experience in certain areas than is actually the case.

Supervisor Qualifications

Therapists in training, while in graduate school, frequently receive plentiful supervision and close guidance in learning to provide therapy. Upon graduation, therapists are not likely to receive as close supervision. Therapists must start making more independent decisions, ideally in conjunction with a supervisor, about clinical work. Sometimes these supervisors have different professional backgrounds, such as social worker, mental health counselor, or psychologist. Therapists in these situations need to decide about their scope of practice—this is also true when being supervised by a marriage and family therapist. The line between practicing outside of one's scope of practice is not always clear; some areas that may be seen as requiring further training include eye movement desensitization and reprocessing (EMDR), Applied Behavior Analysis, etc.

Meeting State Requirements

Therapists on a quest to meet their prelicensure requirements often seek employment in which they can accrue client contact hours and, ideally, receive free supervision on their cases by a qualified supervisor located at their employment site. It may be difficult to find this ideal scenario, and in some cases, therapists seek to open their own private practices prior to being licensed. It is prudent to check state laws to ensure that this is allowed, and that client contact hours accrued will be allowed to count toward licensure. Finding a supervisor to provide supervision in such cases is a critical step; therapists need to be mindful of balancing the need for hours (and the allure of making money from one's own practice) and the need to find a supervisor who will challenge the therapist to grow clinically. Regardless of where therapists acquire their client contact hours, they need to receive clinical supervision and it is imperative that therapists notify clients that they are receiving supervision. Details that should be provided to clients about supervision include the name of the supervisor, who else will have access to client data (for example, a co-supervisee), any raw data supervision that will be acquired (live supervision, video or audio recordings), and how that raw data will be used, including length of time this material will be stored.

Establishing a Supervisory Contract

Therapists receiving supervision need to think about how supervision will unfold, particularly if the supervisor providing supervision is independent of (i.e., not employed by) the same agency in which the therapist is working (Ungar & Costanzo, 2007). Therapists working toward supervision are working under the license(s) of those who are supervising them; being supervised by a professional outside of the field can present some challenges. For example, there may be two or more sets of ethics codes to abide by, which may conflict in various ways. Therapists may also receive different case conceptualization directives if they are being supervised by two or more professionals. Ethical dilemmas may arise if one supervisor is tied to the supervisee's employer, whereas the other supervisor is aligned with the supervisee's professional field. Having a supervision contract in place that anticipates these dilemmas can be an important step in handling conflictual situations that may arise from this arrangement (Korinek & Kimball, 2003).

Maintaining the License

Achieving licensure is a goal that many therapists revere. However, maintaining the license is an important process that some therapists overlook. Therapists must consult their state's rules and regulations around maintaining the license, including earning continuing education units, informing the licensing board of changes in name or address, and renewing the license in a timely fashion. Because of budget cuts, some states have stopped mailing reminder cards to license holders, thereby placing the onus on the licensee to remember to renew. Therapists can also keep in mind that involvement with the law often needs to be reported to licensing boards, which may trigger an inquiry into the therapist's license. Any accusation of therapist misconduct by the licensing board—whether founded or not—is likely to negatively affect the therapist's relationships with colleagues, supervisors, and employers (Coy, Lambert, & Miller, 2015), and may have an impact on the public's view of the profession as a whole.

Supervision

Supervisees' Ethical Uses of Power

Supervision of student therapists' clinical work is required until licensure is achieved. Supervisees have quite a bit of power in the supervisory relationship (Murphy & Wright, 2003), which they must be sure to ethically manage. In other words, supervisees must use their power in an ethical manner; they have a responsibility to the supervisory relationship as well as to their clients and the field. Training therapists must keep in mind that they practice under the license of their supervisor, meaning the supervisor is held accountable for the supervisee's actions. Supervisors rely on supervisees' accounts of their work with clients because it is not possible for supervisors to be with supervisees at all times. As a result, one ethical responsibility supervisees have is to keep the supervisor up to date on all cases. Supervisees have the power to *not* share information about cases with supervisors, for example, cases in which the supervisee has done something "wrong." However, failing to provide this information to a supervisor is unethical—supervisees must risk being viewed negatively by their supervisor, even if temporarily, for the benefit of their clients. Supervisors can make clear in a supervisory contract that is set up before the start of supervision the level of contact and types and frequency of updates so that supervisees are clear about expectations. Similarly, supervisees can often choose which clients to present for supervision, or they can choose which video clips can be shown in supervision. These decisions have ethical implications for clients and supervisees. Supervisees may want a positive evaluation for a course or for licensure; although a positive evaluation is important, supervisees should consider what is best for clients as they navigate the learning process.

By virtue of evaluation, supervisors have more power in the supervisory relationship; however, this does not exempt student therapists from being responsible for recognizing ethical situations which arise. That is, the supervisee cannot rely exclusively on the supervisor for recognizing and acting on ethical situations. Developmentally, students take on increasing levels of responsibility for their clients, including detecting ethical dilemmas (Stoltenberg & McNeill, 1997). Similarly, student therapists can independently recognize when they need to excuse themselves from supervision (when in group supervision) based on a dual relationship with another client who is being discussed. The supervisee must keep confidential the client's identity and presence in therapy, even if one has excused oneself from supervision. Of course, the supervisee can discuss the need to remove oneself with the supervisor, yet it is the supervisee's responsibility to alert others to the dilemma and then take action.

Many times when accruing client contact hours, supervisees see their colleagues more often than they see their supervisor. This situation can lead to obtaining what is considered to be informal supervision from colleagues (Farber & Hazanov, 2014). Although consulting with colleagues on cases can be helpful, the dangers in taking guidance from colleagues are many. First, colleagues are not responsible for cases, as are the therapist and supervisor; indeed, therapists and supervisors are the parties that will be held accountable if unethical acts occur. Second, colleagues generally do not have the experience and training that supervisors have, so they may end up unintentionally giving poor guidance on a case. Third, the supervisee may end up taking action and not informing the supervisor about steps taken on a case. That is, supervision by colleagues may be helpful in the moment, but the supervisor may not ever be informed of actions taken, leading the supervisor then to perhaps provide conflicting guidance on a case. Likewise, student therapists must be careful not to provide pseudo-supervision to their colleagues.

Part of the danger of supervision provided by colleagues is that supervisees may unintentionally end up practicing outside the scope of the supervisor's competence. Colleagues may be trained in specialty areas, and offer helpful interventions on cases that is beyond the scope of the supervisor's competence or license. In the moment, such suggestions can feel very helpful when a therapist is stuck on a case; however, it is the supervisor's responsibility to monitor the case and to assist the therapist to grow in supervision. Alternatively, therapists who are licensed will need to develop a network of colleagues to consult with on ethical matters (Brennan, 2013).

Conflict Management

Appropriate management of conflict is crucial to the supervisory relationship (Korinek & Kimball, 2003). Ultimately, being evaluated can be uncomfortable for student therapists, but it is also part of the process of growth and learning. Conflict can also arise when therapists and supervisors have different ideas (or values) about how to move forward in a case. Ethical dilemmas may emerge from differing perspectives on what needs to be done with a case, such as whether a report of abuse/neglect needs to be made, or whether police need to be involved on a case. Ideally, avenues for resolving conflict would be present in a supervisory contract that both parties agree to before this kind of ethical dilemma emerges.

It could be said that training therapists need to invest themselves in the training process, and sometimes make difficult changes in order to grow and learn. Bringing concerns directly to the supervisor instead of venting to colleagues is an important step in acting ethically. In the course of evaluation, the supervisor may instruct the supervisee to enter into therapy as a means of working through some personal issues that are seen as preventing the student therapist from growing as a therapist. Students have an ethical responsibility to engage in therapy when personal issues continually interfere or become a block from moving forward with their training. Therapists can take this responsibility seriously and not necessarily wait for a supervisor to say that attending therapy is necessary for the therapist's training progress. Therapists can keep in mind that supervisors have a gatekeeping responsibility, with their first responsibility to clients, followed by responsibility to supervisees.

Ethical Misconduct by a Supervisor

As discussed previously, supervisees have many ethical responsibilities related to the training process; they are not exempt from responsibility just because they are receiving supervision. On the other hand, supervisees may experience ethical misconduct by a supervisor. One clear-cut ethical mandate in many professional codes of ethics is the prohibition of sexual relationships between supervisors and supervisees while there is a training or evaluative period in supervision. This is a critical mandate because the integrity of the training relationship is destroyed when there is a sexual relationship between supervisor and trainee. Any semblance of objectivity, particularly in regard to evaluation of the supervisee, is gone. Moreover, the supervisor in such cases is abusing power bestowed upon the role of supervisor—exploiting the supervisee for sexual pleasure. Supervisees need to know that sexual relationships with supervisors are *never* acceptable under any circumstance. Sexual attraction that is experienced by either supervisor or supervisee should be discussed in supervision (Murray & Sommers-Flanagan, 2014), or with a peer, if necessary.

Supervisors must use their evaluation power in an ethical fashion. Negative evaluations of supervisees can lead to job loss, failure of a practicum course, expulsion from a graduate program, or denial of licensure. It is unethical for supervisors to threaten supervisees with use of negative evaluation when the evaluation is not tied to actual concerns or competencies. Likewise, supervisors must be timely in their delivery of evaluations for ultimate effectiveness (Ladany, Lehrman-Waterman, Molinaro, & Wolgast, 1999).

Supervisees may observe unethical behavior on the part of the supervisor (Ladany, 2014), including but not limited to inappropriate billing practices, lack of supervision provided yet the supervisor signs off on supervisory hours provided, boundary crossings with clients and/or other supervisees, and practice outside accepted scope of practice. Observing these behaviors poses an ethical dilemma for the supervisee in how to respond to the concern. Ideally, supervisees would be able to approach another clinical supervisor for guidance on these issues. Barring this possibility, supervisees may need to take a risk and discuss their concerns with their supervisor, knowing that this may negatively impact the supervisory relationship.

Advertising

Beyond the master's degree, many therapists work on earning advanced credentials, or they go on for further study in a doctoral program. Therapists have an ethical responsibility to educate others about their credentials, as well as not to mislead others about their credentials. For example, therapists should not use initials ABD after their names; ABD is an abbreviation for "all but dissertation" that is frequently used in academic circles to indicate that a doctoral student has completed all work for the doctorate except the dissertation. Yet, the public is not likely to know what these letters mean and indeed they do not indicate any professionally recognized level of achievement. Therapists would be wise to avoid using this kind of abbreviation on their professional business materials.

Additionally, it is important to maintain awareness of current state laws and requirements regarding use of promotional materials in representing oneself through advertising. Some states consider misleading, fraudulent, deceptive, or false statements to be violations of both criminal and public health laws. Therapists are prudent to consistently ensure what is put into advertising efforts is straightforward and accurately represents their profession and training. If false or misleading information is found to exist, therapists follow ethical guidelines to correct errors in advertising. For example, if one is introduced before a presentation as possessing a doctorate but is a master's-level clinician, they should correct the misrepresentation at first chance with the audience.

Publication and Research Ethics

Client Confidentiality

Therapists may wish to conduct research or publish in professional journals as a way to make scholarly contributions to the field. It is important to take steps to protect confidentiality of clients when making professional publications or publishing work about clients (Campbell, Vasquez, Behnke, & Kinscherff, 2010). In protecting confidentiality—whether in publications or when communicating about clients—therapists must take steps to ensure that clients cannot be identified via a combination of specific information. For example, when constructing a demographics table, the use of pseudonyms is important, as is concealing information that may reveal participants' identities, such as the name of the town in which they live combined with their occupation. An ethical dilemma may arise between protecting client confidentiality and maintaining research integrity. Details about clients may need to be obscured to the point in which readers of research may not be provided with information needed to understand the study. Therapist researchers need to think about what is best for clients in these situations. This can sometimes be a difficult decision if therapists feel pressure or desire to publish results of a study. Therapists can also keep in mind that publishing includes research done for a thesis or dissertation; even if that work is not published in a therapy journal in the field, the thesis or dissertation can be found online and is available to the general public. If identifying information is provided about clients, then securing permission from all clients is necessary.

Institutional Review Board Approval

Therapists associated with a university need to get Institutional Review Board (IRB) approval before beginning the research process. Depending on the university, recruitment may not begin until IRB approval is given. However, therapists have an obligation to review the ethics of their studies if related to the clinical or supervisory realm, above and beyond that of getting their university's IRB approval. IRBs serve as one mechanism to evaluate the ethical nature of the proposed study in relation to federal and state rules and regulations. Therapists are responsible for reviewing their studies to ensure compliance with their profession's code of ethics. If an IRB is not a resource relevant to the therapist's setting, then consulting with members of the field is prudent before undertaking a study. When developing the procedures for a study, it is important to consider if there is any undue influence on clients to participate. Clients should never be placed in a situation in which they feel that they have to choose between attending therapy and participating in a study or not receiving therapy at all. Therapist researchers must clearly make this separation clear to clients. Again, therapists have to distinguish their own needs from the needs and best interests of their clients. A conflict of interest may be present if a therapist stands to benefit from a client's participation in a study that may bring the therapist recognition or other reward, such as publication, promotion, or pay increase. In accordance with practicing professionally, therapists should discuss research plans with others potentially impacted, including employers and colleagues. For those therapists operating outside of a university setting, the formation of an Ethics Advisory Board that includes therapists, community members, and former clients can be helpful in evaluating the ethical nature of a proposed research study.

Informed Consent Process

Similar to the informed consent process when conducting therapy, therapist researchers should engage in a process of obtaining informed consent for research studies involving clients or supervisees. More than simply having participants sign a piece of paper, the informed consent process involves allowing time for potential participants to read the informed consent document and ask questions. Potential participants must be given time to consider the risks and benefits of participation. Ideally, the informed consent process includes a discussion between the therapist researcher and participant about the procedures, risks, benefits, and implications for therapy. The sometimes blurred lines between therapy and research should also be considered. Procedures should be explicitly detailed regarding what happens to confidentiality if the participant reveals information involving harm to self or others in the course of the research study. Therapist researchers need to be clear about which role(s) they are taking on when conducting research with client participants.

Authorship Considerations

Authorship issues are another frequent area for ethical consideration. Typically, authorship is ordered with the person making the largest or most significant contribution first, followed by the person with the second most significant contribution, etc. Authorship order follows a linear progression, as is commonly understood in the field. Some authors who truly collaborate together use an asterisk to signify that all authors made equal contributions; however, we do not currently have a mechanism to recognize shared authorship in this manner, as someone is still always listed first, followed by second, etc. Following American Psychological Association (APA) guidelines is a start for determining authorship, yet even those guidelines do not always help determine authorship, particularly when there are power differences between authors. Student therapists can be most vulnerable to being listed last on publications, if at all, even with substantial contributions to manuscript or study development. It is generally accepted for students to be first author on publication of their thesis or dissertation in a research journal, even if faculty have done significant work on manuscript development.

Conclusion

It can be overwhelming to think of all the details that go into maintaining an ethic of professionalism. Many elements of professionalism overlap with other ethical topics discussed in this book. Following are some highlights of what it means to be professional:

- Consider how you are viewed by others,
- Appearance is important,
- Have respect for others,
- Timeliness is key,

- Maintain boundaries,
- Be mindful of your use of technology,
- Be honest and transparent,
- Talk through concerns with others, and
- Maintain confidentiality.

When using a frame of relational ethics, the impact on others is considered as well as the impact on self. In addition, context is always central when considering ethics—this impacts ethics of professionalism. Questions to ponder include: How do we present ourselves to others? How might clients or other professionals in the field view our actions? How do our actions reflect and impact the larger field? More than the larger ethical dilemmas that we face, our day-to-day and moment-to-moment actions can affect the field and others' perceptions of our competence and abilities.

References

Brennan, C. (2013). Ensuring ethical practice: Guidelines for mental health counselors in private practice. *Journal of Mental Health Counseling, 35*(3), 245–261. doi: 10.17744/mehc.35.3.9706313j4t313397.

Campbell, L., Vasquez, M., Behnke, S., & Kinscherff, R. (2010). *APA ethics code: Commentary and case illustrations.* Washington, DC: American Psychological Association.

Coy, J. S., Lambert, J. E., & Miller, M. M. (2015). Stories of the accused: A phenomenological inquiry of MFTs and accusations of unprofessional conduct. *Journal of Marital and Family Therapy, 42*(1), 139–152. doi: 10.1111/jmft.12109.

Devi, S. (2011). Facebook friend request from a patient? *The Lancet, 377*(9772), 1141–1142. doi: 10.1016/S0140-6736(11)60449-2.

Farber, B. A., & Hazanov, V. (2014). Informal sources of supervision in clinical training. *Journal of Clinical Psychology: In Session, 70*(11), 1062–1072. doi: 10.1002/jclp.22127.

Jordan, N., Russell, L., Afousi, E., Chemel, T., McVicker, M., Robertson, J., & Winek, J. (2014).The ethical use of social media in marriage and family therapy: Recommendations and future directions. *The Family Journal: Counseling and Therapy for Couples and Families, 22*(1), 105–112. doi: 10.1177/1066480713505064.

Kilgore, J. E. (1979). The marriage and family therapist's use of media for public education. *Journal of Marital and Family Therapy, 5*(4), 87–92. doi: 10.1111/j.1752-0606.1979.tb01285.x.

Korinek, A. W., & Kimball, T. G. (2003). Managing and resolving conflict in the supervisory system. *Contemporary Family Therapy, 25*(3), 295–310. doi: 10.1023/A:1024559321634.

Ladany, N. (2014). The ingredients of supervisor failure. *Journal of Clinical Psychology: In Session, 70*(11), 1094–1103. doi: 10.1002/jclp.22130.

Ladany, N., Lehrman-Waterman, D., Molinaro, M., & Wolgast, B. (1999). Psychotherapy supervisor ethical practices: Adherence to guidelines, the supervisory working alliance, and supervisee satisfaction. *The Counseling Psychologist, 27*(3), 443–475. doi: 10.1177/0011000099273008.

Murphy, M. J., & Wright, D. W. (2005). Supervisees' perspectives of power use in supervision. *Journal of Marital and Family Therapy, 31*(3), 283–295. doi: 10.1111/j.1752-0606.2005.tb01569.x.

Murray, K. W., & Sommers-Flanagan, J. (2014). Addressing sexual attraction in supervision. In M. Luca (Ed.), *Sexual attraction in therapy: Clinical perspectives on moving beyond the taboo* (pp. 97–114). Malden, MA: Wiley.

Shaw, E. (2011). Relational ethics and moral imagination in contemporary systemic practice. *Australian and New Zealand Journal of Family Therapy, 32*(1), 1–14. doi: 10.1375/anft.32.1.1.

Stoltenberg, C. D., & McNeill, B. W. (1997). Clinical supervision from a developmental perspective: Research and practice. In C. F. Watkins (Ed.), *Handbook of psychotherapy supervision* (pp. 184–202). New York, NY: Wiley.

Taylor, L. A. (2012). Ethics and social networking sites. In C. E. Stout (Ed.), *Getting better at private practice* (pp. 214–229). Hoboken, NJ: Wiley.

Ungar, M., & Costanzo, L. (2007). Supervision challenges when supervisors are outside supervisees' agencies. *Journal of Systemic Therapies, 26*(2), 68–83. doi: 10.1521/jsyt.2007.26.2.68.

Zur, O. (2012). The Google factor: Ethical considerations for therapists practicing in the digital age. In C. E. Stout (Ed.), *Getting better at private practice* (pp. 230–238). Hoboken, NJ: Wiley.

Index